READER'S DIGEST

THE
MAKE IT
YOURSELF
GIFT
BOOK

GIFTS TO MAKE AT HOME FOR ALL
YOUR FAMILY AND FRIENDS

The Make-it-Yourself Gift Book is an adaptation by
The Reader's Digest Association Limited, London, of The Make-it-Yourself Gift Book (1995)
edited and designed by Reader's Digest (Australia) Pty Limited

First edition Copyright © 1996
Reprinted 1997
The Reader's Digest Association Limited,
11 Westferry Circus, Canary Wharf, London E14 4HE
Copyright © 1996 Reader's Digest Association Far East Limited
Philippines copyright © 1996 Reader's Digest Association Far East Limited

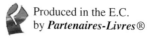
Produced in the E.C.
by *Partenaires-Livres*®

ISBN 0 276 42251 1

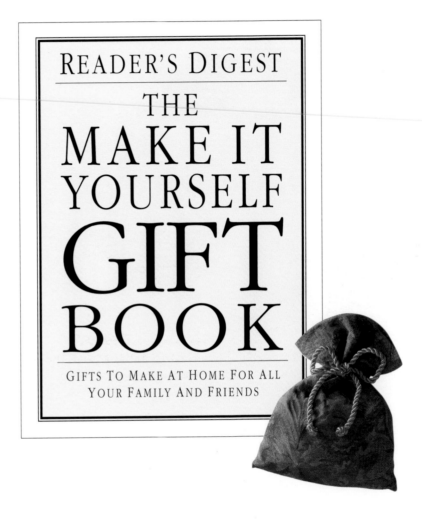

READER'S DIGEST

THE
MAKE IT
YOURSELF
GIFT
BOOK

GIFTS TO MAKE AT HOME FOR ALL
YOUR FAMILY AND FRIENDS

PUBLISHED BY THE READER'S DIGEST ASSOCIATION LIMITED
LONDON · NEW YORK · SYDNEY · CAPE TOWN · MONTREAL

CONTENTS

Sweethearts, brides & grooms

Parents

Homemakers, hosts & hostesses

Edible gifts

Techniques

Indexes

READER'S DIGEST GENERAL BOOKS

EDITORIAL DIRECTOR
Robin Hosie

ART DIRECTOR
Bob Hook

EXECUTIVE EDITOR
Michael Davison

MANAGING EDITOR
Paul Middleton

EDITORIAL GROUP HEADS
Julian Browne · Noel Buchanan · Cortina Butler

PICTURE RESEARCH EDITOR
Martin Smith

EDITORS:
Janet Healey, Rosemary Wilkinson

DESIGNERS:
Kate Finnie, Mike Spiller

CRAFT CONSULTANTS:
Sally Milner, Hilary More, Tonia Todman

CRAFT ADVISERS:
Robyn Baker & Margaret Broun (Hornsby College of TAFE), Laurine Croasdale,
Maureen Holmes, Barbara Lennon (Coats Patons Crafts), Marilyn McCann, Effie Mitrofanis (DMC),
Lucia Ruffo, Phillip Searle, David Thompson, David Zaikowski

EDITORIAL ASSISTANTS:
Maggie Aldhamland, Tom Cabot

ILLUSTRATORS:
Gerry Blake, Stephen Dew, Kalliopi Papageorgiou, Colin Seton, Mike Spiller

STYLISTS:
Mary-Anne Danaher, Louise Owens

PHOTOGRAPHERS:
Andrew Elton, Mark Gatehouse

PATTERN MAKER:
Lesley Griffith

The publishers would also like to thank Dover Publications, Mineola, NY,
for permission to use the images on the printed T-shirts (pages 100–1).

ABOUT THIS BOOK

Throughout history and in every culture, gifts have always been a traditional way of expressing love, regard, thanks and good wishes, and of celebrating life's many happy occasions. Giving a gift means giving part of yourself.

In this busy modern world, buying gifts can be a boring chore, but with this book you'll put the joy back into giving by making your own gifts for every occasion. And you'll rediscover the great pleasure that even the simplest handmade gift can bestow on both giver and receiver.

How often have you spent hours trudging around the shops looking in vain for just the right gift? Now you can spend that time much more enjoyably and profitably in making your own gifts at home. At the same time, you'll be honing the craft skills you already have and learning new ones. And you'll have the satisfaction of putting your creativity to work, because making the gifts in this book will give you lots of ideas for designing and making your own absolutely unique and original gifts.

The projects in the *Make-it-Yourself Gift Book* cover a range of crafts that you can do easily at home – needlecraft, yarn crafts, woodwork, découpage, papier mâché, stencilling, folk art ... and many more. If you've done only basic sewing, you'll find simple gifts to make, either by hand or with a sewing machine, and you'll be learning more about sewing at the same time. And if you're a keen and experienced sewer, you can extend your skills even further by finding out how to make exquisite heirloom-style garments and luxury items such as crazy patchwork.

USING THE BOOK
Each chapter contains gifts specially designed to suit a particular kind of recipient. There are gifts for children, young people, partners, parents, friends, homemakers, hosts and hostesses, and more. Each chapter has gifts suitable for various occasions, and each includes some 'quick and easy' gifts and some that are more difficult to make, so you can choose a gift according to your skills and the time you have to spare. And, of course, many of these gifts can be made for people other than the recipients described by the chapter title.

CHOOSING WHAT TO MAKE
To find the perfect gift to make for that special person in your life, look through the relevant chapter. Are you looking for something to give an extra special infant? How about a hand-made christening gown, modelled on a Victorian design and made of delicate lace and Swiss batiste. Or for a beloved Dad, you could make a wine rack to hold his favourite vintages.

A special feature of the book is the range of 'Quick and easy' gifts. These are gifts that a beginner can tackle with confidence, and that can be made in three hours or less – just the thing for a wet afternoon or a free evening. Most of the quick and easy gifts need little equipment and can be made in the comfort of an arm-chair or a garden seat. Find the quick and easy gifts by looking for the symbol ● at the top of the page and in the contents and index listings.

MAKING THE GIFTS
Read through all the instructions carefully, including the hints and notes, before you begin to make your gift. This is important because you need to understand exactly how the gift is made and how long it will take you. Think how frustrating it would be to start a découpage project for a birthday present in a week's time,

only to discover that you need weeks, or even months, to apply all the layers of varnish!

The instructions for making the gifts are written so that they are easy to follow and will give you the best possible result. The tinted boxes contain hints and notes to make the work easier, and variations on the gifts illustrated – use these to spark your imagination and create your own craft works.

A list of **what you need** is the first information you will come to, so that you will know what equipment and materials you already have and what you need to buy. In some projects we have listed trade names and specific colours for paints or knitting yarns. These were the materials used to make the gifts illustrated. However, remember that the colours of paints and yarns change from time to time, sometimes every year, so you may not be able to find the exact colours specified. Craft shops and other suppliers have colour charts for the major manufacturers and will be able to advise you how to choose a suitable substitute.

For most projects, the list of what you need is followed by a reference to the **technique pages** at the back of the book. These contain basic instructions for the major crafts you need to make the gifts. If you have not attempted a particular craft before, or are not completely confident about your skills, read the relevant techniques section before beginning to make the item.

Then come the **instructions** for making the gift. These are divided into sections, each containing a numbered sequence of steps. There are also step-by-step diagrams illustrating the procedures to follow.

The first section is usually to do with the **preparation** of your materials. Preparation is a very important part of making any craft project. If you try to save time or money by taking short cuts or using inferior materials, you may be disappointed with the final product, so be as careful with the preparation as you are when you are making and finishing the project.

After preparing the materials, you are ready for the exciting part – **making the gift**. For simple projects, this part may consist of only one section, but for more complex projects there may be several sections. Just follow the numbered sequence of steps and the diagrams.

Finally, there's a section on giving your gift **a truly professional finish**. Again, follow the numbered sequence of steps and you can't go wrong.

USING THE INDEXES

There are three indexes: a gifts and crafts index, a techniques index and a general index. The gifts and crafts index lists all the projects in alphabetical order and shows which crafts you need to make them and whether there is a master pattern. The techniques index provides a quick ready reference to the techniques section in case you need to look up a particular stitch or folk art stroke, for example. The general index divides the gifts into categories of use – for example, 'kitchen gifts' has the sub-categories 'equipment', 'furniture', and 'picture', so that you can quickly find a gift for a keen cook.

USING THE MASTER PATTERNS

Supplied with this book are five sheets of master patterns, printed on both sides. The instructions for each gift tell you whether you need a master pattern and what its number is. Identify the pattern pieces on the sheet and trace them carefully to make an individual pattern that you can keep in case you want to use it again. On page 351 you'll find a key to the master pattern pieces, so that you can be sure you have found all the pieces of the pattern.

GENERAL HINTS

Just as important as the preparation of the materials for making a specific item is the organisation of your working time, space and equipment. Follow a few simple rules and achieve good results every time.

Always leave yourself **time** to do the job properly. For needlecraft and woodwork, allow enough time to mark and cut pieces accurately. Many crafts require you to wait while glue, paint or varnish dries before you can proceed to the next step – and don't forget that high humidity can slow down the drying process. If you are in too much of a hurry, you risk wasting the time you have already put in and having to start again.

Your **working space** needs to be well organised too. If possible, dedicate a room – or even part of a room if space is a problem – to the craft you are currently working on, so that you don't have to clear everything out of the way every time you stop work. Remember too that it is important that the area where you do craft work is free of dust, well lit but protected from strong sunlight, and well ventilated.

Buy the **best-quality equipment** you can afford, especially if you plan to do a lot of craft work – it will save you money in the end. Scissors, scalpels, pins and needles, and saws, chisels and hammers should be kept sharp and rust-free. Make sure you have the right equipment for the job; craft and hardware shops are very helpful in finding the right equipment or suggesting suitable substitutes.

If you are trying out a new craft, **practise the techniques** using scraps until you are satisfied that you have mastered them. It takes a little extra time, but you will be quicker and more proficient when you come to make the gift itself.

The *Make-it-Yourself Gift Book* is more than a source of great ideas for gifts; you can also use it to improve your craft skills and learn new ones. And everyone in the family will find something that they can enjoy making and giving. With some adult supervision, children can make many of the simpler projects – an excellent way of introducing them to the delights of making items that are beautiful as well as useful, which is what craft is all about.

BABIES

We all want to express our joy when a new baby is born. In this chapter you'll find a great selection of gifts that you can make to welcome a new arrival and to delight the baby's parents.

Classic christening gown

What parent could resist this beautifully crafted heirloom, which will certainly be handed down for generations to come? The design is adapted from a Victorian christening gown.

WHAT YOU NEED

Master pattern A3(a–e) • 1.5 m Swiss batiste, 115 cm wide • Swiss or suitable fabric laces: 12 m beading with entredeux, 10 mm wide, 5.6 m fabric insertion lace, 30–40 mm wide, 2.8 m faggoting, 5–10 mm wide, 9 m edging lace, 40 mm wide • 13 m satin ribbon, 2 mm wide (for beading insertion) • 3 small pearl buttons • fine machine thread • coloured tacking thread • needles: fine sharp, fine machine • lace pins • tracing paper • pencil • scissors • sewing machine
● *Technique pages 292–301, 303–4, 343–4*

❶ CUTTING OUT THE FABRIC

1 Using tracing paper and a pencil, trace all the pattern pieces from the master pattern and cut them out. Make sure you transfer all markings.
2 Pull a thread at each raw edge of the batiste to find the straight grain. Following the cutting guide, pin all pattern pieces except the front panel to the fabric and cut them out.
3 Cut a 12.5 cm strip the width of the fabric and a 12.5 cm strip half the width of the fabric. Join these strips selvage to selvage with a small flat seam to make a strip 12.5 cm by 1.7 m (this will be used to make the tucked insert for the heirloom fabric). The rest of the fabric is used for bias and straight grain strips for the neck binding and the placket.

❷ MAKING THE LACE FABRIC

See the box 'Heirloom sewing techniques' (page 16) for the methods of assembling the heirloom fabric.

Tucked insert

1 From one long edge of the 1.7 m strip of batiste, measure three intervals 2.5 cm apart. Pull a thread the whole width of the fabric at each interval. (This is to ensure that the tucks are stitched on the straight grain.)
2 Press folds along the pulled threads and machine 5 mm from the folds. Roll and whip the top and bottom edges of the tucked inserts, using heirloom sewing method 1.

Lace inserts

1 Cut four pieces of beading with entredeux 2.8 m long, two pieces of insertion lace 2.8 m long, and a piece of edging lace 4.8 m long.

2 Gather the edging lace until it measures 2.8 m, using heirloom sewing method 4.
3 Following steps A to H below, and using the appropriate heirloom sewing method, assemble a composite lace fabric about 2.8 m long by joining: **A** beading (method 2) to **B** insertion lace (method 2) to **C** beading (method 3) to **D** faggoting (method 3) to **E** beading (method 2) to **F** insertion lace (method 2) to **G** beading (method 2) to **H** gathered edging lace.

Adjusting the skirt length
Having made the lace fabric, you can adjust the length of the skirt.
1 Measure the finished width of the lace fabric. If you are making a skirt with tucks and lace edging, subtract 3.4 cm (this allows for three 5 mm tucks and a 4 mm seam allowance to roll and whip). Cut this amount from the hem of the skirt.
2 For a skirt with lace edging only, subtract 4 mm (this allows a 4 mm seam allowance to roll and whip). Cut this amount from the hem of the skirt.

❸ MAKING THE FRONT PANEL

1 From both the lace fabric and the tucked fabric, cut the following pieces: one 40 cm wide, one 35 cm wide, one 29 cm wide, one 23 cm wide, and one 18 cm wide. (The rest of the lace fabric is for the hem of the skirt.)
2 Using heirloom sewing method 2, join the pieces of lace fabric and tucked fabric of equal width to each other. Find the vertical centres of all five pieces of heirloom fabric and mark them using a needle and coloured tacking thread.

Cutting guide
Pin all the pattern pieces except the centre front panel to the folded batiste as shown, and cut them out. From the remaining fabric, cut one strip 12.5 cm × 115 cm, and one strip 12.5 cm × 57.5 cm; these strips will be joined and pin-tucked to make the tucked inserts for the heirloom fabric. Use the fabric left over to cut the strip for the placket and the bias strip for the neck. Cut out the centre front panel from the assembled heirloom fabric.

3 Starting with the widest piece and keeping the tucked part uppermost, match the tacked centre lines and join all pieces together with the edging

lace overlapping, using method 2. Press the edging lace down.

4 Place the centre front of the front panel pattern piece on the tacked centre line of the heirloom fabric. Pin the pattern piece to the fabric and cut out.

5 Thread the ribbon through all the beading. Trim 6 mm of the 1 cm seam allowance from both sides of the front panel and roll and whip down each edge (heirloom sewing method 1), ensuring that the ends of the ribbon are caught in the stitching.

6 Cut two pieces of edging lace one-and-three-quarter times the length of the front panel (about 1.75 m). Roll and whip one short end of each piece.

7 Roll, whip and gather the two pieces of edging lace, using heirloom sewing method 4, and then stitch them to the long edges of the front panel with the rolled and whipped short ends at the hem, using heirloom sewing method 2.

HEIRLOOM SEWING TECHNIQUES

To create the heirloom fabric, you will need four basic machine sewing techniques. These are referred to in the instructions as heirloom sewing methods 1, 2, 3 and 4. If you have not attempted heirloom sewing before, practise these techniques on scraps of fabric and lace before starting to make the christening gown.

All the techniques use the sewing machine's zigzag function, and the aim is to join the components of the heirloom fabric together with as little bulk as possible. Set the stitch length short enough to hold the fabrics together securely, but not so short as to form a closed satin stitch.

To make laces easier to handle when machine stitching, spray them with a commercial fabric stiffener or starch.

1 **Roll and whip:** Place the cut edge of the fabric about 2 mm to the right of the centre of the machine foot. Set the zigzag width at 3–5 mm so that the needle will come down on either side of the cut edge, thus forming the fabric into a fine roll.

2 **Joining beading with entredeux to**

fabric or fabric insertion lace: With the right sides together, machine zigzag a fine seam along the raw edges.

3 **Joining two straight edges (for example, beading with entredeux to faggoting):** Trim the edges of the laces and butt them together. Do not overlap them. Set the zigzag width to catch both laces and machine with the right sides facing up.

4 **Roll, whip and gather (for example, gathering lace):** Proceed as for roll and whip, but place a strong thread – buttonhole twist or quilting thread – under the centre of the machine foot. Guide the thread through the centre of the zigzag as you work. Pull the thread up to gather the lace to the required length.

❹ ASSEMBLING THE GOWN

When you are assembling the christening gown, use a 1 cm seam allowance for all standard seams.

Skirt placket

1 Make the placket by machine stitching about 4 mm down either side of the centre back to the point, taking one stitch across to turn at the point. Cut between the lines of stitching.

2 Cut a strip of batiste 22 cm x 3 cm along the straight grain. Open the placket right out so that the stitching is in a straight line. With the right side of the strip to the wrong side of the skirt, machine along the previous line of stitching. When you reach the point, leave the needle down, raise the presser foot and push the excess fabric back out of the way. Lower the presser foot and finish the stitching.
3 Press down 5 mm along the raw edge of the strip. Fold the strip over to the right side of the skirt, place the pressed edge over the machine stitching, and machine topstitch as close to the edge as possible.

4 Machine stitch the end of the placket diagonally to reinforce it, and press the placket into place.

Skirt hem

1 If you are making tucks at the lower edge of the skirt, sew three tucks following the steps for tucked inserts in 'Making the lace fabric'.

2 Join the remaining piece of lace fabric to the hem of the skirt, using heirloom sewing method 2.

Skirt to yokes

1 On both the back yoke pieces, press creases along the fold line of the self-interfacing and the fold line of the button extension.

2 Machine two rows of large gathering stitches along the top edges of the front and back skirt. With right sides together, match the dots on the four yoke pieces and the skirt piece. Align the placket edge with the fold line of the button extension. Adjust the gathers and machine stitch the seams.

3 Press the self-interfacing to the wrong side along the fold line. Fold the back yoke over the skirt along the button extension line and stitch the skirt to the yokes through all layers along the seam line.

4 Neaten the edges with a fine zigzag stitch and press the seams towards the yokes. The finished seam will be about 4 mm wide.

Front panel to garment

1 Trim the front seam allowances of the side panels to 4 mm.

2 With right sides together, attach the front panel to the garment, using heirloom sewing method 2. Widen the zigzag to catch all three layers.

Shoulder seams and neck binding

1 With right sides together, machine stitch the shoulder seams. Neaten the edges with a narrow zigzag.

2 Cut a bias strip of batiste 4 cm wide and about 35 cm long. Press it in half lengthwise, wrong sides together.

3 Trim a 1 cm seam allowance from the neck and machine stitch the bias strip to the right side of the garment using a 5 mm seam. Wrap about 1 cm of binding around to the wrong side at either side of the back opening. Fold the binding over to the wrong side and slipstitch it into place.

Sleeves

1 Using heirloom sewing method 2, join 70 cm of beading with entredeux to 70 cm of edging lace. (Do not gather the edging lace.) Cut the piece in half and attach one piece to each sleeve hem, using heirloom sewing method 2.

2 Sew two rows of gathering stitches around the shoulder line of the sleeves between the dots.

3 With right sides together and the lace edging aligned, machine stitch the underarm seams and neaten them with a fine zigzag stitch. The finished seams will be about 4 mm wide.

4 With right sides together, set the sleeves into the armholes, matching the dots and notches and adjusting the gathers evenly. Machine stitch the seams and zigzag to neaten.

5 FINISHING THE GOWN

1 Machine three horizontal buttonholes in one back yoke buttonhole extension, in the positions marked on the master pattern. Sew the buttons to the other back yoke on the centre back line, in positions to correspond with the buttonholes.

2 Cut the remainder of the ribbon in half and thread the pieces through the beading on the sleeves. Use the threaded ribbons to gather the sleeves slightly, and tie the ribbons in a bow.

NOTE
If the laces you choose are wider or narrower than those specified, work out a plan for sewing the laces together that will give you a piece of lace fabric about 10 cm wide.

Jingle bears

The bright colours, contrasting stitching and jingling bells of this string of soft bears are sure to hold a baby's attention and will not drive mum crazy!

WHAT YOU NEED

Master pattern **A7(a)** • 2 m each of red, yellow and blue Russia braid • 3 pieces of different coloured fabric, each 15 cm **x** 20 cm • polyester stuffing, 50 g • small quantities of stranded embroidery cotton: green, yellow, blue, brown, black • sewing thread to match the fabric • 1 m red embroidery ribbon, 4 mm wide • 50 cm blue embroidery ribbon, 4 mm wide • strong sewing thread • needles: size 8 crewel, size 20 tapestry • 4 bells (enclosed safety variety) • tracing paper • pencil • scissors
● *Technique pages 292–301, 307–14, 343–4*

❶ PLAITING THE BRAID

1 Place the three braids side by side. Knot them together 4 cm from one end and knot them again a further 4 cm along. This forms a loop for attaching the toy to the pram.
2 Plait the three braids together to make a length as wide as the pram and tie off the braids. (Two metres of braid will make just over a metre of plait.) Tie off the braid to form another loop. Trim surplus braid.

❷ CUTTING OUT THE BEARS

1 Trace the design from the master pattern, including the dots that indicate the turning holes.
2 Fold the fabric in half, pin the pattern to the fabric and cut out to make two identical bear shapes. Repeat for each piece of fabric.

❸ EMBROIDERING THE BEARS

1 Using two strands of embroidery cotton and following the stitch guide, embroider the bears' eyes in black and their mouths and noses in brown.
2 Following the stitch guide, embroider the tummies of the bears with the ribbon and embroidery cotton. Work the tummy design on the blue bear and the yellow bear with red ribbon in spider's web stitch, and on the third bear work the tummy design in lazy daisy stitch using blue ribbon.
3 Embroider the stems of the small flowers in fly stitch using two strands of green cotton. Form the flowers with French knots, using two strands of yellow embroidery cotton for two of the bears and two strands of blue embroidery cotton for the third.

`--- Backstitch	● French knot
▲ Satin stitch	✦ Spider's web stitch
Y Fly stitch	ℚ Lazy daisy stitch

Stitch guide
Silk ribbon is best for ribbon embroidery, as it sits and folds more smoothly and is easier to manage than synthetic ribbon.

❹ FINISHING

1 Using thread to match the fabrics and with right sides facing, stitch around each bear to join the backs to the fronts, leaving the sections between the dots open.
2 Trim and clip the curves and turn the work right side out.
3 Fill the bears with polyester stuffing. Close the opening with ladder stitch and then sew across the ears, close to the head, using running stitch.
4 Position the bears along the braid and sew each paw to it. Sew the bells to the braid between the bears. Use strong sewing thread and attach the bells and bears very firmly.

VARIATION

*To adapt this toy for a cot, lengthen the plaited braid to match the width of the cot and add extra bears as required. For each additional bear you will need 15 cm **x** 20 cm of coloured fabric and a bell, plus a small quantity of filling.*

New baby sampler

The birth of a baby is a very special time for parents, and what better way to mark the occasion than with this cross-stitch sampler? Mounted in a suitable frame, it makes a unique and lasting gift.

Master pattern **J68(a–b)** •
50 cm **x** 45 cm 14 gauge aida
cloth • stranded cotton: Anchor
colours 1 (white), 11 (red), 24
(pink), 216 (green), 293 (yellow),
313 (orange), 355 (light brown),
382 (dark brown), 9159 (blue) •
coloured tacking thread • needle:
size 24 tapestry • embroidery
hoop • picture frame with an inside
measurement of 41 cm **x** 36.5 cm •
A2 white backing board • A2
mounting board • linen carpet
thread or fine, strong string (for
mounting) • craft knife • steel rule •
tracing paper • scissors • pencil •
tape measure • spray glue
● *Technique pages 309, 343–4*

❶ MAKING THE SAMPLER

1 Iron the aida cloth and hand over-sew or machine zigzag the raw edges.
2 Mark the vertical and horizontal centre lines with tacking stitches.
3 Following the stitch and colour guide on the master pattern, work the border design. This becomes a reference point for the rest of the design.
4 Complete the design, working one small area at a time and following the stitch and colour guide carefully.

❷ PERSONALISING THE SAMPLER

1 On tracing paper, rule a straight line to act as a guide. From the master pattern for cross-stitch letters, trace the letters of the baby's name and the date of birth. Leave a space the width of two cross-stitches between letters and a space equivalent to four cross-stitches between words. You will not

be able to fit more than 12 characters across the sampler, so use only the child's given name if necessary. Mark the mid-point of your tracings.
2 Match the mid-point of the name to the centre point of the design in the space provided at the top of the sampler. Embroider the letters using colours of your choice, starting from the middle and working outwards.
3 Repeat step 2 for the date of the baby's birth, embroidering in the space provided at the base of the sampler. You may need to shorten the name of the month.

❸ FRAMING THE SAMPLER

1 Press the sampler on the wrong side through a damp cloth, being very careful not to stretch the fabric or the stitching.
2 To frame the sampler, follow the steps described in 'Wedding day sampler' (pages 194–5).

NOTE

For some tips on counted cross-stitch, turn to 'Wedding day sampler' (pages 194–5).

When you are embroidering the baby's name and date of birth, begin at the mid-point of the line of text and work outwards to the sides of the sampler.

Benjamin Bear

Every young child loves a teddy bear as a friend. This appealing mohair bear is fully jointed and stands 27 cm tall. A colourful neck bow is the perfect finishing touch.

Master pattern **C23(a–j)** • 65 cm **x** 30 cm mohair fabric • two 8 mm perspex safety eyes • joint set: two 30 mm wooden discs, eight 25 mm wooden discs, five M5 **x** 25 mm machine screws, five M5 lock nuts, 10 small washers • 15 cm **x** 15 cm felt • sewing thread to match mohair fabric • black and brown embroidery cotton • coarse thread or waxed dental floss • polyester stuffing, about 300 g • needles: general sewing, size 22 chenille (for embroidery), size 18 tapestry (for closing seams) • dressmaking pins • 50 cm ribbon, 25 mm wide • tracing paper • pencil • fabric marker • sewing machine • fine-pointed scissors • pocket spanner (for lock nuts) • screwdriver • chopstick

● *Technique pages 292–301, 343–4*

Cutting guide
Cut the body pieces from mohair fabric and the paws and foot pads from felt.

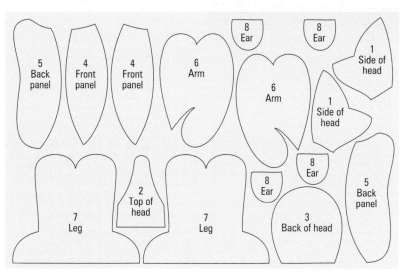

1 TRACING THE PATTERN

1 Trace the pattern pieces from the master pattern on to tracing paper, tracing reverse pattern pieces where indicated. Transfer all the arrows, markings, lettered points and symbols.
2 Cut carefully around the outline of each piece.

2 CUTTING OUT

1 Establish the direction of the pile of the mohair fabric by running your hand over it. It will feel smooth when your hand is moving in the direction of the pile. Lay all the pattern pieces in the same direction as the pile.

NOTE

A 6 mm seam allowance is included in the pattern. As you pin the pieces of fabric together, push the pile away from the cut edge. You can sew the bear with a sewing machine (except for the last stages) or by hand, using backstitch and strong thread.

2 With the wrong side of the mohair fabric facing up, pin each pair of pattern pieces 1 to 8 on to the fabric, following the cutting guide in the panel on page 18. Make sure the arrows marked on the pattern pieces follow the direction of the pile.
3 Trace around each pattern piece with the fabric marker. Transfer all markings, including the positions of joints and eyes.
4 Cut out the mohair pieces with the fine-pointed scissors, taking care not to cut through the pile of the mohair.
5 Pin pairs of pattern pieces 9 and 10 to the felt, trace around them with the fabric marker and cut out.

❸ SEWING
Head and ears

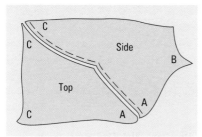

1 With the right sides of the fabric together, pin and stitch the centre front seam under the chin from A to B and the top of the head to the sides of the head from A to C.

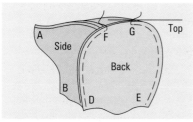

2 Pin and sew the back of the head to the front and side head piece, sewing

from D to F and E to G. Pin across the opening FG at the top of the head, but do not stitch.
3 Using a strong thread, run a gathering stitch by hand around the base of the neck. Draw up the ends of the thread tightly and secure.
4 Turn the work right side out and make small holes with pointed scissors at the positions marked for the eyes. Push the shafts of the safety eyes through the holes and click the safety discs on to the shafts on the wrong side of the fabric.
5 With right sides facing, pin ear pieces together in pairs. Sew around the curved edge of each ear, but not along the base. Turn right side out.
6 At the base of each ear, fold the raw edges approximately 5 mm to the inside and oversew by hand. Put the ears aside for later use.

Arms and legs

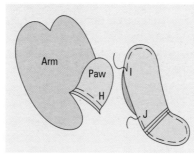

1 Matching H on the felt paw pad to H on the arm, and with right sides of the fabrics together, pin and sew the paw to the inner arm.
2 Fold the arm in half lengthwise, so that the right sides of fabric are facing. Pin and sew around the top of the arm and down around the felt paw pad, leaving an opening between I and J. Turn the work to the right side.
3 Repeat steps 1 and 2 to sew a paw pad to the other arm.

4 Fold the leg in half lengthwise, so that right sides of the fabric are facing.

Pin and sew from K to L and M to N leaving an opening between L and M.

5 Match the foot pad centre O to the centre seam of the leg (N). Ease the foot pad to fit the leg snugly, and sew. Turn the work to the right side.
6 Repeat steps 3 and 4 to sew the pad to the other leg.

Body

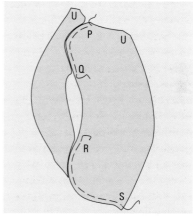

1 With right sides of fabric facing, pin and sew the back panels together from P to Q and R to S, leaving an opening between Q and R.
2 With right sides of fabric facing, pin and sew the front panels together from T to S.

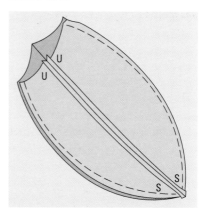

3 With right sides facing, pin and sew the front body piece to the back body piece, matching the points at U on both sides and also matching the seams at the crotch (S).

BEAR PERSONALITY

When you embroider the face on to your bear, give some thought to the expression you want to achieve. Try sketching the face on paper first, experimenting with the shape and position of the nose and mouth. Keep the shapes simple and when you are happy with your face, start embroidering from the centre of the nose, following your sketch.

4 With a strong, coarse thread, run a gathering stitch by hand around the top of neck. Draw up the ends tightly and secure with a knot. Turn the work to the right side.

❹ ASSEMBLING THE BEAR

1 On to a screw, put a washer and then a 30 mm wooden disc and a ring of felt cut a little larger than the disc. The felt will prevent the disc from rubbing and weakening the fabric.
2 Place the screw into the head through the opening at the top. Push the shaft through the gathered edge of the neck so that the end of the screw protrudes from the base of the head. Then push the protruding screw through the gathered neck opening at the top of the body.
3 Reaching through the back body

opening, place on the screw another piece of felt, a 30 mm wooden disc, a washer and a lock nut.
4 Finger-tighten the lock nut. Using a single socket spanner, continue to tighten the lock nut until it feels snug. Use a screwdriver, through the opening at the top of the head, to prevent the machine screw from turning.
5 Using fine-pointed scissors, carefully make holes through the fabric at the joint marks on the inner arms and legs and on the body.
6 Follow steps 1 to 4 above to make the arm joints. Use the smaller wooden discs and position the joints by working through the openings in the limbs and back. Make sure that the joints are screwed firmly together, otherwise the arms and legs will soon begin to flop.

You can buy a joint set from specialist craft stores. The set consists of five joints, used to make the neck, arm and leg joints rigid. Assemble the joints as shown in the diagram. Make sure the bottom nuts are firmly screwed home, or the limbs will tend to flop.

❺ FINISHING

1 Using the chopstick, stuff the arms and legs firmly, making sure that the polyester filling is pushed well down into the paws and feet. Be careful not to push the stuffing tool through the felt paw pads.
2 Close all seam openings in the limbs with ladder stitch, using coarse thread or waxed dental floss. Embroider black claws on the paws with straight stitch, securing the thread with tiny backstitches.
3 Stuff the body firmly, being careful to push plenty of stuffing around the neck, arm and leg joints. Close the opening in the back in the same way as for the limbs.
4 Stuff the head firmly, moulding it into shape as you go. Close the opening on top of the head.
5 Work the nose with brown embroidery cotton. Secure the thread with a knot in the centre of the nose area. Using closely spaced satin stitch, go over and over the same area until the nose is built up. To finish, fasten off the thread by running the needle back and forth underneath the satin stitches to catch the material.
6 Pin the ears into position and ladder stitch them to the head. Remember that different positions for the eyes and ears can completely change the look of the bear.
7 Tie the ribbon in a bow round the bear's neck. Choose ribbon in a bright colour or a bold pattern, such as tartan or Paisley.

Washer
Felt
Bolt
Wooden disc
Nut

Embroidered baby's vests

Buy inexpensive cotton vests and transform them into a beautiful, personalised present for a small baby by working simple designs on the vests using coloured cottons and a few easy stitches.

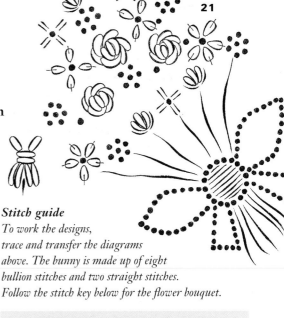

When you are working the embroidery, use the straw needle for the bullion knots and the crewel needle for all other stitches.

① BUNNY VESTS
Embroidering the armholes
1 Fold the vest in half to find the centre. Using the embroidery marking pen, mark positions for the French knots so that they are evenly spaced around the armholes. Avoid the armpit area, as the embroidery may irritate the baby's skin.
2 With three strands of embroidery cotton in your chosen colour, work French knots at the marked positions, running the thread behind the fabric and on to the next stitch.

Embroidering the bunnies
1 Find the centre front point of the neck. Using an embroidery marking pen, mark the positions of the bunnies. Place the centre bunny slightly lower than the other two.
2 Using three strands of embroidery cotton in your chosen colour, work the bodies with four bullion knots, turning the thread around the needle 10 times. Make the necks with two bullion knots, turning the thread six times. Make one bullion knot for each ear, turning the thread five times.
3 Work the tail using three strands of white embroidery cotton and straight stitch.

② LONG-SLEEVED VEST
Embroidering the neckline
Using two strands of embroidery cotton in your chosen colour, work chain stitch around the neckline.

Embroidering the sleeves
1 Mark the positions of the seven bullion rosebuds so that they are evenly spaced around the wrists.
2 Embroider the rosebuds in the colours of your choice, turning the

Stitch guide
To work the designs, trace and transfer the diagrams above. The bunny is made up of eight bullion stitches and two straight stitches. Follow the stitch key below for the flower bouquet.

🌿 Padded satin stitch		🌀	Bullion rose
✳ Satin stitch flower		🌀	Lazy daisy stitch
⚫ French knot flower		＼	Backstitch
🌿 Bullion rosebud		●	French knot

thread five times round the needle for the centre bullion knots and seven times for the two outer bullion knots.

Embroidering the body
1 Following the stitch guide, and using colours of your choice, work the design on the body of the vest.
2 To make the bow, backstitch the outline with two strands and work the centre in padded satin stitch using three strands. Make the surrounding French knots using three strands.
3 Work the roses in bullion knots, turning the thread around the needle six times for the centres and 12 times for the outside petals.
4 Work the half-open roses with three bullion knots.
5 Make the French knot flowers with three strands. Start by working a central knot, and then make five or six knots around the edge.
6 To make the lazy daisy flower petals, use two strands. Repeat for the other three petals. The bud is one French knot using three strands.
7 To make the satin stitch buds, work a central French knot using three strands of embroidery cotton. Work the four surrounding petals in satin stitch using two strands.
8 Work the individual French knots using three strands.

'B is for Baby' quilt

This quilt, measuring 90 cm x 125 cm, is embroidered in traditional cream on cream using simple embroidery stitches. It is an ideal gift for either a girl or a boy.

WHAT YOU NEED

Master pattern **A2**(a–h) • 2.5 m quilter's muslin or calico, 150 cm wide • 7 m heavy, double-edged, cream cotton lace, 60 mm wide • Coton à broder (the same colour as the fabric) • 100 cm x 150 cm batting • cream quilting thread • cream machine sewing thread • needle: chenille size 22 • dress-making pins • large embroidery hoop • tracing paper • black felt-tipped pen • water-erasable fabric marking pen • scissors • sewing thread to match calico and lace • sewing machine
● *Technique pages 292–301, 307–12, 343–4*

❶ PREPARING THE FABRIC

1 Fold the quilter's muslin in half lengthwise, selvage to selvage, and cut out the following pieces, as shown in the diagram *Cutting out the fabric:*
A one 100 cm x 150 cm piece

(backing); **B** six 36 cm squares (embroidery blocks); **C** two 92 cm x 13 cm strips (end borders); **D** two 104 cm x 13 cm strips (side borders); **E** two 95 cm x 9 cm strips (end bindings); **F** two 128 cm x 9 cm strips (side bindings).
2 Fold and quarter the embroidery blocks and borders to find the centres, and mark the centre of each piece.

❷ EMBROIDERING THE FABRIC

1 Using tracing paper and the black felt-tipped pen, trace a working design from the master pattern.
2 Match the centre of each embroidery block and border with the centre of the appropriate working design and pin them together with the fabric on top. Note that the bunny, bear and bluebird look best if they face into the centre of the quilt.
3 Place the fabric and design on a light box or tape it firmly to a window. Using the fabric marking pen, trace the design on to the fabric.
4 Embroider the designs, following the stitch guides given on the master pattern pieces.
5 When the embroidery is complete, wash out any transfer marks. Dry the work flat and press the pieces from the back on a towel.

❸ ASSEMBLING THE EMBROIDERED FABRIC

1 Arrange the blocks in position. With right sides facing, stitch the blocks together in pairs, then join the pairs, matching the seam lines.
2 With right sides facing, sew the side border strips to the centre panel. Then sew the top and bottom borders to the centre panel and side borders. Trim if necessary.
3 Place the work face down on a towel and press from the back.

❹ ATTACHING THE LACE

1 Wash and press the lace to preshrink it. From the 7 m length of double-edged lace, cut two 70 cm strips and one 104 cm strip.
2 Fold under 5 mm at each end of the lace strips. Using a medium zig-zag stitch, machine down the centre of the lace in the least obvious place, attaching the two shorter strips along the horizontal seam lines of the centre panel and the long strip down the vertical seam of the centre panel. The folded ends of the lace, which will extend beyond the edges of the centre panel, will be secured in step 3.

CUTTING OUT THE FABRIC

Pattern pieces include a 1 cm seam allowance. The sizes given are those you need to construct the quilt. You can cut the fabric blocks larger for easy handling in a large embroidery hoop, then trim them to the correct size after rinsing and pressing. Cut the border strips a little longer to allow a safety margin, and trim them to size after sewing each pair of strips to the blocks.

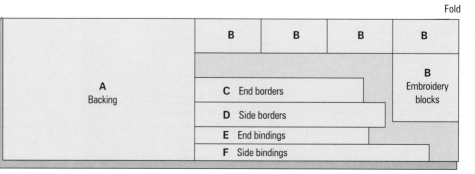

Allow plenty of time to measure, cut and mark the pattern pieces accurately. You will save yourself time and frustration later on, and the result will be a professional finish that will delight you.

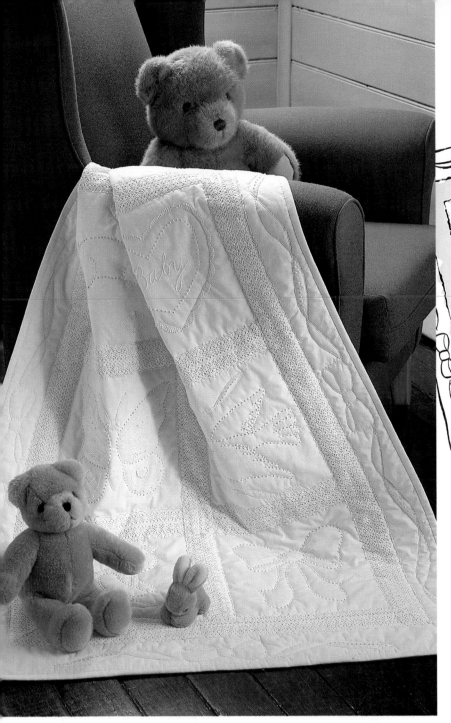

The six motifs are worked on separate blocks of fabric that are stitched together. The whole panel is framed with long strips of fabric and then the embroidered blocks are bordered with lace.

3 Use the remainder of the lace to stitch a border around the centre panel, securing the ends of the other lace strips in the process and mitring the raw edges neatly.
4 Carefully press the finished piece from the back over a towel.

⑤ ASSEMBLING THE QUILT

1 Lay the backing piece out flat with the wrong side facing up. Tape or pin the wadding on to it and then lay the embroidered fabric over the top, right side facing up. Pin all the layers together, matching the centres. Note that the backing and the wadding are larger than the top fabric. Tack all three layers together by hand.
2 Using a small running stitch, hand quilt around the outlines of the motifs.
3 Hand quilt around each block, securing the lace edges as you go. Handstitch any remaining loose edges of lace to the top layer.
4 Fold all the binding strips in half lengthwise, wrong sides facing, and press, then open the pieces out again.
5 Working first with a short piece of binding, pin the binding to the top edge of the quilt, right sides facing, and machine stitch through all layers, allowing a 1.5 cm seam.

6 Repeat step 5 to attach the binding to the bottom edge of the quilt. Trim the wadding and the backing fabric at the top and bottom edges of the quilt and fold the bindings to the back.
7 Turn under a 1.5 cm hem and slipstitch the back of the binding strips into place along the row of machine stitching. Trim the ends of the binding level with the edges of the quilt.
8 Repeat steps 5 to 7 to attach the long pieces of binding to the sides of the quilt, trimming the ends of the binding so that they extend about 1.5 cm beyond the edge.
9 Fold the ends back into the binding and slipstitch them neatly into place, keeping the stitching at the back of the quilt and the corners square.

Soft animal toys

The soft and simple animal toys in this project are designed to stimulate a baby's senses. You can make them as clutch toys for tiny babies or rattle toys for older babies, or as flat bath toys or teething aids.

Master pattern B13(a–f)
Clutch toys
Scraps of closely woven fabric • fabric scraps: seersucker, taffeta, satin or heavily napped fabric • sewing thread • polyester stuffing • fabric paints or black embroidery cotton • needles: size 6 sharp, size 7 crewel • dressmaking pins • scissors • blunt implement (e.g. chopstick) • tracing paper • pencil • sewing machine • small ball-shaped bell and piece of 6 mm foam sheeting 3 cm x 6 cm (for a bell), or small plastic screw-on lid 3–4 cm in diameter, small flat button and piece of interfacing or firmly woven fabric (for a rattle)
Bath toys
60 cm x 30 cm terry towelling or 2 flannels, 30 cm x 30 cm • 6 mm foam sheeting, 30 cm x 30 cm • needles: size 6 sharp, size 7 crewel • sewing thread • embroidery threads • tracing paper • pencil • scissors • dressmaking pins • sewing machine
● *Technique pages 292–301, 307–12, 343–4*

These toys are an ideal gift for a new baby. They are portable, washable, and inexpensive to make using scraps from the ragbag or the remnant bin.

Clutch toys

❶ MAKING THE TOY
1 Using tracing paper and scissors, trace and cut the shape you have selected from the master pattern.
2 Cut a pair of shapes from the fabric, making sure that the straight grain runs the same way for both shapes.
3 Using fabric paints or embroidery thread, add facial details or decorative features to the right side of the fabric. Remember that the larger the area covered by paint, the more difficult the shape will be to turn right side out. Do not paint within the 5 mm seam allowance. Let the paint dry.

4 With right sides of the fabric facing, pin the shapes together, leaving a 4 cm opening on a straight, gently

VARIATION
The simple shapes that make up this set of toys can be part of a whole range of matching gifts. They can be used as motifs for quilts, pillowcases and curtains, or as stencils for furniture, to give a baby's room that totally coordinated look.

curving section. Machine stitch along the seam line, 5 mm from the edges. Stitch again for strength.
5 Clip the curves and notch the seam allowance in the tight corners, taking care not to cut the stitching. Tie and cut off the loose threads.

❷ MAKING THE BELL OR RATTLE
The bell
Enclose the bell in a little pillow of foam sheeting so that the toy will be safe for the baby to play with.

1 Using a needle, attach a double thread to the bell. Place the bell on the foam and fold the foam over so that the bell and the thread are enclosed in the fold.

2 Securely handstitch the edges of the foam together to form a little pillow containing the bell.

The rattle
1 Cut a circle of fabric or interfacing 5 mm larger in diameter than the container lid and another circle 5 mm larger in diameter than the first.

2 Place the lid on the smaller circle of fabric, put a button in the lid, and cover with the larger circle.

3 Using doubled thread, handstitch the circles together to enclose the lid and the button.

4 Sew around the circles again to make the fabric fit tightly against the lid. If the fabric is not pulled tight, the stuffing will push into the lid and the rattle will not work.

❸ FINISHING THE TOY

1 Turn the fabric shape right side out. You will need to use the blunt implement to push out the pointed sections at the extremities.

2 Fill the toy with the polyester stuffing. Start with the extremities and make sure not to overstuff. The toy should be flattish, not bulky.

3 Insert the bell or rattle. Complete the stuffing and then close the opening with ladder stitch or whip stitch.

Bath toys

❶ MAKING THE BATH TOY

1 Using the tracing paper and scissors, trace and cut a broad, simple shape from the master pattern.

2 Place two flannels or pieces of terry towelling together, right sides facing.

Pin the paper pattern in position and cut out the shape. Keeping the shapes together, pin them to the foam sheeting. Cut the foam to shape.

3 Keeping all layers pinned together, machine stitch along the seamline 5 mm from the edges, leaving a 4 cm opening on a gently curving section. Stitch again for strength.

4 Turn the toy right side out, using the blunt implement to push out any pointed sections. Close the opening by hand, using ladder stitch.

5 Topstitch with matching or contrasting thread 5 mm from the edge. Add details with embroidery.

HINT
A terry towelling bath toy can be an excellent teething aid. Simply dampen the fabric and chill the toy in the refrigerator to make a safe, soothing object for a teething baby to suck on.

Rocking horse overalls

Designed for an energetic one-year-old, these overalls are a practical and attractive gift to make for a busy baby.

WHAT YOU NEED

Master pattern **A4(a–e)** • 1.5 m light to medium weight fabric, 115 cm wide • 15 cm **x** 40 cm even-weave linen for cross-stitch (26 threads to 2.5 cm) • 30 cm lightweight iron-on interfacing • 2.5 m fine piping cord • 2.5 m bias binding, to complement the main fabric • 2 buttons (15 mm), to match bias binding • Anchor stranded embroidery thread: 376 (beige), 380 (brown), 109 (mauve), 928 (duck egg blue) (or a colour scheme of your choice) • sewing thread to match fabric • needles: tapestry, general sewing • embroidery frame (optional) • scissors • tracing paper • pencil • dressmaker's pencil • sewing machine • dressmaking pins
● *Technique pages 292–301, 309, 343–4*

❶ CUTTING OUT THE FABRIC

1 Using tracing paper, pencil and scissors, trace all the pattern pieces from the master pattern. Make sure that all markings are transferred.
2 Pin the pattern pieces on to the main fabric, following the cutting guide, and cut them out. Do not cut the linen for the front panel piece.
3 From the interfacing, cut out one front yoke, one back yoke and two leg bands.

❷ MAKING THE FRONT PANEL

1 To centre the cross-stitch design, measure and mark the horizontal and vertical centre lines of the linen with coloured tacking thread. The intersection of the lines is the centre point.
2 Using two strands of embroidery thread, follow the stitch and colour guide to work the rocking horse.
3 When you have finished the cross-stitch, place the work face down, cover it with a damp cloth and press it carefully with a warm iron.
4 Centre the pattern piece for the cross-stitched panel on the cross-stitched linen by matching the centre front of the pattern piece with the vertical tacked line. Pin the pattern piece to the linen and cut out the panel. Remove the tacking threads.
5 Cover the piping cord with bias binding, using the machine zip foot and machining close to the cord. On the right side of the neck edge of the embroidered panel, lay the piping along the seam allowance line. Using the zip foot, machine the piping to the panel.
6 Fold and press the seam allowance to the back so that the piping lies along the edge of the fold.

> **NOTES**
> ● *Seam allowances are 1 cm.*
> ● *Finish all seams with over-locking or zigzag.*

❸ SEWING THE YOKE

1 Fuse the yoke interfacings to the wrong sides of one main fabric front yoke and one main fabric back yoke.

2 With the right sides of the two main fabric front yokes together, start machining the armhole 5 cm below the shoulder. Sew up to the shoulder, along the shoulder, around the neckline and along the other shoulder, finishing at the same point on the other armhole. Notch and clip the seam.
3 Turn the front yoke right side out and press. Ensuring that the front yoke piece is sitting free of the interfaced front yoke and that the neck turnings are pressed down, tack the cross-stitched panel to the right side of the front yoke piece just below the horizontal edge of the neckline so that the piping sits up over the

finished edge. Topstitch the cross-stitched panel into place across the front yoke from armhole to armhole.

4 Turn the front yoke inside out as far as necessary. With right sides facing, sew the front of the yoke to the back along the side seams. Repeat for the yoke facings. Press seams open.

5 Machine the remainder of the yoke to the facing in one continuous seam, blending the seam into the previous stitching at the upper front armholes. Press the lower edge of the yoke facing up 1 cm. Attach piping around the lower edge of the right side of the main yoke along the seam line, as for the embroidered panel in step 3.

6 Clip and notch the armhole and neckline turnings. Turn the work right side out and press.

❹ SEWING THE PANTS

1 With right sides together, machine the front and back inside leg and side seams. Zigzag to finish, and press the seams towards the back.

2 With right sides together, place one leg inside the other and stitch the crotch seam from the centre front to the centre back. Zigzag to finish, and press to one side.

3 Machine two rows of gathering stitches around the upper edge and the calf edges of the pants.

❺ SEWING THE YOKE TO THE PANTS

1 With right sides facing, pin the lower edge of the outside yoke to

STITCH AND COLOUR GUIDE

Embroider the linen panel before sewing it on to the front yoke of the overalls. Find the centre of the panel by tacking the horizontal and vertical centre lines, and then follow the colour and stitch guide below.

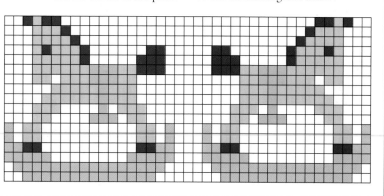

the top edge of the pants, matching centre points and side seams. Pull up the gathering and adjust the gathers evenly. The piping will be sandwiched in the seam. Using the zip foot, stitch around the seam. Trim the seam and press it up into the yoke.

2 Slipstitch the pressed edge of the interfaced yoke over the seam.

❻ LEG BANDS

1 Iron the leg band interfacings to the wrong sides of two of the leg bands. With right sides facing, stitch all four leg band seams. Press open.

2 Pin and stitch covered piping cord to the right sides of the long edges of the outside leg bands (not interfaced), using the zip foot.

3 With right sides together, and using the zip foot, machine the

interfaced leg bands to the lower edges of the piped leg bands. Press down a 1 cm hem along the other edges of the interfaced leg bands.

4 Around the calf edges, match the inner leg seams of the pants to the leg band seams, with right sides together and raw edges aligned. Pull up the gathers and adjust evenly. Using the zip foot, stitch the leg bands to the legs in the same way as you stitched the yoke to the top of the pants.

5 Slipstitch the pressed edges of the interfaced leg bands to the wrong sides over the seam line.

❼ FINISHING

Machine stitch vertical buttonholes in the back shoulder straps. Sew the buttons to the front shoulder straps, aligning them with the buttonholes.

Cutting guide

Cut two of each piece from the main fabric. To cut the yokes, trace around the pattern pieces on to the fabric with the dressmaker's pencil and then flip the pattern pieces, as shown by the dotted lines. For the embroidered panel, use a piece of linen 25 cm x 40 cm and work the cross-stitch embroidery before cutting out the pattern.

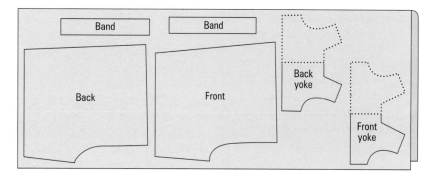

Cot blanket

Made by embroidering crocheted panels, this attractive little blanket will keep baby warm during those first months and then will become a treasured 'cover-up' for naps. It measures about 75 cm x 110 cm.

Yarn: 19 balls Patons 4 ply Fairytale (50 g balls) • Anchor stranded embroidery cotton: 8 skeins 336 (apricot), 3 skeins 976 (pale blue), 3 skeins 978 (dark blue), 1 skein 338 (terracotta), 1 skein 403 (black) • crochet hook: 3.50 mm (no. 9) • needle: size 20 chenille • dressmaker's pencil
● *Technique pages 307–12, 320–2, 327*

CHECKING THE TENSION

Before you begin, check your tension for both plain and lace crochet so that the measurements of the finished article will be as close as possible to the specified size. Using a 3.50 mm crochet hook, you should have 24 double crochets and 27 rows to a 10 cm square of plain crochet and 11 patterns and 12 rows to a 10 cm square of lace crochet. If you have fewer stitches, use a smaller hook; if you have more, use a bigger hook. The

SPECIAL TERMS

Cluster: ★ yoh, draw up a loop in next 2 ch sp, yoh and draw through first 2 loops on hook, rep from ★ twice in same 2 ch sp, yoh and draw through all 4 loops on hook.
Crab stitch: Crab stitch is like double crochet, except that it is worked from left to right instead of right to left, so that the stitches are worked backwards.

STITCH AND COLOUR GUIDE

Find the centre of the square you intend to work in and match it with the centre of the motif on the grid below. Starting from the centre point, cross-stitch the motif in the colours specified by matching the stitches in your crocheted square to the squares on the grid below.

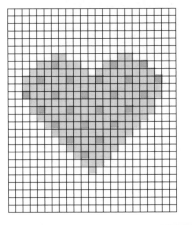

blanket has been designed to be worked on a bigger hook at a looser tension than is usually recommended.

CROCHETING THE PANELS

The blanket is made up of seven panels, each consisting of 10 alternating squares of plain and lace crochet. The first panel begins with a plain square and the second begins with a lace square. Make four of the first panel and three of the second.

❶ FIRST PANEL

Plain square
Loosely work 24 ch.
1st row: Miss 1 ch, 1 dc in each ch to end to make 23 dc.
2nd row: ★★ 1 ch, 1 dc in each dc to end.
Rep 2nd row 25 times.

Lace square

1st row: 2 ch, 1 htr in each of first 2 dc, ★ 2 ch, miss 1 dc, 1 htr in next dc, rep from ★ to last dc, 1 htr in last dc to make 10 sps.
2nd row: (1 dc, 1 ch) in first htr, 1 tr in next htr, cluster in first 2 ch sp, ★ 1 ch, miss 1 htr, cluster in next 2 ch sp, rep from ★ to last 2 htr, 1 tr in each of last 2 htr.
3rd row: 2 ch, 1 htr in each of first 2 tr, 2 ch, miss cluster, ★ 1 htr in next 1 ch sp, 2 ch, miss cluster, rep from ★ to last 2 sts, 1 htr in next tr, 1 htr in top of turning ch.
Rep 2nd and 3rd rows 5 times. †

Plain square

1st row: 1 ch, 1 dc in each of first 2 htr, ★ 1 dc in 2 ch sp, 1 dc in next htr, rep from ★ to last htr, 1 dc in

④ EMBROIDERING THE DESIGNS

1 Find the centre of each of the squares to be embroidered by using the dressmaker's pencil to mark the point where the diagonals cross. Match these centre points to the centre points of the embroidery designs and work the embroidery, treating the rows and stitches on the square as the cross-stitch grid.
2 Following the stitch and colour guide, and using the diagram below for the position of each motif, work the cross-stitch designs on the plain squares in the four first panels.
3 Using the black stranded cotton, outline the hands and faces in back-stitch and French knots, as shown on the stitch and colour guide.

⑤ FINISHING OFF

With the right side of the work facing, work three rounds of double crochet and then one round of crab stitch around the outside edge of the blanket to make a border. Increase or decrease as necessary to keep the work flat.

The blanket consists of seven panels, with 10 squares in each panel. Alternate panels start with a plain square or a lace square. Embroider the motifs on the blanket after sewing the panels together.

last htr to make 23 dc. ★★
Rep from ★★ to ★★ 4 times, finishing at † at end of last rep.
Fasten off.
(Make 4 of these panels altogether.)

② SECOND PANEL

Lace square
Loosely work 25 ch.
1st row: Miss 2 ch, 1 htr in each of next 2 ch, ★ 2 ch, miss 1 ch, 1 htr in next ch, rep from ★ to last ch, 1 htr in last ch to make 10 sps.
2nd and 3rd rows: ★★★ Work as for 2nd and 3rd rows of lace square in 1st panel 6 times.

Plain square
1st row: 1 ch, 1 dc in each of first 2 htr, ★ 1 dc in 2 ch sp, 1 dc in next htr, rep from ★ to last htr, 1 dc in last htr

to make 23 dc.
2nd row: 1 ch, 1 dc in each dc to end.
Rep 2nd row 25 times. ††

Lace square
1st row: 2 ch, 1 htr in each of first 2 dc, ★ 2 ch, miss 1 dc, 1 htr in next dc, rep from ★ to last dc, 1 htr in last dc to make 10 sps. ★★★

Rep from ★★★ to ★★★ 4 times, finishing at †† at end of last rep.
Fasten off.
(Make 3 of these panels altogether.)

③ MAKING UP

1 Arrange the seven panels, alternating first and second panels as shown. Do not press.
2 Join the panels using a flat seam and matching yarn.

Daisy & bee baby's outfit

A bright bee and delicate daisy motif attracts the eye immediately on this dainty dress and bonnet. The embroidery design is worked mainly in shadow stitch. The outfit consists of a plain dress of Swiss batiste and a bonnet and an embroidered sheer collar trimmed with lace. It is designed to fit an average one-year-old.

WHAT YOU NEED

Master pattern **A1**(a–i) • fine sewing machine thread • stranded embroidery cotton: 3 shades green, 2 shades pink, yellow, orange black, pale grey • embroidery hoop • 20 cm **x** 40 cm non-woven interfacing (to protect fabric) • fine embroidery needles • dressmaking pins • water-soluble marker pen • tracing paper • scissors • pencil • tape measure • sewing machine
Dress
1.2 m Swiss batiste, 115 cm wide • 30 cm pure cotton organdie or pure silk organza, 115 cm wide (for the collar) • 1 m woven cotton edging lace, 9 mm wide • 2 mother-of-pearl shank buttons (for the collar), 6 mm diameter • 3 flat mother-of-pearl buttons (for the yoke), 6 mm diameter
Bonnet
18 cm **x** 36 cm pure cotton organdie or pure silk organza (for the brim) • 30 cm Swiss batiste, 115 cm wide (for the crown) • 1.6 m woven cotton edging lace, 9 mm wide (to match the collar lace) • 50 cm narrow entredeux • 1.5 m double-faced satin ribbon, 5 mm wide • 1.3 m double-faced satin ribbon, 7 mm wide
● *Technique pages 292–301, 307–12, 343–4*

① PREPARING THE COLLAR
1 Using the tracing paper and pencil trace a working pattern for the collar from the master pattern. Trace all markings, including the embroidery design. Do not cut out the pattern.
2 Pin a rectangle of organdie, 25 cm **x** 15 cm, over the traced pattern, pinning around the edges of the fabric so that the pin marks will not show on the finished collar.

3 Using the water-soluble marker, trace the front collar pattern on to the organdie. Then lightly trace the embroidery design on to the organdie.
4 Remove the traced paper pattern. To allow for the fabric to be held in the embroidery hoop, do not cut out the collar piece yet. If you are using silk organza, overcast the edges of the rectangle to minimise fraying.

② EMBROIDERING THE COLLAR
Work the whole design with two strands of embroidery cotton. The leaves are worked in three shades of green and the daisies are worked in two shades of pink.

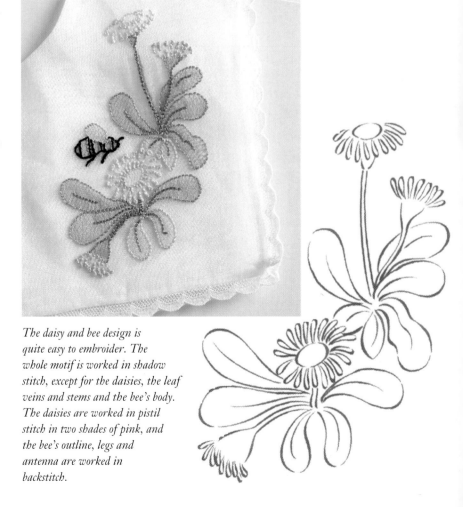

The daisy and bee design is quite easy to embroider. The whole motif is worked in shadow stitch, except for the daisies, the leaf veins and stems and the bee's body. The daisies are worked in pistil stitch in two shades of pink, and the bee's outline, legs and antenna are worked in backstitch.

1 Place the organdie in the embroidery hoop, making sure that the fabric is protected by the interfacing circles and the design is centred in the hoop. (See page 32 for a note on working with sheer fabrics in a hoop.)

Daisies
1 Choose a pale pink for open flowers and mid pink for closed flowers and use a 50 cm long thread to complete a whole flower.
2 Work the daisy centres in shadow stitch using yellow thread. Work the petals in pistil stitch. Begin from the centre of the blossom on the right side of the fabric. Follow only one line of

the petal at a time.

3 Work one or two tiny backstitches, and then take the thread down to the wrong side, bringing it up again a few stitches from the tip of the petal.

4 Backstitch on the right side of the fabric to the tip, ending with a two-turn French knot. Your needle and thread are now on the wrong side. Bring them up at the start of the next

petal, and repeat the process.

Stems and leaves

1 Work flower stems in backstitch using the darkest shade of green. At the same time, shadow stitch the calyx at the top of each stem using the same green. Work two rows of backstitch to complete each stem.

2 Shadow stitch the leaves, working from the tips to the bases. Use pale

Shadow stitch is worked like herringbone stitch, but from the back of the fabric, producing a

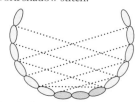

subtle and charming effect. Turn to page 311 for details of how to work shadow stitch.

On the leaves, start with several backstitches before beginning to work the shadow stitch.

On the bee's wing, start at the pointed end and make sure the cross-over stitches are even.

NOTE

When working on fine fabric in an embroidery hoop, protect the fabric from damage by placing two rings of non-woven interfacing between the fabric and the hoops. The outer circumference of each interfacing ring should be 5 cm larger in diameter than the hoop and the inner circumference 4 cm smaller.

green for the smaller leaves and mid green for the larger leaves.

3 Work the leaf veins in backstitch using the darkest shade of green. Start stitching at the stalk end and work towards the tip.

Bee

1 Work the wing in shadow stitch using pale grey cotton.

2 Shadow stitch the body in alternate vertical stripes of orange and black. Outline the body and work the legs and antenna with backstitch using black thread.

❸ MAKING THE COLLAR

1 Cut out the embroidered front collar to the size of the pattern. Then cut one plain front collar (for the lining) and four back collar pieces (two for the lining) from the organdie.

2 Using small French seams, stitch the front and a left and right back together at the shoulders. Do the same with the lining pieces.

3 Pin the lace to the outside edge of the collar on the right side, with the lace heading on the seamline and the scalloped edge towards the centre. When pinning, follow the outer

perimeter of the collar, allowing extra fullness at the corners so that the collar will sit properly when it is turned right side out. Do not run the lace up the centre backs, as the collar will overlap here. Tack the lace in place.

4 Place the collar lining on top of the collar, right sides together. Starting near the centre of one of the back overlaps, and stitching through all layers, sew around the entire collar, including the neck edge and back, to 5 cm from the starting point. (This opening will be used to turn the collar through to the right side.)

5 Machine sew a fine line of zigzag stitching beside the seam before trimming the seam closely and turning the collar to the right side.

6 Neatly sew up the opening with a few handstitches.

7 Make two horizontal buttonholes in the left back in the positions marked on the pattern. Sew the two

Rock-a-bye doll's cradle

Delight a youngster with this easy-to-make rocking cradle. Fit it with mini bed linen made with fabric scraps and it's ready for a favourite toy.

Master pattern **C21(a–c)** • plywood: 800 mm **x** 420 mm **x** 18 mm (for the head and foot); 700 mm **x** 520 mm **x** 10 mm (for the sides and base) • 2 lengths of scrap timber, 310 mm **x** 10 mm **x** 10 mm (for the base supports) • PVA glue • 30 mm lost head nails • sandpaper: medium, fine • 2 paintbrushes, 13 mm • timber undercoat • gloss paint • tracing paper • pencil • masking tape • scissors • hand plane • drill and 6 mm drill bit • jigsaw • hammer
● *Technique pages 338–42, 343–4*

❶ PREPARING THE PLYWOOD

1 Carefully trace all the pattern pieces from the master pattern on to the tracing paper.
2 Cut out the pattern pieces. Cut the heart-shaped holes from the pieces for the head and foot.

Cutting guide
Place your traced pattern pieces on the sheets of plywood as shown below: 18 mm plywood (top), 10 mm plywood (bottom).

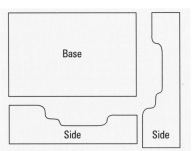

3 Lay the pieces on the plywood as shown in the cutting guide, and secure them with masking tape. Mark a base piece 500 mm x 305 mm on the 10 mm plywood.
4 Trace around the pattern pieces with pencil and then remove them from the timber. Cut out all the pieces with a jigsaw.
5 Inside the heart shapes, drill holes large enough to take the jigsaw blade. Insert the blade and cut out the heart-shaped holes. Sand the cut edges with medium-grade sandpaper.

❷ MAKING THE CRADLE

1 Plane the outside of the lower edges of the sides so that the angle between the sides and the base will be slightly greater than 90°.
2 Glue and nail the sides of the cradle to the head, driving four or five nails straight down through the end into the sides. Support the sides in a vice.
3 Turn the cradle on to its head and glue and nail the foot down on to the sides. Use three or four nails for each join. Let the glue set completely before proceeding to the next step.
4 Turn the cradle upside down and glue the lower edges of the sides. Position the base and hammer in four or five nails on each side, spacing them evenly and allowing for the angle of the sides to the base.

CRADLE CONSTRUCTION

Sides — Foot — 100 mm
Base — Support — 140 mm

Sides — 30 mm — 240 mm — 140 mm
Base — Support — 140 mm — Head

Lower edges of sides are planed to make angle greater than 90°.

5 Glue and nail the two base supports on to the end pieces as shown on the plan. Leave the glue to set.

❸ FINISHING

1 Sand all surfaces thoroughly with fine-grade sandpaper.
2 Ensure that all surfaces are clean and free of dust, and apply undercoat.
3 When dry, apply gloss paint in a colour of your choosing.

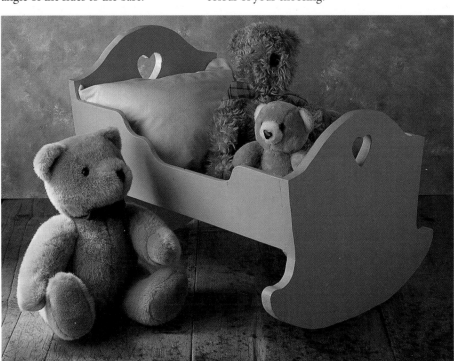

Dolls' house

Dolls' houses are a perennial source of delight and entertainment for children. This house should keep a small child happily and creatively absorbed for hours. You can furnish the house with the dolls' house furniture on pages 54–5, or children can create their own.

WHAT YOU NEED

Medium density fibreboard (MDF):
565 mm x 370 mm x 18 mm,
605 mm x 600 mm x 9 mm,
1145 mm x 505 mm x 6 mm,
980 mm x 600 mm x 3 mm • PVA
woodworking glue • plastic wood •
chipboard screws: eight 6 gauge
(30 mm), two 6 gauge (20 mm) •
acrylic paints • paintbrush •
panel saw • jigsaw • drill, 3 mm
drill bit, countersink drill bit •
router • medium and fine-grade
sandpaper • screwdriver • pencil •
ruler • square • 60 cm broderie
anglaise, 50 mm wide
● *Technique pages 338–42, 343–4*

❶ CUTTING THE FIBREBOARD

Use a pencil, ruler and square to measure and mark all pieces, following the cutting guide. Mark the pieces clearly, using a light pencil so that the labels will not show through the paint.

1 Cut out and label the following pieces from the 18 mm MDF:

A one base, 560 mm x 300 mm; **L** two battens, 560 mm x 18 mm; **M** one door runner, 200 mm x 18 mm.
2 Cut out and label the following pieces from the 9 mm MDF:
B/C two sides, 540 mm x 300 mm;
G one balcony, 570 mm x 55 mm.
3 Cut out and label the following pieces from the 6 mm MDF:
D one front, 570 mm x 450 mm;
E one floor, 570 mm x 220 mm;
F one divider, 380 mm x 200 mm;
J one front door, 150 mm x 100 mm;
H one railing, 565 mm x 50 mm.

NOTE

It is important to paint the door its final colour before you slide it into place. Do not paint the bottom edge, and make sure that the paint is completely dry before slotting the door into the runners, otherwise the paint will stick and the door will not slide back and forth smoothly.

4 From the 3 mm MDF, cut out and label the following:
K one roof, 600 mm x 340 mm;
I eight tile lengths, 600 mm x 60 mm;
N one ridge cap, 600 mm x 20 mm;
O 14 shutters, 100 mm x 35 mm.

❷ PREPARING THE PIECES OF FIBREBOARD
Base (A)

1 Using the router, cut a groove 6 mm wide and 5 mm deep along the full width of the base, 65 mm from the front edge and parallel to it.

CUTTING GUIDE

Four thicknesses of MDF are used in this project. With the diagram (right) as a guide, measure and mark the pieces listed in 'Cutting the fibreboard' on the appropriate boards, and cut the pieces out with a panel saw. Label each piece lightly in pencil, so that the marks will be concealed when you paint the house. The base and side walls are grooved and the room divider and upper floor are slotted so the pieces slide easily together.

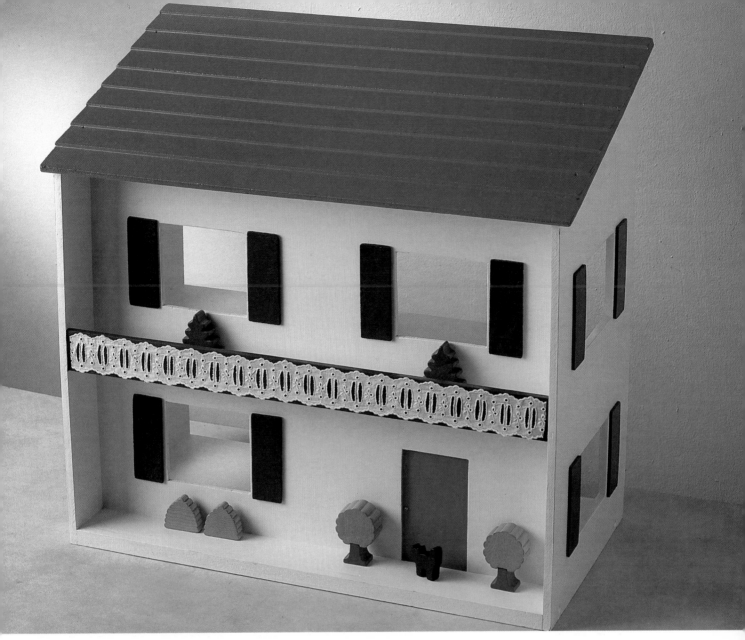

2 To accommodate the sliding door, widen the right-hand 200 mm of the groove to 12 mm by cutting another groove immediately behind the first.
3 Cut a second groove 6 mm wide and 5 mm deep at right angles to the first groove, starting at the centre point of the first groove and stopping 20 mm from the rear edge.

Sides (B and C)

The wall in the diagram (right) is for the left-hand side, and steps 2 and 3 below refer to the left-hand wall. Make the right-hand wall as a mirror reflection of the left-hand wall.
1 Clamp B and C together. Mark the angle of the roof on one piece and, with the panel saw, cut through both boards along this line. Unclamp the pieces and mark them 'left' and 'right'.

540 mm

400 mm

210 mm

65 mm

300 mm

2 On the inside face of each side, 65 mm parallel to the front edge, use the router to cut a full-length vertical groove 6 mm wide and 5 mm deep.
3 On each side, 210 mm parallel to the lower edge, starting 10 mm in

HINT
Instead of painting the interior, you could use wallpaper with a small motif and place carpet or lino scraps on the floor.

from the front edge and finishing 10 mm from the rear edge, use the router to cut a horizontal groove 6 mm wide and 5 mm deep.

Front (D)

1 Using a ruler and pencil, draw the doors and windows on the front and side panels, following the measurements in the diagram 'Cutting the windows and door' (page 52).
2 Cut out the door and the windows with a jigsaw. Sand all edges smooth.

Assembling the dolls' house

Measure, cut and prepare the fibreboard with care, and the dolls' house will be easy to assemble. Four countersunk screws secure the side walls to the base, and then the balcony, the front and the interior walls are slotted in. Finally, the roof is secured with four more countersunk screws.

CUTTING THE WINDOWS AND DOOR

To cut the windows, drill holes in the window spaces large enough to take the jigsaw blade, and then work from the drilled holes to cut out the windows.

Floor (E)

Starting at the centre of one of the long edges and using the router, cut a slot 120 mm long and 6 mm wide, at right angles to the edge.

Room divider (F)

Starting at the centre of one of the long edges, use the router to cut a slot 110 mm long and 6 mm wide, at right angles to the edge.

Balcony (G)

Using the router, cut rebates 5 mm wide and 5 mm deep at both ends.

Balcony railing (H) and door (J)

Using the medium-grade sandpaper, sand all edges smooth.

Door runner (M)

Beginning and finishing 10 mm from each end, use the router to cut a rebate 7 mm wide and 7 mm deep.

Roof (K), roof tiles (I) and ridge cap (N)

1 Glue the two roof battens to the underside of the roof, 30 mm from the top and bottom edges and 20 mm in from the sides. Sand all edges.

2 Glue the eight roof tile sections to the main roof piece, beginning at the lower edge and lapping each section 20 mm on to the previous section – i.e., leaving 40 mm of each roof tile section exposed. Glue the ridge cap to the uppermost edge of the top roof tile section.

3 Plug the gaps between the main roof piece and the roof tile sections with plastic wood.

③ ASSEMBLING THE DOLLS' HOUSE

1 Using the drill and the 3 mm drill bit, make a pilot hole at each corner of the side walls (B and C), 30 mm from the front and back edges and 9 mm from the top and bottom edges.

2 Use the countersink bit to enlarge the drill holes on the outer surfaces so that the screws can be countersunk.

3 Screw the side walls (B and C) to the base (A) through the lower pilot holes, using four 30 mm 6 gauge screws. Make sure that the corners are perfectly aligned.

4 Position the rebated edges of the balcony (G) in the horizontal grooves on the side walls and slide the balcony to the front of the house.

5 Slide the front wall (D) down the vertical grooves cut into the side walls, making sure that the doorway is positioned at the right-hand side.

6 Turn the house on to its front on a horizontal surface. Position the door (J) in the door groove in the house base, just inside the door frame. Hold the rebated runner over the top of the

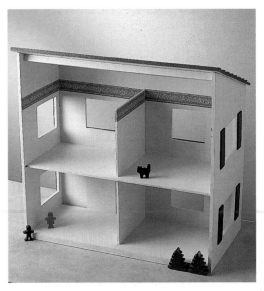

door and against the inside of the front wall, so that the door is held upright but can slide freely. The end of the runner should be 20 mm from the corner. Check that the door fills the door frame when closed and clears it when open, and mark the position of the runner with the pencil. Fix the runner to the wall with the two 20 mm 6 gauge screws.

7 Join the room divider (F) to the floor (E) by meshing the two slots at right angles until they lock into position. Ease the bottom edge of the room divider into the centre groove on the base, at the same time carefully working the side edges of the floor into the horizontal grooves in the side walls (B and C).

8 Place the roof (K) in position. Attach the roof to the walls through the upper pairs of drilled and counter-sunk holes using four 30 mm 6 gauge screws. The screws should enter the ends of the roof battens.

9 Glue the balcony railing (H) and the window shutters (O) in position.

④ FINISHING

1 Sand all surfaces well and paint and decorate the house. Choose good strong colours for the roof and the doors and shutters and paler colours for the interior. Place miniature trees and shrubs on the verandahs.

2 Glue the length of broderie anglaise to the balcony railing to simulate wrought iron work.

HOME BEAUTIFUL

The gift of a dolls' house can be an inspiration for other gifts – there are so many things you can make or buy to add to the house as the years go by. Try the following ideas.

• Make a movable chimney with a piece of timber measuring 50 mm x 50 mm x 60 mm. Cut one 50 mm x 50 mm face at an angle so that the piece will sit on the roof tile sections. Sand it, and paint it in a colour to match the door and shutters.

• Buy stylish little wooden trees and animals from a good toyshop – or design and make them yourself.

• Make the set of dolls' furniture (pages 54–5), and look in toyshops and gift shops for miniature kitchen and bathroom equipment, musical instruments, and a host of other home improvers and beautifiers.

• Provide the proud home owner with a car, a bicycle, a wheelbarrow, and even a garden shed.

Miniature furniture

Add a touch of elegance to a youngster's dolls' house with these home-crafted furnishings that you can make a room at a time as gifts for different occasions. All you need is imagination, scraps of timber, and odds and ends from the sewing basket.

Scraps: timber, plywood, fabric, lace, ribbon, aluminium foil, small images (for pictures) • acrylic paint • small paintbrushes • tiny brass screws • small transfers • pencil • ruler • PVA glue • medium and fine-grade sandpaper • fretsaw • small chisel • drill, fine drill bits
● *Technique pages 338–42*

❶ THE KITCHEN
Sink

1 Using a fretsaw, cut a block of timber 90 mm x 45 mm x 35 mm. From 3 mm thick plywood, cut one piece 45 mm x 30 mm and two pieces 45 mm x 25 mm.
2 Glue the plywood strips to the timber block to make the cupboard doors.

3 Make handles by gluing three small scraps of timber to the doors or by screwing small brass screws to them.
4 On the top of the sink unit, in the centre third, use a drill and a small chisel to scoop out a depression for the sink. It should be no larger than 25 mm x 20 mm.

5 For the draining boards, cut two pieces of very thin plywood, 25 mm x 20 mm. Glue these pieces on either side of the sink.

6 Make the tap spindle from a scrap of timber and glue it to the back edge of the sink. Screw brass screws on either side of this for the tap handles.
7 Sand the surfaces smooth. Using acrylic paints and a small paintbrush, paint the sink and the draining boards silver. Paint the unit and doors in colours of your choice.

Refrigerator

1 Using a fretsaw, cut a block of timber 90 mm x 35 mm x 35 mm.
2 Sand all sides and then apply two coats of white acrylic paint, sanding gently between coats.
3 Glue on a small scrap of black-painted wood for a handle.

Table and chairs

1 Use a fretsaw to cut a table top measuring 90 mm x 52 mm from 3 mm thick plywood.

2 For the legs, cut two plywood rectangles measuring 90 mm x 35 mm, and from these cut out rectangles 60 mm x 25 mm. Discard the smaller rectangles. Each remaining shape forms two legs and a cross-piece. At the mid-points, cut out a 6 mm semi-circle from the upper edge of one piece and a 6 mm semi-circle from the lower edge of the other piece.

3 If you wish, use the fretsaw to shape the legs and the table top, as shown in the photograph at the left. Glue the legs to the table top.
4 For each chair, use a fretsaw to cut,

from 3 mm thick plywood, one back 60 mm x 25 mm, one seat 25 mm x 25 mm, and one front leg 25 mm x 20 mm. Use the fretsaw to cut a small rectangular section from the top of the back piece.

5 Glue the seat and the leg together at right angles and let the glue dry. Then glue the seat to the back, making sure that the back and the leg will sit evenly on the floor.

6 Sand the surfaces smooth. Using acrylic paint and a small paintbrush, paint the table and chairs in a colour of your choice.

❷ THE LIVING ROOM
Lounge suite

1 From 9 mm thick plywood, use the fretsaw to cut one base 100 mm x 36 mm, one back 100 mm x 35 mm and two arms 45 mm x 40 mm. Round off one corner of each arm with sandpaper.

2 Glue the back and the base together at right angles, and let the glue dry. Glue the arms to the base and back, aligning the top edges of all pieces. The arms should extend 5 mm below the base to form the legs.

3 For each armchair, cut one base 40 mm x 36 mm, one back 40 mm x 35 mm, and two arms 45 mm x 40 mm. Make up as for the sofa.

4 Sand the surfaces smooth. Using acrylic paint and a small paintbrush, paint the lounge suite in a colour or colours of your choice.

❸ THE BEDROOMS
Wardrobes

1 To make the small wardrobe, use the fretsaw to cut a block of timber 125 mm x 75 mm x 35 mm. Then, from 3 mm plywood, cut two strips measuring 125 mm x 36 mm for the wardrobe doors.

2 Glue the doors to the front, leaving a 3 mm gap between them.

3 For the door handles, glue a small scrap of timber to the centre edge of each door, about 55 mm from the top edge.

4 For the large wardrobe, cut a timber block 170 mm x 105 mm x 30 mm and, from 3 mm thick plywood, three pieces 105 mm x 55 mm for the doors and, the centre panel. Assemble the wardrobe following steps 2 and 3 above. The gaps on either side of the centre panel should be 3 mm.

5 Sand the surfaces smooth. Using acrylic paint and a small paintbrush, paint the wardrobes in a colour or colours of your choice.

Beds

1 To make the small bed, use a fretsaw to cut from 5 mm thick plywood one bed head 45 mm x 40 mm and one bed foot 45 mm x 20 mm. From 9 mm thick plywood, cut one base 105 mm x 45 mm.

2 Glue the bed head and foot to the base, allowing the foot and head to extend 3 mm below the base.

3 For the large bed, cut a block of timber 130 mm x 80 mm x 20 mm for the base and from 3 mm plywood cut two rectangles, one 90 mm x 55 mm (head) and one 80 mm x 40 mm (foot). To assemble, repeat step 2.

4 Sand the surfaces smooth. Using acrylic paint and a small paintbrush, paint the beds in colours to match or complement the wardrobes.

MORE THINGS TO MAKE OR BUY

- Once you have made these pieces of furniture for the dolls' house, it will be easy to work out how to make other pieces, such as a stove, dressing tables, sideboard, or television set. Remember to keep the sizes in proportion.
- You can buy miniature toys, musical instruments, cooking equipment and crockery, even bathroom fittings, from toy shops, gift shops and novelty shops. Exterior items such as trees, plants, animals, cars and farm equipment are also readily available.

❹ THE FINISHING TOUCHES

1 Decorate some of the furniture by applying small decorative transfers, or paint designs by hand. For the furniture illustrated, we used a design of fruit and flowers for the fridge and a classic bow design for the centre panel of the large wardrobe.

2 Using very thin plywood and a fretsaw, cut out little motifs and glue them to wardrobes and beds before painting. We used a simple heart motif on the blue bedroom furniture.

3 Make rugs, cushions, bed linen and a table runner from scraps of printed fabric. Use aluminium foil pasted on thin plywood for mirrors and cut images from postcards for pictures.

4 Make planter boxes by drilling small holes in pieces of wooden moulding 25–30 mm long. Paint the moulding if desired, and insert a tiny sprig of dried flowers in the hole.

Edward Bear suit

A great idea for a fancy dress or special party, this outfit
has separate mittens and a large opening for ease of dressing.
The finished suit measures 95 cm from the back neck to the
toes and 80 cm from the underarm to the toes.

WHAT YOU NEED

Master pattern B12(a–h) • 1.6 m
fake fur, 140 cm wide • contrasting
felt, fleecy fabric or vinyl (for soles
and mittens) • small quantity of
ribbing (for mitten welts) • 35 cm
zip • sewing thread to match fur
fabric • sewing needle • dressmaking
pins • tracing paper • pencil • dressmaking scissors • sewing machine
● *Technique pages 292–301, 343–4*

SEWING FAKE FUR

Fake fur is awkward to sew, as
the pile tends to slip against itself.
To minimise problems, use the
following techniques.
• This project involves curved
seams, so do not choose a fabric
with a thick, heavy pile – these
fabrics are very prone to slipping.
• Cut fur fabric with extreme
care, making sure that the pile
does not cause the fabric base
to move and distort the shape
of the pattern piece.
• Tack all seams firmly before
machining them; pinning alone
is not adequate to prevent the
fabric from moving.
• As far as possible, stitch in
the direction of the pile.
• Use the eye end of a heavy,
blunt needle to release pile
caught in the stitching.

❶ CUTTING OUT THE FABRIC

1 Trace all the pattern pieces from
the master pattern on to tracing paper
and cut them out. Ensure that you
also transfer all markings.

2 Pin the pattern pieces to the fur
fabric, following the cutting guide.
Make sure that all the pattern pieces
are running in the same direction (the
direction of the pile).

3 Cut out the ears, mittens and paws
from the contrasting material, as
shown on the cutting guide.

❷ ASSEMBLING THE BODY

1 Using the sewing machine,
staystitch around the front and back
neckline 1 cm from the neck edge to

Cutting guide

From the fur fabric, cut one back hood piece and two of all the other pattern pieces. If you prefer, you can cut all four ear pieces from the fur fabric. Ensure that the fur pieces are all cut in the same direction, so that the pile on the suit will lie from head to shoulder, from shoulder to ankle and from shoulder to wrist. All seam allowances are 1.5 cm.

prevent the fabric from stretching while you are working with it.

2 To fit the zip, place the right sides of the front together and machine the centre front seam from the dot towards the inside leg seam for a short distance. Backstitch to reinforce the stitching at the dot.

3 Press down the seam allowances along the centre front zip opening and lay the zip face down along the seam line over the pressed seam allowances. Using the zip foot, machine stitch the entire length of the zip tape on both sides, stitching as close as possible to the zip teeth.

4 Tack the contrasting paw pads to the lower legs of the two back pieces with right sides together, and machine stitch the seams.

5 With right sides together and raw edges aligned, tack and machine stitch the shoulder seams. Press open.

6 Matching the dots, tack and machine stitch the sleeves to the armholes, with right sides together and raw edges aligned. Press the seams towards the sleeves.

7 Place the front piece and the back piece right sides together and machine stitch from the inside leg seam at the crotch around the leg and foot to the wrist in one continuous seam. Repeat for the other side of the suit.

8 With right sides together, place one body piece within the other and tack and machine the seam from the centre back neckline to the crotch. Carry the seam on up the remainder of the front crotch seam to the zip.

❸ ASSEMBLING THE HOOD

1 To sew the ears, match a fur with a fabric piece and place right sides together. Tack and machine around the ears, leaving the bottom edges open. Trim and clip the seams.

2 Turn the ears right side out and press. Tack the open edges of the ears to the edge of the right side of the back hood piece, at the top of the curved edge. Stitch 1 cm from the edge of the fabric.

3 Tack the right sides of the front hood together at the top, stitch and press open. With right sides together, tack the joined front hood piece to the back hood, matching centres and dots. Sew in place. (The ears will be sandwiched in the seam.)

4 Tack and machine the hood to the front and back necklines, matching shoulder seams to head seams. Press the hood face opening and the ends

of the zip opening to the wrong side along the seam line. Topstitch around the pressed area.

❹ SEWING THE MITTENS

1 With right sides together, tack and machine the two fabric mitten pieces to the two fur mitten pieces, leaving the wrist edges open. Trim and clip the seams.

2 From the ribbing, cut two strips measuring 12 cm in the direction of the rib and 16 cm in the opposite direction. Machine in the direction of the rib to sew each strip into a tube.

3 Fold both of the tubes in half, wrong sides matching, to make double-thickness tubes 6 cm long. Divide each tube equally into four, marking the quarter points with pins.

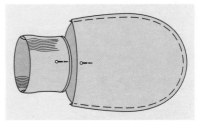

4 Mark the centre points between the mitten seams with pins and match the four pins in the ribbing to the seams and the pins in the mittens. Use a zigzag or overlock stitch to machine the ribs to the mittens, stretching the ribbed fabric so that the marked points will meet.

A very special Christmas stocking

For young children, the thrill of hanging up a Christmas stocking is matched only by the excitement of opening it on Christmas morning. Delight a toddler with this stocking, which is sure to become an indispensable part of the family's festive decorations for years to come.

WHAT YOU NEED

Master pattern C16(a–c) • 1 m red fabric, 90 cm wide • 40 cm x 30 cm fabric with Christmas print • 30 cm x 20 cm green print fabric (for tree appliqué) • Christmas print fabric scraps (for present appliqués) • 2 pieces polyester wadding, 40 cm x 30 cm • sewing thread: red, green, gold lamé • 50 cm ribbon, 10 mm wide • pencil • tracing paper • scissors • sewing machine

● *Technique pages 292–301, 302, 343–4*

❶ CUTTING OUT

1 Trace the pattern pieces for the stocking and the stocking collar from the master pattern on to tracing paper and cut them out. Trace the tree pattern on to another piece of tracing paper and cut that out.
2 Fold the red fabric in four. Pin the stocking pattern piece to the folded fabric and cut out four stocking shapes. Put one pair aside for the lining and work on the other pair to make the outer stocking.
3 Cut a collar piece 40 cm x 30 cm from the Christmas print fabric.
4 Cut the Christmas tree from the green fabric and the shapes of the presents from scraps of suitable Christmas print fabric.
5 Pin the main stocking pattern piece (not the collar) to the wadding and cut out two stocking shapes.

❷ SEWING THE APPLIQUÉ

1 Using the master pattern as a position guide, tack the appliqué shapes in place on the right side of one outer stocking piece.

2 Stitch the shapes in place with machine satin stitch (closed zigzag), using the green thread for the tree and the red for the presents.
3 Thread the sewing machine with gold lamé thread and use a long, straight machine stitch to add such details as Christmas tree decorations and ribbon ties to the appliqués.

❸ MAKING UP THE STOCKING

1 Pin the cut-out wadding stocking pieces to the wrong sides of both outer stocking pieces.
2 With right sides facing and allowing a 1.5 cm seam, sew the back and front stocking pieces and the wadding together, leaving the top open. Trim and clip the seams and press flat. Turn the work to the right side and press.
3 Repeat step 2 to sew the inner stocking pieces (the lining) together.
4 With wrong sides together, slip the lining inside the outer stocking. Tack the lining to the outer stocking along the upper edge.
5 With right sides facing, stitch the short ends of the collar together to form a cylinder. Press the seam open.

Lining

Fold collar here

6 With the right side facing the outside of the stocking, match the seam of the collar to the back seam of the stocking. Pin and tack the collar to the upper edge of the stocking and machine stitch it in place.
7 On the unsewn edge of the collar, press down a 1.5 cm double hem. Fold the collar over to the inside of the stocking and slipstitch it into place, covering the line of stitching on the inside of the stocking. Turn the collar down to the outside to form the stocking top and press.
8 Make a loop for hanging the stocking up by oversewing the ends of the ribbon to the back seam on the inside of the top of the stocking.

Party pinafore dress

With some simple embroidery stitches and a little lace, you can transform a plain pinafore dress into a party outfit. Choose a dress made of plain-coloured fabric to set off the embroidery.

WHAT YOU NEED

Plain pinafore dress • stranded embroidery cottons: DMC colours 3053 (pale green), ecru (cream), 814 (rose red), 815 (mid-red) • needles: size 7 crewel, size 7 straw or milliner's • embroidery marking pen • small drinking glass • dressmaking pins • sewing machine • stretchy self-gathered lace
● *Technique pages 292–5, 307–12*

❶ EMBROIDERING THE DESIGN

1 To mark out the design, fold the front of the dress in half to find the centre. Place a small drinking glass over the crease and mark out a circle by drawing around the glass using the embroidery marking pen.
2 Work the rosebuds in bullion knots, using the crewel needle. For the centre of every second rosebud, use three strands of rose red cotton and wind around the needle seven times. Work the alternate centres in the same way with mid-red.
3 Use three strands of cream cotton and wind nine times around the needle to make the outer petals.
4 With two strands of green cotton and the straw needle, work the bud cases in straight stitch, the stems joining the rosebuds in stem stitch, and the leaves on either side of the stems in lazy daisy stitch.

> Bullion rosebud
> Stem stitch
> Lazy daisy stitch

Stitch guide
The circle of rosebuds is formed by bullion knots. The rosebud centres are stitched alternately in rose red and mid-red, and the outer petals in cream. The leaves and bud cases are worked in lazy daisy stitch.

❷ FINISHING
Sew stretchy self-gathered lace by hand around the armholes.

Toddler's table & chairs

Some lucky child will have hours of fun with this practical gift. The table and chairs are sturdy enough for all those toddler activities – tea parties, art and craft projects and meetings with friends over milk and biscuits.

WHAT YOU NEED

Master pattern C15(a–g) • plywood or MDF, 2400 mm x 1200 mm x 18 mm • 8 gauge wood screws: 32 mm, 38 mm • 30 mm lost head nails • PVA woodworking glue • masking tape • wood filler • timber undercoat • gloss paint: yellow, blue • small stencil • tracing paper • transfer paper • jigsaw • wood rasp • scissors • pencil • hammer • nail punch • drill, drill bits • paintbrush • medium-grade sandpaper

● *Technique pages 337, 338–42, 343–4*

❶ PREPARING THE PLYWOOD

1 Trace the pattern pieces from the master pattern on to the tracing paper, including all markings. Cut out the pattern pieces.
2 Lay out all the pattern pieces on the plywood, as shown in the cutting guide, and secure them in place with the masking tape.
3 Trace around all the pattern pieces with a pencil, and then remove the pattern pieces from the plywood.
4 Cut out the pieces with a jigsaw and round off the edges and corners with a wood rasp.

5 From the leftover plywood, cut a strip 120 mm long x 18 mm wide x 18 mm thick. Cut this strip into four pieces 30 mm long. (These are the glue blocks.)

❷ MAKING THE CHAIRS

1 Glue and screw the cross bar supports to the leg pieces with two

CAUTION
Because this project is for small children, all surfaces must be finished smoothly so that there is no danger of splinters or rough edges hurting small hands.

38 mm screws at each join in the positions shown on the master pattern.

2 Stand the assembled leg and cross bar unit the right way up, and then glue and screw the seat into position. Use two screws through the seat into the top of each leg and cross bar support (eight screws per seat).

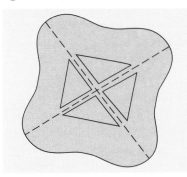

3 Glue and screw the back into position, using two screws on each side.

4 Repeat steps 1 to 3 to make the second chair.

❸ MAKING THE TABLE

1 Turn the table top upside down. With a pencil, mark the positions of the legs and triangular leg supports.

2 Place plywood offcuts in the channels between the pencilled positions for the supports – these will help you

---

CUTTING GUIDE

Trace the pattern pieces from the master pattern on to tracing paper, cut them out and lay them on the plywood as shown in the diagram. Attach the pattern pieces with masking tape and trace around them. Cut out the pieces with a jigsaw.

---

to space the supports correctly. Push four of the leg supports up against the spacers and glue and screw them in place with the 32 mm screws.

3 Glue and nail the other four leg supports directly on top of the first four leg supports.

4 Glue the tops of the table legs. Knock out the spacers and slide the legs into the channels, making sure that the curved edges of the legs face in towards the centre. While the glue is drying, hold all the pieces in place with masking tape. Since the leg pieces do not touch one another, there should be a small square space left at the middle of the table.

5 Glue and nail the four 30 mm glue blocks (cut from the leftover pieces) to the inside corners created

by the meeting of the table legs. With the table still upside down, the blocks rest on the built-up table leg supports.

❹ FINISHING

1 Fill in any holes and rough spots with wood filler, sand all surfaces and wipe them clean. If necessary, round off the edges further with a rasp.

2 Apply the timber undercoat and allow it to dry completely, and then paint the table and chairs with several coats of the yellow gloss paint.

3 Stencil your chosen shape on each corner of the table and each side of the chair backs, using the blue paint.

NOTE

Screw the table and chairs together with 8 gauge 38 mm and 32 mm wood screws. Drill a 2.5 mm pilot hole through the top piece into the section to which it will be fastened, and then enlarge the hole through the top piece with a 4 mm bit to make a clearance hole, which is then countersunk.

Balloon shorts

In these colourful shorts, your favourite young person will be the best dressed toddler at the party or the beach. The basket of the largest balloon forms a small pocket for keeping little treasures safe.

Master pattern **C22(a)** • 50 cm white, medium-weight fabric, 115 cm wide (for the shorts) • 20 cm **x** 15 cm white fabric (for the large balloon) • 10 cm **x** 12 cm fawn fabric (for the basket) • 20 cm **x** 15 cm lightweight wadding (for the large balloon) • 25 cm **x** 25 cm tear-off backing (for the small balloons) • 1.5 m fawn braid, 2 mm wide • 6 novelty buttons (e.g. cars, planes) • 55 cm non-roll elastic, 15 mm wide • sewing thread to match the fabrics • dark brown sewing thread (for outlining the small balloons) • fabric paints: red, brown, yellow, green, blue • paintbrushes • tracing paper • dressmaker's carbon paper • pencil • scissors • dressmaking pins • safety pin • sewing needle • sewing machine
● *Technique pages 292–301, 302, 343–4*

The pattern fits an average four-year-old (waist 53 cm, outside leg 38 cm, inside leg 11 cm).

❶ MAKING THE PATTERNS
1 Using tracing paper, pencil and scissors, trace and cut out a working pattern for the shorts from the master pattern, including all markings.
2 Trace and cut out working patterns for the large balloon and its basket (drawn in a solid line on the master pattern), adding an extra 1.5 cm seam allowance all round the basket.

❷ PREPARING THE FABRIC
1 Wash, dry and iron all fabric – this removes fabric conditioners so that the paint will fix more satisfactorily.
2 Fold the fabric for the shorts in half, selvage to selvage. Pin the shorts pattern piece to the folded fabric, with the straight grain parallel to the selvage, and cut the shorts out. You will have two identical sides that will be joined at the centre front and back and the inside leg.
3 Separate the pieces and, using dressmaker's carbon paper, transfer the patterns for the large balloon and its basket (drawn in a solid line) on to the left-hand piece. Transfer the small balloon patterns (drawn in broken lines) on to the right-hand piece.
4 Pin the patterns for the large balloon and its basket to the appropriate fabrics and cut them out. Then pin the large balloon pattern to the wadding and cut it out, allowing an extra 5 mm around the edge.
5 For each of the three small balloons, cut a piece of tear-off backing slightly larger than the whole motif, including the basket and ropes.

❸ MAKING THE BALLOONS
1 On the fabric piece for the large balloon, use the red, green, yellow and blue paints to make each of the four panels a different colour.
2 Working directly on to the shorts fabric, paint the tiny balloon green, the slightly larger balloon yellow and the remaining balloon red. Paint all three baskets brown.
3 Set the fabric paints according to the manufacturer's instructions.
4 Pin or tack the pieces of tear-off backing to the wrong side of the fabric behind the painted shapes of the three small balloons.
5 Either by hand or by machine, use brown thread to stitch around the painted balloons, down the ropes and around the baskets. Still using the brown thread, stitch a row of scallops across the centre of the yellow balloon. Stitch vertical curves on the red balloon to form panels, and stitch a basket weave pattern on its basket.

Painted balloons
Use brown sewing thread to machine stitch along all design lines.

6 Remove the pins (or tacking stitches) and carefully tear away the backing from the back.

❹ APPLIQUÉING THE LARGE BALLOON
1 Pin the wadding for the large balloon to the wrong side of the previously painted fabric. Machine or handstitch the layers together, 5 mm from the edge.

HINTS
● *Look for the type of tear-off backing that can be stitched on to the fabric and torn off later. Do not use non-woven iron-on interfacing or wadding as these will wash badly and may irritate delicate skin.*
● *The three small balloons on the shorts illustrated are painted directly on to the white shorts fabric. If you want to use coloured fabric for the shorts instead of white, you will need to paint these balloons on to pieces of white fabric and then cut them out and appliqué them to the coloured fabric, using the method described for appliquéing the large balloon.*

1 With right sides together, pin and sew the two pieces of the shorts together at the crotch seams, and then pin and sew the inside leg seam. Finish the seams and press.

2 Turn the raw edges of the legs under 6 mm to the wrong side, making sure that you also turn the lower edge of the appliquéd balloon basket. Sew with straight stitch. Turn under a further 1.5 cm and sew the hem, either by hand using slipstitch or by machine using topstitch.

3 To make the waist casing, fold down the raw edge of the waist 6 mm to the wrong side and press. Fold the waist over a further 4 cm and press.

4 Topstitch the waist casing in place, leaving a 3 cm gap near a seam to thread the elastic through.

5 Topstitch 2 mm from the top edge, using a large machine stitch or back-stitching by hand.

🕖 FINISHING

1 Using a large safety pin, thread the non-roll elastic through the waistband. Pull the ends of the elastic together and stitch them securely, first ensuring that the elastic is not twisted Close the opening with small slipstitches.

2 Stitch the novelty buttons at random on the shorts, the cars near the bottom of the shorts and the planes near the top, as though flying around the balloons.

Appliqué balloon
Paint the panels and stitch narrow fawn braid along all the design lines except the top and bottom of the basket.

2 Trim away the excess wadding. Fold the raw edge of the fabric to the wrong side and pin or tack it down.

3 Place the padded balloon motif on the right side of the shorts fabric, in the position marked, and pin it in place. Topstitch around the outer edge of the balloon.

4 Finish the edges of the fabric for the large basket with zigzag stitch to prevent fraying. Turn under a 1.5 cm hem along the top and side edges and press it into place. Topstitch the top edge 2 mm and 8 mm from the fold – this will be the pocket opening. Pin and tack the basket to the fabric, aligning the raw edge at the bottom of the basket with the raw edge at the bottom of the shorts fabric.

5 Topstitch the basket in place along the sides only, leaving the top and bottom open. (The bottom edge will be caught in the leg hem later.) Reinforce the sides with a second row of stitching, 6 mm from the first.

🔂 ATTACHING THE BRAID

1 Using straight stitch, sew single rows of braid between the panels and around the edge of the large balloon.

2 Starting at a lower corner of the basket, stitch a single row of braid up the side of the basket to a point midway up the side of the balloon. Loop the braid in shallow scallops across the middle of the balloon, then stitch down to the bottom corner of the basket, opposite where you started.

🔂 SEWING THE SHORTS
The seam allowance is 1.5 cm.

Push-along duck

This amusing toy makes a very satisfying noise as it is wheeled along. It encourages crawling children to get up and toddle and delights them with its novel walking action.

WHAT YOU NEED

Master pattern B10(a–d) • plywood, 500 mm x 500 mm x 15 mm • 570 mm dowel, 12 mm diameter (for handle shaft) • 130 mm dowel, 25 mm diameter (for handle grip) • 60 mm dowel, 12 mm diameter (for axle) • heavy duty rubber gloves (for feet) • PVA glue • epoxy resin glue • sandpaper • undercoat paint • gloss paint in your chosen colours • tracing paper • transfer paper • pencil • scissors • jigsaw or coping saw • clamps • drill and drill bits
● *Technique pages 338–42, 343–4*

❶ PREPARING THE PLYWOOD

1 Trace and transfer the pattern pieces from the master pattern on to the plywood, being careful to transfer all details. Note that you need to cut two body pieces.

2 Using a jigsaw or coping saw, cut the shapes from the plywood and sand them smooth. Make sure the slits in the wheels are the right size for the thickness of the feet.

DUCK CHARACTER

Toy ducks are traditionally coloured plain bright yellow, which appeals to very small children. For a slightly older child you may like to base your paint colours on a real duck. Shown below are colour schemes based on the mallard (right), which has a dark emerald head and a white collar, and the chestnut teal (left), with its green-black head and black tail.

HINT

You can use scraps of leather or felt instead of rubber to make the duck's feet.

❷ MAKING THE DUCK

1 Glue the two body pieces together, making sure that all edges are aligned exactly. Clamp them together until they are dry. Sand the edges to remove any irregularities.

2 In the position indicated on the plan, drill a hole in the duck's back, 12 mm in diameter and 40 mm deep, to take the handle shaft. Push the pre-glued dowel end into the hole and allow to dry.

3 Round off the ends of the handle grip with sandpaper and drill a 12 mm diameter hole in the centre; this hole should not be more than 12 mm deep. Glue the end of the handle shaft into the hole. Allow to dry.

4 Glue the wings to the body in the position shown on the master pattern.

5 Cut open the rubber gloves and trace and transfer the duck foot from the master pattern to the rubber six times. Transfer three foot shapes, flip the tracing and transfer the next three reversed. Squeeze a small amount of epoxy glue into the slits cut in the wheels and insert the rubber feet.

6 Using a 13 mm or 14 mm drill bit, drill the axle hole through the duck's body at the position marked.

7 Using a 12 mm drill bit, drill a hole in the centre of each wheel.

8 Push a pre-glued axle end into one of the wheels, pass it through the body, and glue the other end into the other wheel. Do not butt the wheels right up to the body – leave enough play for the wheels to move freely.

❸ FINISHING

1 When the glue is thoroughly dry, sand, undercoat and paint the duck in acrylic gloss paint.

2 Decorate the duck's neck with a bright ribbon tied in a bow and sewn securely together.

Cutting guide

Cut two body pieces and glue them together. The wing piece fits into the square notch behind the head.

CHILDREN & YOUNG ADULTS

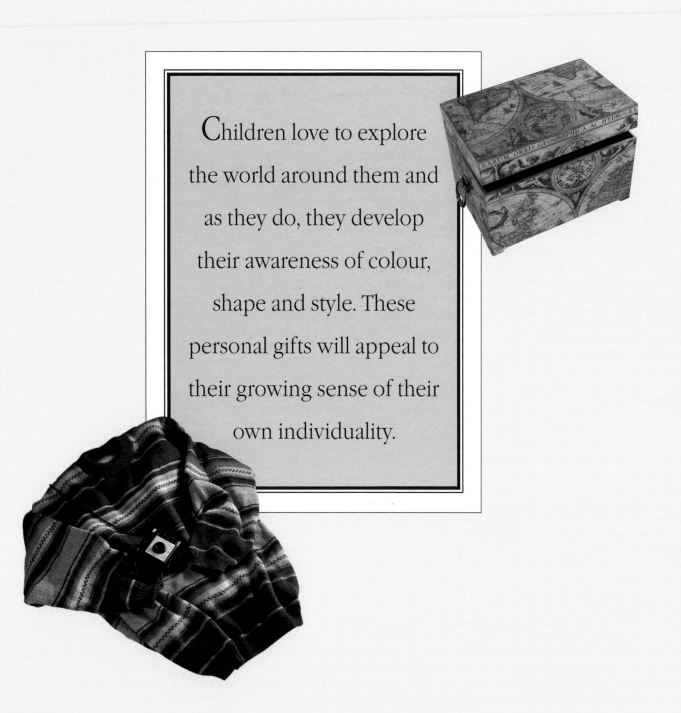

Children love to explore the world around them and as they do, they develop their awareness of colour, shape and style. These personal gifts will appeal to their growing sense of their own individuality.

Cuddly cow sweatshirt

A plain sweatshirt becomes an eye-catching and novel garment with this simple appliqué and embroidery design.

WHAT YOU NEED

Master pattern **C18(a)** • sweatshirt • lightweight iron-on interfacing, 40 cm **x** 35 cm • non-woven tear-off backing, 35 cm **x** 25 cm • white fabric, 28 cm **x** 18 cm • black fabric, 25 cm **x** 10 cm • pink fabric (for the udder, nose and ears), 10 cm **x** 10 cm • sewing thread: black, pink • stranded embroidery cotton: black, green, bright pink, lemon, blue, gold, white • cardboard, 3 cm **x** 2 cm • needle: medium crewel • tracing paper • dressmaker's carbon paper • hard pencil • dressmaking pins • scissors • sewing machine
● *Technique pages 302, 307–12, 343–4*

① PREPARING THE COW

1 Trace the cow outline from the master pattern on to the tracing paper. Trace the black patches and pink features on to a separate piece of paper.
2 Using dressmaker's carbon paper and a pencil, transfer all the shapes to the shiny side of the interfacing.
3 Cut out all the shapes, making sure that you separate the shapes that will be cut from black fabric from those to be cut from pink fabric.
4 Place the interfacing shape for the complete cow silhouette, shiny side down, on the wrong side of the white fabric. Fuse the shape to the fabric with a hot iron and cut out.
5 Place the interfacing shapes for the black patches, shiny sides down, on the wrong side of the black fabric. Fuse them to the fabric with a hot iron and cut them out.
6 Fuse the udder, nose and ear shapes on to the pink fabric with the iron and cut out these shapes too.

CREATING YOUR OWN MOTIF

You can use any animal shape for the appliqué motif, as long as it is fairly rounded and has no thin, protruding pieces that would be hard to cut and sew. This cat shape is perfect, as all

details except one or two of the whiskers are within the silhouette. Embroider the whiskers in straight stitch after you have appliquéd the cat shape to the sweatshirt.

② APPLIQUÉING THE COW

1 Position the pieces for the nose, udder, ears and black patches on the cow and tack them in place.
2 With a machine satin stitch (closed zigzag), sew the pieces on to the cow. Remove the tacking thread.
3 Using the master pattern as a guide, straight machine stitch any elements that need to be defined – for example, the line between the legs and the side of the face. At this stage, do not stitch any of the outline; this will be worked when you appliqué the cow to the sweatshirt.
4 Embroider the facial features, using satin stitch for the pupils and nostrils and straight stitch for the eye outlines and eyelashes.

5 To make the end of the tail, cut out a piece of cardboard 3 cm x 4 cm. Wind black and white stranded cotton round the cardboard about 30 times, and then cut through one end. Bunch up the threads in the middle of the bundle and tightly wind a piece of black stranded cotton a few times

HINTS

For appliqué work, choose smooth fabrics of light or medium weight. Very bulky fabrics or fabrics with a loose weave are not suitable. It is important to iron fabrics flat before you begin working.

around the bundle. Thread the end of the cotton on to a needle and push it through the end of the tail on the appliqué. Stitch through the interfacing several times to secure. The tail will be sewn on more securely when you attach the cow to the sweatshirt.

③ ATTACHING THE COW

1 Decide where to place the cow appliqué on the sweatshirt. Mark the top, bottom and side positions with pins. Using the pins as guides, lightly tack the non-woven tear-off backing to the wrong side of the sweatshirt, covering the place where the cow will

Sweatshirt material

Stabiliser

be attached. This will stabilise the knit fabric while you sew the appliqué, and will be removed later. Tack the cow into position on the right side of the sweatshirt, making sure that the tear-off backing is behind the appliqué cow.

2 Using a machine satin stitch, sew around the outline of the cow, making sure that the cotton threads at the end of the tail are securely sewn on to the fabric. Cut and peel the backing from the back of the shirt.

Stitch guide
Use the diagram above and the key at the right as guides when you are embroidering the flowers.

o	French knot
/	Straight stitch
⬯	Lazy daisy stitch

3 Referring to the stitch guide above and the photograph below, embroider the flowers around the cow's feet. Embroider the flowers in lazy daisy stitch and put a French knot in the centre of each flower. Work the stems in straight stitch.

Delectable lace collar

Made from fine crochet cotton, this lacework collar would please any little girl. It is designed to sit around the neckline without sewing, so it can be worn over several outfits.

1 ball Greek butterfly crochet cotton no. 50 • no. 3 darning needle • 1 m satin ribbon, 3 mm wide
● *Technique page 328*

❶ MAKING THE COLLAR
Work 64 basic loops over a double strand of cotton. Turn.
2nd row: Work a basic loop into each loop. Turn.

Double strand of cotton

3rd row: Work a small turning loop and a long closed loop into the first loop. Work a long closed loop into each loop to the end of the row. Turn.
4th row: On top of the large loops work a foundation row in a multiple of three-plus-one basic loops. Turn.
5th row: Work a turning loop into the first basic loop and work a basic loop into each loop to the end of the row. Turn and repeat this row twice. (Ribbon-threading edge made.) Turn.

8th row: Work a turning loop into the first loop. Make a large loop by missing two loops and working into the next loop. Repeat to the end of the row. Turn.

9th row: Work a large turning loop and three long picots into the first large loop. Insert the needle through the three picots and join them together with a closed loop knot. (In this way, you have made joined picots.) ★ Work a large loop and three joined picots into the next large loop. ★ Repeat from ★ to ★ until the end of the row. (The last large loop is worked into the turning loop of the previous row.) Turn.

10th row: Work a large turning loop and three joined picots into the first large loop. Work another row of joined picots.

11th row: Turn and work a large turning loop into the first large loop. Work large loops into each large loop to the end of the row. Turn.
12th row: Work a foundation row of basic loops in a multiple of three-plus-one basic loops on to the large loops.

Repeat 5th row five times.
Repeat 7th row through to 12th row once.
Repeat 5th row five times.
Repeat 7th row through to 12th row once. Pull the last knot very tight and trim the thread close to the knot.

❷ WORKING THE EDGING FOUNDATION
1st row: With the wrong side of the lacework facing, join thread into the first loop on the neck edge and work basic loops in a multiple of seven-plus-six loops to the corner. Work a corner loop, then work basic loops in

Worked lace collar

a multiple of seven-plus-three loops on to the large loops. Work a corner loop. Work basic loops in a multiple of seven-plus-six loops to the neck edge. Turn.

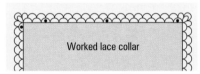
Worked lace collar

2nd row: Work a turning loop into the first loop and a basic loop into each basic loop, increasing in both corner loops. Turn.
Repeat 2nd row twice.

❸ WORKING THE EDGING

Worked edging foundation

1st row: Work a small turning loop into the first loop and a basic loop into the next six basic loops. ★ Make a large loop by missing one loop and working into the next loop. Work five basic loops. ★ Repeat from ★ to ★ to the end of the row. Work one basic loop and turn.

Worked edging foundation

2nd row: Work a small turning loop into the first loop and a basic loop into the next five basic loops. ★ Make a

ORDER OF WORKING
The first three rows make up the neckline of the collar, through which the ribbon will be threaded. Then the main part of the collar is worked as a long, straight piece. Finally, the edging is worked around the three outer sides of the collar; the fourth side is the neck edge, where the ribbon is to go.

bridging loop and four long picots into the large loop. Bridge into the next loop then work four basic loops. ★ Repeat from ★ to ★ to the end of the row. Work one basic loop. Turn.

Worked edging foundation

3rd row: Work a small turning loop into the first loop and a basic loop into the next four basic loops. ★ Make a large loop by missing the bridging loop and then working into the first long picot. Join the next three long picots with basic loops. Miss the bridging loop and work a large loop into the next loop. Work three more basic loops. ★ Repeat from ★ to ★ to the end of the row. Work one basic loop and turn.

Worked edging foundation

4th row: Work a small turning loop into the first loop and a basic loop into the next three basic loops. ★ Miss the large loop and work into the next basic loop. Work two basic loops. ★ Repeat from ★ to ★ to the end of the row. Work one basic loop and turn.

Worked edging foundation

5th row: Work a small turning loop into the first loop and a basic loop into the next two loops. ★ Miss the large loop and work one large loop into the next basic loop. Work one

basic loop. ★ Repeat from ★ to ★ end of row. Work one basic loop and turn.

Worked edging foundation

6th row: Work a small turning loop into the first loop and a basic loop into the next basic loop. ★ Bridge into the first large loop and work five small picots. Into the basic loop on top of the motif, work a bridging loop and three long picots. Bridge into the next long loop and work five small picots. Work a bridging loop and two small picots into the next basic loop. ★ Repeat from ★ to ★ to the last two loops. Bridge into the second last loop. Make a basic loop into the last loop, pull knot tight and trim thread. Thread ribbon through neck edge.

Flower seeds in homemade packets

This is a gift that will delight youngsters who are keen to try their hand at growing flowers. Children can make the paper packets to give to their friends.

WHAT YOU NEED

Brown paper • artist's paints • paintbrushes • clear craft glue • flower seeds • paper punch • ribbon, 5 mm wide • scissors • pencil • ruler
● *Technique pages 334–5*

❶ MAKING THE PACKETS

1 From brown paper, cut rectangles measuring 36 cm x 13 cm.
2 Fold the rectangles in half width-wise and make firm creases along the fold lines. Unfold the rectangles.
3 Fold 1 cm strips down the two long sides of each rectangle.

4 Cut halfway down each side crease and cut away the 18 cm x 1 cm strips.

5 Refold the rectangles in half along the original folds, and then glue the 1 cm flaps over the cut edges.
6 At the tops of the packets, fold down 5 cm flaps to the back.
7 Use the hole punch to make two holes through all thicknesses, about 2 cm from the tops of the packets.

❷ FINISHING THE PACKETS

1 On the fronts of the packets, paint flowers to identify the seeds inside. Experiment on scrap paper, keeping the designs simple. Alternatively, you can trace the designs reproduced on this page (bottom left) and transfer them to the fronts of the packets. Then paint over the designs in one or two colours of your choice and write the names of the seeds beneath.
2 Place the appropriate seeds in the packets, fold the tops of the bags over and secure them with a dab of glue.

3 Thread short lengths of ribbon through the holes and tie them in bows at the fronts of the packets.

VARIATION

Decorate the fronts of your homemade packets with the illustrations from bought packets of seeds, or with pictures cut from magazines – this is an excellent quick and easy way for small children to make this gift with little help.

Flower designs
If you do not feel confident about drawing the flower yourself, trace and transfer one of the generic designs above on to the packet, paint it, and write the name of the seeds below.

6 Use the scalpel or craft knife to carefully separate the lid of the box from the base, starting from one of the corners. Trim excess paper from the edges and corners so that the paper is as flat as possible, with no ridges or bumps. If any paper lifts or tears as you work, apply a little more glue and gently massage the paper back on to the surface of the box.

④ VARNISHING THE BOX

1 Work in a well ventilated area, as varnish fumes can be toxic. Apply about 10 coats of varnish to the paper on the box, making sure that each coat is thoroughly dry before applying the next (at least 24 hours).
2 Using no. 600 wet-and-dry abrasive paper wrapped around the sanding block and a little water, lightly sand the box, paying attention to the corners and the join in the paper, where the varnish may have built up. Wipe over the box with a lint-free cloth and apply another coat of varnish.

3 Apply another four or five coats of varnish, and then repeat step 2. The idea is to sand back the varnish where it is building up in the corners or seams and to build up the varnish elsewhere, until eventually the entire box feels smooth and seamless.
4 Repeat steps 2 and 3 until you are satisfied that the surface of the box is absolutely flat and smooth.
5 Apply three further coats of varnish, polishing the surface with no. 1200 wet-and-dry abrasive paper between applications to achieve a very smooth, dull finish.

⑤ FINISHING

1 Paint the rims of the box and the lid with gold paint, and paint the inside gold or a colour of your choice.
2 When the paint is dry, attach the hinges and handles.
3 For a shiny, lasting finish, wax the box, following the instructions given in the techniques section for découpage.

3 Using the rubber roller and working from the centre outwards, smooth the surface, squeezing out air bubbles and excess glue. Wipe off any excess glue with a damp sponge.
4 When the glue is dry, use a scalpel or craft knife to trim the edges of the paper to fit the lid top exactly.
5 With the lid in position, and working on one side at a time, repeat steps 2 to 4 to stick the paper to the sides of the box.

COVERING THE BOX

It is best to use the type of wrapping paper that is sold in rolled sheets. If you use a folded paper, do not use any part that has fold creases in it, as they will show through the finish. Seal the paper on both sides with acrylic gloss medium before you begin.

Decide where on the box you want the design elements to appear: for example, the paper used on the box illustrated features old maps of the world and includes a lettered border, which looks very effective around the upper edge of the lid.

Covering the lid
Cut a sheet of paper to the exact size of the top of the lid. If the paper stretches when it is glued, you can trim away the excess later.

Covering the sides
Put the lid on the box and wrap the paper around the sides. Position the design to your satisfaction, and trim the paper to cover the sides exactly; it should not overlap or extend over the edge of the box. Place the join inconspicuously on a corner or at the back of the box. When the glue is dry, carefully run a scalpel between the box and the lid to separate them.

Child's hat & scarf

Your favourite niece or nephew will be as warm as toast on chilly winter days in this wool crepe hat and scarf. Make them in colours that complement the child's jumper or jacket.

WHAT YOU NEED

Size	A	B
Age (years)	4–8	10–14
Hat fits (cm)	52–54	56
Scarf length (cm)	100	120

The yarn used in this project is Patons 4 ply Diploma Gold (50 g balls). The colours for both garments are: main colour (mc), 4282 (cream); 1st contrast (cc1), 4291 (cornflower); 2nd contrast (cc2), 4220 (light blue); 3rd contrast (cc3), 4219 (pink).

Hat

Main (mc)	2	2
1st contrast (cc1)	1	1
2nd contrast (cc2)	1	1
3rd contrast (cc3)	1	1

Scarf

Main (mc)	4	5
1st contrast (cc1)	1	1
2nd contrast (cc2)	1	1
3rd contrast (cc3)	1	1

Knitting needles: 4.00 mm (no. 8), 3.75 mm (no. 9), 3.25 mm (no. 10) • wool sewing needle
● *Technique pages 323–7*

CHECKING THE TENSION

Before you begin, check your tension so that the measurements of the finished garment will be as close as possible to the size specified. You should have 27.5 stitches and 28 rows to a 10 cm square over Fair Isle using 4.00 mm needles, and 26.5 stitches to a 10 cm width over stocking stitch using 3.75 mm needles. If you have fewer stitches, use smaller needles; if more, use bigger needles.

❶ KNITTING THE HAT

Using 3.25 mm needles and mc, cast on 161 (169) sts.

NOTE

Do not weave colours in Fair Isle knitting. Instead, carry colours not in use loosely across on the wrong side of your work. Always carry colours to ends of rows, and always carry the main colour above the contrast colours.

1st row: K2, ★ P1, K1, rep from ★ to last st, K1.
2nd row: K1, ★ P1, K1, rep from ★ to end.
Rep 1st and 2nd rows 4 times, inc once in last row…162 (170) sts, making 10 rows rib in all.

Change to 4.00 mm needles. Work 19 rows of patt from graph A. Change to 3.75 mm needles and work 3 rows in mc, dec 6 (0) sts evenly across last row…156 (170) sts.
★★ Change to 4.00 mm needles and work 5 rows of patt from graph B, dec 4 (0) sts evenly across last row…152 (170) sts.
Work 5 rows from graph C, inc 2 (0) sts evenly across the last row…154 (170) sts.
Work 5 rows from graph D, inc 2 (0) sts evenly across the last row…156 (170) sts. ★★

Work 5 rows from graph B, dec 2 (0) sts evenly across the last row...154 (170) sts. Change to 3.75 mm needles and work 0 (2) rows in mc.

Shaping the top
Working in mc only:
1st row: K1, ★ K2 tog, K2, rep from ★ to last st, K1...116 (128) sts.
2nd and alt rows: Purl.
3rd row: K1, ★ K2 tog, K1, rep from ★ to last st, K1...78 (86) sts.
5th row: K1, ★ K2 tog, rep from ★ to last st, K1...40 (44) sts.
7th row: ★ K2 tog, rep from ★ to end...20 (22) sts.
Break off yarn, carefully run end through rem sts, draw up tightly and fasten off securely.

❷ MAKING UP THE HAT
1 Press lightly with a warm iron through a slightly damp cloth.
2 Using wool sewing needle and backstitch, join the two edges together. Press seam.
3 Using mc, make a pompom and sew it to the top of the hat.

❸ KNITTING THE SCARF
Using 3.75 mm needles and mc, cast on 22 (23) sts.
1st row: K1, ★ inc in next st, rep from ★ to last st, K1...42 (44) sts.
2nd and 4th rows: Purl.
3rd row: K1, ★ inc in next st, K1, rep from ★ to last st, K1...62 (65) sts.
5th row: K1, ★ inc in next st, K2, rep from ★ to last st, K1...82 (86) sts.
6th row: Purl.
Change to 4.00 mm needles.
Work 19 rows of patt from graph A.
Change to 3.75 mm needles and work 3 rows in mc, inc 4 (0) sts evenly across last row...86 sts.
Work as for hat from ★★ to ★★, omitting inc and dec.
Change to 3.75 mm needles and work in stst until scarf measures 84 (104) cm from beg, ending with a purl row.
Change to 4.00 mm needles and work 5 rows of patt from graph D.
Work 5 rows of patt from graph C.
Work 5 rows of patt from graph B.
Change to 3.75 mm needles and work 2 rows in mc, dec 4 (0) sts evenly

across last row...82 (86) sts.
Change to 4.00 mm needles.
Work 19 rows of patt from graph A.
Change to 3.75 mm needles.
Working in mc only, shape the end:
1st row: K1, ★ K2 tog, K2, rep from ★ to last st, K1.
2nd and 4th rows: Purl.
3rd row: K1, ★ K2 tog, K1, rep from ★ to last st, K1.
5th row: K1, ★ K2 tog, rep from ★ to last st, K1...22 (23) sts.
Break off yarn, carefully run end through rem sts, draw up tightly and fasten off securely.

❹ MAKING UP THE SCARF
1 With a slightly damp cloth and warm iron, press lightly.
2 With wrong side outside, back-stitch the side seam to form a tube. Turn the scarf to the right side and gather the cast-on edge, pulling it up

KNITTING GRAPHS
Reading knit rows from right to left and purl rows from left to right, work from the graph. Strand the colours loosely across the back of the work to the end of the row.

Graph A

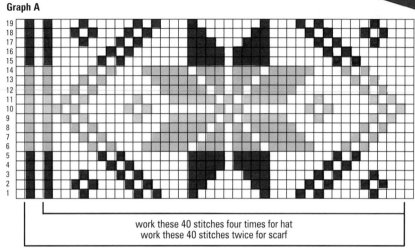

work these 40 stitches four times for hat
work these 40 stitches twice for scarf

work these 42 stitches four times for hat
work these 42 stitches twice for scarf

Graph B

Repeat these 14 stitches

Graph C

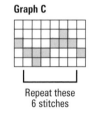

Repeat these 6 stitches

Graph D

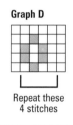

Repeat these 4 stitches

tightly. Fasten off the ends securely.
3 Make two pompoms and sew one to each end of the scarf. Press the seam through a damp cloth.

VARIATION
A plain scarf makes an excellent introduction to knitting for a child who would like to make a gift for a special friend.

Use five (six) balls of yarn and needles as specified in the pattern. Cast on and work the first five rows as given in the pattern. Continue working in stocking stitch (beginning with a purl row) until the work measures 98 (118) cm from the beginning, ending with a purl row. Work the last five rows and finish off as in the pattern.

Sculpted floral hair slide

Decorate a plain plastic hair slide and create a colourful accessory for a little girl. Older children could make this pretty floral hair slide themselves for a special friend.

and carefully follow the directions for making the dough. If you find the dough is too crumbly to manipulate easily, add more glue, or, if it is too sloppy, add more breadcrumbs. Before you begin the project, you may need to practise making and rolling

Hair slide • 6 slices white bread (a few days old, with the crusts removed) • PVA glue • artist's acrylic paints: white, green, and 2 or 3 colours of your choice for the flowers • 4 cake-decorating flower stamens • water-based clear matt varnish • plastic food wrap • sticky tape or Blu Tack • piece of A4 paper • electric blender or hand grater • bowl • small wooden stick (for mixing the dough) • smooth laminated board • scissors • knife • pencil • paint palette • 2 small paintbrushes (for varnishing and gluing) • piece of dowel about 8 cm long (for a rolling pin) • selection of small cake-decorating cutters in the shapes of stars, leaves and flowers

White breadcrumbs kneaded with PVA glue form a wonderfully elastic and pliable modelling dough. The dough, which requires no baking, can be tinted with acrylic paints to create stunning jewellery and knick-knacks.

To achieve the best results, use the ingredients in the quantities specified

Cutting the shapes

Any small cake-decorating cutters can be used for cutting the shapes from the dough. To make this project, the cutters illustrated below were used. They are shown to exact size.

the dough and cutting shapes from it until you are happy with the result.

❶ MAKING THE DOUGH

1 Using a blender, a grater or a food processor, reduce the bread to very fine crumbs.

NOTE

It is important to add white acrylic paint to the basic dough mixture – otherwise, the dough will become transparent and will crack when it dries. The paint also helps to improve the texture of the dough for easy working.

2 Place the breadcrumbs in a bowl with 60 ml of PVA glue and mix with a wooden stick.

3 Place the dough on the laminated board and knead it with your hands, working the dough until it is smooth and quite free of lumps. The dough will become softer and smoother as you knead it.

4 Add a small amount of white paint and knead this through the mixture, adding more paint if necessary until the dough is an even white colour.

5 Wrap the dough in plastic food wrap until you are ready to use it so that it does not dry out. The dough should be used within 12 days.

❷ PLANNING THE DESIGN

1 Using a pencil, trace the shapes of your cutters on to a piece of paper. Cut out at least two of each shape. Draw a template the size and shape of the part of the hair slide where the design is to be placed.

2 Arrange the paper cut-outs on the template until you are happy with the design. Fix them in place on the template with sticky tape or Blu Tack.

3 Decide what colour each shape is to be. (You can create more colours by mixing the paints on the palette before adding them to the dough.)

❸ CREATING THE DESIGN

It is important to press all the dough shapes on to the slide before the dough hardens, in order to allow for greater manipulation of the elements in the design.

1 Using a knife, scratch all over the top surface of the hair slide. This will roughen the surface so that the dough will stick to it.

2 Break off a piece of dough large enough to cover the top of the hair slide. Knead some green paint into it until the colour is evenly spread through the dough.

3 Using the dowel, roll out a flattish sausage of dough large enough to cover the top of the slide. Fix the green dough base to the slide with a little PVA glue, and score the dough at either end with a knife or pencil to create leaf shapes.

4 Break off enough dough to cut out all the shapes of one colour. Knead in paint of the chosen colour, and then roll out the dough thinly. Use the cutters to cut out the shapes.

5 Repeat step 4 until you have coloured and cut out all the shapes.

6 Cut the artificial stamens into short lengths (about 1 cm) and press them into the centres of the two largest flowers. In the middle of the other flowers, press little balls of dough in contrasting colours to make inner petals. Flatten the balls into petals with the end of a pencil.

7 Glue the flower shapes into place following the design of your paper plan.

❹ FINISHING

Leave the slide in a warm place (not in direct sunlight) to dry for two or three days. When it is completely dry, coat it with clear varnish using a small paintbrush.

Mouse bookends

Sturdily made with long base plates, these novel bookends will brighten up a child's shelves and keep books tidy.

WHAT YOU NEED

Master pattern **C17(a–e)** • plywood: 290 mm **x** 250 mm **x** 18 mm; 250 mm **x** 250 mm **x** 4 mm • two dressed timber blocks, 120 mm **x** 70 mm **x** 70 mm (for the cheese) • eight 20 mm lost head nails • six 35 mm lost head nails • timber undercoat • gloss paint: colour to suit decor, yellow (for cheese) • 40 cm **x** 25 cm soft kid leather or suede • 8 small toy eyes • 4 small beads • large bath sponge • 25 cm nylon fishing line • compass • handsaw or jigsaw • hammer • drill and drill bits of various sizes (5 mm to 15 mm) • medium-grade sandpaper • PVA glue • clear craft glue • paintbrush • steel ruler • scissors • craft knife • darning needle • clothes pegs • pencil

● *Technique pages 338–42, 343–4*

CUTTING THE BASES

Cutting lines

120 mm

140 mm

18 mm plywood

120 mm

Cutting line

250 mm

4 mm plywood

❶ MAKING THE BOOKENDS

140 mm

Bookend upright

120 mm

1 Trace an arc with a diameter of about 140 mm at one end of two of the rectangles of 18 mm plywood, using a pencil and a compass or a guide such as the rim of a saucer.
2 Using a handsaw or a jigsaw, cut around the tops of the circles to make the arched uprights of the bookends. The other two 18 mm thick rectangles form the bases for the bookends.
3 With medium-grade sandpaper, sand the edges and surfaces of the uprights, bases and base plates (the two rectangles of 4 mm plywood).

VARIATION
You can vary the mice by using leather or felt scraps of different colours or textures, by making them bigger or smaller, or by changing the shape of their ears or the set of their eyes.

4 Using PVA glue and four nails, glue and nail the base to the base plate for each bookend. Using three 35 mm nails at each join, glue and nail the upright to the base and base plate for each bookend.

❷ MAKING THE CHEESE

35 mm 35 mm

120 mm

70 mm

70 mm

1 Mark up and cut the two dressed timber blocks as shown.

2 One at a time, clamp the timber wedges firmly in a vice, and carefully drill holes at random through the wedges, using a variety of drill sizes and angles of approach.

3 Sand all surfaces smooth and wipe them clean and free of dust.

③ MAKING THE MICE

1 Trace the pattern pieces and all markings on them from the master pattern on to tracing paper and cut them out. Place the pattern pieces on the leather, and mark and cut out four sets of all pattern pieces.

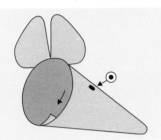

2 Roll the head piece into a cone shape to form the nose. Apply clear craft glue where indicated and clamp the leather with a clothes peg until dry. Glue the eyes to the head.

3 Cut small slits in the body with a craft knife, where indicated on the pattern piece. Insert the ends of the arms into the nicks, adjust them to the desired length, and glue.

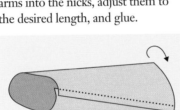

4 Form the body shape by gluing the straight sides together with a 5 mm overlap. Glue the head to the body. Clamp the join firmly with a clothes peg until the glue dries.

5 Using the darning needle, make a hole right through the snout, just

Cutting guide
Cut eight arms and four of all other pieces, remembering to transfer markings. To make bigger or smaller mice, enlarge or reduce the master pattern on a photocopier.

behind the nose. Push two 3 cm lengths of fishing line through the hole to make the whiskers. Glue a bead at the end of the nose cone.

6 Glue the base of the tail in place inside the body. With a craft knife, cut a cone from the sponge to fit inside the body. Glue the feet to the base of the foam cone so that the toes are visible, and then glue the sponge cone inside the mouse's body.

7 Repeat steps 2 to 6 three times to make three more mice.

④ FINISHING

1 Apply the timber undercoat to the bookends and the cheese and leave all the pieces to dry.

2 Paint the cheese yellow and the bookends in a colour of your choice. Allow to dry thoroughly.

3 Glue the cheese wedges in place on the bookends. Glue the mice to the cheese and the bookends as illustrated.

Beginner's flower press

Encourage a child's interest in botany by making this attractive flower press as a gift, perhaps accompanied by a little book on wild flowers. Pressed flower arrangements are ideal for craft projects such as cards or bookmarks.

WHAT YOU NEED

Plywood, 400 mm x 200 mm x 12 mm • timber, 200 mm x 200 mm x 9 mm (for the base plate) • 2 pieces felt, 200 mm x 200 mm • 4 bolts, 6 mm diameter, about 200 mm long, with matching washers and wing nuts • 15 mm lost head nails • PVA woodworking glue • clear craft glue • medium and fine-grade sandpaper • Folk Art acrylic paints: wicker white, poetry green • wrapping paper (for cut-out flower motifs) • 2 small paintbrushes • varnish • drill and drill bits • scrap timber • clamp • hammer • nail scissors • handsaw

● *Technique pages 338–42*

❶ PREPARING THE TIMBER

1 Cut the plywood into two pieces, each measuring 200 mm x 200 mm.
2 Sand smooth the cut edges of the plywood and the timber with medium-grade sandpaper.

❷ MAKING THE PRESS

1 Clamp together one of the 200 mm x 200 mm pieces of plywood (this will be the lid) and the timber base plate.
2 About 10 mm in from each corner, and with a drill bit to suit the diameter of the bolts, drill four bolt access holes right through the plywood and the base plate into a piece of scrap timber. Unclamp the wood.
3 Using a drill bit with a larger diameter, enlarge the bolt access holes on one side of the base plate so that the bolt heads can be recessed into the base plate.
4 Insert the bolts through the holes drilled in the base plate. Using the PVA glue and bullet head nails, glue and nail the undrilled piece of plywood to the bottom of the base plate, trapping the bolt heads.
5 Sand the corners of the press with medium-grade sandpaper until they are gently curved.
6 Using fine sandpaper, sand all surfaces smooth, including the lid (the plywood with the holes drilled in it).

❸ FINISHING THE PRESS

1 Using a small decorating brush, paint all surfaces with a base coat of wicker white and then two coats of poetry green. Allow each coat to dry thoroughly before applying the next.
2 Cut out suitable flower motifs from the wrapping paper with nail scissors, cutting neatly around the outlines.
3 Glue the paper motifs to the flower press lid, using the clear craft glue. Allow the glue to dry.
4 Apply a coat of varnish, allow to dry thoroughly, and then apply a second coat. Allow to dry.
5 Using the nail scissors, trim the corners of the two pieces of felt to match the rounded corners of the press. Cut a hole at each corner to accommodate the bolts.
6 Sandwich the two pieces of felt between the top plate and the base plate of the flower press.

NOTE

The flowers are pressed between sheets of blotting paper enclosed between sheets of card. With the gift, include a supply of blotting paper and cardboard, cut to about 150 mm square.

6 Repeat steps 3 to 5 until you have stuck down all the images. Allow the glue to dry thoroughly.

7 Apply two coats of artist's acrylic medium (sealer) to the découpaged surfaces. Allow the sealer to dry for one hour between coats and before starting to apply the varnish.

❸ VARNISHING AND SANDING

1 Using the imitation sable brush, apply 5 to 10 coats of varnish to all the découpaged surfaces. It is important to work carefully and to let the varnish dry for at least 24 hours between coats, otherwise lumps and drips of varnish will form.

2 When you are sure that the images are well protected with varnish, begin sanding between each third coat, using no. 600 wet-and-dry abrasive paper wrapped around a rubber sanding block and moistened with a little water. Sand lightly in one direction, and aim to allow the varnish on the background to build up to the level of the images. Before applying a new coat of varnish, use a lint-free cloth to remove any dust.

3 Continue varnishing and sanding until the découpaged surface is completely smooth and flat and you cannot feel the edges of the images – they should appear to be submerged in the layers of varnish. You may need as many as 30 coats of varnish to achieve the desired effect, although on a flat surface 10 coats may be enough.

4 Apply three more coats of varnish, sanding the surface between coats with no. 1200 wet-and-dry abrasive paper. This will give the box a very smooth, dull finish.

❹ FINISHING

1 Leave the pencil box to stand for two weeks to allow the varnish to harden and cure completely.

2 Make a mixture of equal parts of clear beeswax and cabinetmaker's polish and warm it slightly. Working on a small area at a time, rub the mixture evenly into the découpaged surfaces with a soft, lint-free cloth. Wipe the waxed area vigorously with a damp cloth and then polish it with a soft, dry cloth.

3 Repeat steps 2 and 3 if necessary.

CAUTION

Because the many layers of varnish used in découpage will increase the thickness of the lid, it is important to sand the lid right back so that it slides easily and very loosely in the grooves. For the same reason, do not paint or varnish in the grooves, and do not attempt to fit the finished lid into the box until you are satisfied that the varnish on both the box and the lid is completely dry and cured.

Stylish soft rucksack

Smart enough for any outing and strong enough to carry quite a load, this quilted rucksack will please the fussiest of teenagers. Made from two contrasting fabrics, it is easy to make up using a standard sewing machine.

WHAT YOU NEED

Master pattern **D27(a–c)** • **1 m main fabric, 115 cm wide** • **50 cm contrasting fabric, 90 cm wide** • **50 cm lining fabric, 115 cm wide** • **75 cm craft wadding, 115 cm wide** • sewing thread • sewing needle • 2 buttons • 10 large eyelets • dressmaking pins • tracing paper • pencil • dressmaker's pencil • scissors • tape measure • sewing machine
● *Technique pages 292–301, 305–6, 343–4*

① CUTTING OUT THE RUCKSACK

1 Using the tracing paper and pencil, trace the pattern pieces for the base, the bag flap, and the pocket flap. Cut the pattern pieces out.
2 Cut out the fabrics as follows.

Main fabric

One main piece, 87 cm x 44 cm; two straps, 8 cm x 75 cm; one reinforcing strip, 5.5 cm x 25 cm; one handle, 8 cm x 24 cm; one base (from master pattern); one bag flap (from master pattern); one pocket flap bias strip, 4 cm x 38 cm; one bag flap bias strip, 4 cm x 70 cm.

Contrasting fabric

One pocket, 32 cm x 32 cm; one bottom band, 5.5 cm x 87 cm; one cord, 90 cm x 3.5 cm; two pocket flaps (from master pattern); one bag flap (from master pattern).

Lining fabric

One main piece, 87 cm x 36 cm; one base (from master pattern).

Wadding

One main piece, 90 cm x 48 cm; one base (from master pattern) – cut this piece 1 cm larger all around; one bag flap and one pocket flap (from master pattern); two straps, 8 cm x 75 cm; one handle, 8 cm x 24 cm.

② QUILTING THE PIECES

Use iron-on or regular craft wadding.

1 Iron or tack the wadding to the wrong side of the main piece cut from the main fabric, and machine-quilt them together in a 7 cm grid pattern. Trim away the excess wadding.
2 Repeat step 1 to quilt the base piece cut from the main fabric.
3 Iron or tack the wadding to the wrong side of one of the pocket flaps cut from the contrasting fabric. Lay

VARIATION

Instead of making the rucksack with contrasting prints, you could use plain fabrics in either complementary or contrasting colours – for example, purple and pink or black and white. You could also buy the cord rather than making it.

② KNITTING THE FRONT

Work as for back to ★★.
Work 21 (21-21-19-19-19) rows patt.

Shaping the neck

Next row: Patt 19 (20-22-22-23-24) sts, cast off 23 (23-23-25-25-25) sts, work in patt to end.
Cont on last 19 (20-22-22-23-24) sts.
Dec at neck edge in alt rows until 13 (13-15-16-17-17) sts rem, then in every foll 4th row until 8 (8-10-10-11-11) sts rem.
Work 7 rows. Cast off.
Join yarn to rem sts and work other side to correspond.

③ CROCHETING THE BAND

First motif

Using 3.50 mm crochet hook and Gem cotton, work 8 ch, join with a slst to form a ring.
1st round: 3 ch, 1 tr in ring, (Picot 3, 2 tr in ring) 11 times, Picot 3, slst in 3rd ch at beg.
Fasten off.

Second motif

Using 3.50 mm crochet hook and Gem cotton, work 8 ch, join with a slst to form a ring.
1st round: 3 ch, 1 tr in ring, ★ 2 ch, drop loop from hook, insert hook in any picot of 1st motif, draw dropped loop through picot, 1 ch, slst in last tr of 2nd motif (to complete the picot) ★, 2 tr in ring, rep from ★ to ★ once in next picot of 1st motif, complete as for 1st motif.
Fasten off.

Continue joining motifs in this way, leaving 4 picots free before joining the next motif, until there are 20 (21-22-23-25-26) motifs.
Make 1 more motif, joining it (as before) to the previous motif and also to the first motif with the 7th and 8th picots.
Make another 21 (22-23-24-26-27) motifs, joining each (as before) to the previous motif and also to a 1st round motif with 4th and 5th picots. Join the final motif to the previous motif, the 1st round motif and the 1st motif of the 2nd round.

④ FINISHING THE TOP

Using Stonewash cotton and wool sewing needle, join side and shoulder seams with backstitch. It is best not to press this garment, because of its textured pattern.

Waist

Using 3.50 mm crochet hook and Gem cotton, work 1 rnd of dc evenly around lower edge. Fasten off. Using a flat seam, sew picots of midriff band to dc rnd.

Neckline and armholes

1st round: Using 3.50 mm crochet hook and Gem cotton, work 1 rnd dc evenly around the neck edge, taking care to keep work flat and working an even number of sts.
2nd round: 1 ch, 1 dc in the first dc, ★ Picot 2, 1 dc in each of next 2 dc, rep from ★ to last dc, Picot 2, 1 dc in next dc, slst in first dc. Fasten off.
Work the same edging around the armholes.

⑤ CROCHETING THE HAT

Check your tension before you begin. You should have 24 dc and 28 rows to 10 cm over double crochet fabric, using a 4.00 mm hook.

This hat is designed to be worked with a bigger hook at a looser tension than is usually recommended.

Using 4.00 mm crochet hook and Gem cotton, work 4 ch, join with slst to form a ring.
1st round: 1 ch, 12 dc in ring, slst in first dc.

MOSS STITCH

Moss stitch is sometimes called seed stitch. It produces a firm, textured fabric that keeps its shape. It can be used to make a whole garment or as a contrast.

2nd round: 1 ch, 2 dc in same place as slst, 2 dc in each dc to end, slst in first dc...24 dc.
3rd round: 1 ch, 1 dc in same place as slst, 1 dc in each dc to end, slst in first dc.
4th round: 1 ch, 1 dc in same place as slst, 2 dc in next dc, ★ 1 dc in next dc, 2 dc in next dc, rep from ★ to end, slst in first dc...36 dc.
5th round: As for 3rd round.
6th round: 1 ch, 1 dc in same place as slst, 1 dc in next dc, 2 dc in next dc, ★ 1 dc in each of next 2 dc, 2 dc in next dc, rep from ★ to end, slst in first dc...48 dc.
7th round: As for 3rd round.
8th round: 1 ch, 1 dc in same place as slst, 1 dc in each of next 2 dc, 2 dc in next dc, ★ 1 dc in each of next 3 dc, 2 dc in next dc, rep from ★ to end, slst in first dc...60 dc.
9th round: As for 3rd round.
10th round: 1 ch, 1 dc in same place as slst, 1 dc in each of next 3 dc, 2 dc in next dc, ★ 1 dc in each of next 4 dc, 2 dc in next dc, rep from ★ to end, slst in first dc...72 dc.
Rep 3rd round twice.
13th round: 1 ch, 1 dc in same place as slst, 1 dc in each of next 4 dc, 2 dc in next dc, ★ 1 dc in each of next 5 dc, 2 dc in next dc, rep from ★ to end, slst in first dc...84 dc.
Rep 3rd round twice.
16th round: 1 ch, 1 dc in same place as slst, 1 dc in each of next 5 dc, 2 dc in next dc, ★ 1 dc in each of next 6 dc, 2 dc in next dc, rep from ★ to end, slst in first dc...96 dc.
Cont inc in this way (working 1 more dc between inc each time) in each foll 3rd rnd, until there are 132 dc.
Rep 3rd rnd until work measures 17 cm from beginning. (The length may be varied at this point to suit individual requirements.)
Next round: 1 ch, 1 dc in same place as slst, miss 2 dc, 5 tr in next dc, miss 2 dc, ★ 1 dc in next dc, miss 2 dc, 5 tr in next dc, miss 2 dc, rep from ★ to end, slst in first dc.
Fasten off.

Liberty-print hair accessories

Cover elastic, hair clasps, bands and combs with pretty fabrics in colours to complement her favourite outfit – they're sure to be a hit with a fashion-conscious young woman.

Strong sewing threads to match the fabrics • invisible thread • needle: fine sharp • sewing machine (optional) • scissors • tape measure • long knitting needle • craft glue
Scrunchie
Liberty-print fabric strip, 12 cm **x** width of fabric • 30 cm narrow elastic
Ruffled clasp
Liberty-print fabric strip, 15 cm **x** width of fabric • hair clasp
Narrow hair band
Liberty-print bias strip, 3 cm **x** 33 cm • plastic hair band, about 10 mm wide, with no teeth or grips on the underside
Ruffled hair band
Liberty-print bias strip, 6 cm **x** 122 cm (join short bias strips as described in 'Bias binding', page 299) • plastic hair band, about 15 mm wide, with no teeth or grips on the underside • wadding (enough to cover the hair band)
Side comb
Liberty-print bias strip, 3 cm **x** 50 cm • plastic side comb, with no teeth or grips on the underside
● *Technique pages 292–5*

❶ MAKING THE SCRUNCHIE

1 Fold the fabric in half lengthwise, with right sides together.
2 Leaving 4 cm open at each end, sew the long sides together. Turn the tube right side out, using a long knitting needle to push the end through.

3 Place the two short ends together and, with right sides facing, sew them together so that the fabric forms a closed tube. Leave the opening on the long side unstitched at this stage.
4 Thread the elastic through the tube and sew the ends together with strong thread. Slipstitch the opening in the scrunchie with invisible thread.

❷ MAKING THE RUFFLED CLASP

1 Fold the fabric in half lengthwise, with right sides together, and sew along the entire length. Leave the ends open.
2 Turn the tube right side out and press it with an iron so that the seam

lies flat in the middle of the tube.
3 Fold the corners into a triangular point at one end. Fold the point down to the middle of the base of the triangle formed by the previous folds and

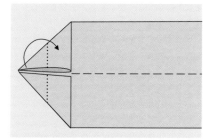

slipstitch the fold down at the point, using strong thread. Repeat this step at the other end of the tube.

4 Using strong thread, sew long gathering stitches along the entire length of the stitched seam, being careful not to catch the top layer of fabric with the needle.

5 Oversew one end of the fabric to one end of the clasp base at the point where you slipstitched the fold down. Sew through the holes in the clasp to keep the fabric in place.

6 Draw up the gathering stitches until the ruffle is the same length as the clasp. Arrange the gathers evenly. Oversew the free end of the ruffle to the end of the clasp, as in step 5.

7 Oversew the ruffle to the clasp along the gathered seam, again being careful not to catch the top layer of fabric with the needle. Finish off securely, and arrange the ruffle evenly over the clasp.

❸ COVERING THE NARROW HAIR BAND

1 Fold the strip of fabric in half lengthwise, with right sides together.

2 Sew the long sides together leaving a 5 mm seam allowance, so that the tube formed is slightly wider than the hair band. (This will allow the hair band to fit snugly inside the fabric.)

3 At one short end, sew the sides together. Trim the seams and turn the tube right side out, using a long knitting needle to push the fabric through.

4 Feed the hair band into the tube, smoothing the fabric over the band as you work. Trim any excess fabric from the open end.

5 Turn in the raw edges to fit snugly over the end of the hair band. Close the hair band cover using slipstitch and invisible thread.

❹ COVERING THE RUFFLED HAIR BAND

7 cm

1 Fold the bias strip in half lengthwise, with right sides together.

2 Begin stitching the long sides together with a curved, tapering seam, so that the tube is about 1 cm wide at the end and broadens to about 2.5 cm with a 5 mm seam allowance at a point 7 cm from the end. Then continue sewing a straight seam to 7 cm from the other end. Fasten off.

3 Trim the seam at the tapered end of the tube, and use a knitting needle to turn this end of the tube in on itself for about 15 mm.

HINTS

- *To glamorise the narrow hair band for evening wear, glue on ribbon roses or a matching bow, or wind and glue a satin ribbon around the band.*
- *When a favourite outfit becomes too old to wear, save fabric from the least worn areas to make these hair accessories.*

4 Spread a thin coat of glue evenly on the top surface of the hair band and attach a layer of wadding. Trim the batting to the shape of the band.

5 Spread a thin layer of glue on the last 5 cm of the underside of one end of the hair band and push this end into the tapered end of the fabric tube, pulling the fabric smooth. Push all the fabric on to the band, turning it right side out along its entire length as you work, and keeping the seam on the underside of the band.

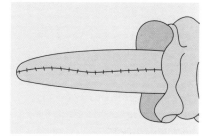

6 Scrunch the fabric into an even ruffle along the wide part of the band.

7 Fit the open end of the fabric tube to the band by overlapping the edges of the fabric very tightly and using the invisible thread to sew them together with fine stitches. This end must be stitched very firmly to hold the ruffled band cover in place.

❺ DECORATING THE SIDE COMB

1 With wrong sides together, fold the two long edges of the fabric strip in 5 mm and press the folds. Again with wrong sides together, fold the strip in half lengthwise and press.

2 Apply a small amount of glue to one end of the underside of the bar of the comb, and glue one end of the bias strip to the comb. Allow the glue to dry completely.

3 Hold the comb in your left hand and, from the glued end, wind the bias strip over the bar and through to the right side of the comb. Keeping the fabric taut, wind the bias strip neatly between each tooth of the comb and around the bar until you reach the other end.

4 Trim away any excess fabric and glue the raw end to the inside of the bar.

Rainbow jumper

Delight a young person by knitting them this vibrant striped jumper, which appeals equally to both girls and boys.

WHAT YOU NEED

Size	A	B	C
Chest (cm)	75	85	95
Jumper measures (cm)			
Chest	100	110	120
Length	68	69	70
Sleeves	43	43	43

The yarn used in this project is Patons Diploma Gold DK (50 g balls) and the colours are: main colour (mc), 3149 (slate); 1st contrast colour (cc1), 6143 (natural); and 1 ball each 6139 (cherry), 6140 (ever green), 6212 (medium green), 6198 (pale green), 6199 (pale grey), 6219 (pale pink), 6158 (medium pink), 6203 (rose pink), 6214 (plum), 6217 (navy blue), 6169 (medium blue), 6120 (pale blue), 6151 (orange red), 6208 (maroon), 6226 (purple), 6224 (mauve), 6196 (lemon), 6205 (tan), 6150 (yellow).

mc	6	7	7
cc1	3	3	3

Knitting needles: 4.00 mm (no. 8), 3.25 mm (no. 10) • wool sewing needle • 2 stitch holders
● *Technique pages 323–7*

CHECKING THE TENSION

Before you begin knitting the jumper, make a sample square to check the tension of your knitting so that the measurements of the finished garment will be as close as possible to the size specified in the pattern.

You should have 22.5 stitches to a 10 cm width over stocking stitch, using 4.00 mm knitting needles. Check very carefully. If you have fewer stitches, use smaller needles; if more stitches, use bigger needles.

COLOUR SCHEMES

Colours can look very different, depending on the colours that appear in combination with them.

In a harmonious colour scheme, all the colours come from the same part of the colour wheel. Each colour tones down the impact of the others, which produces a sophisticated effect of understated richness.

In a contrasting colour scheme, the colours come from opposite segments of the colour wheel. This heightens and intensifies each colour and creates a striking and dramatic effect.

Try this alternative colour scheme as a variation on the jumper shown in the photograph.

❶ BACK

Using 3.25 mm needles and mc, cast on 113 (125-137) sts.
1st row: K2, ★ P1, K1, rep from ★ to last st, K1.
2nd row: P1, ★ K1, P1, rep from ★ to end.
Rep 1st and 2nd rows 5 times...12 rows rib in all.
Change to 4.00 mm needles.
Work in stst in stripes as foll:
3 rows mc, 1 row cherry, 1 row natural, 1 row ever green, 15 rows mc, 1 row ever green, 1 row natural, 1 row cherry, 3 rows mc, 2 rows ever green, 2 rows medium green, 2 rows pale green, 2 rows pale grey.
36th row: P1 natural, ★ P1 mc, P1 natural, rep from ★ to end.

37th row: K1 mc, ★ K1 natural, K1 mc, rep from ★ to end.
Cont in stripes as foll: 2 rows pale pink, 2 rows medium pink, 2 rows rose pink, 2 rows plum, 3 rows mc, 1 row cherry, 1 row natural, 1 row ever green, 16 rows natural, 1 row ever green, 1 row natural, 1 row cherry, 3 rows mc, 2 rows navy blue, 2 rows medium blue, 2 rows pale blue.
80th row: Rep 36th row.
81st row: Rep 37th row.
Cont in stripes as foll: 2 rows natural, 2 rows orange red, 2 rows cherry, 2 rows maroon, 3 rows mc, 1 row natural, 1 row ever green, 1 row cherry, 15 rows mc, 1 row cherry, 1 row ever green, 1 row natural, 3 rows mc, 2 rows purple, 2 rows mauve, 2 rows pale pink.
123rd row: Rep 37th row.
124th row: Rep 36th row.
Cont in stripes as foll: 2 rows lemon, 2 rows tan, 2 rows yellow.
Last 130 rows form patt.
Cont in patt until work measures 65 (66-67) cm from beg, ending with a purl row.

Shaping the shoulder

Keeping patt correct, cast off 10 (12-13) sts at beg of next 6 rows, then 12 (11-13) sts at beg of foll 2 rows. Transfer rem 29 (31-33) sts on to a stitch holder.

❷ FRONT

Work as for back until there are 22 (24-26) rows fewer than there are in the back to shoulder shaping, ending with a purl row.

Shaping the neck

Next row: Keeping patt correct, patt 49 (54-60), then turn and cont on these sts.
Dec at neck edge in alt rows until 42 (47-52) sts rem.
Work 7 (9-9) rows.

Shaping the shoulder

Cast off 10 (12-13) sts at beg of next and alt rows 3 times in all.
Work 1 row. Cast off.
Slip next 15 (17-17) sts on to stitch holder and leave.

Join yarn to rem sts and work the neck and shoulder of the other side to correspond.

❸ SLEEVES

Using 3.25 mm needles and mc, cast on 49 (49-51) sts.
Work 13 rows rib as for back.
14th row: Rib 6 (4-6), ★ inc in next st, rib 1, rep from ★ to last 7 (5-5) sts, rib to end...67 (69-71) sts.
Change to 4.00 mm needles.
Working in patt as for back, inc at each end of 5th and foll 6th (6th-4th) rows until there are 73 (73-105) sts, then in foll 4th (4th-alt) rows until there are 103 (107-113) sts.

Cont until work measures 43 cm from beg, ending with a purl row.
Cast off loosely.

❹ NECKBAND

Using backstitch, join right shoulder seam. With right side facing, and using 3.25 mm needles and mc, knit up 97 (105-109) sts evenly around the neck, incl sts from stitch holders.
Work 21 rows rib as for back, beg with a 2nd row.
Cast off loosely in rib.

❺ MAKING UP

1 Press the garment pieces with a damp cloth and a warm iron.

2 Tie a coloured thread at sides of back and front, 44 cm up from lower edge, to mark armhole positions.
3 Backstitch sleeve and side seams to the coloured threads. Sew in sleeves.
4 Fold neckband in half to the wrong side, and slipstitch into place.
5 Press the seams.

HINT

To add that extra special touch to this gift, knit a plain fringed scarf in one of the contrast colours. Or look for a pair of warm socks in a plain colour to match one of the colours featured in the jumper.

Painted mat

Rather than opting for a ready-made floor mat, you can brighten a teenager's room with a mat you have painted yourself. Teenagers may like to make this gift themselves to give to friends.

1 m primed 10 oz canvas, 150 cm wide, hemmed around edges • 2 m fringing • white acrylic house paint, matt or semi-gloss • Jo Sonja's artist's colours: yellow light, green oxide, jade, raw sienna, gold oxide, ultramarine, dioxazine purple, titanium white, napthol crimson • paintbrushes: 50 mm decorating, no. 12 round • toothbrush • metal spatula (or old table knife) • water-based clear matt varnish • PVA glue • soft pencil
● *Technique pages 334–5*

❶ PREPARING THE CANVAS

1 Apply two coats of white acrylic house paint to the canvas, allowing the paint to dry between coats.
2 Using a soft pencil, rule a 10 cm border around the edge of the mat. Sketch in the border design, following the painting guide or inventing your own pattern. The design looks most

MAKING A WALL HANGING

This design could also be used to make a wall hanging, either the same size as the mat or somewhat smaller – simply scale down the elements of the design to suit whatever size of hanging you want to make.

Follow the instructions for making the painted mat, omitting the fringing at one end and making the hem at that end large enough to take a piece of strong, flat dowelling about 10 cm longer than the width of the canvas. When the design is painted and finished, push the dowelling through the wide hem and attach a strong cord for hanging. Trim with tassels if desired.

2 Dry-brush over the leaves with jade paint. This will add dimension, depth and light.

Nuts

1 Paint the nuts with gold oxide, leaving patches of canvas unpainted to create highlights.
2 Dry-brush the nuts in raw sienna to define and shape them.

Background

1 Leaving a 1 cm border around the nuts and leaves, lightly cover the background with ultramarine and allow to dry.
2 Dry-brush over the same area with dioxazine purple. In some places allow the colours to blend into each other, and in other places allow single colours to stand out.
3 Paint around each leaf and nut in yellow light, allowing the edges to blend into the blue paints.

Border

1 Following the painting guide, paint the border design. Paint the background to the design in green oxide.
2 Using a toothbrush and a spatula, spatter blue paint over the mat by sliding the paint-loaded spatula across the mat and releasing the paint particles with light toothbrush strokes.

Painting guide

The design illustrated is based on the shapes and colours of nuts and leaves. The border motif is created from abstract motifs and designs.

However, this design and the colours specified are meant as suggestions only. The free style of painting used offers you plenty of scope for your own ideas. Before starting to paint the canvas, use wallpaper lining paper to experiment with colour and design and develop your own style.

❸ FINISHING

1 When the paint has dried, apply two or three coats of clear varnish.
2 Coat the back of the mat with a mixture of one part PVA glue and one part water. Allow to dry.
3 If the fringing has not already been attached by the supplier of the canvas, stitch it to the ends of the mat.

HINT
Ready-primed canvas bought from a sailmaker or chandler is the most economical material for this project. Heavy-duty canvas is difficult to sew, so ask the sailmaker to stitch the hems around the edges and attach the fringing to the short ends.

effective if the border has a free appearance rather than a precise geometrical look.
3 In the centre area of the mat, sketch in nuts and leaves.

❷ PAINTING THE CANVAS
Leaves

1 Paint the leaves in green oxide, leaving a thin unpainted strip down the centre of each leaf to represent the vein of the leaf. Allow to dry.

Printed T-shirts

Personalise a T-shirt for a young friend with this simple method. You don't have to be an artist to create eye-catching designs – all you need is access to a photocopier and a good eye for suitable images.

WHAT YOU NEED

T-shirts • images to photocopy • photocopy acetate • turpentine • fabric paints: red, blue, yellow, black • dessertspoon • paintbrushes: medium round, small liner • sticky tape • chopping board • old tea-towel • old towel • iron • plate

❶ PREPARING THE IMAGES

1 Any illustration or photograph is suitable for printing on a T-shirt, so long as it photocopies well in black and white and the image is clear with good lines and shading.
2 Photocopy the image, enlarging or reducing until you have a size appropriate to the size of the T-shirt. It is best to make the copies fairly dark.
3 If you want to include text with the picture, you need to make a mirror image of the writing so that it prints the correct way on the fabric. To make a mirror image, photocopy the image on acetate film. Then place the sheet of acetate back to front on the photocopier glass and photocopy the reversed image on to a sheet of paper.

❷ FIXING THE IMAGES ON TO THE T-SHIRT

1 Lay the T-shirt on an old towel on a flat working surface. Have the turpentine, dessertspoon, sticky tape, photocopies and paintbrush within easy reach.
2 Wrap an old tea-towel around a chopping board and secure it with some sticky tape. Place the wrapped board inside the T-shirt, beneath where you plan to place the design. This provides a firm, slightly absorbent surface against which

HINTS

● *For added interest, put smaller versions of the image on to the sleeves or back of the shirt.*
● *Centre the image on the top two-thirds of the T-shirt so that it is shown to its best advantage. Remember that the bottom of a T-shirt is often tucked into jeans or a skirt.*
● *Practise on an old T-shirt or other fabric scrap first until you have perfected the technique.*

to apply the photocopied design, and prevents the dye running through to the other side of the shirt.
3 Cut around the photocopied image, leaving at least 2 cm of blank paper all around. Place the photocopy face down on the T-shirt and secure it with sticky tape, taking care not to cover any of the design.
4 Paint turpentine over the back of the image until it is saturated. You should be able to see the image through the paper quite clearly, but there should be no pools of liquid on the surface.
5 Rub firmly all over the image area with the back of the spoon, holding the paper and T-shirt down securely as you go so that the image doesn't move around. Go over the whole area about three times. If the turpentine evaporates before you have finished, reapply and continue rubbing.
6 Lift one corner of the paper to see whether the image has transferred to the fabric. If you can see any areas that are missing, replace the corner and rub the entire image again. With experience you will be able to judge the correct degree of pressure, rubbing and saturation of turpentine to achieve the best effect.
7 Remove the paper carefully, starting from one corner and slowly peeling it back. Some makes of T-shirt are slightly fluffier than others; if any pieces of blackened fluff appear as you peel the paper back, pick them off the surface with your fingers or a brush. If fragments land on clean areas of the shirt, don't remove them until the turpentine has evaporated.
8 To fix the image, iron the shirt at a temperature suitable for the fabric.

Look for suitable images in art books and magazines. If you prefer, you can photocopy the images on this page. The text has already been reversed for you. Enlarge or reduce the images to fit the size of your T-shirt.

❸ APPLYING THE COLOUR

1 Decide what colours to use on the images. Place the chopping board behind the images to protect the other side of the shirt.

2 Mix the fabric paints on a plate with a small amount of water. It is a good idea to experiment on scraps of fabric first until you have a good consistency. If the paint is too runny, the colour will 'bleed' over the edges of the image. If the paint is too dry, it will create a rough, caked-on effect.

3 Paint the images by filling in different areas with flat colours and outlining the image with a small liner brush. Alternatively, create more unusual effects. See folk art techniques (pages 334–5) for suggestions for creative brush strokes and shading.

4 Follow the manufacturer's instructions for fixing the paints and washing.

VARIATION

This method of transferring images can be used to make unusual curtains, cushions or a bedspread for a teenager's room. You can repeat the same image across the fabric or print several different images at random.

Brilliant bead jewellery

Jewellery design is limited only by your imagination. With a selection of interesting beads and some basic equipment, you can make a gift that will delight any young person.

WHAT YOU NEED

Selection of decorative beads of your choice • wire cutters • pliers: long-nosed, round-nosed
Necklace or bracelet
nylon-coated wire (tiger tail), 5 cm longer than finished length of necklace or bracelet • 2 crimps for each item • barrel or ring clasp
Earrings
2 headpins for each pair of earrings • 2 eyepins for each pair of earrings (for double-section earrings) • screw-on or clip-on fittings, or pierced-ear wires

❶ MAKING THE NECKLACE OR BRACELET

1 First thread a crimp on to one end of the wire, positioning it about 2 cm from the end.
2 Take one half of the clasp and

thread the short end of the wire through the loop of the clasp and then back through the crimp.
3 Making sure that the crimp and clasp are fitted snugly together, squeeze the crimp with the pliers until it locks the wire securely.
4 Thread the beads of your choice on to the wire, leaving the last 3 cm of wire free.
5 Thread the free end of the wire through the second crimp, then through the other half of the clasp and back through the crimp. Do not squeeze the crimp shut yet.
6 Push the excess wire back through the last two or three beads. Pull the end of the wire as tightly as possible, so that there are no gaps between beads, crimp and clasp. Squeeze the crimp firmly with the pliers to lock the wire in place. Carefully snip off any excess wire.

EXTRA LONG EARRINGS

• You can make really long earrings by adding a further eyepin threaded with one or more beads before you attach the earring fitting.
• Try adding several eyepins, each threaded with a single bead for a different effect.
• The wires may also be bent into interesting shapes to add variety to the designs.

❷ MAKING THE EARRINGS

1 Thread the selected beads on to the headpin, leaving the last 1 cm of wire bare. The headpin wire can be cut to any length, depending on how long you want the earrings to be.

2 With the long-nosed pliers, bend the end of the wire to make a slightly open loop.

3 Pass the loop through the hole on the earring clips or wires and close with the round-nosed pliers.

BEST FRIENDS &
RELATIONS

It's often hard to find just
the right thing for a
dear friend or close relative.
In this chapter there are
some delightful ideas for
gifts that you can make
to show a loved one how
much you care.

Herb-filled sleep pillow

The delicate heirloom-style fabric of the outer pillow allows the relaxing aroma of the herbs inside to slowly release during sleep.

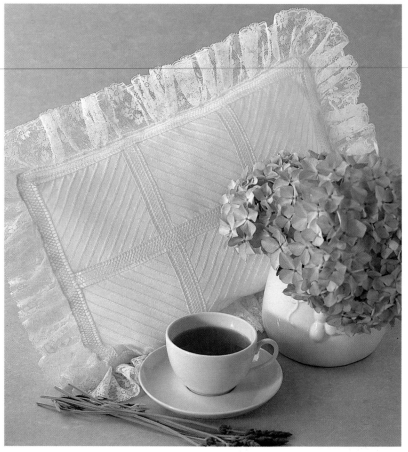

WHAT YOU NEED

24 cm voile, 115 cm wide • 2.5 m insertion lace, about 20 mm wide • 4 m edging lace, 50 mm wide • loose-weave fabric for inner cushion, about 38 cm x 48 cm • 2 spools white sewing thread • sewing machine with double needle and zigzag setting • scissors • tape measure • aromatic herbs or a herb pot pourri (see 'Fragrant pot pourri', pages 214–15)
● *Technique pages 292–301, 303–4*

❶ SEWING THE PILLOWCASE

1 To make the front, fold the fabric in half and cut six 12 cm squares of voile, as shown in the cutting guide. The rest of the fabric is for the back.
2 Using a double sewing machine needle, stitch each square in a pattern of diagonal lines.

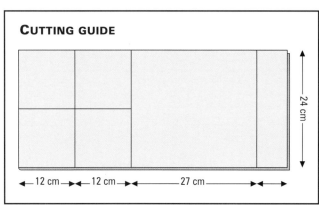

CUTTING GUIDE

← 12 cm → ← 12 cm → ← 27 cm →

24 cm

3 Press down a 1 cm hem all around each square. Using a medium zigzag setting and a fairly long stitch, join the squares together with insertion lace. Make two rows of three squares and then join the rows to form a rectangle. Edge the rectangle with insertion lace.
4 Measure the finished front piece. (It should measure 24 cm x 36 cm, but there may be some variation depending on the width of the insertion lace and how closely you have joined the squares.) From the voile, cut two pieces 24 cm wide and 27 cm long, or as long as the short edge of the front piece plus 3 cm (see cutting guide). These pieces will form a lapped back.
5 Turn under 1 cm on one 27 cm edge of each piece and machine hem. Turn under 1.5 cm on the remaining three sides of each back piece and press flat.
6 Lay one back piece on the front piece, wrong sides together, and then lay the second back piece right side up over the first, so that the hemmed edges overlap

to form a flap at the back through which to insert the pillow.
7 Tack the three layers together, and then topstitch all around the pillow-case as close to the edges as possible.
8 Using a gathering stitch, sew along the inside edge of the edging lace. Gather the lace until it fits around the outside of the pillowcase. Use a medium zigzag stitch to attach the gathered lace around the insertion lace border.

❷ MAKING THE INTERIOR

1 Using any fine, loose-weave fabric, make an inner pillow slightly smaller than the cover (about 22 cm x 34 cm), leaving one end open.
2 Fill the pillow with a mixture of aromatic herbs or a herb pot pourri, stitch up the open end, and insert the pillow in the lace cover.

Chic fabric necklace

Make this charming and unusual necklace to coordinate with a friend's or relative's favourite dress, or create it from a more neutral-coloured fabric that will complement several outfits.

Fine lawn or silk, 1 m x 8.5 cm •
18 round wooden beads about 1 cm
in diameter • 19 ceramic beads with
large holes, in a colour suitable for
the fabric • matching sewing thread
• knitting needle • invisible thread •
protective fabric spray • sewing
machine • sewing needle: sharp size
12 • scissors
● *Technique pages 292–301*

❶ PREPARING THE FABRIC

1 With right sides facing, fold the
fabric in half lengthwise. Beginning
10 cm from the end, cut both ends of
the fabric at an angle to create a point.
2 With a 1 cm seam allowance,
machine stitch around the open edges,
leaving a 5 cm opening at one end of
the long side for turning out.

3 Trim the excess fabric from the
tapered ends and turn the fabric to the
right side, pushing the tapered points
out neatly with a knitting needle.

❷ THREADING THE BEADS

1 Thread a ceramic bead on to the
fabric tube, positioning it 15 cm from
the end furthest from the opening.

> **NOTE**
> *It is essential to choose a very
> fine, soft fabric that will thread
> easily through the ceramic beads
> and lie smoothly against the
> large wooden beads. Liberty
> tana lawn is an ideal choice,
> giving excellent results.*

2 Push a wooden bead through the
opening in the fabric tube and guide
it down the fabric until it is butting
up against the ceramic bead. Make
sure that the hole in the wooden bead
fits snugly against the ceramic bead.
Manipulate the beads and the fabric
so that the fabric covers the wooden
bead as smoothly as possible.

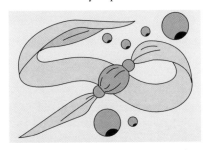

3 Thread on another ceramic bead,
pushing it up against the wooden bead
inside the tube. Again, adjust the fabric to lie as smoothly as possible.

4 Repeat steps 2 and 3 until you have
used all the beads. Finish with a
ceramic bead, leaving a tail of about
15 cm of fabric without beads.

❸ FINISHING

1 Using invisible thread, close the
opening in the tube with slipstitch.
2 Iron the fabric tails and treat all the
fabric with a protective spray. Tie the
tails together in a loose knot.

Raffia sunhat

A cloche-shaped raffia sunhat makes a thoughtful gift for a dear friend or relative who enjoys being out in the sun, but is careful about her skin.

WHAT YOU NEED

About 400 g raffia • 20 cm raw silk or similar fabric, 90 cm wide • 70 cm petersham ribbon, 20 mm wide (optional) • clear PVA craft glue • small bunch of old-fashioned dried flowers (optional) • sewing thread to match silk and petersham ribbon • needles: very large-eyed tapestry, general sewing • small, sharp scissors

● *Technique pages 292–5*

❶ MAKING THE RAFFIA PLAIT

It is important that the weaving pattern is the same as that shown in the diagram. Untangle the raffia strands as you work, and keep the plait the same width – about 2 cm. With practice you will be able to work with more than one strand at a time.

1 Untie and untwist the hank of raffia and draw out 20–25 strands. Bind and

NOTE

It is important to know or estimate the size of the recipient's head. If you want your gift to be a surprise, measure your own head size and then guess at any differences between your head and the recipient's, or look for someone who has a similar head size. The hat should sit just above the ears.

If you cannot estimate the size accurately, make the hat larger rather than smaller, and adjust the size by threading a strand of raffia through the crown in a running or gathering stitch. Draw up the thread and tie it in a bow, which will be covered with the silk band.

tie them together firmly at one end with another strand of raffia and attach the bundle to a stable, solid object, such as a door handle.

2 Divide the bundle of raffia strands into four equal sections. Take the left-hand strand (1) and pass it over the second strand (2), then under the third strand (3) and over the last strand (4). Start again on the left-hand strand (which is now strand 2), and weave over, under and over again.

3 Continue weaving until the plait starts to become thinner as some of the strands begin to run out. Weave in more strands of raffia to make a continuous plait, adding a few strands of raffia at a time. Take the thinning section to one side and over-lap the new strands along its length, allowing the ends to protrude about 10 cm. Continue plaiting.

4 Repeat steps 2 and 3 until you have about 8 metres of plaiting, and then trim the ends of the raffia strands to the same length and bind them loosely so that they do not get in the way while you are working on the hat.

5 Untie the start of the plait and fix the ends together by applying craft glue across all strands. Allow the glue to dry and trim off the excess raffia. (The loose strands at the other end of the plait will be woven into the hat when you have finished making it.)

6 Carefully trim the excess raffia away from the points where you added new strands to the plait.

❷ TO MAKE THE HAT

If you are right-handed, the plait will run clockwise; if you are left-handed, it will run anti-clockwise.

1 To make the crown of the hat, start in the middle by forming the raffia plait into a tight circle. Tuck the start of the plait under the first coil and stitch it firmly into place with a tapestry needle and a strong raffia strand.

2 Still using the tapestry needle and a strong strand of raffia, begin stitching the plait to itself in a smooth, sloping coil. Take the needle straight across, making the stitches at such an angle that they hardly show. Stitch through one section only on each side. When the strand you are stitching with runs out, weave it back through the raffia plait and start another strand.

3 Keep stitching the raffia to itself in a coiled circle, and form the rounded top crown of the hat by leaning the plait over slightly to slope the coil. The top crown should measure about 24 cm across, which will take six or seven rounds of raffia plait.

4 Begin to slope the raffia coil a little more sharply to form the sides of the crown. The sides should measure about 7 cm – four or five rounds

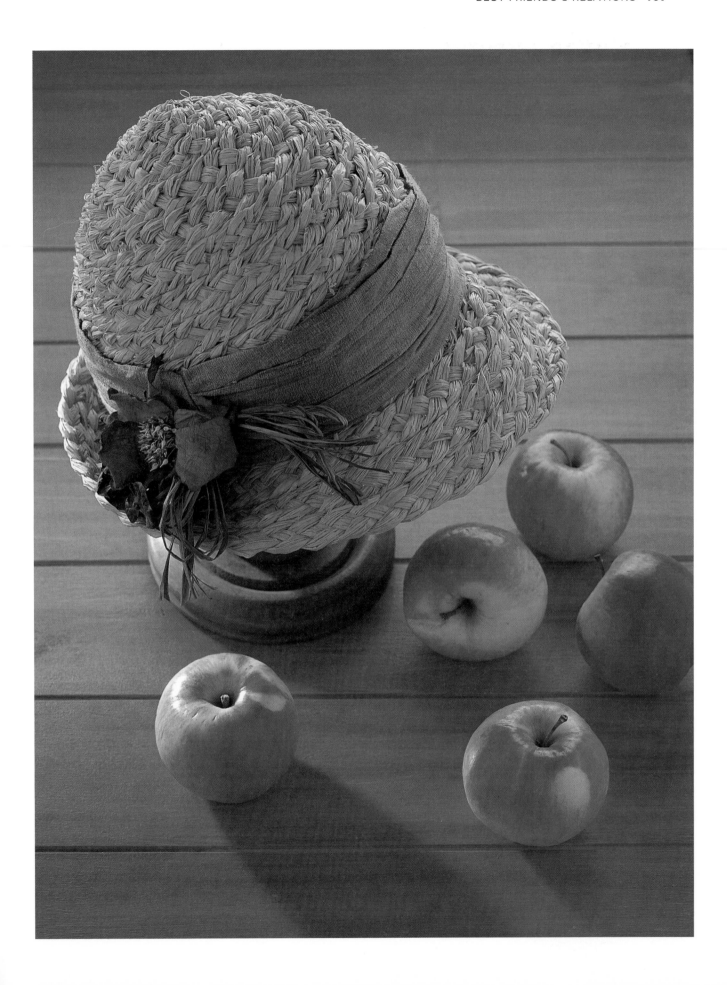

of raffia plait. Adjust the angle of the plait to achieve the right size. Keep trying the hat on as you work, allowing for any difference in head size. It is preferable to undo a small amount of work and adjust it until the size is right than to finish the hat and find that it doesn't fit.

5 Begin to form the brim of the hat by angling the next round of raffia plait out from the side crown. Mould and shape the plait as you work.
6 Complete the brim by adding three or four more rounds of raffia plait,

HINTS
• *Raffia varies considerably in quality. Spend a little extra and choose a high-quality product – the result will be well worth it.*
• *When you are coiling the plait, keep the circle as round as possible. This is necessary because an oval shape will distort the overall shape of the hat.*
• *Loose stitching will result in a floppy hat, so stitch the plaits together tightly.*

continuing to stitch the plait at a gentle angle. Trial and error will achieve the result you want.
7 To secure the end of the raffia plait, stitch the final coil to within about 10 cm of the centre back of the hat. Cut the plait, beyond the 10 cm, and taper it down to half its width by cutting out some of the pieces of raffia and then threading each of the four strands back into the brim with the tapestry needle. Follow the weave of the raffia plait so that the finishing doesn't show.

❸ FINISHING THE HAT
1 To make the hat band, stitch the petersham ribbon around the inside of the crown, just where the hat will encircle the head. Stitch only the lower edge, leaving the upper edge lying free. Overlap the ends of the ribbon 1 cm at the back of the hat. To prevent fraying, turn the raw ends under and handstitch them together with hemming stitch, using a sewing thread that matches the ribbon. Alternatively, cut the ends of the ribbon at an angle. (It is not essential to insert this ribbon, but it does make the hat more comfortable to wear.)
2 Stitch a narrow hem along each long side of the silk and wrap the silk around the hat to measure the length you will require. With right sides facing, join the two short ends of the fabric to form a circle to fit the hat.
3 Turn the silk to the right side and press. Ruche the silk band around the base of the crown with the seam at the back. (If you are trimming the hat with dried flowers, position the seam where the flowers will be placed.)
4 Stitch the silk into place with a few backstitches in matching thread.
5 If you are using dried flowers, stitch them in place over the seam of the silk band with a strand of raffia.

RAFFIA HAT STYLES

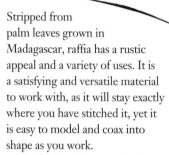

Stripped from palm leaves grown in Madagascar, raffia has a rustic appeal and a variety of uses. It is a satisfying and versatile material to work with, as it will stay exactly where you have stitched it, yet it is easy to model and coax into shape as you work.

A raffia hat, being made of a natural fibre, is cool in summer and gives maximum protection from the sun.

The hat illustrated has a rustic, handmade look that suits raffia and is very attractive. However, you may prefer your hat to have a smoother, more even finish. To achieve this, steam iron the plait between damp cloths before you begin to make the hat. Another variation that you could try is to dye the raffia before you begin to make the plait. Any commercial fabric dye is suitable, or use natural dyes (see 'Natural dyeing methods', page 118).

As you gain experience in working with raffia, you will want to make different shaped hats. You can modify the hat illustrated by giving it a flatter crown or a snap brim. For a flatter crown, make a flatter coil when you are working the top of the crown and increase the angle when you come to the sides. For a snap brim, bring the last three or four rounds up at a sharp angle.

Découpage picture frame

Use the art of découpage to decorate a wooden frame with images selected to set off a favourite family photograph.

WHAT YOU NEED

Wooden photograph frame with large frame area • suitable printed images • artist's gesso • artist's acrylic paint in a colour to tone with images • artist's acrylic gloss medium (sealer) • polyurethane gloss varnish • paintbrushes: 3 small (for sealing, gluing and painting), 25 mm imitation sable (for varnishing) • wet-and-dry abrasive paper: nos 280, 600, 1200 • sanding block • wallpaper paste • PVA glue • gilding cream • clear beeswax • cabinetmaker's polish • small natural sponge • lint-free cloth • Blu Tack • pieces of thick kitchen sponge • fine, curved scissors
● *Technique pages 329–31*

❶ PREPARATION

1 Cut out the images. Seal them with artist's acrylic gloss medium and allow them to dry.
2 Remove the backing and glass from the frame and sand the frame surface with no. 600 sandpaper, smoothing out rough spots and edges. Apply a coat of artist's gesso and allow to dry. Sand with no. 280 sandpaper, apply a coat of the sealer and allow to dry.
3 Sponge the acrylic paint on to the frame with a natural sponge to achieve a textured effect. Leave it to dry.
4 Apply the gilding cream along the inside and outside edges of the frame.

❷ FIXING THE IMAGES

1 Make a paper template of the shape of the frame and arrange the images on it, attaching them with Blu Tack and rearranging them until you are satisfied with the design.
2 Apply a mixture of three parts wallpaper paste and one part PVA

NOTE
If you are unfamiliar with découpage techniques, read the appropriate technique pages before starting this project.

glue to the surface of the frame where the first image is to go and a small amount to the right side of the image.
3 Massage and mould the image on to the frame, adding more glue if necessary. Repeat until all images are glued in place. Remove excess glue with a wet sponge and allow to dry.
4 Apply two coats of sealer to the surface, allowing each coat to dry thoroughly before applying the next.

❸ VARNISHING AND SANDING

1 Wipe the frame with a lint-free cloth and, allowing at least 24 hours between coats, apply as many coats of varnish as necessary – six to 10 coats – to make sure the images are protected from sanding damage.

2 Apply further coats of varnish, sanding with no. 600 wet-and-dry abrasive paper between coats. Make sure the abrasive paper is wet, and sand in one direction only. Wipe with a lint-free cloth. Always allow at least 24 hours between applications.
3 When you are satisfied that the varnish is evenly applied and the surface has no shiny patches, sand lightly with the no. 1200 abrasive paper and wipe with a lint-free cloth.
4 Apply three more coats of varnish, sanding with the no. 1200 abrasive paper between coats to achieve a very smooth, dull finish.

❹ FINISHING

1 Mix equal parts of beeswax and cabinetmaker's polish and warm the mixture. Apply the wax to the surface a little at a time.
2 Wipe over vigorously with a damp cloth, and polish with a soft, dry cloth.
3 Apply a light coat of gilding cream with a natural sponge, encroaching only slightly on the images.

Dried flower wreath

A floral wreath captures nature's beauty, and is a welcome gift for a friend or relation who loves flowers but has no garden. Flowers from your own garden make this gift extra special.

WHAT YOU NEED

Vine wreath base (available from florist's suppliers) • hot glue gun • maidenhair fern • line-establishing flowers: delphinium, larkspur, hidcote lavender • filler flowers: daisies, Japanese anemones, straw flowers, white and blue statice, soft white daisies • focal-point flowers: dahlias, shasta daisies, gerberas, Canterbury bells

● *Technique pages 332–3*

❶ SELECTING THE FLOWERS

Plan your choice of flowers with regard to the range of hues and the strength of tones. Keep the colours balanced, and remember that warm, light colours – such as yellows and pinks – will come forward, while cool, dark colours – such as blues and violets – will recede.

Select flowers at different stages of growth so that you have buds as well as half-open and full blooms. Include different sizes, shapes and textures – for example, flat, smooth leaves will counterpoint delicate, lacy flowers, and slender, pointed leaves will complement full-bodied flowers.

You could buy fresh flowers from a florist and supplement them with flowers from your own garden or with wild flowers.

❷ DRYING THE FLOWERS

Dry the plant material according to the methods outlined in 'Flower and foliage drying'. Note that drying methods vary according to the type of flower.

If you want to make this project at short notice, buy flowers and foliage already dried from a florist or florist's suppliers.

❸ ASSEMBLING THE WREATH

1 Make small bundles of maidenhair fern, apply glue to the ends of the stems and attach them to the vine wreath base. Add ferns until the vine base and sides are completely covered. If the effect is too flat, give the wreath depth by adding individual leaves or small bunches here and there, in more upright positions.
2 Place the line-establishing flowers around the wreath, varying the length and direction of the stems in order to achieve a balanced, rounded effect. Do not glue the flowers down until you are happy with the arrangement.
3 Glue the ends of the stalks and press them into the layer of maidenhair fern. Hold the blooms in place until the glue hardens.
4 Turn the wreath constantly as you work and look at it from all angles to make sure that the arrangement is well balanced.
5 Being careful to keep within the established height and width of the

NOTE

Remember to tell the recipient of this gift that the flowers are more likely to retain their natural colours if the wreath is displayed away from direct sunlight or fluorescent lighting.

VARIATIONS

The flowers and foliage shown below are suggestions only; you can vary them to produce many different effects. For a harvest wreath, choose blooms in autumn tonings – orange and yellow tea roses, chrysanthemums and buttercups. Try leaving some parts of the vine wreath base uncovered. Or wire small sprays of flowers at intervals around the base, then wind matching ribbons in between.

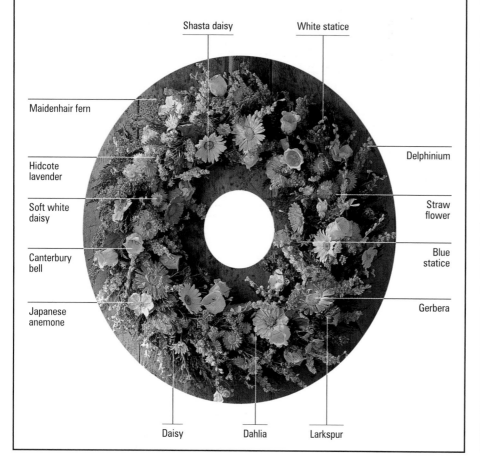

Shasta daisy

White statice

Maidenhair fern

Hidcote lavender

Soft white daisy

Canterbury bell

Japanese anemone

Delphinium

Straw flower

Blue statice

Gerbera

Daisy

Dahlia

Larkspur

wreath, position and glue filler flowers to fill in the outline. Push some of the filler flowers in among the maidenhair fern, so that they seem to be growing out of the foliage.

6 Position the focal-point flowers around the wreath, arranging them to face in various directions. Nestle some of them deeply among the fern fronds. Do not use too many focal-point flowers – just a few, strategically placed, will give the best effect. When you are satisfied with the arrangement, glue them in place.

7 Add a few filler stems of white and blue statice to lighten the overall effect, and glue into position. Position and glue bunches of daisies evenly around the wreath.

Starting the wreath
First the vine wreath base is covered completely with small bundles of maidenhair fern. Depth and fullness are achieved by placing some fern fronds in an upright position.

Crinolined lady lampshade

This stencilled lampshade, featuring ladies with crinolines and parasols strolling amid spring flowers, will brighten any bedroom. It would also be charming in a small sitting room.

Master pattern **E74(a–d)** • stencil film or treated manila cardboard • plain lampshade in a truncated cone shape, about 34 cm across the base and 21 cm high • spray adhesive • fabric spray paints: pale blue, deep blue, deep red • artist's acrylic paints: deep green, bright yellow, ultramarine, burgundy • paint palette • paintbrushes: 4 small stencilling, no. 4 round • tracing paper • transfer paper • pencil • fine permanent marker pen • craft knife • cutting mat or board • lightweight card (for masking) • masking tape • light-coloured chalk • paper towels • spray-on fabric protector
● *Technique pages 337, 343–4*

1 MAKING THE STENCILS

1 Trace and transfer the stencil designs from the master pattern on to the sheet of stencil material and cut them out using the craft knife and the cutting mat or board. If you are using stencil film, trace the design straight on to the film with a fine permanent marker pen.

2 Use masking tape to stick pieces of lightweight card around the edges of the stencil. This is to protect the lampshade from paint drift while you are spraying.

2 STENCILLING THE CRINOLINED LADIES

1 With chalk, mark the positions on the lampshade where you plan to place the crinolined lady motif. On a lampshade this size, you should be able to repeat the design three times.

The lamp base makes all the difference to the appearance of this gift – choose plain blond wood for a simple cottage style, or plastic in a clear primary colour for an ultra-modern look.

CRINOLINED LADY COORDINATES

Stencilling is a popular home-decorating technique, and a coordinated set of furnishings using the crinolined lady stencil would be a very welcome gift. Find out what a friend's new colour scheme will be, and choose the colours for the stencils accordingly.

As well as making the lampshade, you could stencil the motifs on sheets and pillowcases for a guest room, or on a pair of cushion covers for a sitting room. And, as a final touch, why not complete your gift with a pair of crinolined lady curtains?

Use a photocopier to enlarge or reduce the master stencil pattern to sizes suitable for the various items.

The crinolined lady stencil could even provide the perfect inspiration for someone who is looking for decorating ideas. The lampshade might suggest a colour scheme, and the stencils could be used to create a wall frieze. Stencil the lampshade in colours to the recipient's taste, and present your gift along with the stencils, brushes and paints, and a set of instructions for stencilling. General stencilling techniques are described in the technique pages, and some stencilling tips are given in 'Oak & acorn drawer liners' (pages 128–9).

2 Apply spray adhesive lightly to the back of the stencil. Place the stencil in position on the lampshade and press it firmly down. Shake the can of paint well before spraying and test it on a piece of scrap paper to make sure the nozzle is not clogged. Spray the stencil with pale blue paint, holding the can upright at an angle of 90° to the shade to prevent the paint from drifting under the edge of the stencil. Aim to achieve a soft, even tone.

HINT
It is not necessary for all the stencilled figures to be identical. Part of the charm of stencilling lies in the slight variations among basically similar motifs.

VARIATION
You could devise different colour schemes to suit the recipient's taste. For example, imagine the effect of black stencilled motifs on a white ground, reminiscent of Victorian silhouette pictures. A simple lamp base in black wood or metal would provide a dramatic finishing touch.

3 Using the deep blue spray paint, add more colour here and there.
4 Finally, spray small amounts of deep red very lightly on selected areas to create further shades of colour.
5 Wipe the stencil clean before fixing it in the next position. Repeat steps 2 to 4 for the other crinolined ladies.

❸ STENCILLING THE FLOWERS
1 Lightly mark the lampshade with coloured chalk where you intend to place the daisies, forget-me-nots and grape hyacinths.
2 Apply spray adhesive lightly to the back of each flower stencil and place in position over the appropriate chalk marks. Work one flower at a time. Using the acrylic paints and the stencilling brushes, gently pounce on deep green for the leaves and yellow, ultra-

marine and burgundy for the flowers. Repeat each flower motif as desired.
3 To stencil the grass, mask the flowers on the grape hyacinth stencil with small pieces of masking tape. Use the remaining parts of the stencil to paint scattered tufts of deep green grass here and there.

❹ FINISHING
1 Place masking tape evenly around the top and bottom of the lampshade, 1.5 cm from the edge.

Masking tape

2 Using the masking tape as a guide, paint a 1.5 cm cuff around the top and bottom of the shade with the dark green paint and a no. 4 brush. Allow the paint to dry and remove the tape.
3 Spray the entire surface of the lampshade with fabric protector.

Crazy patchwork evening bag

Made from scraps of luxury fabric, this unusual bag is richly embroidered and trimmed. The bag measures 22 cm x 24 cm and is designed to be carried on the shoulder.

WHAT YOU NEED

Master pattern **D26(a)** • 30 cm x 30 cm main evening fabric (e.g. satin, shantung, taffeta) • 30 cm x 50 cm lining fabric • 90 cm satin bias binding in a shade to match the lining • 30 cm x 50 cm light-weight iron-on craft wadding • 6 scraps evening fabrics, about 26 cm x 15 cm (for the patchwork) • 26 cm x 6 cm evening fabric (for the front binding) • 30 cm x 10 cm chiffon • 2.5 m gimp (furnishing braid) (for the strap) • 2 tassels • suggested trimmings: embroidery, ribbons, braids, decorative buttons, seed beads, metallic ornaments • sewing thread to tone with the colour scheme • needles: sharps and crewels, in sizes to suit the fabrics and trimmings • craft glue • tracing paper • dressmaking pins • pencil • scissors • dressmaker's pencil • tape measure • sewing machine

● *Technique pages 292–301, 343–4*

❶ CUTTING OUT THE FABRICS

1 Using the tracing paper and pencil, trace a working pattern for the patchwork from the master pattern. Make sure you mark the numbers on each shape in the patchwork pattern. Do not cut out the individual pieces yet.

2 From the main fabric cut a rectangle 26 cm x 27 cm, and from both the lining fabric and the iron-on wadding cut rectangles 26 cm x 44 cm.

3 Before you cut out the patchwork shapes from the scrap fabric, study the pattern and decide how you want to arrange the fabrics. Using the dress-maker's pencil, number each fabric to correspond with the numbering on the pattern. Cut up the working pattern along the lines so that you have a pattern for each patchwork piece.

4 Pin the patchwork patterns on to the corresponding numbered fabrics and cut them out, adding a 1 cm seam allowance all round.

5 Near your work area, lay out the pieces as in the master pattern to avoid confusion when joining them.

HINT

It is easy and fun to create your own crazy patchwork, and this bag would be an excellent beginner's project. Choose fabrics and trimmings that complement each other – they don't need to be of similar weight or weave but don't include too many prints.

❷ SEWING THE BACK

1 Tack and then iron the wadding to the wrong side of the lining.

2 With right sides together, sew the main fabric to the lining along one 26 cm edge. Press the seam towards the main fabric. Turn the work to the right side and topstitch through the main fabric and the seam allowance close to the seam line.

3 Fold the main fabric over the seam so that 1cm of the main fabric is on the inside (the lining side) of the bag. Press down the fold.

❸ SEWING AND TRIMMING THE PATCHWORK

1 With right sides facing, sew fabric 1 to fabric 2. Then sew joined fabrics 1 and 2 to fabric 3, fabric 3 to fabric 4, and fabric 5 to joined fabrics 1, 3 and 4. Finally, sew fabric 6 to joined fabrics 1 and 5. The basic patchwork is now complete.

2 Sew fabric 6 to the main fabric, and press the seams open.

3 With the wrong sides together, pin and then tack the lining to the joined patchwork and main fabric piece along the raw edges, making sure that the 1 cm of main fabric that was folded over previously is still on the lining side of the work.

4 Quilt the patchwork by machining your chosen ribbons and braids along the seam lines of the patchwork.

5 Sew on the chiffon overlay following the steps outlined in 'Adding the chiffon overlay'.

6 Decorate the bag as desired with embroidery, ribbon, braid, buttons and beads, and metallic ornaments attached with craft glue.

❹ BINDING THE FRONT EDGE

1 With wrong sides facing, fold the 26 cm x 6 cm fabric strip in half lengthwise. Press. Placing all the raw edges together, stitch the binding strip to the right side of the patchwork, 1 cm down from the front edge.

2 Turn the folded edge of the strip over to the wrong side and slipstitch it to the lining along the row of machine stitching.

3 If you have trimmed the patchwork with seed beads, use a fine needle to sew a row of seed beads just below the binding at 1 cm intervals.

❺ SEWING THE SIDE SEAMS

1 Fold the completed fabric piece in half widthwise, right sides together, ensuring that the top edges are even.

2 Starting at the top, and using a 2 cm seam allowance, sew a 10 cm seam down both sides. Backstitch to finish these seams and then complete the side seams with a 1 cm seam allowance. This method of joining the sides will form a pleat that will give the bag a slightly tapered shape.

3 Turning the edge of the binding under at each end, bind the edges of the seams with satin bias binding. First bind the edges of the 2 cm side seams separately, and then bind the edges of the 1 cm seams together.

4 Press the large bound seams open and slipstitch them to the inside of the bag at the top.

5 Turn the bag right side out.

❻ ATTACHING THE SHOULDER STRAP

1 Cut the gimp in half and sew the two lengths together, wrong sides facing, with a row of straight stitches along each edge.

2 Place one end of the strap along each side seam, about 8 cm from the top of the bag. Slipstitch around all the edges of the strap to attach it firmly to the bag.

3 Oversew the tassel cords to the sides of the bag, immediately below the strap ends, adjusting the length of the cords so that one tassel hangs lower than the other. Cover the joins by attaching braid or buttons to match the trimmings on the patchwork.

ADDING THE CHIFFON OVERLAY

When you are slipstitching the chiffon to the underlying fabric, ensure that the raw edges are turned under 1 cm.

1 Lay one 10 cm raw edge of the chiffon along the raw edge of patchwork fabric 1 and tack it into place along the seam allowance.

2 Slipstitch one 30 cm side along the seams joining fabric 1 to fabrics 2 and 3, and about 2 cm along the seam joining fabrics 5 and 3. Leave the rest of this side and the remaining 10 cm side free.

3 Starting at the bottom of the tacked 10 cm raw edge, slipstitch the first 7 cm of the remaining 30 cm side to fabric 1 at an angle of 30° to the seam joining fabrics 1 and 6. Leave the next 9 cm of chiffon free.

4 Slipstitch the remaining 16 cm of chiffon into place, bunching it loosely as you go to fit along the last 7.5 cm of the seam joining fabrics 1 and 6.

5 Loosely ruche the chiffon on to fabric 1, pleating and gathering it and then catching it here and there with small backstitches.

6 Ruche the rest of the chiffon to extend over the seam between fabrics 5 and 1.

Pastoral poppy tray

With its delicate poppy illustration – reminiscent of a medieval Italian herbal picture – this recycled timber tray would be an ideal gift for someone who values traditional design.

Master pattern **D29(a)** • rectangular wooden tray, about 36 cm x 50 cm, preferably made of old timber • paint stripper (if necessary) • artist's acrylic paints: green, cadmium red medium, vermilion, raw sienna, black, white, burnt umber shades • Jo Sonja's artist's colour: Turner's yellow • clear sealer • water-based matt varnish • paint palette • paintbrushes: nos 2 and 5 round, no. 000 liner, small decorating • fine-grade sandpaper • pencil • eraser • tracing paper • transfer paper • hard pencil (or empty ballpoint pen)
● *Technique pages 334–5, 343–4*

❶ PREPARING THE TRAY
1 Use the paint stripper to take off any old paint or varnish. Sand the tray well to create a good, smooth surface on which to paint the design.
2 Seal the tray with clear sealer mixed with water according to the manufacturer's instructions.

❷ TRANSFERRING THE DESIGN
1 Trace the design from the master pattern on to the tracing paper.
2 Transfer the design to the centre of the inside surface of the tray, using the transfer paper and the hard pencil or ballpoint pen.

❸ PAINTING THE DESIGN
Stems and leaves
1 Using the medium round brush, paint the stems and leaves of the poppy in green. To vary the tone of the leaves, make some of them lighter

Painting guide
Simple and dramatic, this classic poppy design shows the flower in all its phases. The plant is painted mainly in dark green and shades of brilliant red, highlighted with yellow, umber and sienna.

by adding a touch of Turner's yellow to the green. Apply a second coat if necessary.
2 When the paint is dry, erase any carbon lines that show through.
3 Using the fine liner brush and black paint that has been watered down, outline the stems and leaves.

Roots
1 Using the small round brush and burnt umber, paint the roots.
2 Use the liner brush and raw sienna to add the fine roots and root hairs.

Open poppies
1 Load the medium round brush with cadmium red and take a heavy side-load of vermilion. Place the brush down next to the edge of the petal, with the vermilion side-load facing towards the outside. Wiggle the brush along the design line of each petal, pushing the side-load off the brush and on to the petal.
2 Reload with cadmium red. Place the brush down on the petal near the side-load and press on the brush to open it up like a fan. Gently drag the brush towards the centre of the flower, using about three strokes to fill each petal. The fewer strokes you use, the better the effect. Leave to dry.
3 Using the small round brush loaded with black, paint the centre of the petals on the open poppy. Use the liner brush to paint the stamens with Turner's yellow, then add tiny dots of white around the edge of the black.

A MODERN VERSION
The tray illustrated was made from old mortised wood panelling; the knots and nail holes and some of the original paint were left untreated, giving a delightfully rustic quality.
  For a more modern look, buy or make a new tray. Sand it very smooth and paint it white or cream. When the tray is dry, transfer and paint the poppy design. Finish with several coats of high-gloss varnish.

Framed memories

Photographs keep memories alive, and a montage of photographs celebrating a dear one's life makes a special and personal gift for a family member or a close friend.

WHAT YOU NEED

Selection of photographs • large picture frame • mounting board, cut to fit the frame • scalpel or craft knife • ruler • square • jar lid or saucer, with a circumference large enough to frame several of the photographs • invisible or masking tape • sheet of rub-off decorative corners and borders • hard pencil (or empty ballpoint pen)

❶ CHOOSING THE PHOTOGRAPHS

1 Select a series of images that are related thematically. You will need one main photograph, such as a large portrait, as a focal point for the arrangement. For the montage illustrated here, the focal point is a favourite photograph of the recipient's grandfather; the other images reflect various aspects of his life – his wife, his daughter, his home and his first car.
2 Experiment with the positions of the photographs on the mounting board until you are happy with the arrangement. Remember that symmetrical arrangements are the most pleasing to the eye.
3 Decide which images you would like to place in a circular opening. (Circular openings make excellent frames for displaying portraits, especially old black-and-white or sepia portrait photographs.)

❷ CUTTING THE OPENINGS

1 Working on the back of the mounting board, mark the cutting lines for the frames with a pencil. Use a ruler and a square to mark the square-edged frames and an inverted jar lid or saucer of the appropriate size for the circular frames. You can cut each frame to display either the whole image or only part of it, but the frame must be smaller than the photograph so that the photograph will sit behind

the mounting board. Start by marking the frame for the focal image, and measure the distances between images carefully to keep them uniform.
2 With the scalpel or craft knife, cut out the frames. Cut the square-edged frames first, using the steel ruler. To cut out the circular frames, take the lid or saucer that you used to trace the shape and place it over the tracing. Gently score around the shape with the craft knife, as you would with a pencil. Remove the lid or saucer and cut out the circle along the score line. Work slowly and carefully and do not press the scalpel too hard.

PICTURE FRAMES

Select a large picture frame so that there will be enough space to display the photographs to the best advantage. The frame shown here is made of recycled timber, which suits the subject perfectly.

You can buy picture frames with holes already cut in various shapes in the mounting boards.

NOTE

Work on a clean surface with clean hands. If a smudge occurs, remove with an ordinary pencil eraser; if this doesn't work, use the rub-on border to hide it.

❸ MOUNTING THE PHOTOGRAPHS

1 When you have cut out all the frames, carefully fix the photographs in position with invisible tape or masking tape. Use only one piece of tape along the top edge of each photograph – this allows the photographic paper to expand and shrink with the weather, which prevents the photographs from wrinkling.
2 With the hard pencil, transfer the rub-on borders on to the mounting board around the photographs. Place them to accentuate the focal image and embellish the secondary images.

❹ FINISHING

Make sure that the glass is clean, and carefully fit the mounting board with the photographs into the picture frame. Secure the back of the frame according to the manufacturer's or frame-maker's instructions.

Cream-on-cream cushion

This stylish calico and lace cushion with self-colour embroidery uses simple embroidery stitches and is made from inexpensive materials. It would be a delightful addition to any room.

② TRACING AND TRANSFERRING THE DESIGN

1 Trace the design from the master pattern with tracing paper and the black felt-tipped pen.
2 Match the centre of the fabric with the centre of the working design and pin them together with the fabric on top. Place the fabric and the design on a light box or tape it to a window. Using the fabric marking pen, trace the design on to the fabric.

③ EMBROIDERING THE FRONT

Place the fabric with the marked design in the embroidery hoop, pulling it taut. Embroider the design following the stitch guide, completing one section at a time.

Large flowers

1 With a double strand of candlewick cotton, work the outlines of the petals in a double row of colonial knots. Work several colonial knots in the centre of the flower.
2 Work the stamens in stem stitch, placing a single colonial knot at the end of each stamen.

Medium flowers

1 With a double strand of candlewick cotton, outline the petals with a single row of colonial knots.
2 Complete the centres of the flowers in the same way as the large flowers.
3 Work the small sprays of buds below the flowers in colonial knots, using a single strand of cotton.
4 Work the flat leaves below the sprays in chain stitch.

WHAT YOU NEED

Master pattern E32(a) • calico, 75 cm x 150 cm • 2 m cotton lace, about 40 mm wide • 40 cm x 40 cm cushion insert • candlewick cotton (same colour as calico) • needle: size 22 chenille • coton à broder • embroidery hoop • tracing paper • black felt-tipped pen • water-erasable fabric marking pen • scissors • sewing thread to match calico and lace • sewing machine
● *Technique pages 292–301, 307–14*

① PREPARING THE FABRIC

1 Before cutting out the cushion, prewash and then iron the lace and the calico.
2 From the calico, cut out a 45 cm square for the front, two pieces 45 cm x 25 cm for the back, and two strips 15 cm x 150 cm for the frill.
3 Fold the 45 cm square in half and then in quarters to find the centre. Using dark-coloured thread, tack along the straight grain of the folds to mark the centre horizontal and vertical lines.

HINT

You can work the embroidery in any order you prefer, but it is best to complete one section at a time so that you do not have to clamp the fabric in the embroidery hoop too often.

5 Place colonial knots on both sides of the lower lines of the heart.

Daisies and other small flowers

1 Work the daisies in straight stitch with a single strand of cotton, and place a single colonial knot in the centre of each one.
2 Work the small petalled flowers, the foliage surrounding these flowers and the foliage around the daisies in lazy daisy stitch.

Foliage

Work the scrolled stems and the outlines of the leaves in stem stitch using a single strand of cotton. Work the veins of the leaves in feather stitch.

❹ FINISHING THE FRONT

1 Wash the fabric to remove all traces of the marking pen. Gently steam press from the wrong side.
2 Pin and tack the lace around the right side of the embroidered square, 1.5 cm from the outer edge and with the scalloped edge of the lace facing toward the embroidered heart. Mitre the corners and sew the lace in place.
3 Sew another row of stitching just below the scalloped edge of the lace to keep the lace flat against the fabric.

4 Join the two long frill pieces together to form a continuous band and press the seams open.
5 Press the band in half lengthwise with wrong sides facing.

6 Divide the frill into quarters. In each quarter, sew two rows of gathering stitches through both sides, 5 mm from the raw edge, starting and finishing at quarter marks.

7 Pin the frill to the front of the cushion, outside the lace border. Match the quarter marks on the frill to the corners of the cushion. Pull up and adjust the gathers to fit.
8 Stitch the frill to the cushion front, leaving a 1.5 cm seam. Remove the gathering threads.

❺ MAKING UP THE CUSHION

1 Sew a double hem along one 45 cm side of each back piece.
2 Place the two back pieces on top of the embroidered front, right sides facing and with the hemmed edges of the back overlapping in the middle.

▪▪▪•• Colonial knot	⁚⁝⁚	Straight stitch
ℰ Stem stitch	✐	Lazy daisy stitch
✐ Chain stitch	ꝡ	Feather stitch

Stitch guide

The design is created with just a few basic stitches worked in cotton thread.

Pin, tack and stitch the cushion front to the back, leaving a 1.5 cm seam allowance all round.
3 Trim the seams, iron with a damp cloth, then turn the cushion through to the right side. Iron the right side with a damp cloth.
4 Insert the cushion pad and close the back opening with slipstitch. This can be opened for washing.

CUTTING GUIDE

Made of calico and cotton lace, the cushion will wash and wear well. For the best results, buy good-quality calico. Prewash both the fabric and the lace to allow for shrinkage, and be sure to cut along the straight grain.

Frill		
Frill		
Front	Back	Back

Handmade hatboxes

Hats are back in fashion, and these functional yet stylish fabric-covered boxes provide decorative storage for them.

The measurements given first are for making the larger box, and those in brackets are for making the smaller box.
Heavy cardboard: A1 sheet • light cardboard: A1 sheet, A0 sheet • 50 cm (30 cm) lightweight, firmly woven cotton fabric, 115 cm wide • about 35 cm x 35 cm lightweight wadding • 1.2 m (2 m) braid • 1.2 m cord, 10 mm diameter • PVA glue • pencil • ruler • compass • scissors • scalpel • wide masking tape • spring clothes pegs (or bulldog clips)

❶ CUTTING OUT THE CARDBOARD
1 Using the pencil, compass and scalpel, mark, label and cut the following shapes from the heavy cardboard: **A** one circle radius 153 mm (115 mm) for the lid; **B** one circle radius 150 mm (112 mm) for the base.
2 With the pencil, compass, ruler and scalpel, mark, label and cut the following shapes from the light cardboard: **C** one circle radius 153 mm (115 mm) for the lid liner; **D** two circles radius 146 mm (108 mm) for the base liners;

E two strips 1020 mm x 42 mm (750 mm x 40 mm) for the lid rims; **F** one strip 1020 mm x 38 mm (750 mm x 36 mm) for the lid rim liner; **G** one rectangle 990 mm x 180 mm (730 mm x 170 mm) for the base wall; **H** one strip 990 mm x 176 mm (730 mm x 166 mm) for the base wall liner.

❷ CONSTRUCTING THE LID
1 Apply a strip of masking tape along one edge of one lid rim (E), so that half the width of the tape overhangs the edge of the cardboard.
2 Cut V-shaped notches along the overhanging tape.

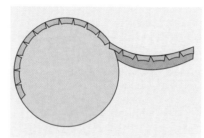

3 With the rim at right angles to the lid (A), roll the rim around the edge of the lid and attach it by pulling the notched masking tape on to the lid and pressing it firmly into place.
4 Overlap the ends of the rim and tape them together.

❸ COVERING THE LID
1 Apply glue to the lid top and place it on the wadding. Smooth out the wadding and trim it to fit exactly.

2 Trace the outline of the lid on to the wrong side of the fabric, adding a 1.5 cm seam allowance. Cut the traced shape from the fabric and notch the seam allowance.

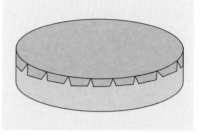

3 Glue the fabric and place it over the wadding, pulling it taut as you work. Glue the notched seam allowance down on to the rim.
4 Trace the shape of the second lid rim (E) on to the wrong side of the fabric. Add a 1.5 cm seam allowance all around and cut out.
5 Glue the lid rim and place it on the wrong side of the fabric. Turn over and glue the seam allowance to the wrong side along one long edge only.

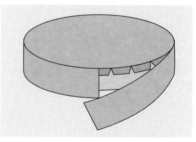

6 Glue the second rim over the first, with the glued-down seam allowance sitting over the notched lid cover. Trim one end so that the cardboard ends sit flush. Glue the remaining seam allowance over the join.
7 Glue the lower edge of the seam allowance to the inside of the rim. Clamp the fabric to the rim with clothes pegs until the glue has dried.

❹ LINING THE LID
1 Place the lid rim liner (F) on the wrong side of the fabric and trace around it, adding a 1.5 cm seam allowance. Cut out the traced shape from the fabric.
2 Glue the lid rim liner and place it on the wrong side of the cut-out fabric. Glue the 1.5 cm seam allowance to the wrong side along both long

---

CUTTING THE CARDBOARD PIECES
Cut the fabric using the cardboard pieces as templates.

Heavy cardboard

Light cardboard

Light cardboard

lid rim to the lid. Overlap the ends of the wall and secure with masking tape.
3 Coat the base wall with glue and centre it on the wrong side of the fabric. Roll the base wall along the fabric piece until it is covered, smoothing out any wrinkles as you go.
4 Glue the top seam allowance to the inside of the base wall.
5 Notch the seam allowance along the lower edge and glue it to the base.

6 ATTACHING THE CORD HANDLES
1 Using sharp scissors, pierce two holes in the base wall, opposite each other and about 5 cm from the top.
2 Measure and cut enough cord to form a handle running from hole to hole across the top of the box. Thread the ends of the cord through the holes from the outside and hold them in place by gluing and taping them flat to the inside of the box.

7 LINING THE BASE
1 Place the base liners (D) on the wrong side of the fabric and trace around them, adding a 1.5 cm seam allowance. Cut out the traced shapes from the fabric.
2 Working on one at a time, coat the base liners with glue and place them on the wrong sides of the fabric circles. Notch the seam allowances and glue them to the wrong sides of the cardboard liners.
3 Glue one of the covered base liners to the outside of the base of the box and the other to the inside.
4 Trace around the base wall liner (H) on the wrong side of the fabric, adding a 1.5 cm seam allowance, and cut the traced shape from the fabric.
5 Glue the base wall liner to the wrong side of the cut-out fabric. Turn and glue the seam allowance to the wrong side along the upper and lower edges. Trim off the seam allowance at one short end.
6 Glue the wrong side of the liner and fit it inside the box, pressing it into place. Lap the remaining seam allowance over the join. Hold the liner against the base wall with clothes pegs until the glue dries.

edges. Glue the covered lid rim liner to the inside of the lid rim, trimming one end to fit snugly and gluing the seam allowance over the join.
3 Trace around the lid liner (C) on the wrong side of the fabric, adding a 1.5 cm seam allowance. Cut out the traced shape from the fabric.

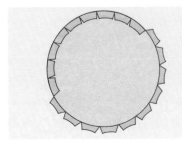

4 Glue the lid liner and place it on the wrong side of the cut-out fabric. Notch the seam allowance and glue it around the edge of the lid liner. Glue the liner to the inside of the lid.
5 Glue the braid around the outside edge of the rim. (The smaller hat box illustrated has two rows of braid.)

5 CONSTRUCTING AND COVERING THE BASE
1 Trace the shape of the base wall (G) on to the wrong side of the fabric, adding 1.5 cm all around for the seam allowance. Cut out the traced shape.
2 Join the base wall (G) to the base (B) in the same way as you joined the

Hand-covered photograph album

Most people have photographs lying around waiting to be mounted. Here is a simple method of converting an inexpensive, purchased photograph album into a distinctive and useful gift.

WHAT YOU NEED

Photograph album with spiral binding • craft wadding, a little larger all round than the complete cover (back and front) of the album • fabric, 4 cm larger all round than the complete cover of the album • 1 m ribbon, 25 mm wide, to coordinate with fabric • wrapping paper to coordinate with fabric • sewing thread • sewing needle • tape measure • scissors • PVA glue • clean scrap paper
● *Technique pages 292–5*

❶ APPLYING THE WADDING

1 Evenly coat the outside of the front cover of the album, including the edges and the spine, with a thin layer of PVA glue.
2 Lay the piece of wadding flat and position the glued front cover of the album on it, with the edges just inside the edges of the wadding.
3 Repeat step 1 for the outside back cover of the album.
4 Bring the wadding over the spine, keeping it taut and smooth, and press it down over the glued back cover.
5 If necessary, trim the wadding so that it will just wrap around the edges of the cover. Clip the corners so that they will not be bulky, and press the wadding down on to the glued edges. Allow the glue to dry.

❷ COVERING THE ALBUM

1 Cut the ribbon in half. With right sides facing, lay one piece of ribbon over the fabric with the end centred on one short edge of the fabric. Stitch a 2 cm x 3 cm rectangle to hold the ribbon flat and secure.

2 Repeat step 1 to attach the second piece of ribbon to the opposite edge of the fabric, and then trim the ribbon ends at an angle to prevent fraying.

3 Open the album. On the inside cover, mark the centre point of the vertical edge. Run glue along this edge from top to bottom. Press the wrong side of one short edge of the fabric on to the glued area, aligning the stitched end of the ribbon with the centre point. Let the glue dry.
4 Turn the album over and repeat step 3 on the other side, pulling the fabric firmly over the cover with the album as nearly closed as possible.

Close the album, placing sheets of clean paper between the cover and the pages in case of glue leakage. Let the glue dry thoroughly.

5 If necessary, trim the fabric at the spine so that it will tuck down flat behind the spiral binding. Glue the top and bottom of the inside of the spine and stick the fabric down.
6 Apply glue to the top and bottom edges of the inside front cover. Stick the fabric down, mitring the corners and ensuring that the fabric covers the outside of the album smoothly. Repeat this step on the inside back.

❸ FINISHING

1 To make endpapers, cut two pieces of wrapping paper 5 mm smaller all round than the inside dimensions of the cover. Glue the endpapers to the insides of the covers to conceal the raw edges of the fabric.
2 When the glue is dry, close the album and tie the ribbon in a bow.

Garden sculpture

Give this sculpture to a friend who has a shady garden nook. The painted faux finish on an ordinary plaster or concrete bust or statue will give it the appearance of weathered bronze and verdigris.

❶ PREPARATION

1 Scrub the statue quite clean and allow it to dry thoroughly.
2 Gently sand it to remove any old paint, grime or surface irregularities, and wash it again. Allow it to dry.

❷ APPLYING THE FAUX FINISH

1 Using the 25 mm decorating brush, paint the entire surface of the statue with the brown acrylic paint. Add a little water to the paint, so that it flows well but retains its opacity.
2 Allow the paint to dry thoroughly, and then apply another coat of brown paint. Leave the statue to dry for at least 24 hours.
3 Squeeze a small amount of the aqua blue paint on to the palette and add water until the paint has a smooth, light, creamy consistency.
4 Dip the stencil brush lightly into the paint. Then tap the brush on

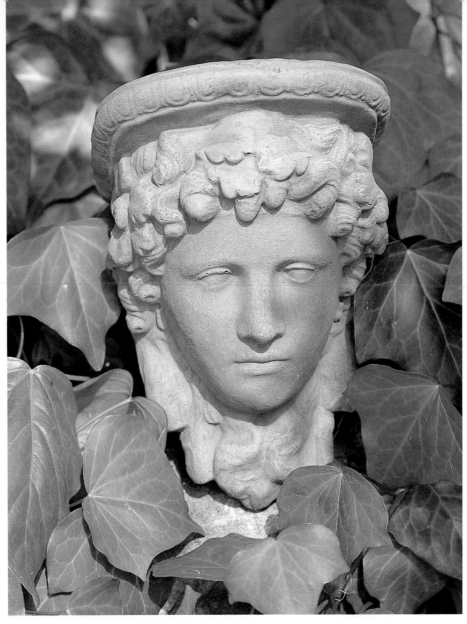

paper towelling to remove any excess paint until there is only a small amount left in the brush.
5 Using an up-and-down pouncing motion, stipple the blue very lightly over the entire surface of the statue. Pay special attention to crevices or folds, which may need a little extra paint. Allow to dry for 24 hours.
6 Mix a small amount of acid green paint with water to make a mixture of light consistency, like the aqua blue mixture, and take a small amount of the paint on to the brush.
7 Stipple the entire surface very lightly – be exceptionally sparing with this colour. If the colour is too strong, pounce a small amount of the brown paint on the affected areas. Allow the statue to dry out for at least 24 hours.
8 Seal all surfaces with a coat of matt polyurethane varnish. This will give

the statue a dry, flat look, like that of weathered bronze, which is very attractive nestled among foliage.

> **NOTE**
> *For the example illustrated, a Roman-style cement head was bought from a second-hand shop. Garden statues suitable for this treatment are also available from plant nurseries and garden shops.*

PAINT COLOURS

Any good quality artist's acrylic paint can be used for this project. Choose colours that match the colour swatches below.

Deep brown

Aqua blue

Acid green

Oak & acorn drawer liners

The geometric design of bows and diamonds framing oak leaves and acorns adds a touch of class to these drawer liners – a gift that should prove popular with house-proud friends.

WHAT YOU NEED

Master pattern G49(a–b) • 1 roll wallpaper lining paper • stencil film or treated manila cardboard • spray adhesive • artist's acrylic paints: gold, pale olive green, red violet • paint palette • paintbrushes: 2 small stencilling, 1 medium stencilling • metre ruler • tracing paper • transfer paper • pencil • gold pen • fine, permanent marker pen • craft knife • cutting mat or board • paper towels • eraser • lint-free cloth

● *Technique pages 337, 343–4*

NOTE
Wallpaper lining paper was used for this project, but any heavy paper with a smooth finish would be suitable. Cream or off-white paper is the best.

① MAKING THE STENCILS

1 Trace and transfer the stencil designs from the master pattern. For stencil film, trace the designs straight on to the film using a fine, permanent marker pen. For treated cardboard, trace the designs and

transfer them to the cardboard using transfer paper. Cut the designs out using the craft knife and cutting mat.
2 Transfer the centre lines from the master pattern on to the gum leaf stencil. These are used to help place the stencil accurately.

② PREPARING THE PAPER

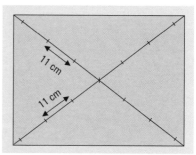

1 Cut pieces of wallpaper lining paper 60 cm wide and 42 cm deep,

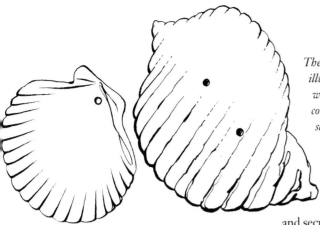

The wind chimes illustrated are decorated with two shells, one conch-shaped and one scallop-shaped. Instead of shells, you could use small bells, large beads, or even little mirror balls.

3 Using the 2.5 mm bit, drill a hole through the middle of the disc.
4 Sand the disc until it is smooth. Wipe it clean with a lint-free cloth.
5 Apply at least four coats of varnish to the disc, ensuring that each coat is fully dry before applying the next.

❸ PREPARING THE SHELLS
1 Using the 2.5 mm bit, carefully drill a hole through the scalloped shell, about 15 mm from the top.
2 Drill two holes in the back of the conch-shaped shell, 20 mm apart.

❹ ASSEMBLING THE CHIMES

1 Cut 90 cm of fishing line. Leaving 5–10 cm of line sticking out of the top, thread one end through one hole in the disc, through the drilled holes in one of the pipes, and then back up through the same hole in the disc, suspending the pipe 1 cm beneath the disc. Take the end of the line over the top of the disc, thread it down the next hole, and secure another pipe in the same way as the first.
2 Continue weaving the line through the disc and pipes in this manner until all five pipes are evenly suspended. Tie the ends of the line together with a double knot.
3 Cut 60 cm of fishing line. Tie the scalloped shell to one end of the line

and secure it with a double knot. Thread the other end through one of the holes in the conch-shaped shell, out through the other hole, and then back through the first hole. Make sure that the shell is hanging horizontally. Adjust the position of this shell so it hangs about 30 cm above the scalloped shell.
4 Thread the free end of the fishing line through the middle hole of the wooden disc. Pull through sufficient line so that the conch-shaped shell is hanging level with the centre of the shortest pipe. Knot the line several times until the knot is slightly bigger than the hole. Trim the end of the line and put a small quantity of glue on the knot to secure it inside the hole, just below the surface.
5 Trim the end of the line on the scalloped shell and secure it with glue.

❺ HANGING THE CHIMES
1 Knot one end of the white cord and thread the other end through one of the holes from the underside of the disc, pulling it all the way through.

2 Carry the cord across and then down the next hole, leaving a 75 cm loop between the holes. Carry the cord across the underside of the disc and up through the next hole. Carry the cord down again through the next hole, once again leaving a 75 cm loop.

Carry the cord across the underside and up through the last hole. The free end of the cord will be a little longer than the doubled loops – about 50 cm.

3 Thread the loops and the free end of the cord through one of the large wooden beads, positioning the bead about 8 cm above the wooden disc. Make sure the two loops are even and the chimes are hanging straight.

4 Fold the free end over so that there are three even loops. Bind this free end to the other cords with white sewing thread. Trim if necessary.
5 Push the ends of the loops through the remaining large bead, positioning it over the bound cords. Place a small quantity of glue around the top of the bead to secure it.

❻ FINISHING
1 Trim the end of the fishing line that is holding the chimes and push the knot down into the nearest hole, securing it with a little glue.
2 To finish off the middle hole, glue the small wooden bead over it.

NOTE
When cutting or drilling, use the clamps or the vice to hold the work steady.

Quilted oven cloth & mitt

Make this colourful gift for a friend and teach yourself to make quilted patchwork at the same time. Once you have worked out how to piece the patchwork, the project is easy to make.

Master pattern G48(a) • coloured fabric strips, 250 cm long, in varying widths (these will be joined to make a piece 250 cm x 20 cm) • 1 m backing fabric, 114 cm wide, in a toning or contrasting shade • 1 m wadding, 90 cm wide • sewing thread to match the fabric • large wooden bead • tracing paper • pencil • scissors • tape measure • sewing machine
● *Technique pages 292–301, 305–6*

❶ MAKING THE FABRIC

1 Sew the strips of fabric together along their long edges to make a strip measuring 250 cm x 20 cm.

2 Trim the short ends of the strip so that they are straight and even.
3 Cut off a piece 160 cm long for the oven cloth. The remaining piece will make the mitt.

❷ CUTTING THE FABRIC BLOCKS FOR THE CLOTH

1 Measure and cut the 160 cm strip into eight 20 cm x 20 cm squares (step A in the diagram opposite).

NOTE
Use a 6 mm seam allowance, unless otherwise specified, and press the fabric and the seams as you go.

2 Cut each square into quarters diagonally and, following step B in the diagram, number the triangles on the wrong side of the fabric in the sequence shown. Make sure the stripes are running in the same direction as the stripes in the diagram.

❸ ASSEMBLING THE BLOCKS

1 Working with two squares' worth at a time, join the triangles together as follows to make four different blocks. The first block is shown in step C of the diagram. Join triangles 1 and 3, triangles 1 and 4, triangles 2 and 3, and triangles 2 and 4. With right sides facing, sew the quarters together.
2 Repeat step 1 with the other triangles, working with two squares worth at a time. Stack together blocks of the same

COMBINING THE SQUARES

The pattern on the cloth is created by cutting eight identical 20 cm x 20 cm squares into triangles and then combining them as shown in step D. Combining the triangles in different ways will create other designs, and you may like to experiment. To make the design illustrated, make sure the stripes are running vertically (as in step B) before you number the triangles. If you divide the finished cloth into four squares, you will see that there are two distinct combinations of triangles.

Step D

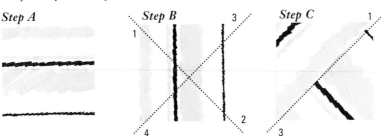

Step A *Step B* *Step C*

HINT

Do not use synthetic fabrics for this project, as they are not always heat or flame resistant. Use firmly woven cotton fabrics of about the same weight.

combination. You should end up with four blocks of each kind.

3 Following step D of the diagram, arrange your 16 blocks in the order shown, referring to the numbers you wrote on the back of each triangle.

4 With right sides facing, pin and sew the blocks together. Press all seams flat.

④ QUILTING THE OVEN CLOTH

1 Cut pieces of backing fabric and wadding a little larger than the assembled main fabric.

2 Lay out the backing wrong side up, then the wadding, then the main fabric right side up. Tack the three layers together firmly along the outside edge.

3 With a long machine stitch, quilt along the seam lines joining the blocks, and along the diagonal seams joining the triangles. Trim all edges.

⑤ FINISHING THE OVEN CLOTH

1 From the backing fabric, cut four strips 50 cm x 5 cm along the straight grain. These are for the binding.

2 With right sides facing, align one raw edge of one of the binding strips with the raw edge of the quilted cloth. Machine stitch through all layers 6 mm from the edge.

3 Turn the remaining raw edge of the binding strip to the back of the cloth, fold it under and slipstitch it into place along the line of machine stitching. Trim the ends of the binding level with the edges of the cloth.

4 Repeat steps 2 and 3 at the opposite edge of the cloth.

5 Bind the two remaining edges of the quilted cloth in the same way, tucking in the raw edges of the binding at the corners and neatening them with a few hand stitches.

⑥ MAKING THE OVEN MITT

1 Using the master pattern and tracing paper, pencil and scissors, trace and cut out a working pattern for the oven mitt. Cut out one mitt shape from the main fabric strip and put it to one side.

2 From the backing fabric cut out three mitt shapes, and from the wadding cut out two.

3 Take the main fabric mitt shape and the matching mitt shape cut from the backing fabric. Place these pieces together, with wrong sides facing. Place one of the wadding shapes between them. Then pin or tack all three layers together.

4 Repeat step 3 with the two remaining mitt shapes.

5 With a long machine stitch, quilt diagonal lines across each of the layered shapes, with the rows of quilting stitches 2 cm apart.

6 With the right sides of the quilted pieces facing and using a 1 cm seam allowance, sew the two quilted shapes together around the outside of the mitt, leaving the wrist end open.

7 Trim the seam, clip the curves and turn the work to the right side.

8 Cut a strip of backing fabric 30 cm x 5 cm along the straight grain and use it to bind the raw wrist edge, following the same procedure as for binding the oven cloth.

⑦ FINISHING THE OVEN MITT

1 From the backing fabric cut a strip 12 cm x 5 cm along the straight grain. Fold the long edges in 1 cm and press.

2 Fold the strip in half lengthwise with the wrong sides facing and topstitch the folded edges together.

3 Thread on the wooden bead. Double the strip over to form a loop and stitch the raw ends to the inside of the thumb seam at the wrist.

NOTE

If the backing fabric has an obvious right side, make sure that two mitt shapes make up one complete pair and the third shape pairs with the mitt shape cut from the main fabric.

Elegant Victorian bows

Decorative bows can be mounted on a board for hanging on the wall or used to add a finishing touch to curtain ties. One of these Victorian-style bows would give great pleasure to a friend who values the sumptuous elegance of an age that is past.

WHAT YOU NEED

Tape measure • scissors • sewing thread to match fabric • sewing needle • sewing machine
Wall-mounted bow
Suitable fabric: 1 strip 40 cm x 115 cm (for the bow), 1 strip 12 cm x 20 cm (for the hanging loop), 2 strips 14 cm x 43 cm (to cover the hanging board) • 2 pieces firm cardboard, 10 cm x 40 cm and 9.5 cm x 38.5 cm • 1 piece polyester wadding, 10 cm x 40 cm • PVA glue • 3 decorative metal charms • 1 brass ring
Angel-trimmed bow
Suitable fabric: 1 strip 40 cm x 68 cm (for the loops), 1 strip 40 cm x 83 cm (for the tails), 2 strips 12 cm x 20 cm (for the knot) • small plastic, papier mâché or wooden angel • artist's acrylic paints: gold, a colour to match the fabric • small paintbrush • brass or plastic ring • PVA glue
● *Technique pages 292–301*

Wall bow

❶ MAKING THE BOW

If the fabric you have chosen is not suitable for making a tied bow, follow the instructions for making a picture bow instead (page 137).
1 With the right sides facing, fold the 40 cm x 115 cm fabric strip in half lengthwise.
2 Cut the fabric at each end of the strip at a slight angle to shape the tails of the bow.
3 Machine the long side and the two short sides together 1 cm from the raw edge, leaving an opening in the middle of the long side for turning.
4 Pull the fabric right side out through the opening. Press the fabric,

then close the opening by hand using slipstitch or by machine.
5 Tie the strip into a good, plump bow, making sure that both loops and ends are symmetrical.

❷ MAKING THE HANGING BOARD

1 To make the loop for hanging the bow, fold the 12 cm x 20 cm fabric strip in half lengthwise, right sides facing, then proceed as in steps 3 and 4 of 'Making the bow'.
2 Using PVA glue, attach the wadding to one side of the 10 cm x 40 cm piece of cardboard.

3 Lay one 14 cm x 43 cm strip of fabric on a hard surface, wrong side facing up, and centre the cardboard, batting side down, on top. Fold the edges of the fabric around the cardboard and glue them in place, mitring the corners if necessary to give a smooth appearance.
4 Cover the other piece of cardboard with the remaining fabric in the same way. (This piece of cardboard is not padded with wadding.)

NOTE

The method of constructing a bow depends partly on personal preference and partly on the type of fabric you are using. Picture bows are especially suitable for very stiff fabrics that cannot easily be knotted or for crisp fabrics that may crease when knotted. The wall-mounted bow illustrated is a knotted bow and the angel-trimmed bow is a picture bow.

5 Thread the brass ring on to the fabric hanging loop. Glue the ends of the loop to the middle of the larger piece of cardboard on the wrong side (the side not covered with fabric).
6 With wrong sides facing, glue the pieces of covered cardboard together.
7 Centre the bow at the top of the front of the hanging board (the side with the batting) and glue it in place.
8 Glue the metal charms on to the board, in a line under the bow.

Angel bow

1 Make a large picture bow with the fabric, following the instructions for 'Making a picture bow'.
2 Firmly stitch the brass ring to the centre top of the knot so that the bow can be hung up.
3 Paint the angel the same colour as the bow and allow the paint to dry.
4 Use the gold paint to add highlights to the angel.
5 When the paint has dried, glue the angel to the knot of the bow.

MAKING A PICTURE BOW

1 *Cutting out the fabric:* For the loops, cut a strip of fabric twice the width of the finished bow by twice

the depth, plus a seam allowance. For the tails, cut a strip twice the length of one tail by twice the width of the tail plus a seam allowance. For the knot, cut two strips about 30 cm long and twice the width of the finished knot plus a seam allowance.

2 *Making the loops:* With right sides together, fold the fabric in half lengthwise. Machine stitch the long edges together. Turn the work to the right side and press. Fold a 1 cm hem into the inside of the fabric at one end and press it down. Slide this end over the other end and sew through all thicknesses, easing the inside fabric slightly to fit. This seam will be at the back of the bow.

3 *Making the tails:* Fold the fabric for the tails in half lengthwise, right sides facing. Shape the tails of the bow by cutting the fabric at each end of the strip at a slight angle. Machine stitch around the raw edges, leaving an opening in the middle of the long side for turning. Pull the fabric right side out, through the opening. Press the fabric, then close the opening, by hand using slipstitch or by machine stitching.
4 *Making the knot:* With right sides facing, machine stitch the two strips of fabric for the knot together along the 30 cm edges. Turn the work to the right side and press.

Fold the strip you have made in half, seam edge to seam edge. Make a line of firm running stitches through all layers of fabric, parallel to the fold at half the width of the folded strip. Open out the strip and press the stitched section into a box pleat.

5 *Attaching the knot:* Lay the knot piece on a hard surface, box pleat downwards, and lay the bow loop over the top with its centre seam facing upwards. Position the tail on top of the back seam of the loops. Fold the ends of the knot over the bow loops and tails, pulling the knot to bunch the loops and tails.

Pin the ends of the knot at the back, then pleat the loops and tails evenly under the knot. Trim the knot piece if necessary. Slipstitch the ends together at the back of the bow.

Luxury handkerchief bag

You can use remnants to make this quick and easy fabric bag for storing handkerchiefs, stockings, scarves or luxury soaps. Put a miniature bottle of perfume and some lace-edged handkerchiefs inside it to complete your gift.

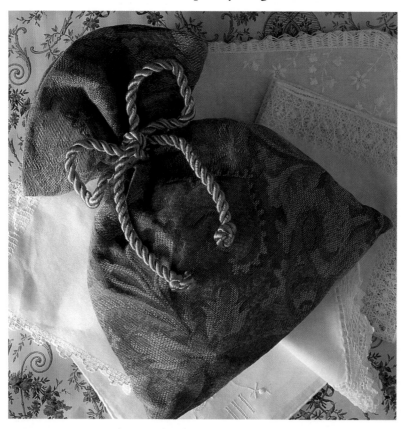

VARIATIONS

● *Adapt the bag for storing soap, perfume or cosmetics by lining it with shower curtain fabric instead of silk.*

● *The bag can also contain an inner bag filled with pot pourri, and can be hung in wardrobes or from door handles or tucked in among cushions. Make a sachet of tulle to fit into the bag, leaving a small opening in one side. Turn the sachet right side out, fill it with pot pourri, and close the opening with slipstitch. Place the sachet in the bag and tie the cord. Sew a fabric loop to the bag for hanging.*

❷ MAKING THE LINING

1 Using the lining fabric, proceed as for steps 1 and 2 of 'Making the bag'.
2 At the top, turn down a 1 cm double hem to the wrong side. Sew it down by machine or with slipstitch.

❸ ASSEMBLING THE BAG

1 Turn the bag right side out and leave the lining wrong side out.

WHAT YOU NEED

25 cm **x** 80 cm heavy upholstery fabric (chintz, tapestry or damask) ●
25 cm **x** 60 cm silk lining fabric ●
90 cm thick silk upholstery cord, in a shade to tone with the fabric ●
sewing thread to match the fabric ● tape measure ● dressmaking pins ●
sewing needle ● sewing machine
● *Technique pages 292–301*

❶ MAKING THE BAG

1 Use the sewing machine to zigzag around the raw edges of the upholstery fabric to prevent fraying.
2 Fold the fabric in half widthwise with the right sides together, and straight machine stitch the sides together with a 1 cm seam allowance. Press the seams open.
3 To make a deep hem along the top edge, fold the top raw edge over 1 cm

NOTE

It is important to neaten the raw edges by zigzagging or overlocking them because heavy upholstery fabric often has a complex weave that frays easily.

to the wrong side and press. Fold over a further 9 cm to the wrong side and slipstitch in place.

2 Insert the lining into the bag and tack it into place just below where the large hem folds over. Slipstitch the lining to the inside of the bag, easing it to fit if necessary. Remove the tacking stitches.
3 Fold the upholstery cord in half and mark the mid-point. Measure about 9 cm down from the top of the bag along a side seam and stitch the mid-point of the cord to the side seam. Bring the cord to the other side of the bag and tie it in a bow.

Draw the threads from the centre

accidentally draw a thread too far, you can carefully weave it back in, but as this is a tedious job, it is best to work in very short sections as you approach the corners.

4 When the inner square of drawn threads is complete, weave the loose threads back into the wrong side of the fabric for about 2 cm. Trim off the ends of threads after weaving.

❷ MONOGRAMMING THE INITIAL

1 Trace and transfer the chosen letter from the master pattern on to one corner of the fabric. Before you start embroidering, study your chosen monogram. Some letters, for example 'B', require two separate lines of embroidery. The letter 'A' requires three lines.
2 Thread the tapestry needle with a piece of crochet cotton twice the length of the first design line to be stitched, plus an extra 25 cm.
3 Bring the crochet cotton up from the wrong side of the fabric at one end of the design line, leaving a tail of about 10 cm on the wrong side. Remove the needle.

4 Using the crewel needle and fine sewing thread, take a small backstitch to secure the thread at point A. Work the first stitch from A to B, holding the crochet cotton in place on the design line with your other hand.

5 Stitch back from B to A and bring the needle out at C, which is just above the crochet cotton. Work the next stitch from C down to B, bringing the needle out at D.

6 Stitch back from D to B and bring the needle out at E. Repeat this stitch sequence until the crochet cotton is anchored to the design line.

7 At the end of the design line, make a few anchoring stitches over the crochet cotton, then turn the crochet cotton and lay it back along the design line. Make a further anchoring stitch and continue as before, making sure that you stitch into the holes that were made on the first pass, so that a textured, hemstitched look is achieved.
8 When you have returned to the beginning of the stitching line, thread the crochet cotton into the tapestry needle again and take it back through to the wrong side of the fabric. Make several overcasting stitches with the fine cotton thread over the crochet cotton to anchor it, then take the fine cotton to the back also. Stitch into the back of the fabric to end off. Neatly clip the ends of the crochet cotton close to the fabric.
9 Repeat this procedure for the other design lines, as required.

❸ FINISHING THE DRAWN THREAD WORK

1 When the embroidery has been completed, rinse the fabric gently to remove any transfer lines. Dry flat and press well from the wrong side.
2 Press a double hem around the fabric so that the hem edge is one thread from the outer edge of the square of drawn threads. Mitre the corners, tuck any loose threads into the hem and tack the hem in place.

3 Working from the wrong side, start at the left edge and take a small vertical stitch just to the right of the drawn thread work, making sure you catch in the hem. Pass the needle around three or four threads and pull them together in a bundle.

4 Take the needle through to the right side and pass it back to the wrong side so that it catches in the hem again.
5 Continue hemstitching in this manner along each edge.
6 Turn the work the other way around and, still working from the back, hemstitch the opposite edge, catching the same bundles of thread that you caught at the other side. This time there is no hem to catch in.

Before you begin embroidering, study the shape of your letter to decide how many lines you will need to form the letter, and which line you will stitch in place first.

Marble kitchen board

This attractive marble board has a multitude of uses – bread board, cheese or fruit platter, or heat pad – and is a practical gift for a partner who enjoys cooking and entertaining.

WHAT YOU NEED

Marble tile, between 300 mm and 400 mm square • 2 m decorative wooden beading, the same depth as the combined thickness of the tile and the plywood • marine plywood, 400 mm x 400 mm x 18 mm • 4 rubber feet with screws • epoxy resin glue • cellulose or plastic-based filler • wood stain or varnish • paintbrush • pencil • mitre box • handsaw • clamps • drill
● *Technique pages 338–42*

1 MAKING THE BOARD

1 Put the marble tile on the plywood and draw around it with a pencil.

2 Trim the plywood to this traced size, and then glue the plywood to the tile with epoxy resin glue. Clamp together firmly and put aside until the glue has set thoroughly.

3 Measure the edges and use the mitre box to cut four pieces from the wooden beading to the dimensions of the tile. Cut the ends at a 45° angle.
4 Glue the beading into position around the tile and plywood with

the epoxy glue. Again, clamp together until the glue has set.
5 Fill in any gaps between the tile and the beading with cellulose or plastic-based filler.
6 Apply stain or varnish to the wooden beading, taking care not to coat the marble tile.

7 Drill a hole 20 mm from each corner of the plywood base and screw in the four rubber feet.

KNITTING GRAPH

Knit the Fair Isle pattern by following the stitches and colours as indicated on the graph. Odd rows are knit rows and even rows are purl.

In Fair Isle knitting, loop unused yarns quite loosely across the back of the work to the end of the row – otherwise the finished work will pucker.

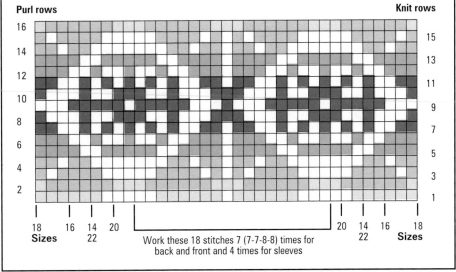

Purl rows

Knit rows

18 16 14 20
Sizes   22

Work these 18 stitches 7 (7-7-8-8) times for back and front and 4 times for sleeves

20 14 16 18
22   **Sizes**

❷ FRONT

Work as for back to ★★.
Work 4 (4-4-4-6) rows patt.

Shaping the neck

Work in patt 53 (55-58-60-62) sts, cast off 27 sts, patt to end.
Cont on last 53 (55-58-60-62) sts.
Keeping patt correct, dec at neck edge in every foll 6th (6th-6th-4th-4th) row until 48 (46-49-57-60) sts rem.

For sizes 14, 20 and 22 only: dec in every foll 8th (6th-6th) row until 45 (50-52) sts rem.

For all sizes: work 4 (4-6-6-6) rows, following the patt.

Shaping the shoulder

Cast off 11 (12-12-12-13) sts at beg of next and alt rows, 3 times in all, until 12 (10-13-14-13) sts rem.
Work 1 row.
Cast off.
Join yarn to rem 53 (55-58-60-62) sts and work other side to correspond, decreasing at the neck edge. Work 1 less row before starting to shape the shoulder.

❸ SLEEVES

Using 3.25 mm needles and mc, cast on 58 (58-62-62-62) sts.
Work 17 rows rib as for back.
18th row: Rib 8 (8-10-10-4), ★ inc in next st, rib 1, rep from ★ to last 8 (8-10-10-4) sts, rib to end...79 (79-83-83-89) sts in total.
Work in patt from graph as for size 14 (14-16-16-18), and, working extra sts into patt, inc at each end of 5th and then alt rows until there are 85 (85-89-89-93) sts. Then inc at each end of every foll 4th row until there are 123 (123-127-127-131) sts in total.
Cont without shaping until work measures 48 cm from beg, working last row on wrong side.
Cast off loosely.

HINT

If this large number of stitches will not fit comfortably on the needle, use a circular needle.

❹ COLLAR

Using 3.25 mm needles and mc, cast on 230 (234-242-246-254) sts.
Work 40 rows rib as for back.
Keeping rib correct, cast off 5 sts at beg of next 16 rows...150 (154-162-166-174) sts.
Next row: Cast off 5 sts, rib 29 (29-31-31-33), (work 2 tog) 41 (43-45-47-49) times, rib to end... 104 (106-112-114-120) sts.
Keeping both ribs correct, cast off 5 sts at beg of next 11 rows.
Cast off rem 49 (51-57-59-65) sts.

❺ MAKING UP

1 With a slightly damp cloth and warm iron, press lightly.
2 Using backstitch, join the shoulder seams, the sleeve seams and the side seams to the coloured threads.
3 Sew in sleeves, and then sew collar in position, crossing left over right at the centre front.
4 Press seams. Do not press ribbing.

Hanging flower basket

Suitable for hanging in a fernery, from a verandah or patio, or in a bathroom, this is a practical gift for a partner who loves potted plants. The wire basket can be flattened or elongated to suit the space it is to fill or to hold a favourite flowerpot.

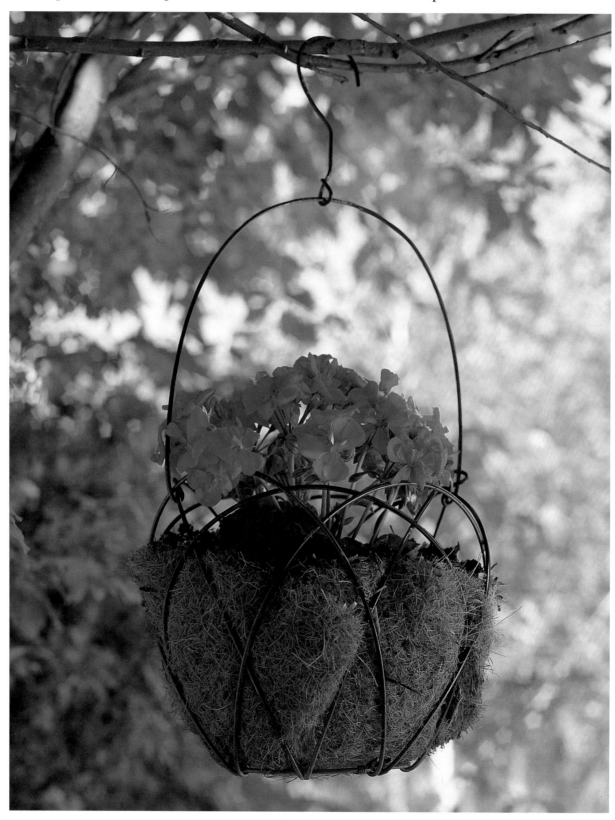

6 m galvanised wire, 3.15 mm diameter • 60 cm galvanised wire, 1.25 mm diameter • pliers • wire cutters • ruler • exterior metal paint

❶ PREPARING THE WIRE

1 Using the wire cutters, cut the 3.15 mm diameter wire into one piece 46 cm long (for the base) and nine pieces 61 cm long (eight pieces for the sides and one for the handle).

2 Cut the 1.25 mm diameter wire in half to make two 30 cm brace wires.

3 Using the pliers, make a hook 2 cm long at each end of the base wire. The hooks should be at right angles to one another so they will loop together.

4 Bend each end of the pieces for the side wires and the handle into 2 cm hooks so that the hooks are facing one another on the same plane.

❷ ASSEMBLING THE BASKET

The base

1 Form the base wire into a circle, hook the ends together and crimp them shut with the pliers.

2 Wind the end of one brace wire three or four times around the base wire near the joined hooks. Keeping

---

HINT

To prepare the basket for planting, line it with sphagnum moss (peat moss) and fill it with good quality potting mixture. Alternatively, buy and fill an attractive pot from a plant nursery and set it in the basket on a bed of sphagnum moss. If you are going to use a plant pot, select the pot before finishing the basket so that you can shape the basket accordingly.

---

the brace wire taut, wind the other end around the base wire directly opposite the first wound end.

3 Using the same technique, wind the remaining brace wire at right angles to the first. The base circle should now be divided into four equal segments by the two brace wires.

The sides

1 Take one of the side wires, one end in each hand with the hooks facing inwards, and draw the ends together until the distance separating the ends equals the diameter of the base circle.

2 Hook one end to the base alongside one of the brace wires. Keeping on the same side of the brace wire, hook the other end of the side wire to the opposite side of the circle. Crimp both hooks shut with the pliers.

3 Take a second side wire. Following the same procedure and keeping to the other side of the brace wire, hook the ends over the base wire.

4 In the same way, hook wire 3 to the base wire alongside one end of the other brace wire (at 90° to wires 1 and 2). Hook the other end to the opposite side of the base, taking care to

---

keep wire 3 underneath wires 1 and 2. Attach wire 4 alongside wire 3 on the other side of the brace wire.

5 Attach the other two pairs of side wires (5 and 6, and 7 and 8) in the same way, filling the spaces between the first two pairs.

The handle

1 Before attaching the handle, you may want to compress the basket to make it more squat or squeeze it to make it longer and thinner.

2 When you are satisfied with the shape, draw the ends of the handle wire together as for the side wires.

3 Hook one end over the intersection of side wires 1 and 5 and the other over the intersection of side wires 2 and 6. Crimp both hooks shut to enclose the side wires.

❸ FINISHING THE BASKET

For a special finishing touch, paint the basket with exterior gloss metal paint in your partner's favourite colour.

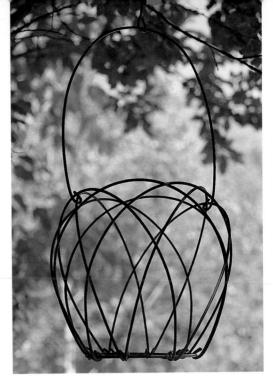

Sewing box

This very practical sewing box is a gift that any keen home dressmaker would be thrilled to receive. The lid of the box opens out to ensure that all sewing equipment is at the user's fingertips.

WHAT YOU NEED

Master pattern **G45(a–i)** • MDF or plywood, 1200 mm **x** 600 mm **x** 12 mm • 650 mm dowel, 6 mm diameter • 2 decorative 20 mm brass hinges, with screws no longer than 12 mm • decorative brass knob, about 20 mm in diameter • 1500 mm length 6 mm quad moulding • 12 rubber grommets (8 mm, with 5 mm diameter holes – they must fit tightly over the 6 mm dowelling) • 25 panel pins (25 mm) • 20 brads (12 mm) • PVA woodworking glue • paint, stain or clear varnish • paintbrushes • fabric, 12 cm **x** 15 cm • thick plastic foam, 11 cm **x** 7 cm • 4 decorative brass upholstery pins • sewing thread • sewing machine • sewing needle: medium sharp • handsaw or circular saw • jigsaw • hammer • ruler • drill and drill bits • mitre box • screwdriver • medium and fine-grade sandpaper • pencil • tracing paper • transfer paper
● *Technique pages 292–301, 338–42, 343–4*

❶ PREPARING THE PLYWOOD

1 Trace all the master pattern pieces on to the tracing paper.
2 Mark out all pattern pieces on the plywood as shown in the cutting guide, taking care to mark all dotted abutment and cutting lines.
3 To avoid confusion later, label all the pieces lightly in pencil.
4 Using the handsaw or the circular saw, cut out all pieces accurately.
5 Use the jigsaw to cut away the lid from the lower front along the curved dotted cutting line.
6 Cut away the triangular lid ends from the sides along the dotted lines.

Cutting guide
Before you begin to cut, ensure that you have marked all dotted abutment and cutting lines. You should also check all measurements and label each piece.

7 Cut the dowelling into 12 pieces, each 50 mm long.
8 Lightly sand all surfaces, being careful not to round joining edges.

❷ ASSEMBLING THE BOX

1 Glue and nail the main pieces in the following order with PVA wood-working glue and 25 mm panel pins:
● shelf front to shelf (shelf front should be at right angles to shelf);
● shelf to inner surface of dividers;
● dividers to base;
● side and back panels to top of base;
● lower front to front edges of base, sides and dividers;
● rear top panel to top of sides, back panel and dividers.
2 Measure and mark the quad moulding to fit around the base and mitre-cut it as required. Apply glue to the moulding and nail it in place with 12 mm brads.

❸ ASSEMBLING THE LID

Cotton reel holder

Base

Back panel

Lid front

Lower front

Lid top

Rear top

Shelf front

Shelf

Lid end

Side

Inside divider

Lid end

Side

Inside divider

1 With a 5 mm bit, drill 12 holes through the cotton reel holder in the positions shown. These holes are for the 12 mm dowel for the cotton reels.
2 Glue and nail the cotton reel holder to the inside of the lid top, centred vertically and horizontally.
3 Glue and nail the triangular lid ends to the inside of the lid top.
4 Glue and nail the lid front to the lid top and to the triangular ends.
5 Glue the ends of the dowels and insert them in the holes drilled in the cotton reel holder.

④ FINISHING

1 Sand all surfaces to a smooth finish. Paint, stain or varnish all surfaces.

2 Put the lid on top of the box in the closed position. Attach the lid to the rear top panel with the hinges, placing the hinges 100 mm from the ends.
3 Screw the brass knob to the lid front as marked on the pattern.
4 Push a grommet on to the top of each dowel to hold the cotton reels on the dowels when the lid is closed.

⑤ PINCUSHION

1 Fold the fabric in half widthwise with right sides facing.
2 Machine stitch along the long side and one short side, leaving a 5 mm seam allowance, and then turn the work right side out.
3 Slide the foam into the fabric and close the opening with slipstitch.
4 Centre the pincushion in the space between the two sets of dowels on the cotton reel holder and fix it in place with an upholstery pin at each corner.

NOTE

Before cutting, it is important to check that you have transferred all the patterns to the wood correctly. The dimensions should be as shown below.

- *lid front/lower front,*
  192 mm x 500 mm
- *lid top, 112 mm x 500 mm*
- *cotton reel holder,*
  70 mm x 400 mm
- *rear top, 92 mm x 500 mm*
- *back panel,*
  180 mm x 500 mm
- *base, 192 mm x 500 mm*
- *sides/dividers,*
  180 mm x 180 mm
- *shelf, 90 mm x 240 mm*
- *shelf front,*
  20 mm x 240 mm

Romantic flowers in a pot

Flowers are a lovely way to say you care. Plant your sweetheart's favourite flower in this decorated pot, and your gift will be a charming reminder of your devotion.

WHAT YOU NEED

Terracotta flowerpot • small flowering plants • potting mix, enough to fill your pot • suitable images from wrapping paper, books or greetings cards • artist's gesso • PVA glue • wallpaper paste • artist's acrylic gloss medium (sealer) • polyurethane gloss varnish • Blu Tack • paintbrushes: 2 small (for gluing and sealing), 20 mm imitation sable (for varnishing) • wet-and-dry abrasive paper: no. 280 • rubber sanding block • rubber roller • pieces of thick kitchen sponge • fine, curved scissors • pencil
● *Technique pages 329–31*

This project uses some découpage techniques. However, it does not require the application of a great many coats of varnish, so it will not have the porcelain-like finish that marks true découpage.

❶ PREPARATION

1 Sand all surfaces of the flowerpot lightly with sandpaper.
2 Apply a coat of artist's gesso to the outside of the pot. Allow the gesso to dry, then sandpaper the surface again. Seal the inside and outside surfaces with artist's acrylic medium.
3 Plan where you will put your images by fixing them to the pot with Blu Tack and rearranging them until you are satisfied with the design. Trim the images with sharp scissors if necessary. Remove the images and lightly mark their positions on the pot.
4 Seal the images on both sides with artist's acrylic medium. Be careful not to make the coat of sealer too heavy, as the images may then become less

NOTE
Remember to choose plants that are suitable for the conditions in which they will be grown.

pliable, so that it will be difficult to mould them around the pot. Allow the images to dry thoroughly.

❷ FIXING THE IMAGES

1 Taking one image at a time, apply a mixture of three parts wallpaper paste and one part PVA glue to the pot where the image is to go, and a small amount to the right side of the image.
2 Massage and mould the image into the surface, adding more glue if neces-

sary. Roll over the image with the rubber roller to get rid of any lumps of glue or air bubbles. Remove the excess glue with a wet sponge.
3 Repeat steps 1 and 2 until all the images are in place.
4 Apply two coats of artist's acrylic medium to the surface, allowing each coat to dry thoroughly before applying the next.

❸ FINISHING

1 Apply at least two coats of varnish, allowing the first coat to dry before applying the next. Leave the pot to dry thoroughly.
2 Fill the pot with potting mix and plant the flower according to the instructions supplied by the nursery.

Aromatic beeswax candles

Make these candles to set the mood for you and your partner on a special occasion. Beeswax is long-burning and does not drip, and when the candles are lit they will fill the room with the delicious scent of natural honey.

WHAT YOU NEED

Sheets of preformed beeswax • length of braided wick, 3 mm wide • ruler • large pair of scissors • hair dryer (in cold weather)

❶ MAKING THE CANDLES

1 Experiment with the shapes and sizes of the candles by cutting out sheets of thin, pliable cardboard and rolling them up in various ways.
2 When you are satisfied with the shape you have achieved, unroll and flatten the cardboard, place it on a beeswax sheet and cut carefully around it. To increase the thickness, add more sheets of wax.
3 Cut a piece of wick 2 cm longer than the finished candle will be.
4 Unless it is a fairly warm day, you may need to soften the beeswax slightly to make it pliable and to prevent the sheet from cracking as you roll. To soften the beeswax, wave a hair dryer over the sheet for about 10 seconds or leave the beeswax near a sunny window for about 10 minutes.

5 Lay the softened beeswax flat on a clean surface. Pinch off a small piece of the wax from the place where you will begin to roll and set it aside. Place the wick along the edge of the sheet and push it gently into the wax.
6 Turn the edge of the sheet over the wick to make a small fold and press lightly to encase the wick.
7 Using the palms of both hands, roll the wax away from you with a light but even pressure, making sure that the base of the candle is level so that it will sit flat when it is finished.

HINTS

When they are alight, beeswax candles give off a natural honey-like fragrance. However, if you would like to add a special scent to the candles, use an eye dropper to drop fragrant oil on to the wick before you roll the beeswax. A small candle requires three or four drops, and a large one between 10 and 20 drops.

CANDLE SHAPES

Tapered candles
To achieve an attractive tapered look, trim one side of the sheet diagonally and roll from the long end.

Square candles
To make a square candle, place a ruler close to the edge of the beeswax sheet and turn the wax around it. Repeat this step each time you turn the sheet.

8 Continue rolling more sheets of beeswax around the first until the candle is the thickness you want. Press the outside edge of the wax against the candle to prevent it from unrolling.
9 If the shape has become a little distorted because of uneven pressure when rolling, you can make the candle perfectly cylindrical by rolling it briskly back and forth a few times.

❷ FINISHING

1 Trim the wick to 1.5 cm and pinch the piece of reserved wax around the base of the wick. This will help it to light more easily.
2 As a final touch to the gift, group a few candles of complementary shapes and include a box of luxury matches.

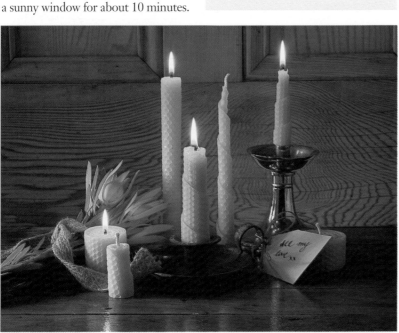

Man's summer nightshirt

Made from cool, pure cotton, this nightshirt will help to keep your man comfortable, even on the hottest nights.

Master pattern **F38(a–e)** • 2.5 m lightweight cotton fabric, 150 cm wide • 80 cm iron-on interfacing • sewing thread to match fabric • 3 medium sized buttons, 15 mm diameter • tracing paper • pencil • scissors • needle: general sewing • dressmaking pins • tape measure • sewing machine

● *Technique pages 292–301, 343–4*

1 CUTTING THE PATTERN

1 Using the tracing paper, pencil and scissors, trace and cut out a working pattern from the master pattern. Transfer all markings.

2 Cut out the pattern pieces from the fabric. Use the collar and front facing pattern pieces to cut the interfacings.

2 MAKING THE COLLAR

1 Staystitch the neckline of the nightshirt 1 cm from the raw edges. With right sides together, machine stitch the front and back shoulder seams.

Zigzag or overlock the edges together and press the seams toward the back.

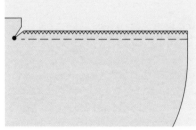

2 Iron the collar interfacing to the wrong side of one collar piece. Zigzag or overlock the outer edges. Place the right sides of the collar pieces together and machine around the unnotched edge, leaving the neck edge open. Trim the seam allowance and the corners. Clip the neck edge of the collar at the large dots to the seamline. Turn down the middle section of the interfaced side and press.

3 Turn the collar to the right side and press. With the right side of the non-interfaced side of the collar to the right side of the nightshirt, staystitch the collar to the neckline, matching the large dots.

NOTES

● *Consult technique pages 295-6 to find out how to match the stripes when you are cutting plaid or striped fabrics.*

● *All seam allowances are 1.5 cm and all seams are overlocked or zigzagged to finish.*

3 ATTACHING THE FRONT FACINGS

1 Starting at the hem, with the right sides of the centre front seams together, machine stitch to the large dot and backtack to reinforce. Clip diagonally to the large dot, overlock or zigzag the edges together, and press the seam toward one side.

2 Iron the interfacings to the front facing pieces. Starting at the large dot on the centre front seam, with right sides together, pin the facings along both sides of the centre front opening and around the neck edges, overlapping the collar. From the large dot

CUTTING GUIDE

Fold the fabric in half lengthwise and lay out the pattern pieces as shown to cut two of each piece. Place the centre backs of the back piece and the two collar pieces on the fold. For the interfacings, cut two front facing pieces and one complete collar piece from the iron-on interfacing.

To make the nightshirt with plaid or striped fabric, you will need extra fabric to match the stripes. If you cannot buy the fabric you want in the 150 cm width specified here, measure the pattern pieces to work out how much 115 cm wide or 90 cm wide fabric you will need to buy.

Fold

Back

Collar

Collar

Front facing

Front

Sleeve

75 cm

2.5 m

at the centre front, stitching through all layers, machine stitch a continuous seam up the centre front opening, around the front and back neck and down the other centre front opening to the large dot. Pivot the needle at the corners, and backtack to reinforce the beginning and end of the seam.

3 Trim the seams and corners and clip the neck edge so that the work will be smooth and neat when it is turned right side out.

4 Clip diagonally through all layers of the neck seam at the shoulders, so that the exposed part of the seam at the back of the neck can be pressed up into the collar.

5 Turn the facings to the inside of the nightshirt and press. Press the exposed back neck seam up into the collar and bring the folded edge of the collar over the machine stitching at the back neck. Stitch the folded edge down by hand or machine, and secure the facings at the shoulder seams.

6 Reinforce the centre front opening at the large dots by topstitching a square and then bisecting it with one diagonal line of stitching.

④ ASSEMBLING THE NIGHTSHIRT

1 With right sides together, pin and machine stitch the sleeves to the armholes. Neaten the raw edges and press the seams toward the sleeves. Neaten the wrist edges of the sleeves.

2 With right sides facing, pin the front and back side seams together, matching the dots and underarm seams. Machine from the dots on the side seams to the wrists. At the side seam openings, clip the front hem to the machine stitching.

3 Starting at one wrist, neaten the side seam and continue around the back hem to the opposite side, finishing at the other wrist. Then neaten the raw edge of the front hem.

4 Press the front, back and sleeve hems to the inside and machine hem at the desired width from the edge.

⑤ FINISHING

1 Mark and machine three buttonholes on the left front in the positions marked on the master pattern.

2 Sew the buttons on the centre line of the right front to match up with the buttonhole positions.

Elegant indoor planter box

This decorative planter box will delight your partner and add a touch of style to any home. The box is large and strong enough to hold a plant pot about 30 cm in diameter and 36 cm high.

WHAT YOU NEED

Exterior quality dressed timber: 70 mm **x** 12 mm (finished size), 2 lengths 4500 mm and 1 length 3300 mm; 50 mm **x** 50 mm (finished size), 1 length 5400 mm; 20 mm **x** 20 mm (finished size), 1 length 3600 mm • 4 decorative wooden door knobs, about 60 mm diameter • galvanised lost head nails, 25 mm, 30 mm and 75 mm long • PVA woodworking glue • wood filler or putty • exterior paint or stain • paintbrush • medium-grade sandpaper • handsaw or power saw • mitre box • combination square • hammer • drill and drill bits • nail punch • ruler • pencil

● *Technique pages 338–42*

❶ PREPARING THE TIMBER

1 Using the handsaw or power saw, accurately cut the 70 mm boards into 24 lengths of 360 mm (for the side panels), and two lengths of 400 mm

NOTE

When ordering timber, if the lengths itemised above are not available, be sure to specify pieces that will supply you with the multiple lengths listed in section 1, 'Preparing the timber'. Also, be sure to measure out all of your pieces before you cut any to length, in order to minimise waste.

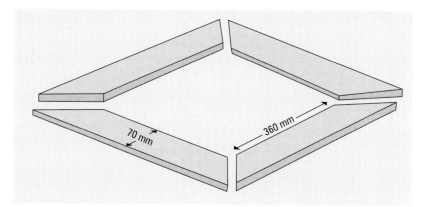

(for the cross bars). From the remaining 70 mm timber, cut the four pieces for the top trim to the dimensions shown above, mitring them at 45°.

2 Using a handsaw or power saw, cut the 50 mm square timber into four 600 mm lengths (for the legs) and eight 360 mm lengths (for the two top rails, the two bottom rails and the four cross rails).

3 Using a handsaw or power saw, cut the 20 mm square timber (inside supports) into eight 420 mm lengths (or lengths equal to six times the width of the side panel boards).

4 If the wooden knobs have any timber protruding from the back, saw them off so that the surfaces are completely level.

5 Sand all cut edges smooth.

❷ ASSEMBLING THE PLANTER

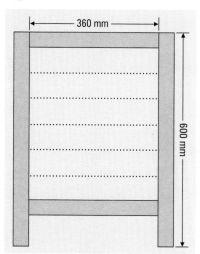

1 Using the glue and 75 mm nails, glue and nail one top and one bottom rail to two of the legs in the positions shown. Make sure that the inside distance between the top and bottom

rails corresponds to six times the actual width of the boards used for the side panels. Repeat this step with the other two legs.

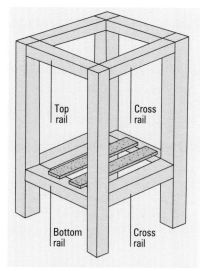

2 Using 75 mm nails, join the two leg units by nailing the legs to the top and bottom cross rails in the positions shown. Glue and nail the two 70 mm cross bar supports from one bottom rail to the other in the positions shown, using 25 mm nails.

3 Attach one pair of inside supports to each leg with PVA glue and 30 mm nails, and then glue and nail the side panels to the inside supports, making sure that there are no gaps between the boards. The panels are recessed from the front edges of the legs and the top and bottom rails, and they should fit snugly between the legs.

4 Fit the mitred 70 mm trim to the top of the planter and fix it in place with PVA glue and 30 mm nails.

5 Glue a decorative wooden door knob to each mitred corner of the top trim, centring the knobs carefully over the legs.

❸ FINISHING

1 Punch all nail holes and fill them with putty or wood filler. Sand all surfaces until they are smooth.

2 Paint or stain all visible surfaces in a colour to complement the decor of the area where the box will stand. If you decide to use stain, finish the planter box with two or three coats of matt polyurethane varnish.

Sweet-scented solutions

Pamper your partner with a gift of homemade fragrant bath oil, hand cream or cologne, presented in an attractive glass container with a decorative label. The ingredients are available from alternative health shops and pharmacies.

WHAT YOU NEED

Eye dropper (1 ml capacity) • measuring cup, graduated in millilitres • non-aluminium double boiler • stainless steel spoons • stainless steel or ceramic bowls • stainless steel whisk • fine muslin • coffee filter papers • sterilised, coloured glass bottles and jars (for sterilising directions see 'Tips for making cosmetic preparations' in the box on this page.)

Bath oil
30 ml sweet almond oil • 5 ml avocado oil • 5 ml wheatgerm oil • essential oils: 6 drops chamomile, 6 drops rose, 18 drops lavender

After-shower body oil
10 ml jojoba oil • 10 ml wheatgerm oil • 40 ml hazelnut oil • 40 ml apricot kernel oil • essential oils: 12 drops frankincense, 12 drops geranium, 6 drops jasmine, 24 drops lavender

Nourishing hand cream
10 g beeswax • 5 g anhydrous lanolin (wool fat) • 60 ml almond oil • 5 ml sweet wheatgerm oil • 20 ml distilled water • 20 ml aloe vera juice • essential oils: 10 drops carrot, 5 drops rose, 2 drops lemon, 2 drops frankincense, 1 drop geranium

Protective hand cream
Handful chopped lemongrass (*Cymbopogon citratus*) • 300 ml boiling water • 15 g anhydrous lanolin (wool fat) • 10 g beeswax • 70 ml almond oil • 5 ml wheatgerm oil • 20 ml aloe vera juice • 2 tsp strained lemon juice • 3 drops friar's balsam

Body cologne
140 ml vodka • essential oils: 3 ml bergamot, 3 ml lemon, 1.5 ml orange, 20 drops neroli, 10 drops rosemary • 60 ml distilled water

❶ BATH OIL
1 Pour the ingredients into a bottle and shake well until all the oils are thoroughly blended. Store the mixture away from heat and direct sunlight.
2 Ten drops will provide a deliciously fragrant bath. The mixture should be used within six months.
● Makes about 50 ml.

❷ AFTER-SHOWER BODY OIL
1 Pour the ingredients into a bottle and shake well until all the oils are thoroughly blended. Store the mixture away from heat and direct sunlight.

> **NOTE**
> *Essential oils are quite expensive to buy – but once you have acquired a good selection of them, you will be able to make wonderful gifts for all your family and friends.*

2 The oil is poured into the palm of the hand and smoothed all over the body when it is towel-dry after a bath or shower. The mixture should be used within six months.
● Makes about 150 ml.

❸ NOURISHING HAND CREAM
1 Melt the wax and the lanolin in a double boiler over a medium heat.
2 Keeping the double boiler over the heat, add all the remaining ingredients, except for the essential oils, and stir gently until the mixture is thoroughly blended.
3 Pour the mixture into a ceramic bowl and allow it to cool slightly.
4 Add the essential oils, and use a whisk to beat the mixture until it is creamy in texture.
5 Transfer the cream to the sterilised jar and label the jar.
6 The cream is rubbed into the hands when the skin feels dry. The mixture should be used within two months.
● Makes about 200 ml.

❹ PROTECTIVE HAND CREAM
1 Place the lemongrass in a ceramic bowl and cover it with the boiling water. Steep for two hours, and then strain the liquid through fine muslin into the other ceramic bowl.

TIPS FOR MAKING COSMETIC PREPARATIONS

For the best results, and to avoid contaminating the mixtures, observe the following rules.

● Measure all your ingredients as accurately as possible. When you are measuring essential oils, use good-quality graduated droppers, which are available from pharmacies. A standard dropper holds 1 ml and is graduated in tenths of a millilitre.

● Use only stainless steel, glass or enamel pans for warming and boiling (never use aluminium pans), and use stainless steel spoons for mixing.

● Keep all your equipment spotlessly clean, and use it only for making up cosmetic preparations.

● Always use distilled water – this is essential to prevent creams and lotions from becoming rancid. Water from the tap contains chemicals and impurities that are likely to contaminate the other ingredients.

● For filtering the mixtures, use coffee filter papers (unbleached if possible), or sterilised fine muslin.

● Store creams and oils in coloured glass jars – amber glass is best. It is essential to sterilise jars and lids properly before using them to store cosmetic preparations. Wash them thoroughly in warm, soapy water and then boil them for 10 minutes. Leave them upside down to dry.

● Label all preparations with their names, the ingredients used, the use-by date and, if applicable, how much to use and how often.

HINT

With your gift, include a card describing how to patch-test new cosmetics before using them to ensure that there is no allergic reaction to the ingredients. Tell the recipient to apply a small quantity of the preparation to the underside of the forearm – if the skin reddens, blisters, burns or becomes itchy, the person should not use the product without professional advice.

2 Put the lanolin, beeswax, almond oil and wheatgerm oil in the top part of a double boiler, and warm the mixture over a gentle heat until all the ingredients are melted.

3 Keeping the double boiler over the heat source, add the aloe vera juice

and 20 ml of the strained lemongrass infusion. Stir until well blended.

4 Remove the mixture from the heat and pour it into a ceramic bowl. Allow the mixture to cool slightly.

5 Add the lemon juice and the friar's balsam, and beat the mixture with the whisk until it is cool and creamy.

6 Store the cream in the sterilised jar.

7 The protective cream is rubbed into the hands before using detergents or cleaners. The mixture should be used within two months.

● Makes about 400 ml.

5 BODY COLOGNE

1 Pour the vodka into a sterilised glass jar and add the essential oils, stirring slowly until the oils are

completely blended. Seal the jar and let the mixture stand for 48 hours.

2 Add the distilled water, stirring slowly to mix thoroughly.

3 Leave the mixture to steep in the jar for 48 hours to four weeks, depending on how strong you want the fragrance to be. If you feel that the fragrance is too strong, dilute the mixture with a little more distilled water.

4 When the scent has matured, drip the mixture through a coffee filter into a decorative, sterilised glass bottle; one with a ground glass stopper is ideal.

5 The cologne makes a refreshing pick-me-up when it is splashed on to the body. The mixture should be used within six months.

● Makes about 250 ml.

Man's scarf & hat

To keep the man in your life warm and cosy, make him this scarf and matching hat. The hat is shaped like a beanie and the scarf is finished off with tassels.

WHAT YOU NEED

Length of scarf	**160 cm**
Width of scarf	**22 cm**
Hat fits a 59 cm circumference	

The yarn used in this project is **Patons Diploma Gold DK (100 g balls)**, and the colours are: main colour (mc), 7233 (college grey); 1st contrast (cc1), 7266 (berber); 2nd contrast (cc2), 7260 (charcoal).

Hat

Main (mc)	1
1st contrast (cc1)	1
2nd contrast (cc2)	1

Scarf

Main (mc)	3
1st contrast (cc1)	1
2nd contrast (cc2)	1

Knitting needles: 3.75 mm (no. 9), 4.00 mm (no. 8) • crochet hook (for fringe) • wool sewing needle
● *Technique pages 323–7*

CHECKING THE TENSION

Before you begin to knit, test your tension to ensure that both the scarf and the hat will be as close as possible to the size specified. You should have 22 stitches to 10 cm in width over pattern, using 4.00 mm needles. If you have fewer stitches, you should use smaller needles; if you have more stitches, use larger needles.

❶ KNITTING THE SCARF

Using 4.00 mm knitting needles and mc, loosely cast on 46 sts.

NOTE

You will need only one ball of each of the contrasting colours to make both the scarf and the hat.

1st row: K2, ★ P2, K2, rep from ★ to the end.
2nd row: P2, ★ K2, P2, rep from ★ to the end.
3rd row: As for 2nd row.
4th row: As for 1st row.
(These 4 rows form patt.)
Cont in patt until work measures 140 cm from beg, working the last row on the wrong side.
Cast off in patt.

❷ FINISHING THE SCARF

Using mc, cc1 and cc2, make a fringe about 10 cm long at both ends.

❸ KNITTING THE HAT

Using 3.75 mm needles and mc, cast on 130 sts.
1st row: (right side of the brim) K2, ★ P2, K2, rep from ★ to end.
2nd row: P2, ★ K2, P2, rep from ★ to the end.
Rep 1st and 2nd rows 4 times, then 1st row once, in stripes of 2 rows cc1, 2 rows cc2, 2 rows cc1, then 3 rows in mc. Change to 4.00 mm needles. Beg patt.
1st row: (right side) K2, ★ P2, K2, rep from ★ to end.

2nd row: P2, ★ K2, P2, rep from ★ to end.
3rd row: As for 2nd row.
4th row: As for 1st row.
(These 4 rows form patt.)
Cont in patt until the work measures 19 cm from the beg, ending with a 4th row.

Shaping the top

1st row: K2, ★ P2 tog, K2, rep from ★ to end...98 sts.
2nd and 3rd rows: P2, ★ K1, P2, rep from ★ to end.
4th and 5th rows: K2, ★ P1, K2, rep from ★ to end.
6th row: As for 2nd row.
7th row: P2 tog, ★ K1, P2 tog, rep from ★ to end...65 sts.
8th and 9th rows: K1, ★ P1, K1, rep from ★ to end.
10th and 11th rows: P1, ★ K1, P1, rep from ★ to end.
12th row: As for 8th row.
13th row: K1, ★ work 3 tog, rep from ★ to last st, K1...23 sts.
Break off yarn. Run end of yarn through rem sts, draw it up tightly and fasten it off securely.

❹ MAKING UP THE HAT

1 Using the wool sewing needle, join the seam with backstitch, reversing the stitching for the ribbed section.
2 Turn back the ribbed edge to form a brim around the hat.

MAKING A FRINGE

1 Wind the yarn round a piece of cardboard as wide as the desired length of the finished fringe plus 2–3 cm, and cut along one edge.
2 Take three strands of yarn of one colour and fold them in half.
3 With wrong side of the knitting facing, push the crochet hook through the knitting and draw the folded loop through one stitch in the edge of the knitted piece.
4 Without removing the crochet hook from the loop, draw the cut ends through the loop and pull gently to form a knot. Adjust the knots so they are evenly tied.

Master pattern 161(a–d) • 3 wooden rectangular kitchen canisters, the largest about 30 cm tall • Folk Art acrylic base coat: porcelain white • Folk Art pure pigment: alizarin crimson, ivory black, yellow light, phthalo green, Prussian blue • Folk Art acrylic colour: Paisley blue, harvest gold, plum pudding, southern pine, raspberry wine, bayberry, calico red, persimmon, chocolate fudge, wicker white • drying retarder • water-based clear varnish • paint palette • paintbrushes: sponge brush (about 40 mm), no. 5 round, no. 12 flat, no. 00 liner • medium and fine-grade sandpaper • lint-free cloth • tracing paper • transfer paper • fine-tipped marker pen • stylus (or empty ballpoint pen) • masking tape • palette • paper towels
● *Technique pages 334–5, 343–4*

❶ PREPARING THE CANISTERS

1 Lightly sand all the outside surfaces of the canisters with medium-grade sandpaper and wipe away all residue with a lint-free cloth.
2 Using the sponge brush, apply two coats of porcelain white base coat to the outsides of the canisters and lids, sanding between coats with fine-grade sandpaper. Be careful not to get paint on the insides of the canisters or on the surfaces where the canisters and the lids meet.
3 Allow the paint to dry thoroughly.

4 With the flat brush, paint a thin coat of drying retarder on the lower third of each canister and then a coat of porcelain white over the retarder.
5 Side-load the flat brush with phthalo green and float a band of colour 2–3 cm wide around the base of each canister.

❷ TRANSFERRING THE DESIGN

1 Using tracing paper and the fine-tipped marker pen, trace the designs from the master pattern.

2 Using masking tape, position the vine leaf design on the front of the large canister, near the top. If the canister is the type with a lid extending over the side of the canister (as used in this project), place the design so it falls over both lid and canister.
3 Using transfer paper and stylus, transfer the design to the canister.
4 Remove the design carefully and attach it to the adjoining side of the canister, making sure that the beginning of the second design matches the end of the first design to form a continuous vine pattern.

HINTS

● *When painting the designs, use a round brush to apply two coats of the specified base colour.*
● *Do all further work using a 'wet-on-wet' technique, so that shading and highlights are blended with the central colour.*
● *Use a round brush when blending the shading on the small fruit. Change to a flat brush for the larger plums, apples and pears, using short, patting strokes to give the fruit a rounded appearance.*

5 Repeat step 4 until the design appears right around the upper edge of the canister. Then repeat steps 2 to 5 on the other two canisters.

6 Find the centre of the front of each canister by lightly ruling two diagonal lines from opposite corners. Where the lines cross is the centre of the canister. Fix the relevant fruit design to each

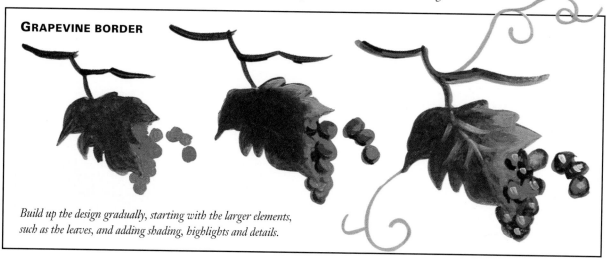

GRAPEVINE BORDER

Build up the design gradually, starting with the larger elements, such as the leaves, and adding shading, highlights and details.

BLUEBERRIES

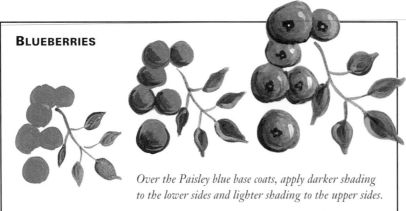

Over the Paisley blue base coats, apply darker shading to the lower sides and lighter shading to the upper sides.

PEARS

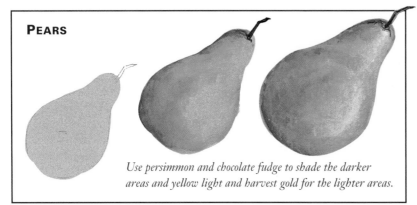

Use persimmon and chocolate fudge to shade the darker areas and yellow light and harvest gold for the lighter areas.

canister in turn, using masking tape and aligning the centre mark on the design with the centre mark on the canister. The bottom of the design should be about 3.5 cm from the bottom of the canister, just above the phthalo green band. The design may extend around the corners. Then transfer the design on to the front and sides of each canister.

❸ PAINTING THE DESIGNS

Grapevine border

1 Base-coat the leaves with southern pine and allow them to dry.

2 Apply a coat of phthalo green to the centre of each leaf, then shade with southern pine along the lower edge and bayberry along the upper.

3 Paint the grapes with Paisley blue. Shade them with Prussian blue and raspberry wine, then add highlights of phthalo green and wicker white. Using the liner brush and wicker white, paint in the veins of the grapevine leaves.

4 Using the liner brush, paint the grapevine stems in ivory black and chocolate fudge and the vine tendrils in chocolate fudge.

String bag

1 Base-coat the string bag with phthalo green.

2 Using rough comma strokes, paint the first and fourth stripes in harvest gold, the second in raspberry wine and the third in southern pine. Highlight each stripe by mixing wicker white into paint of the appropriate colour.

3 Paint the strap in bands of southern pine and yellow light commas, highlighted in the same way as the stripes.

Blueberries

1 Base-coat the blueberries with Paisley blue.

2 Shade one side with Prussian blue mixed with a touch of raspberry wine, and shade the other side with Paisley blue mixed with wicker white. Add wicker white highlights.

3 Paint the blossom ends with ivory black highlighted with wicker white, and the leaves with southern pine highlighted with bayberry.

Oranges

1 Base-coat the oranges with harvest gold. Shade them with chocolate fudge and persimmon, then brush-mix

harvest gold, yellow light and wicker white to paint the highlights.

2 Paint in the stem ends using ivory black, bayberry and a mixture of ivory black and bayberry.

Plums

Base-coat the plums with plum pudding. Shade them with a mixture of plum pudding and Prussian blue and highlight them with raspberry wine, plum pudding and wicker white.

Apples

1 Base-coat the apples in calico red.

2 Shade the dark sides and the bases of the stems with chocolate fudge and raspberry wine.

3 Add a rosy glow to the centres using alizarin crimson, and then highlight the other sides with persimmon and harvest gold. Dry-brush light wicker white highlights.

4 Paint the stems in ivory black, with chocolate fudge and wicker white highlights.

Pears

1 Base-coat the pears with two coats of harvest gold.

2 Blend chocolate fudge and persimmon in the darker areas of the fruit, and blend yellow light and harvest gold in the lighter areas. Dry-brush highlights with wicker white.

3 Paint the stems in ivory black and highlight them with chocolate fudge and wicker white.

❹ FINISHING

1 When the paint is quite dry, erase all transfer lines.

2 Wipe all surfaces thoroughly with a lint-free cloth before applying three coats of varnish with a flat brush.

> **NOTE**
> *The fruit folk art pattern has been designed so that it flows from one canister to the next. When the canisters are displayed, the tallest one should be on the left and the smallest one on the right.*

Ribbon & lace bridal garter

A beautifully crafted white garter is an important part of a traditional wedding outfit, and the bride is sure to treasure a garter you have lovingly made especially for her.

WHAT YOU NEED

1.6 m satin ribbon, 25 mm wide •
1.7 m entredeux, 10 mm wide •
1.7 m edging lace, 25 mm wide •
non-roll elastic, 20 mm wide, cut to
the leg measurement plus 1.5 cm •
20 cm satin ribbon, 5 mm wide •
fine sewing thread • sewing machine
• fine sewing needle • scissors •
dressmaking pins
● *Technique pages 292–301, 303–4*

❶ PREPARING THE RIBBON AND LACE

1 Cut the 1.6 m of satin ribbon
into two equal pieces.
2 With right sides together, and
using a 5 mm seam, stitch the ends
of one piece of ribbon together to
form a circle. Press the seam open.
Set this piece aside.

3 Join the second piece of ribbon into
a circle in the same way, but on this
piece, sew only a scant 5 mm in from
each edge, leaving a 15 mm gap in the
centre of the seam to thread the elastic
through. This piece forms the inside
of the garter.
4 Cut the entredeux and edging lace
in half and press all four pieces.

HINT

*The satin ribbon that was used
in this project has a floral motif
embroidered on it. Look for a
ribbon with a pretty variation
like this to add that extra touch
to the garter.*

Carefully trim away one batiste edge
of each piece of entredeux.
5 Butt the trimmed edge of one piece
of entredeux to one piece of lace edging and, using a fine machine zigzag
stitch, sew them together. Press well.
Repeat this step with the second
pieces of entredeux and lace.

❷ SEWING THE GARTER

Wrong side

1 Pin the untrimmed edge of the
entredeux to one edge of the wrong
side of the inside piece of ribbon (the
piece with the opening) so that the
entredeux holes are just visible at the
ribbon's edge. Fold the raw edges of
the joined entredeux and lace under at
the seam and trim away any excess.

2 Sew the joined entredeux and lace
in place along the edge of the ribbon,
using a straight machine stitch.
3 Repeat steps 1 and 2 on the
other side of the ribbon.
4 With wrong sides facing, pin the
two circles of ribbon together, making
sure the seams on both pieces match.
5 Sew the pieces together along both
edges of the ribbon using a straight
machine stitch.
6 Handstitch the ends of the lace
together at the seam, using a fine
seam. Neaten the edges and trim
any loose threads. Press well.
7 Thread the elastic through the
opening, overlap the ends and handstitch the elastic firmly to secure it.
Close the opening with slipstitch.
8 Tie the 5 mm ribbon in a small
bow and sew it by hand to the centre
of the garter, opposite the seam.
9 Trim the ends of the ribbon
at an angle to prevent fraying.

VARIATION
*Use blue ribbon in the garter if
you want to give the bride the
traditional 'something blue'.*

Coat-hanger for a wedding dress

A special dress requires special care when storing, and this padded coat-hanger covered with silk shantung is perfect for the purpose. The embroidery is adapted from a Brazilian pattern.

WHAT YOU NEED

Master pattern l66(a) • wire coat-hanger • 25 cm white silk shantung, 90 cm wide • 2 pieces polyester wadding, 18 cm x 50 cm • needles: size 7 straw, size 7 embroidery • white silk embroidery thread • 30 cm white silk ribbon, 4 mm wide • tracing paper • dressmaker's carbon paper • fabric marking pen • pencil • dressmaking pins • scissors
For lace trimming: Bouc linen lace thread no. 50 • no. 3 cotton darning needle
● *Technique pages 292–301, 307–12, 328, 343–4*

❶ PREPARATION

Using tracing paper and scissors, trace and cut out the master pattern pieces. Trace the embroidery guidelines on to the larger piece.

Cover back

1 Pin the larger pattern piece to a single thickness of the silk shantung and cut carefully around it.
2 Fold the lower edge over 1 cm to the wrong side of the fabric and press. Put this piece to one side.

Cover front

1 Using a fabric marking pen, lightly trace the outline of the larger pattern piece on to the remaining shantung. Do not cut the fabric yet.
2 Using the dressmaker's carbon paper, transfer the embroidery guidelines on to the right side of the fabric.

VARIATION

Instead of working the knotted lace trimming, buy 50 cm of edging lace and trim and slipstitch the lace to the turned lower edge of the front hanger cover before sewing the back and front together.

Padding

1 Pin the smaller pattern piece to a double thickness of wadding and cut out the two pieces.
2 Place the two wadding pieces on either side of the wire coat-hanger, leaving the hook sticking out at the top. Use a double thread to oversew the pieces together.

Hook cover

1 From the silk shantung, cut a bias strip 14 cm long and 3 cm wide.

1 cm

Old-fashioned botanical picture

Traditionally, pressed flowers and leaves have been used for the identification of plants. This old-fashioned botanical picture is an unusual wedding gift that will be very handy for reference.

WHAT YOU NEED

This is a large picture. To fill the framed area you will need to collect quite a number of plants.

A selection of flowers and leaves of medicinal and culinary herbs, cultivated and wild, such as achillea, ageratum, basil, bellflower, catmint, chives, coriander, daffodil, dandelion, delphinium, dill, dogwood, fern, feverfew, geranium, hyssop, jonquil, lavender, love-in-a-mist, nasturtium, parsley, pennywort, rose, rosemary, snowdrop, violet • picture frame with glass (inside measurement 56 cm x 76 cm) • A1 sheet of white handmade textured paper • A1 sheet of 5 mm white mounting board • scissors • spray adhesive • clear craft glue • craft knife • steel ruler • tweezers • cocktail stick or paintbrush • eraser • soft pencil • ruler • Indian (permanent) ink

● *Technique pages 332–3*

❶ PREPARATION

1 Press the flowers and foliage using the methods described in 'Flower and foliage drying'. Note that drying treatments vary for different plants.
2 Trim the mounting board and paper to fit snugly into the frame.
3 Decide which side of the textured paper to display and apply spray adhesive to the edges of the other side. Position it on the mounting board and leave it to dry completely.

NOTE
Remember to tell the recipient of this gift that the picture will retain its natural colours better if it is displayed away from direct sunlight or fluorescent lighting.

4 With a ruler and pencil, measure and lightly draw a margin around all sides, 2 cm in from the edges.
5 Divide the margin into three vertically and into four horizontally. Lightly mark this three-by-four grid on the paper with the soft pencil.

❷ ASSEMBLING THE PICTURE

1 Arrange the pressed plants evenly over the display area, using the pencilled grid as a guide to help you to space them. Group flowers and leaves of each specimen together and try to place related families of plants next to each other.
2 Some flowers have to be pulled apart for pressing. To put them back together, refer to the guidelines for *Reassembling the flowers* in 'Framed wedding bouquet' (pages 188–9).
3 When you are satisfied with the layout, apply a small amount of craft glue to the back of each flower or herb using the tweezers and a cocktail stick

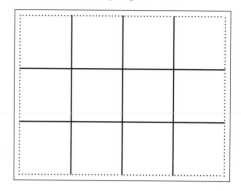

DRAWING UP A GRID
A grid drawn on the backing acts a guide for arranging and aligning the herbs.

or small paintbrush, and lightly press into place. Allow the glue to dry.
4 Lightly label each specimen with a sharpened pencil. When you are satisfied with the lettering, go over the pencilled labels with Indian ink.
5 Carefully erase any pencilled guidelines that are still showing.
6 Insert the picture into the frame and secure the back according to the frame manufacturer's instructions.

Monogrammed towels

Embroidered grub roses add a touch of romance to the monogrammed initials on these bath towels, hand towels and flannels. Either embroider the initials of the bride and groom separately, or intertwine them to create personalised bathroom linen for the newly married pair.

WHAT YOU NEED

Master pattern **E35(a)** • bath towels, hand towels and flannels – preferably with woven bands at each end • stranded embroidery cotton in green and a shade to blend with the towels (second colour) • needle: size 3 straw • coloured tacking thread • scissors • tracing paper • pencil
● *Technique pages 307–12, 343–4*

❶ PREPARING THE MONOGRAMS

1 Using a photocopier, enlarge the initials on the master pattern to the right size for the item to be mono-grammed. A letter 10 cm high is appropriate for a bath towel, and a letter 8 cm high for a hand towel. The flannel has one flower spray and no initial.

VARIATION

Intertwine the monogrammed initials of the bride and groom to make a very romantic gift. Trace one initial on to tracing paper, then place this letter on top of the other initial. Move the tracing paper around until you are satisfied with the inter-twining effect. Trace the second initial over the first.

2 Making one tracing for each towel, trace the initials that you need on to tracing paper.
3 Centre the initials on the end of the towel, placing the bottom of the initial on the woven band.
4 Using running stitch and coloured tacking thread, sew through the paper to mark the initials on the towel. Tear away the paper.

❷ EMBROIDERING THE BATH TOWEL

All the embroidery is worked with six threads. Before you use each piece of embroidery cotton, separate the strands and then put them back together again. This gives the work a textured appearance.

1 Study the lines of the initial you are using on your towel and decide where to place the rose design. As a general rule, the best position will be along the principal line of the letter.
2 Following the bath towel stitch guide, embroider the grub roses first, leaving enough space between the roses to insert the buds.
3 Work stems and foliage in green to form the rest of the initial.

Grub roses

Working in the second colour, make three bullion knots of 12 turns each for the centre of the rose. Around these knots work five more bullion knots of 16 turns each.

Buds

Still working in the second colour, embroider two straight stitches, one on top of the other, to form a bud. On either side of these stitches, and using green embroidery cotton, work two straight stitches, one on top of the other, to form the calyx (the green outer part of the bud).

Hand towel stitch guide
The flower sprays for the hand towels are worked with straight stitch and finished with a French knot in the centre of the spray.

	Grub rose
	Bud
	Stems and leaves

Bath towel stitch guide

Make the grub roses by working three bullion knots for the centres and five longer, curving ones for the petals. Use straight stitch for the buds and leaves. Work a grub rose as the centre of the separate flower spray.

2 To embroider the flower spray, follow the hand towel stitch guide (bottom left), embroidering the buds and leaves in straight stitch in the same way as for the bath towel and placing a French knot in the centre of the design.

Stems and leaves

Using green cotton, work the stems in stem stitch and then embroider the leaves in straight stitch, placing one stitch on top of the other.

4 Following the bath towel stitch guide (top right), embroider a rose spray on each side of the initial. For a standard bath towel, place the rose spray about 10 cm from the letter.

❸ EMBROIDERING THE HAND TOWEL AND FLANNEL

1 The hand towel is worked in the same way as the bath towel, except that the flower sprays on either side of the initial are smaller.

3 Following the bath towel stitch guide for the separate flower spray, embroider a single flower spray in one corner of the flannel.

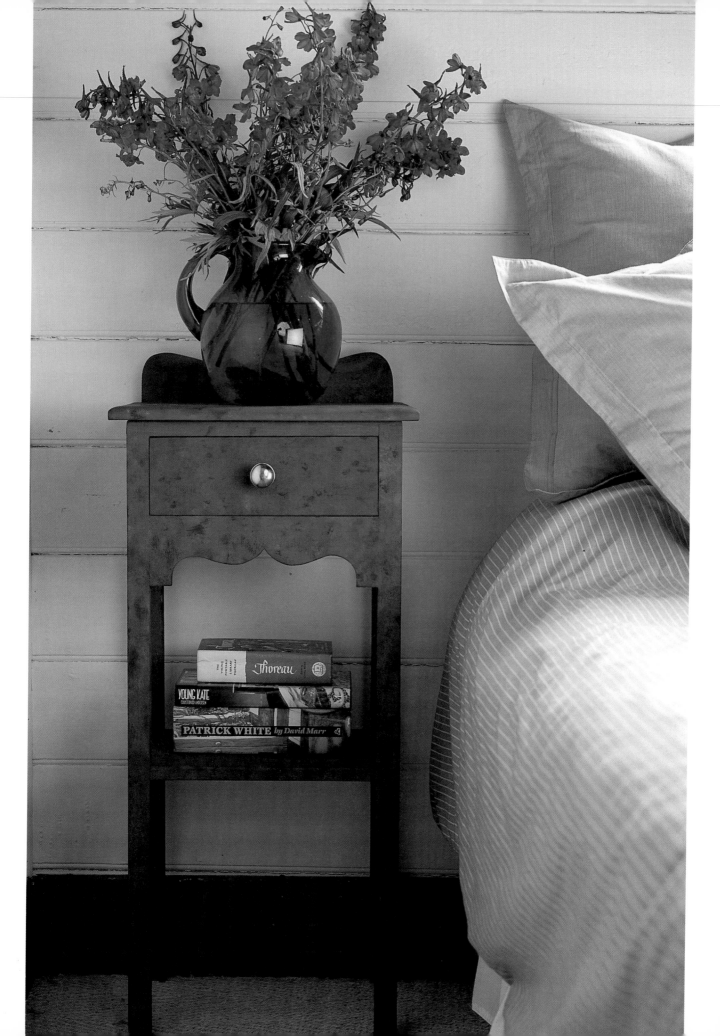

Faux finish bedside table

Applying a faux finish to new or second-hand furniture gives it a stylish look of classic opulence that is sure to appeal to a young newly married couple. This bedside table has been treated to look like granite, but many other effects are possible.

Bedside table, new or second-hand • artist's acrylic paints: black (for base colour), dark grey, mid-grey, light grey • artist's paint medium (sealer) • water-based clear varnish • paintbrush: 50 mm decorating • paint palette • small natural sponge • stripper (for old furniture) • medium-grade sandpaper • baking parchment • lint-free cloth • surgical gloves
● *Technique pages 334–5*

❶ PREPARING THE SURFACES

1 For a new piece of furniture, sand down any rough patches or edges. For a second-hand piece, use stripper to remove old paint or varnish, following the manufacturer's instructions.
2 Using the medium sandpaper, sand all surfaces to a smooth finish and wipe them with a lint-free cloth.
3 Mix the black acrylic paint with an equal quantity of sealer and cover all surfaces, using the 50 mm paintbrush. Allow to dry, then sand lightly and apply another coat of black paint. Lightly sand again and wipe over with a lint-free cloth.

❷ CREATING THE MARBLED GRANITE EFFECT

1 First, rinse the sponge in water and wring it out thoroughly to soften it.
2 Thin the dark grey paint with paint medium. Wearing surgical gloves, dip the sponge lightly into the thinned paint and squeeze out the excess. Take off most of the paint by dabbing the sponge on baking parchment until there are no large globules of paint in the holes of the sponge.
3 Pounce the sponge at random over the surface of the furniture to create a light, speckled effect. Repeat this procedure until you have covered all the surfaces, aiming for an even coverage with some black base coat showing through. If you find you have sponged too much paint on to any area, sponge lightly over the top with the base coat colour. Allow the paint to dry thoroughly.
4 Repeat step 3 using the mid-grey paint, covering less of the area than you did with the dark grey.
5 Allow to dry, and then sponge on the light grey paint in light, drifting strokes. The base coat should still show through in some areas.

❸ FINISHING

Allow the paint to dry, and then apply several coats of varnish. Let the varnish dry thoroughly between coats.

NOTE

Use a natural sponge for this project; synthetic sponges do not give the same softly mottled result. If you have not tried sponging before, experiment with the colours and techniques on an old board or heavy card before painting the furniture.

HINT

Choose your colour combinations carefully. For the best effect, select colours and tones that are close to each other on the colour spectrum. Using colours from opposite ends of the spectrum produces a garish effect.

ALTERNATIVE EFFECTS

Different marbled effects can be achieved with different colours. Study the colours in a piece of marble and then choose similar paint colours. Marble comes in many colours, including white, green, purple and black, so there is plenty of scope. A very attractive finish can be achieved by using a base coat of off-white and then sponging with pink, beige and reddish tones.

There are many other attractive ways to decorate furniture. Outlined below are two simple methods.

Crackle finish
Choose two different colours of water-based paint. Apply a base coat in the darker shade and allow to dry. Apply commercially prepared crackle medium over the base coat and leave to dry. Apply the second, lighter shade of paint in straight, even strokes. The paint will crack as it dries.

Dragging
Mix equal parts of paint, commercially prepared scumbling medium and mineral turpentine. Paint the glaze on with straight even strokes in one direction. Create a textured look by dragging a lint-free cloth in the opposite direction, then dragging a stiff paintbrush in the first direction.

Table centrepiece of dried flowers

For busy newlyweds, this floral centrepiece will ensure that there is always an attractive arrangement of flowers on the table. To keep it looking fresh and colourful do not stand the arrangement in direct sunlight and keep it dust-free by gently blowing over it with a cool hair dryer once a month.

WHAT YOU NEED

Low, round basket or vase • foliage, such as carthamus, nigella, nigella sativa, nigella orientalis or alchemilla • flat-headed flowers in tones of yellow, such as achillea filipendulina, achillea verticor, lonas inodora, marigolds and sunflowers • approximately 20 yellow roses • dry foam bricks (available from florist's suppliers) • florist's spike • adhesive clay • secateurs • craft knife
● *Technique pages 332–3*

❶ PREPARING THE FLOWERS AND FOLIAGE

1 Dry the flowers and foliage using the various methods described in the techniques section 'Flower and foliage drying'.
2 When working with the flowers and foliage you will achieve a more balanced and professional looking arrangement if you use groups of one type of flower or foliage rather than individual flowers or stems. Prepare your materials beforehand and have separate piles of each type of flower or foliage ready trimmed and within reach.

❷ ESTABLISHING THE BASE

1 Use a craft knife to cut a piece of florist's foam to fit the basket or vase. The foam should extend about 3 cm above the rim of the container.

Begin covering the foam base with a group of flowers positioned vertically in the centre, then gradually angle the rest downwards to form a semi-spherical arrangement.

2 Fix the florist's spike to the bottom of the vase with the adhesive clay. Push the foam firmly on to the spike.
3 With the knife, cut off the sharp corners of the foam, and round the top and sides to fit the container.
4 The flowers will be densely arranged and will overlap the container so that the foam will be invisible

HINTS

● *Dried roses, whether dried at home or commercially, have a tendency to close up as they dry. To achieve a 'full-blown' appearance, hold the rose over the spout of a steaming kettle until you see the petals begin to soften and go limp. Using a hairpin or a piece of florist's wire, gently open out the petals, returning the rose to the steam as necessary. Use the steam moderately or the rose may begin to drop some of its petals. This technique may also be used for peonies.*

once the arrangement is complete.

❸ ESTABLISHING THE CENTRE AND OUTLINE

1 The finished shape of the arrangement will echo the shape of the container and this is achieved by working with flowers and foliage with comparatively short stems (approximately 15 cm). This will allow you to control the outline of the arrangement more accurately than is possible with longer stems and will also make it possible to pack the flowers very closely together.
2 In the centre of the container, place a group of carthamus or other foliage to establish the maximum height. The finished arrangement should be twice the height and width of the container.
3 Working from the centre add groups of achillea, roses and foliage tightly around the central group of

in the centre cut away. Thin out sprays of multi-headed blooms.
4 Press the flowers or petals individually, using the methods described in 'Flower and foliage drying'.

❷ PREPARING THE FRAME

1 Press the fabric and remove the backing from the picture frame.
2 Cut the fabric slightly larger than the picture frame backing.
3 Coat the surface and edges of the backing board with spray adhesive and carefully press the fabric on to it, smoothing the fabric out from the centre to make sure there are no wrinkles or air bubbles.
4 Trim the excess fabric away.

❸ REASSEMBLING THE FLOWERS

Reassemble any dried flowers that were dismantled for pressing. The following steps show how to reassemble flowers commonly found in bridal bouquets. You should be able to apply similar techniques to other flowers.

Rosebuds

1 Starting with two small rose petals of similar size, fold the upper edge of each petal over and glue down using clear craft glue and a cocktail stick. Glue the two petals together, overlapping them at the centre.

2 Repeat step 1 with two larger petals. Glue these larger petals behind the two smaller petals.
3 Form the centre of the rosebud by folding a large petal in half and gluing it along the inside of the fold. Then

For orchids, reassemble the petals in a semi-circle using clear craft glue, then glue the throat over the centre of the arrangement.

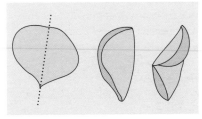

apply a little glue to the outside along the folded edge and fold the upper part to the right at an angle.

4 Glue the folded petal into the centre, behind the assembled petals, with the top protruding and then glue three more petals behind the folded central petal.

5 Finish by gluing three sepals (the green, outer covering of the flower) over the assembled rosebud.

Carnations

1 Arrange the petals in a circle on a piece of adhesive tape, working inwards until the tape is covered.

2 Apply a little clear craft glue to the back of a small petal and place it in the middle to form the centre of the carnation.

❹ RECREATING THE BOUQUET

1 Using the sketch or photograph of the bouquet as a guide, lay the outermost foliage or flowers on the fabric backing. This will form an outline for the rest of the bouquet.
2 Fill in the rest of the bouquet, placing the outer flowers and foliage first and working towards the centre, experimenting with the design. Do not lay out the central, focal-point flowers yet.
3 If the bouquet has trailing pieces, place the flowers so they face outwards, in the direction of the trail.
4 When you are happy with the arrangement, use a cocktail stick or small brush to apply a thin coat of glue to the back of the foliage and flowers and press them gently into place on the fabric.
5 Now add the focal-point flowers and glue them into place. Fill any remaining spaces with small, light foliage or flowers.
6 When the glue is thoroughly dry, turn the picture on its side and gently tap it to dislodge any loose plant material. Mount the finished arrangement in the frame.

HINT

Remember to tell the bride that the framed bouquet will retain its natural colours better if it is displayed away from direct sunlight or fluorescent lighting.

Country-style dish rack

A pine dish rack is an original gift for a couple who are setting up house. Mounted on a wall above a draining board, the rack can be used for draining dishes or for storage.

WHAT YOU NEED

Pine: 1500 mm x 240 mm x 18 mm (finished size), 2100 mm x 290 mm x 18 mm (finished size) • 3600 mm wooden dowel, 12 mm diameter • scrap timber • 30 mm nails • PVA woodworking glue • clear varnish • paintbrush • wood filler • sandpaper: coarse, medium and fine • pencil • ruler • square • handsaw • jigsaw • clamps • wood rasp • drill, 12 mm drill bit • hammer • nail punch

● *Technique pages 338–42*

❶ PREPARING THE TIMBER

1 Using a pencil, ruler and square, and following the cutting guide, measure and mark out the following pieces on the 290 mm timber: **A** one lower rear panel, 622 mm x 290 mm; **B** one upper rear panel, 622 mm x 280 mm; **C** one bottom front rail, 586 mm x 50 mm; **D** one rear support rail, 586 mm x 20 mm; **E** one top shelf, 586 mm x 210 mm.

2 Still following the cutting guide, measure and mark out the following pieces on the 240 mm timber: **F** two side panels, 430 mm x 210 mm; **G** two dividers, 270 mm x 210 mm; **H** two draining rails, 218 mm x 30 mm; **I** two draining rails, 186 mm x 30 mm.

3 Mark the curves on the rear and side panels (A, B and F). On the side panels, make sure the front edge between the curves is straight for 270 mm. Mark the front edge of the bottom front rail (C).

4 Using the handsaw, and the jigsaw for the curved edges of the rear and side panels, cut out all the pieces.

5 Cut the dowel into eight 295 mm lengths and five 186 mm lengths.

6 Clamp the dividers together with all edges aligned. Referring to 'Constructing the dish rack' (opposite), drill the dowel holes through both dividers. Remove the clamps.

7 Clamp the bottom front rail over the top shelf, with the front and side edges aligned. Drill the dowel holes as described in 'Constructing the dish rack', drilling right through the rail but only 9 mm into the shelf.

8 Remove the clamps. Smooth all cut edges with medium sandpaper.

❷ ASSEMBLING THE RACK

Refer to the box 'Constructing the dish rack' while you are putting the dish rack together.

1 Glue the lower rear panel to the upper rear panel. Clamp the panels together and leave them to dry.

2 Glue one end of each of the 186 mm dowels. With a hammer, tap the glued ends into the holes in one of the dividers until the ends of the dowels are flush. Glue the other ends of the dowels.

3 Lay the divider flat on the bench and position the second divider over the dowel ends, manoeuvring it until the drill holes are aligned with the dowels. Gently tap the second divider on to the dowels, hammering evenly until the ends of the dowels are flush with the surface of the divider.

4 Check that the dividers are square, then glue and nail them to the top shelf in the positions shown in the diagram, ensuring that the partially drilled holes are at the front of the top shelf and on its underside.

5 Glue the ends of the 295 mm dowels and tap them into the holes in the bottom front rail until they are flush.

6 Glue the other ends of the dowels. Glue and nail the bottom front rail to the bottom of the dividers, at the same time pushing the dowels into the holes in the underside of the top shelf.

7 Glue and nail the four draining rails to the bottom of the dividers, and the side panels to the partially completed shelf unit. Make sure that all sections of the completed shelf unit are square and then glue and nail it to the rear panels.

CUTTING GUIDE

Label all pieces as you work. Using a pencil, ruler and square, measure and mark the pieces as described in 'Preparing the timber'. Then carefully mark the curves on the lower rear panel (A), the upper rear panel (B) and the two side panels (F). Use a handsaw to cut out the pieces and a jigsaw to cut the curves. To drill the dowel holes in the dividers, the top shelf and the bottom front rail, refer to the box on the opposite page.

NOTES

● *Keep the distance between the dividers equal to 150 mm, the distance between the dividers and the outside edges of the top shelf and the front rail equal to 200 mm, and the inside height between the top shelf and the bottom front rail equal to 270 mm at both ends.*

● *The dish rack should be fixed firmly to the wall above the draining board, using a method suitable for the type of wall surface to which it will be fixed.*

8 Using the rasp, file the front edges of the top shelf and the bottom front rail to match the curves on the side panels. Sand these edges smooth with coarse and then medium sandpaper.

❸ FINISHING

1 Punch all nail holes and fill them with wood filler. Sand all surfaces smooth. Using coarse and then fine sandpaper, round off the outside edges of all exposed surfaces, paying particular attention to the front edges of the dividers, the side panels and the rear panel.

2 Varnish the dish rack, being careful to coat all surfaces to provide a waterproof finish that will prevent dishwater from rotting the timber. You may need several coats.

CONSTRUCTING THE DISH RACK

Drilling the dividers

Clamp the dividers together, one on top of the other, and mark five holes on the top piece in a horizontally centred row. Mark the centres of the outside holes 25 mm in from the edges and allow 40 mm between the centres of the other holes. With a 12 mm drill bit, drill right through both dividers into a piece of scrap timber.

Drilling the top shelf and the bottom front rail

Clamp the bottom front rail to the underside of the top shelf. Mark four holes in a horizontally centred row 30 mm from the front edges with the centre of the first hole 40 mm from the side edge and the centres of the other holes 40 mm apart. With a 12 mm drill bit, drill right through the bottom front rail and halfway through the top shelf. Repeat the procedure at the other end of the shelf and rail.

Draining rails (underside view)

The shorter draining rails are fixed across the dividers and the longer ones extend from the dividers to the side panels. The side panels (shown in cross-section) and the rear panel are attached when the inner parts of the dish rack have been assembled.

Side and rear panels (front view)

The side panels and the rear panel (made by joining pieces A and B) are glued and nailed to the assembled inner components of the dish rack.

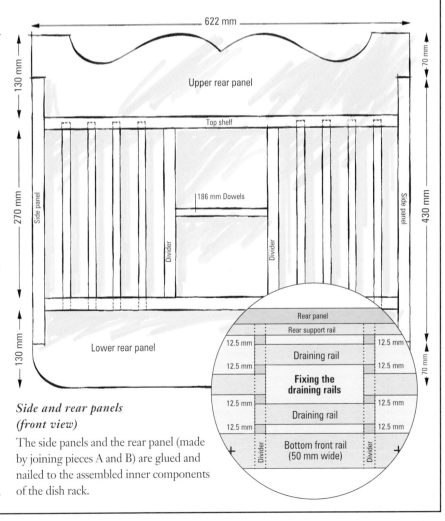

Fast food station for birds

A bird feeding table is one way of attracting birds to a new or existing garden until suitable plants are established to provide a permanent food source for the birds. It can be secured to any pole or post, as long as it is out of the reach of cats.

MARKING THE BASE

Mark the positions for the walls and handles as shown.

WHAT YOU NEED

Master pattern l63(a) • marine plywood, 1500 mm x 500 mm x 10 mm • 600 mm wooden dowel, 19 mm diameter • 2 rounded wooden drawer handles, about 100 mm long (for perches) • 25 plated or galvanised panel pins, 12 mm long • PVA woodworking glue • exterior paint • wood filler or putty • paintbrush • medium-grade sandpaper • hard pencil (or empty ballpoint pen) • square • handsaw or power saw • jigsaw or coping saw • drill, 4 mm and 19 mm drill bits • scrap timber • clamp • screwdriver • nail punch • ruler • tracing paper • transfer paper • pencil

● *Technique pages 338–42, 343–4*

① PREPARING THE TIMBER

1 Tie one end of the string around the pencil. Anchor the other end to the plywood with a panel pin so that the length of the string from pin to pencil point (when pulled taut) is 230 mm. Holding the string taut, draw a circle on the plywood. Remove the pin and mark the centre point clearly. The diameter of the circle you have just drawn (which will form the base of the feeder) should be 460 mm.

2 Using tracing paper and a pencil, trace a working pattern of the side panels from the master pattern. Using transfer paper and a hard pencil, transfer the pattern twice on to the plywood. Neaten the lines with pencil and ruler.

3 With a ruler, pencil and square, mark out two rectangles on the plywood, one 310 mm x 200 mm, and one 310 mm x 190 mm. These will form the roof panels.

4 Using a handsaw, power saw or jigsaw, cut around the outlines of all pattern pieces. Within the large circular shapes to be cut from the side panels, drill an access hole wider than the blade of the jigsaw. Place the blade of the jigsaw in the access hole and carefully cut out the circular shapes.

5 Clamp the side panels together with the edges aligned. Into scrap timber, drill a 19 mm hole through both pieces in the position marked, making the hole big enough so that only light pressure is required to insert the dowel. Remove the clamp.

6 Using the pencil and ruler, carefully draw a diameter line through the centre of the circular base. Using the square for accuracy, draw another diameter line at right angles to the first. The circle is now divided into four equal segments. Mark the diameter lines on the edges of the plywood, turn the base over and rule the diameter lines on the underside, making sure lines on both sides are aligned.

7 Measure and mark the positions of the walls on both the upper and lower surfaces of the base, as shown in 'Marking the base' in the box above.

CUTTING GUIDE

Using string and a pencil, draw a circle 460 mm in diameter for the base. Trace the side panels from the master pattern, and then measure and mark out a left roof panel measuring 310 mm x 200 mm and a right roof panel measuring 310 mm x 190 mm. Cut the pieces with a handsaw or power saw and jigsaw or coping saw.

8 Mark the position of the handles on one surface of the base only. Place the handles on the base and mark the position of the screws. Using the 4 mm drill bit (or a bit to match the diameter of the fixing screws), drill holes for the metal thread screws right through the base into scrap timber.
9 Round the ends of the dowel with sandpaper. Lightly sand the edges of all other pieces.

② ASSEMBLING THE FEEDER

1 Apply glue to the bottom edges of the walls. Holding them steady in the positions marked on the top surface of the base, nail them in place from the underside, using the previously drawn lines as a guide. Glue and nail the roof panels together, making sure that the

long edge of the smaller piece is butted against the long side of the larger one, as shown in the diagram.

2 Centre the roof on the walls so that the overlapping eaves are equal at both sides, and the back and front of the roof protrude equally over the

back and front walls. Glue and nail the roof into place.
3 Tap the dowel gently through both holes until the excess protrudes evenly at both ends. Squeeze glue around the holes to secure the dowel in place. Wipe off any excess glue.

③ FINISHING

1 Punch the nails with the nail punch and then fill all nail holes with putty.
2 Sand all surfaces until they are smooth and paint or stain inside and out. Allow the paint to dry.
3 From the underside, screw the perching handles into position on the upper surface of the base through the pre-drilled holes, as shown in the box 'Marking the base'. Use the screws supplied with the handles.

Wedding day sampler

Commemorate this special day in the bride and groom's lives with a traditional cross-stitch sampler; it will be a gift for the couple to treasure throughout the years to come.

Master patterns J71(a–b) •
47 cm x 51 cm 14 gauge Aida cloth
• stranded cotton: Anchor colours
1 (white), 24 (pink), 38 (dark pink),
214 (light green), 216 (dark green),
343 (light blue), 891 (gold), 921
(dark blue) • coloured tacking
thread and needle • needle: size
24 tapestry • picture frame, with
an inside measurement of 41 cm x
36.5 cm • A2 white backing board •
A2 mounting board • linen carpet
thread or fine, strong string (for
mounting) • craft knife • steel rule •
tracing paper • scissors • pencil •
tape measure • spray glue
● *Technique pages 309, 343–4*

❶ MAKING THE SAMPLER
1 Iron the cloth and hand oversew
or machine zigzag the raw edges.

2 Fold the cloth in half and then in
quarters, and mark the vertical and
horizontal centre lines with tacking.
3 Following the stitch and colour
guide in the master pattern, first
embroider the border design. This
then becomes a point of reference
for the remainder of the design.
4 Complete the design, working
one small area at a time and following
the stitch and colour guide carefully.

**❷ PERSONALISING
THE SAMPLER**
1 On tracing paper, rule a straight
line to act as a guide. Then, using the
master pattern piece for cross-stitch
letters, trace the letters of the bride
and groom's names and the date of
their marriage. Leave two empty
stitches between letters and four
between words. You will probably
be able to fit only about 12 characters
across the sampler, so abbreviate the
names to initials if necessary and use
an ampersand (&). Mark the mid-
point of the tracings.
2 Match the mid-point of the name
to the centre point of the sampler in
the space provided at the top of the
sampler. Embroider the letters using

colours of your choice, starting from the middle and working out.

3 Repeat step 2 for the date, embroidering in the space provided at the bottom of the sampler.

③ FRAMING THE SAMPLER

1 Ensure that the backing board and the mounting board both fit snugly into the back of the frame. If you need to trim them to the correct size, do so by placing the board on an appropriate cutting surface and using the craft knife and a steel rule.

32 mm

27 mm

2 Using the pencil and ruler, mark a rectangle measuring 32 cm x 27 cm on the back of the mounting board. Take care to make the facing margins equal. Using the craft knife and the steel rule, cut along the pencil lines to create a hole in the middle of the mounting board.

3 Press the sampler on the wrong side through a damp cloth, being very careful not to stretch the fabric or the stitching.

4 Lay the sampler right side up on the backing board, ensuring that it is centred on the board.

5 Fold one edge of the canvas back and secure it to the edge of the board with pins, and then do the same with

the opposite edge. Place the cut mounting board over the sampler to check that you have positioned the sampler correctly.

6 Turn the work over and, using linen carpet thread, sew the folded-over edges of canvas together with large herringbone stitches. With each stitch, go back to the beginning and tighten all the stitches to stretch the canvas firmly over the board.

7 Secure the thread at the start and take out the pins. Once again, tighten each stitch in succession. When the canvas is stretched tight, tie off the thread firmly.

8 Stretch the canvas in the other direction by securing and sewing the other two edges in the same way. Fold the corners flat – do not mitre them.

Mark the centre points on your tracings of the text and match them up with the vertical centre lines on the canvas, and then work the lines of text from the centre towards the borders. Leave two empty stitches between letters and four empty stitches between words.

Check constantly that the stitches are progressively tightened and that the canvas is evenly stretched.

9 Place the mount over the sampler and insert mount and sampler into the frame. Close the back according to the manufacturer's instructions.

CROSS-STITCH TIPS

- *Match each colour with its symbol on the stitch and colour guide and fix a small piece of thread against each symbol on the guide before you begin work.*
- *Use an embroidery hoop to keep the tension even.*
- *Count outwards from the centre to the border and begin the embroidery by stitching the border design. Use the border as a reference to locate other stitches. Stitch in any other lines of reference.*
- *Divide the design into small areas and complete one area before moving on to the next.*
- *Always use two strands of embroidery cotton.*
- *Work each cross-stitch so that the top stitch lies in the same direction throughout your work.*
- *Never use knots to finish off a colour. Always fasten your work off by passing the end of the thread under several stitches on the reverse side of the work.*

Broderie anglaise nightshirt

An heirloom nightshirt with pin-tucked inserts is a lovely contribution to a bride's trousseau. The finished nightshirt is 98 cm long and has three-quarter length sleeves.

WHAT YOU NEED

Master pattern l60(a–f) • 2.3 m Swiss batiste, 115 cm wide • 10 m fabric insertion lace, 33 mm wide • 10 m fabric insertion lace with entredeux, 18 mm wide • 10.5 m fabric edging lace, 30 mm wide • 15 cm lightweight iron-on woven interfacing, 115 cm wide • 7 decorative buttons, 10 mm diameter • fine machine thread • fine sewing needle • tracing paper • pencil • lace pins • scissors • tape measure • sewing machine, with fine needle, double needle and pin-tucking foot
● *Technique pages 292–301, 303–4, 343–4*

1 CUTTING OUT THE FABRIC

1 Using the tracing paper and pencil, trace the pattern pieces, including all markings, and cut them out.
2 Following the cutting guide, fold the Swiss batiste in half lengthwise and cut the back skirt and the front bands. Open out the batiste and cut the right sleeve, the left front skirt and the neck bias strips. Then cut a rectangular piece 115 cm x 80 cm, which will be machine pin-tucked before you cut a right front skirt, a left front yoke and a left sleeve from it.
3 Cut out two front bands from the iron-on woven interfacing.

2 MAKING THE LACE FABRIC

1 Cut 23 pieces 40 cm long from both the insertion lace and the insertion lace with entredeux. Use method 2 to join the laces alternately, forming a piece measuring 112 cm x 40 cm. Trim away the excess fabric close to the zigzag stitching.

2 Fold the lace fabric along the centre of one strip of insertion lace to form a double layer the width of the back yoke pattern piece, ensuring that the laces are symmetrical on either side of the fold. Lay the centre back of the back yoke pattern piece along the fold. Place the right yoke pattern piece on the remaining lace fabric with the grain parallel to a lace join.
3 Make sure that the laces will match at the shoulder seams, and then cut out the pieces.

3 PIN-TUCKING

1 Following the settings for your sewing machine, pin-tuck the 115 cm x 80 cm rectangle of batiste along the lengthwise grain of the fabric.
2 Lay the pattern pieces for the left sleeve, the left front yoke and the right front skirt on the right side of the pin-tucked fabric, as shown in the cutting guide, and cut out.

4 ASSEMBLING THE FRONT AND BACK

1 Staystitch the necklines of all the yoke pieces along the seamlines. With right sides together, and matching the insertion laces, join the shoulder seams, using method 1.
2 Cut two 55 cm lengths of edging lace for the front yokes and one 110 cm length for the back yoke.
3 Machine a row of gathering stitches on either side of the seamline on each piece (the seam allowance is 5 mm). Gather up the lace.
4 With the right sides together, machine staystitch the edging lace to the front and back yokes, adjusting

CUTTING GUIDES

Fold the batiste lengthwise to cut the back skirt and the front bands, and then open it out to cut the left front skirt, the right sleeve and the bias strips for the neck. Trim a straight edge on the remaining fabric and machine pin-tuck it along the lengthwise grain. From this pin-tucked fabric, cut out the right front skirt, the left front yoke and the left sleeve.

The back yoke and the right front yoke will be cut from the completed lace fabric.

NOTES

- *Except for the edging lace, the seam allowances for this garment are 1 cm. When you are attaching the edging lace, leave a 5 mm seam allowance on the lace and a 1 cm seam allowance on the fabric to which you are stitching it.*
- *Methods 1 and 2 are the heirloom sewing techniques that you will need to make the nightshirt. For these methods, refer to the box 'Heirloom sewing techniques' on page 14 of 'Classic christening gown'.*

the gathers evenly and matching the 5 mm seam line on the lace to the 1 cm seam line on the yokes.

5 With right sides together, machine stitch the skirts to the yokes, sandwiching the edging lace. Trim the seams, zigzag to neaten, and press the turnings towards the yokes.

6 Cut a 140 cm length of edging lace. Repeat steps 3 and 4 to staystitch the lace to the right front opening of the nightshirt.

7 Iron the interfacings to the wrong sides of two of the front bands. With right sides together and raw edges aligned, machine stitch the interfaced bands to the front openings, sandwiching the edging lace along the right front opening. Press the turnings towards the bands.

❺ ATTACHING THE EDGING LACE

1 Cut 310 cm of edging lace and slipstitch one end to neaten. Gather the lace as before. With right sides together, place the neatened end of the lace on the seam joining the left front band and the neckline. Adjusting the gathers evenly, machine staystitch the lace to the nightshirt in a continuous seam around the neckline, down the right front band and round the right front hemline to the dot.
2 Cut 90 cm of edging lace for the left front hemline and slipstitch one end to neaten. Gather the lace as before. With right sides together and the neatened end aligned with the seamline on the outside long edge of the left front band, machine staystitch the lace around the left front hem to the dot, adjusting the gathers evenly.
3 Cut 140 cm of edging lace. Gather the lace as before, and machine staystitch it around the back hemline between the dots.

❻ ATTACHING THE FACINGS AND NECK BINDING

1 On the remaining two front band pieces, press a 1 cm seam allowance along one long edge. These pieces are the facings for the front bands.

2 With right sides together, lay the band facings along the front bands, sandwiching the edging lace along the right front opening. Starting from the folded seam allowance on the facing at the neckline, machine stitch the facings to the band ends and the front

---

PIN-TUCKING WITH A SEWING MACHINE

Machine pin-tucks are made using a pin-tucking foot and a double machine needle.

Double machine needles are threaded with two threads from the top and are available in various spacings; to make the pin-tucked fabric for the nightgown, use a fine, narrow-spaced double needle. Tucks must be stitched on the straight grain, otherwise they will twist.

The nightgown illustrated is pin-tucked in groups of one tuck, three tucks and five tucks. Try various effects on scraps of batiste to find one that you like.

---

openings. On the left front, take care not to catch the neatened ends of the edging lace at the neck and hem.
3 Join the bias strips for the neck edge, press the seams open and then press the strips in half lengthwise.
4 Trim the seam allowance of the neckline to 5 mm. With all raw edges aligned and right sides together, machine stitch the bias strip to the neckline, sandwiching the edging lace and extending the bias strip slightly into the front bands. Clip the neckline and the corners of the bands.

---

5 Turn the folded edge of the bias strip over to the wrong side and machine stitch it to the nightshirt close to the neckline. Turn the band facings over to the inside of the nightshirt and press. Slipstitch the folded edges of the facings to the seams joining the front bands to the nightshirt.
6 Trim the front and back hem edges to 5 mm and zigzag to neaten.

❼ SEWING THE SLEEVES AND SIDE SEAMS

1 Cut two 30 cm lengths of the 18 mm wide insertion lace with entredeux and two 45 cm lengths of edging lace. Machine two rows of gathering stitches around the lower edges of the sleeves and along the two pieces of edging lace. Gather up.

2 Join the insertion lace to the lower edge of the sleeves and the edging lace to the insertion lace, adjusting the gathers evenly. Roll and whip the seams to neaten (method 1).
3 With right sides together, machine stitch the sleeves into the armholes, matching notches and dots and easing the fabric to fit. Trim seams and zigzag to neaten.
4 With right sides together, machine stitch the sleeve and side seams from wrist edge to hem, taking care to match the sleeve lace trims, the underarm seams and the lace at the hems. Trim seams and zigzag to neaten.

❽ FINISHING

1 Machine stitch seven vertical buttonholes in the right front band in the positions marked.
2 Sew the buttons to the left front band along the centre front line, in positions to correspond with the buttonholes.

PARENTS

Parents usually have everything they need, so it can be difficult to select gifts for them. The perfect solution is something you have made yourself that they can proudly display or use.

Space-saving kitchen tea-towel airer

This is a miniature version of the large drying rack found hanging over many a Victorian kitchen range. It is raised and lowered by a simple pulley system. The tea-towel airer can also be used for drying bunches of herbs or flowers.

WHAT YOU NEED

Master pattern E37(a) • timber, (e.g. pine), 1000 mm x 100 mm x 25 mm • 2400–4000 mm dowel (depending on length of airer), 19 mm diameter • 4 brass eyelet screws, 15 mm diameter • brass cup hooks: 4 of 15 mm diameter, 2 of 20 mm diameter with long threads • 5 m light sash cord • 1 single and 1 double awning pulley, to match diameter of sash cord • 1 rope catch with wall mounting screws • strong thread • varnish • paintbrush • fine-grade sandpaper • PVA glue • tracing paper • transfer paper • pencil • scrap timber • fretsaw or coping saw • clamp • drill, 19 mm drill bit

● *Technique pages 338–42, 343–4*

❶ PREPARING THE TIMBER

1 Trace and transfer the pattern for the end piece from the master pattern twice on to the timber, taking care to transfer all markings.

2 Cut out the two end pieces using the fretsaw or coping saw. Clamp the pieces together firmly and sand all the edges completely smooth.
3 Cut the dowel into four pieces of uniform length.

4 Keeping the end pieces clamped together, drill four 19 mm holes in the positions marked on the master pattern. Drill right through both end pieces into a piece of scrap timber.
5 Sand all the dowels. If necessary, sand the ends down to fit snugly into the holes in the end pieces.

❷ CONSTRUCTING THE AIRER

1 Apply PVA glue to the insides of the dowel holes.

2 Insert one end of a dowel into the first hole of one end piece. With a block of scrap timber, tap the end piece gently until the end of the dowel is flush with the outer face of the end piece. Insert the other three dowels in the same way.
3 Insert the other ends of the dowels into the second end piece and tap into place until the dowel ends are flush.
4 Sand back any protruding dowel.
5 Apply a coat of varnish to the airer. Allow to dry. Sand gently, and apply a second coat. Leave to dry thoroughly.

6 Screw two eyelet screws and two 15 mm cup hooks into each end piece.

❸ SETTING THE SASH CORDS

1 Cut the sash cord into two pieces of equal length.
2 Thread one end of one piece of cord through the two eyelet hooks on one end of the airer. Fashion a triangle by joining the rope to itself

ANTIQUE LINEN AIRER

Make this charming variation of the tea towel airer for someone who has a taste for old-style elegance.

As well as the basic requirements, you will need walnut wood stain, golden shellac and methylated spirits. Instead of the 15 mm cup hooks, use four small drawer handles made of ceramic, brass or pewter-look metal.

1 When you have assembled the airer, sand it smooth and remove dust and wood particles with a tack cloth.
2 Use a rag to apply walnut stain to the airer, following the manufacturer's instructions. Let the stain soak more deeply into the end pieces and

the ends of the dowels than into the parts where the linen will hang. Apply stain until you achieve the effect you want.
3 Dissolve the shellac in methylated spirits following the manufacturer's instructions, and apply one or two coats to the airer using a good-quality paintbrush. Allow to dry.
4 Fit the drawer handles to the end pieces in place of the cup hooks.
5 To give the airer that authentic 'antique' look, use off-white cord and a wooden rope catch finished in the same way as the airer. Bind the cord with gold picture wire.

and binding the join tightly with strong thread. Apply PVA glue to the binding thread to strengthen the join.

3 Repeat step 2 with the other piece of cord and the other end of the airer.

4 Thread one piece of cord through the single pulley, then through the double pulley. Thread the other piece through the double pulley only.

5 Bind the ends of the cords with strong thread and strengthen the binding with PVA glue.

❹ INSTALLING THE AIRER

1 Find a cross-beam or joist in the ceiling that will support the weight of the airer. Drill one tap hole fairly close to the wall end of the beam or

joist. Drill another tap hole further along the beam. The holes should be the length of the airer apart.

2 Screw the two 20 mm cup hooks tightly into the tap holes and test that they will bear the weight of the airer. Hook the pulleys on to the cup hooks.

3 Screw the rope catch to the near wall about a metre below the ceiling.

NOTE

If it is not possible for you to install this gift yourself, copy out the installation instructions and include them with the airer, with the 20 mm cup hooks, the rope catch and the screws.

Rosebud nightgown

This old-time nightgown, made from fine woven wool fabric and Swiss batiste using heirloom sewing techniques, would be the perfect gift for your mother or grandmother. The nightgown is designed to fit sizes 12 to 14.

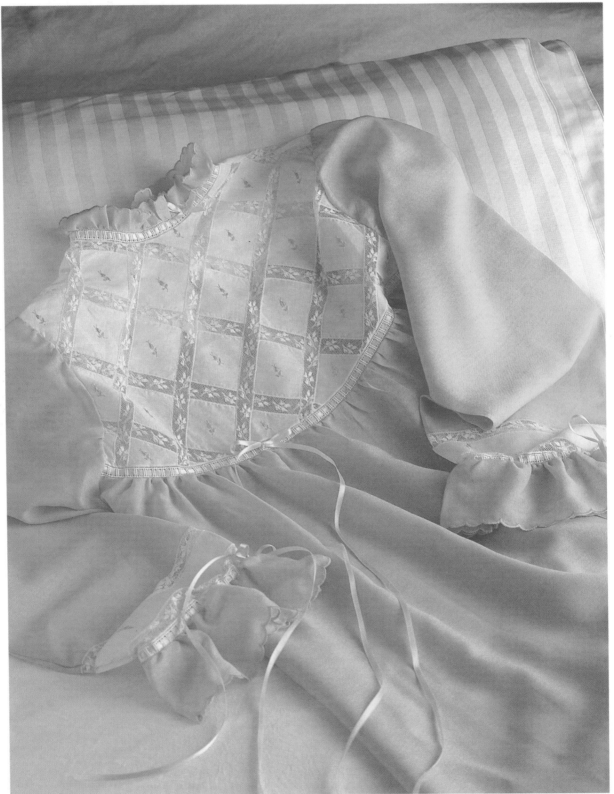

WHAT YOU NEED

Master pattern **F42(a–e)** • 2.5 m
wool challis, 150 cm wide • 1 m
Swiss batiste, 115 cm wide • 17.5 m
woven insertion lace, 15 mm wide •
3.8 m beading with entredeux,
12 mm wide • 8 m satin ribbon,
5 mm wide • 3 flat buttons, 10 mm
diameter • sewing threads: white,
a colour to match the wool challis •
stranded embroidery thread, in a
colour to match the wool challis •
needles: general sewing, fine
machine, fine embroidery • tracing
paper • pencil • lace pins • scissors •
tape measure • sewing machine
● *Technique pages 292–301, 303–4,
307–12, 343–4*

❶ CUTTING OUT THE FABRICS
1 Trace a working pattern from the
master pattern, using a pencil and
tracing paper and making sure you
include all markings. Cut out the
traced pattern pieces.
2 Following the cutting guide for the
wool challis, cut out all the pattern
pieces except the yoke and the back
facing. Still following the wool challis
cutting guide, cut two skirt hem frills
measuring 10 cm x 140 cm, two wrist

frills measuring 10 cm x 70 cm, and
a neck frill measuring 6 cm x 80 cm.
3 Following the cutting guide for
the batiste, cut a straight grain square
measuring 63 cm x 63 cm. Pull a
thread along all edges to ensure that
the square is on the straight grain.
(This square will be used to make
the heirloom fabric for the yoke.)
4 Still following the batiste cutting
guide, use the master pattern piece to
cut the back facings, and then cut two
skirt hem inserts measuring 11 cm x
90 cm and two wrist inserts measuring
6 cm x 45 cm.

❷ MAKING THE YOKE
1 On the square of Swiss batiste, pull
threads at 7 cm intervals across the
width of the square (eight threads in

HINT
*To stabilise the fabric when
you are machining scallops, place
strips of tissue paper between the
fabric and the feed dog and
stitch through both fabric and
tissue paper. After machining,
tear away the tissue paper and
trim off the excess fabric.*

all). Turn the square through 90°
and pull eight more threads, at 7 cm
intervals, at right angles to the first
eight pulled threads.
2 Following the method for mock
lace insertion (page 204), sew insertion lace along all the pulled threads
for the full width of the square.

3 Fold the yoke square diagonally in
half and press lightly to mark the true
bias. Place the centre front line of the
yoke pattern on the bias crease. Move
the pattern along the diagonal until
the lace inserts are identical on either
side of the centre front and do not run
directly along the centre back, the
centre back seamline or the stitching
lines of the back neck.

CUTTING GUIDE
Wool challis: Cut the front and back
skirts in one piece along the fold, and
then cut the sleeves separately. Open
out the remaining fabric and cut out
the hem, neck and wrist frills.

Swiss batiste: Cut all the pieces
from a single layer. Cut the yoke
square first, ensuring that it is cut
on the straight grain of the fabric by
pulling threads along all edges. The

insertion lace will be sewn into place
on this piece before the yolk is cut
from it. From the Swiss batiste, also
cut the back facing, two skirt hem
inserts and two wrist inserts.

4 Pin and cut out the yoke. Machine staystitch around the neckline, the armholes and the yoke curves to prevent stretching.

5 Cut 50 cm of beading with entredeux. Do not trim the fabric from the edges. With right sides together and raw edges aligned, machine stitch the entredeux to the front yoke curve, with a seam allowance the width of the fabric edging of the entredeux. To neaten the edge, machine a fine zigzag over the straight stitching and trim close to the zigzag.

6 Press the back facings in half lengthwise with wrong sides together. Lay the raw edges along the centre backs of the yoke, on the right side of the fabric, and machine stitch along the seam lines through all layers. Trim and zigzag or overlock the seams and press the facings to the wrong side of the yoke along the seamlines. Slipstitch the facings to the wrong side of the yoke.

7 Overlap the left back yoke over the right back yoke, making sure the centre back lines are aligned. Staystitch along the seamline at the yoke curve to hold it in place.

❸ SEWING THE YOKE TO THE SKIRTS

1 Machine two rows of gathering stitches along the upper edges of the front and back skirts.

2 With right sides together and raw edges aligned, match the armhole edges and centre backs of the yoke and the back skirt. Pull up the gathering threads, adjust them evenly and machine stitch the seam. Neaten the raw edges with a fine zigzag stitch and trim.

3 With right sides together and raw edges aligned, match the armholes

and centre fronts of the yoke and the front skirt. Pull up the gathering threads, adjust them evenly and machine stitch the seam, using a seam allowance the width of the entredeux fabric edge. Neaten the edges with a fine zigzag and trim.

4 Cut two 115 cm lengths of ribbon and thread them through the beading around the front yoke, so that the long ends emerge at the centre front. Machine staystitch the ends of the ribbons at the armholes. Roll up the long ends and tie them loosely with thread to keep them out of the way.

5 Join one side seam only. Neaten the seam with a fine zigzag stitch, and then trim.

❹ ATTACHING THE SKIRT AND SLEEVE TRIMS

MAKING THE HEIRLOOM FABRIC

Methods 2, 3 and 4 are the heirloom sewing techniques that you need to make the rosebud nightgown. For these methods, refer to the box 'Heirloom sewing techniques' on page 14 of 'Classic christening gown'. To make the rosebud nightgown, you will also need the method for mock lace insertion.

Mock lace insertion: Pull threads, or use a pencil, to mark the centre of the lace placement lines. With the wrong side of the lace facing the right side of the fabric,

centre the lace over the marked lines. Machine the lace headings to the fabric on either side. Using small sharp scissors and working from the wrong side, cut the fabric only along the marked lines. Press the cut edges back to expose the back of the lace. From the right side, zigzag over the lace headings. Trim the excess fabric from the wrong side close to the zigzag stitching.

To make laces easier to handle when machine stitching, spray them with a commercial fabric stiffener.

1 Join the batiste skirt hem inserts together along one short end. Neaten the seam with a fine zigzag and trim. Fold the joined strip in half lengthwise and press, and then unfold the strip. Centre the insertion lace along the fold and sew it to the batiste, using the method for mock lace insertion.
2 Lay a row of insertion lace along each long edge of the skirt hem insert, matching the centre of the lace with the raw edge of the batiste. Stitch the lace to the batiste, using the method for mock lace insertion.

3 Cut 180 cm of beading with entredeux and trim the fabric mounting from one edge. Sew the trimmed edge of the beading to the insertion lace along one edge of the Swiss batiste, using method 3.
4 Match the centre of the insertion lace along the other edge of the batiste strip with the lower edge of the skirt. Join the lace and the fabric, using the method for mock lace insertion.
5 Repeat steps 2 to 4 to make and attach the wrist trims.

❺ MAKING THE FRILLS

1 Machine stitch the wool challis skirt hem frills together at one short end and neaten the seam.
2 Using thread to match the wool challis, and following your machine settings for making scalloped edges, machine scallop along one long edge of the frill, being careful to form a closed satin stitch.
3 Roll, whip and gather the raw edge of the frill, using method 4.
4 Trim the fabric from the lower edge of the entredeux on the skirt and use method 2 to attach the frill to the entredeux, adjusting the gathers evenly as you work.
5 Repeat steps 2 to 4 to make and attach the wrist frills.

6 Repeat steps 2 and 3 to make the neck frill, machining the scallops in a curve around both corners. Put the neck frill aside to be attached later.

❻ ASSEMBLING THE NIGHTGOWN

1 Join the second side seam, taking care to match up the skirt trim and frill. Neaten the seam with a fine zigzag and trim.
2 Join and neaten the sleeve underarm seams in the same way as the side seam, again taking care to match up the trims and frills.
3 Sew two rows of gathering stitches in the space between the dots on the heads of the sleeves. With right sides together and raw edges aligned, set the sleeves into the armholes, matching the dots, notches and seams. Pull up the gathering stitches, adjust the gathers evenly, and join and neaten the sleeve seams.
4 With right sides together and leaving the entredeux untrimmed, align the raw edges of the entredeux and the neckline of the nightgown. Machine stitch the entredeux to the neckline, with a seam allowance the width of the fabric edging of the entredeux. Neaten the seam with a fine zigzag stitch and trim.
5 To neaten the ends of the entredeux, fold a small hem to the wrong

side, aligning the beading so that the ribbon can be threaded through.
6 Adjust the gathers of the neck frill evenly and trim the fabric from the other edge of the entredeux. Join the frill to the entredeux, using method 2.

❼ FINISHING

1 Machine stitch three horizontal buttonholes on the left back yoke in the positions marked on the pattern. Sew three buttons to the right back yoke in the corresponding positions.
2 Cut 220 cm of ribbon. Starting at the centre front of the skirt, thread the ribbon through the beading in the skirt trim and tie in a bow.
3 Repeat step 2 for each sleeve, using 110 cm of ribbon and starting opposite the underarm seams.
4 Cut a 50 cm length of ribbon and thread it through the beading at the neckline, trimming the ends and securing them with slipstitch. Make a small bow from the remaining ribbon and handstitch it to the centre front of the neckline.
5 Using a single strand of embroidery cotton, work the rosebud design in the centre of each batiste panel of the yoke. Repeat the design at regular intervals on the skirt and sleeve trims.
6 Undo the rolled long ribbons at the centre front of the yoke and tie a bow.

With a single strand of embroidery cotton, work the rosebuds in satin stitch or bullion stitch. Use chain stitch to embroider the leaves and stem stitch for the stems.

Connoisseur's wine rack

For a parent who is a wine buff, this sturdy wine rack would be the ideal gift. Made of solid pine, it can hold up to 18 full-sized bottles.

Master pattern **F40(a–b)** • timber (e.g. pine): 2 lengths, 600 mm **x** 260 mm **x** 18 mm (for the end panels); 6 lengths, 580 mm **x** 65 mm **x** 18 mm (for the racks) • 24 countersunk wood screws, 38 mm, 8 gauge • stain, paint or clear varnish • 2 paintbrushes • tracing paper • transfer paper • hard pencil (or empty ballpoint pen) • pencil • jigsaw or coping saw • coarse and medium sandpaper • sanding block • ruler • drill and 2.5 mm, 4 mm and countersink drill bits • screwdriver
● *Technique pages 338–42, 343–4*

① PREPARING THE TIMBER

1 Using tracing paper and a pencil, trace the patterns of the scallop-edged racks and the heart-shaped cut-out from the master pattern.

2 Using transfer paper and hard pencil, transfer the scallop shape on to the six racks. Then transfer the heart shapes to the end panels, placing them in the positions shown.
3 Using the jigsaw, cut out the scalloped edges.
4 Within the heart shape to be cut out, drill an access hole greater than the width of the jigsaw blade. Place the blade of the jigsaw in this hole and carefully cut out the heart shape.

5 Wrap coarse sandpaper around the sanding block and sand the edges of the end panels so that the square outside edges are slightly bevelled.
6 Sand all surfaces completely smooth with medium sandpaper.

② ASSEMBLING THE WINE RACK

1 Following the dimensions shown, mark the positions of the racks on the end panels, noting that the racks are spaced 200 mm apart vertically and the top of the upper rack is positioned 5 mm from the top edge of the end panel. The outer faces of all racks should be flush with the vertical edges of the end panels.
2 Mark the positions of the screws on both the end panels and the ends of the racks. The centre of each screw should be 10 mm from the outer edge and 10 mm from the top and bottom edges of each rack.
3 Using the 2.5 mm drill bit, drill holes for the screws right through the end panels and about 1.5 cm into the ends of the racks. Use a vice or a clamping system to help you to hold the panels and racks in position each time you drill through.
4 Using the 4 mm drill bit, redrill all the holes in the two end panels.
5 With the countersink bit, countersink the outside face of each hole in the two end panels.
6 Screw the racks to one end panel. Place the other end panel in position and screw it to the racks.

③ FINISHING

1 Lightly sand all surfaces with the medium sandpaper.
2 Apply stain, clear varnish or paint to all the surfaces.

Strawberry garden chair

Personalise a director's chair for a parent who enjoys relaxing in the garden. The design is attractive, yet easy to paint – it would take very little time to decorate a pair.

WHAT YOU NEED

Master pattern **F41(a–b)** • plain canvas director's chair • Jo Sonja's artist's colours: green oxide, teal green, naphthol red light, burgundy, black, titanium white, Turner's yellow • textile medium • paintbrushes: no. 5 round, no. 00 liner • tracing paper • pencil • dressmaker's carbon • hard pencil
● *Technique pages 334–5, 343–4*

❶ TRANSFERRING THE DESIGN

1 Mark the centre of the back rest. Using tracing paper and pencil, trace the designs from the master pattern.
2 Using dressmaker's carbon and a hard pencil, transfer the single strawberry design on to the front left-hand corner of the seat and the large design on to the back rest, matching centres.

❷ PAINTING THE DESIGN
Leaves

1 Using the round brush, paint all the large leaves with green oxide.

HINT
For a very special gift – perhaps for a wedding anniversary – why not team a pair of these chairs with the Iris garden apron (pages 210–11)?

Apply only one coat, allowing the plain canvas background to show through.
2 Using teal green, dry-brush a dark area on the backs of the large leaves, extending down the centre vein.

Strawberries

1 Paint the strawberries in naphthol red light, using as many coats as necessary to completely cover the fabric. Allow to dry.
2 Dry-brush a little burgundy on to the underside of each strawberry. Blend the shading across the fruit so that some of the base colour shows through.
3 Using Turner's yellow, dry-brush some highlights on to the upper side of each strawberry.
4 Load the liner brush with black and paint the seeds, using tiny comma strokes spaced slightly wider apart at the bulge of the fruit than at the tip.
5 Reverting to the round brush, dry-brush titanium white highlights in the centre of the yellow highlights and over some of the seeds.

Painting guide
The larger design (shown below) goes on the back rest, and the complementary smaller version (above right) is for the front left-hand seat corner of the seat.

Flowers

1 Paint the flowers with titanium white, using two joined comma strokes for each flower petal. Using the end of the paintbrush handle, dot the centres of the flowers with Turner's yellow.
2 Load the liner brush with teal green and paint the sepals on the stem ends of the strawberries. With the same paint and brush, outline each leaf, paint in the tendrils, and then loosely outline the blossoms.

❸ FINISHING

1 Allow the paint to dry thoroughly.
2 Fix the painting on the canvas by following the manufacturer's instructions.

Breakfast tea cosy

Crochet a tea cosy to keep a parent's breakfast and mid-morning tea piping hot.

WHAT YOU NEED

2 balls Patons Diploma Gold DK cream wool • crochet hook: 5.00 mm (no. 6) • stranded embroidery cotton: gold, leaf green • needles: size 10 crewel, size 6 calyx-eye • 1 button
The tea cosy fits a 6-cup teapot.
● *Technique pages 320–2, 327*

CHECKING THE TENSION

For the best results, check your tension before you begin crocheting the tea cosy, so that the measurements of the finished article will be as close as possible to the size specified. You should have 18 double crochets and 22 rows to a 10 cm square over double crochet fabric, using a 5.00 mm crochet hook and 8 ply wool. If you have fewer stitches, use a smaller hook; if you have more stitches, use a larger hook. To achieve the effect illustrated, the tea cosy is designed to be worked on a bigger hook and at a looser tension than is usually recommended in crochet patterns.

❶ WORKING THE CROCHET

Make two of these pieces.
Make 41 ch.
1st row: Miss 1 ch, 1 dc in each ch to end...40 dc.
2nd row: 1 ch, 1 dc in each dc to end. Rep 2nd row 26 times.

Shaping the top
29th row: 1 ch, 1 dc in next dc, ★ 'Dec', 1 dc in each of next 2 dc, rep from ★ to last 3 dc, 'Dec', 1 dc in last dc...30 sts.
Work 2 rows in patt.
32nd row: 1 ch, ★ 'Dec', 1 dc in next dc, rep from ★ to end...20 sts.
Work 2 rows in patt.
35th row: 1 ch, ★ 'Dec', rep from ★ to end...10 sts.
Work 1 row in patt.
37th row: As for 35th row...5 sts.
Fasten off.

❷ EMBROIDERING THE DESIGN

1 Fold one crochet piece in half lengthwise to find the centre. Along the centre line, count up 12 rows from the bottom. Match this point with the location point on the stitch guide.
2 Following the stitch guide, work the design in cross-stitch. If you wish, repeat the design on the other piece.

SPECIAL ABBREVIATION

'Dec': *draw up a loop in each of next 2 sts, yoh and draw through all 3 loops on hook.*

❸ MAKING UP THE TEA COSY

1 Do not press. Using a flat seam, join the pieces on both sides, from the beginning of the decreasing row (row 29) to the top row of five stitches.
2 To make the loop at the top, join yarn with a slst in the top edge, make 15 ch for the loop, slst in opposite edge, turn, work 24 dc in loop, slst in the base of 15 ch. Fasten off.
3 Run a thread through the top edge and draw it up tightly.
4 Work a ch to make a button loop at lower edge below the handle and sew on the button. Sew the sides opposite the button together from the bottom, up 4 cm, leaving a hole for the spout.

STITCH GUIDE

Work the design in gold and leaf green, treating the rows and stitches of the crochet fabric as the cross-stitch grid. Because the crochet fabric is thick and soft, use the full hank of embroidery cotton.

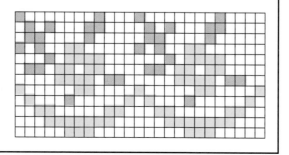

Fragrant pot pourri

Fill pillows and sachets with your own pot pourri mixtures, in combinations to suit a particular recipient's likes and dislikes, to give an added personal touch to this gift.

WHAT YOU NEED

Fragrant flowers and leaves, spices, orange peel (see individual recipes in section 3) • scissors • sheets of newspaper • shoe-box with lid, or large paper bag

1 PREPARING THE DRIED FLOWERS AND LEAVES

1 Gather flowers and leaves from the garden early in the morning (but after the overnight dew has dried, because damp plant material may rot). Pick flowers when they are fully open and before they begin to decay. Pick herbs just as they come into flower.

2 As soon as possible after picking, spread the flowers and leaves on several sheets of newspaper. Leave small flowers, such as tiny rosebuds, daisies or lavender, intact. To prepare larger flowers, remove the petals from the sepals (the green part at the base of the flower). Snip large leaves into several pieces with scissors.

3 Place the newspaper in a dry, airy place, away from wind and direct sunlight. Each day, toss the flowers with your fingertips to make sure that they dry out evenly. The material should be ready in three or four days.

4 When they are leathery to the touch, store the dried flowers and leaves in a lidded shoe-box or closed paper bag until you are ready to make the pot pourri. This protects the plant material from dust and prevents it from becoming mouldy.

2 MAKING THE POT POURRI

1 Put the ingredients for the recipe you want to make in a box or paper bag and shake them together lightly.
2 Fill sachets or pillows with the mixture as soon as possible, and stitch or tie the receptacle shut.

3 RECIPES

Mixed flowers
½ cup mixed heavily scented dried flower petals
¼ cup dried lavender
¼ cup dried lemon verbena leaves
¼ cup dried rosemary
Peel of one orange, cut into slivers and dried

Sweet rose
1 cup dried scented rose petals
Peel of half an orange, cut into slivers and dried
¼ cup crushed cloves and cinnamon sticks
¼ teaspoon nutmeg

Rose and herb
¼ cup dried scented rose petals
¼ cup dried mint
¼ cup dried lemon balm
¼ cup dried lemon verbena

Lemon verbena
1 cup dried lemon verbena

HINTS
● *To crush cloves, place them in a plastic bag and roll gently with a rolling pin.*
● *Crush leaves with your fingers to release the scent before placing them in the sachet.*
● *Unless the dried material you have chosen is heavily scented, (such as scented varieties of lavender, orange blossom, lemon verbena, rosemary, and some of the old-fashioned roses), you will need to add spices, herbs or citrus peel to intensify the fragrance.*
● *You can buy scented oils to boost the fragrance, but this type of pot pourri is not suitable for clothing and linen sachets or for sleep pillows, as the oil will seep through and stain the fabric.*
● *Other suitable ingredients for pot pourri are mimosa, jasmine, apple blossom, camomile, sweet pea, narcissus, honeysuckle, and peel of lemon or lime.*

Old English lavender
1 cup dried very fragrant lavender
5 or 6 crushed cloves

Lavender and rose
½ cup dried fragrant lavender
½ cup dried rose petals
¼ cup dried lemon verbena leaves or dried thyme
10 crushed cloves, or a small stick of crushed cinnamon

Lavender and rosemary
½ cup dried rosemary
½ cup dried lavender
Some slivers of dried orange peel
8 whole cloves

Herb
1 cup dried rosemary
1 cup dried fragrant pine needles

Citrus pot pourri
½ cup lemon verbena leaves
½ cup rose geranium leaves
slivers of orange and lemon peel
10 crushed coriander seeds

SPICY POMANDER
For a deliciously perfumed room or wardrobe, you can substitute pomanders for pot pourri sachets.
1 Stud a few oranges or apples (or both) with whole cloves.
2 In a bowl, mix together ground spices – for example, cloves, cinnamon, nutmeg and orrisroot.

3 Roll the fruits in the ground spices until they are well covered.
4 Place the fruits in individual paper bags for several weeks to dry out.
5 When the fruits are dry, dust them off. Thread a ribbon through them for hanging in a wardrobe, or arrange them in a decorative bowl.

Embroidered table linen

A round tablecloth lovingly embroidered in traditional cross-stitch is a timeless gift that a parent will be thrilled to receive. The rose motif on the tablecloth is repeated on the napkins.

Master pattern J69(a) • 175 cm x 110 cm cream aida cloth (11 gauge) • 3.5 m cream cotton edging lace • stranded cotton: Anchor colours 78 (crimson), 77 (mid-pink), 73 (palest pink), 842 (pale yellow-green), 308 (deep old gold), 890 (old gold), 306 (yellow), 891 (deep cream), 111 (purple), 109 (mauve), 108 (pale mauve), 103 (old rose pink); 2 skeins each of 76 (rose pink), 74 (pink), 261 (grass green); 3 skeins each of 262 (dark green), 215 (mid-green) • needle: size 24 crewel • sewing thread to match the fabric • scissors • tape measure • sewing machine (for zigzagging the lace edge) • dressmaker's pencil • 60 cm string

● *Technique pages 304, 309*

❶ PREPARING THE FABRIC

1 Cut a 110 cm square from the fabric for the tablecloth. From the remaining fabric cut four or six 31.5 cm squares for the napkins.
2 Iron all pieces and oversew or zigzag the raw edges.
3 Fold the fabric for the tablecloth in half and then in half again to find

Cutting guide
Cut a 110 cm square for the tablecloth, and up to six 31.5 cm squares, depending on how many napkins you want to make.

the centre. Using coloured thread, tack along the fold lines to mark the vertical and horizontal centre lines.

❷ EMBROIDERING THE TABLECLOTH

1 To start the embroidery, find the centre of the design on the master pattern and count the number of squares from the centre to the start of the cross-stitch design. Count the same number of squares from the centre of the aida cloth, along one line of tacking. This will give you the starting point for the embroidery.
2 Following the stitch and colour guide on the master pattern, and using five strands of embroidery cotton, embroider the design on to the tablecloth, completing it four times to form a circle.

❸ FINISHING THE TABLECLOTH

1 Press the tablecloth piece and spread it out flat on a clean carpet.

2 Attach the dressmaker's pencil to the end of the piece of string and measure 54 cm from the tip of the pencil along the string. Secure the string at this point to the centre of the fabric.
3 Keeping the string taut, swing the pencil to inscribe a circle on the fabric. Cut along the pencil line to create a circle with a diameter of 108 cm.
4 Attach the lace by machine zigzagging it to the edge of the circle on the right side of the fabric.

4 EMBROIDERING THE NAPKINS

1 To find the starting point for the embroidery, match the edge of the grid on the master pattern with the edge of the cloth and count squares.
2 Using five strands of embroidery cotton, and following the stitch and colour guide on the master pattern, embroider the rose design in one corner of each napkin.

5 FINISHING THE NAPKINS

Turn down all the edges 5 mm and then 1 cm and hemstitch around the napkins, mitring the corners neatly.

> **HINT**
> *For some helpful tips on counted cross-stitch, see 'Wedding day sampler' (pages 194–5).*

Sunflower wall hanging

Lighten your parents' kitchen or breakfast room with this gold and yellow wall hanging.

Master pattern **G77(a–c)** • 3 pieces fabric, 25 cm **x** 16 cm, in shades of gold (for the flowers) • extra piece of one gold shade, 50 cm **x** 30 cm (for the border and loops) • 2 rectangles cream-coloured fabric, 48 cm **x** 35 cm (for background and backing) • fabric scraps (for flower centres) • 20 cm **x** 40 cm green fabric (for stems and leaves) • 48 cm **x** 35 cm wadding, plus a few scraps • 30 cm **x** 25 cm double-sided iron-on webbing • scrap of iron-on non-woven interfacing • sewing thread to match flower centres, stems and leaves • quilting cotton: cream, gold • embroidery cottons: yellow, brown, gold, green • 75 cm gold cord • embroidery hoop (optional) • needles: sewing, quilting, embroidery • 50 cm dowel • tracing paper • pencil • compass • dressmaker's pencil • sharp-pointed scissors • dressmaking pins • sewing machine • iron

● *Technique pages 292–301, 302, 305–6, 307–12, 343–4*

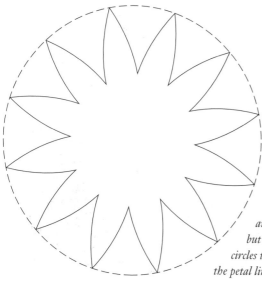

To make the sunflower petals, trace the circles and the petal outlines from the master pattern, but cut out only the circles. Pin the tracing paper circles to the right-sized fabric circles, and cut along the petal lines through the pattern piece and the fabric.

❶ PREPARING THE SUNFLOWERS

1 On the paper side of the webbing, use the compass and pencil to draw nine circles, three with a radius of 4.5 cm, three with a radius of 3.75 cm, and three with a radius of 3.25 cm. Cut out the nine circles.

2 Place one webbing circle of each size, paper side up, on the wrong side of one of the gold fabrics. Fuse the webbing to the fabric by ironing over the paper. Peel the paper away and cut out the fabric circles.

3 Place the three webbing and fabric circles, fabric side up, on the wrong side of the remaining fabric. Fuse the fabric to the webbing with a hot iron and cut out the shapes.

4 Repeat steps 2 and 3 on the other two gold fabrics. You should now have nine double-thickness circles, one of each size from each fabric.

5 From the master pattern, trace the three circles with the petal design. Cut out the circles and pin them to the fabric circles with the tips of the petals touching the edges of the circles. Cut out the flower shapes.

6 Draw three circles with a radius of 1.3 cm on the interfacing and three on the scraps of wadding, using the compass and pencil. Draw one circle with a radius of 1.7 cm on each of the three pieces of scrap material. Cut out all the circles. (They will be used to make the centres of the three sunflowers.)

7 Centre the interfacing circles on the wrong side of the fabric circles and fuse them to the fabric with a hot iron.

8 Separate the layers of wadding to make thinner pads and place them on the top of the interfacing. Clip the edges of the fabric circles and fold them in over the wadding.

❷ PREPARING THE STEMS AND LEAVES

1 Cut three slightly curving 1.5 cm strips of green fabric 22 cm, 16 cm and 14 cm long for the stems. Fold under and press the long edges of the strips so that the stems are about 6 mm wide.

2 On a piece of tracing paper, draw three leaf shapes, two about 7.5 cm long and one about 6 cm long. Cut out the shapes and use them as templates to mark and cut leaf shapes from the interfacing.

3 Iron the three leaf-shaped interfacings to the wrong side of the green fabric. Cut the fabric around the interfacing, leaving a 3 mm border. Fold the border back over the interfacing and press.

❸ ASSEMBLING THE DESIGN

Each sunflower is made up of three petal circles, each of which is a different shade and size.

1 Lay down the largest circle of petals, place the next largest circle on top and the smallest circle on top of that. Arrange the circles so that the petal tips are alternating.

2 Slipstitch the flower centre into position, sewing through all thicknesses. Make sure the edges of the flower centre are neatly turned under.

3 Ensure that the edges of the rectangle of background fabric are square.

4 Position and pin the stems, leaves and flowers in place on the background fabric. When you are satisfied with the arrangement, slipstitch each piece into place.

5 Using six strands of green embroidery cotton, work the stems of the embroidered daisies in stem stitch and the leaves in lazy daisy stitch.

6 Using six strands of yellow cotton, embroider the daisy petals in lazy daisy stitches. Fill the centre of each daisy with French knots, using brown cotton.

7 Work the other flowers in a mixture of yellow, gold and brown, using six strands of cotton.

❹ ADDING THE QUILTING DETAILS

1 To make the backing, press and trim the other rectangle of cream-coloured fabric

2 Place the backing, wrong side up, flat on the table. Lay the wadding over it and the appliquéd fabric, right side up, on top of that. Smooth out any wrinkles. Tack all three layers firmly together around the edges.

3 Following the dotted lines on the appliqué and stitch guide, use small, even running stitches to quilt the details through all layers.

4 When the quilting is complete, machine stitch all layers together around the edge. Remove the tacking.

❺ SEWING THE BORDER

1 Cut four strips 5 cm wide from the border fabric, two 48 cm long and two 37 cm long.

2 Fold each strip in half lengthwise and press the fold. On the long sides of each strip, fold and press down a 1.25 cm hem to the wrong side.

3 Open out the strips. With right sides facing, place the raw edges of the long strips and the sides of the hanging together. Stitch the border to the hanging along the fold lines.

4 Turn the remaining raw edges of the borders to the back of the hanging

Symbol	Meaning	Symbol	Meaning
Cut-out fabric		• French knot	
----- Cream quilting		Stem stitch	
-·-·- Gold quilting		Lazy daisy stitch	

Appliqué and stitch guide
The flowers and foliage are appliquéd first, then the details are embroidered, and finally the quilting lines are sewn.

and fold the seam allowances under. Hem the borders into place on the back by hand.

5 Repeat steps 3 and 4 to sew the shorter strips to the top and bottom edges of the hanging. Make sure that the corners are folded under neatly.

6 Press the wall hanging through a damp cloth, front and back.

❻ FINISHING

1 Cut three strips of the border material, 5.5 cm x 13 cm. Fold down 1 cm around all four edges of each strip and machine sew the hems.

2 Fold the strips in half to form loops and slipstitch them, evenly spaced, to the back of the hanging along the top edge. Thread the dowel through.

3 Attach gold cord to the ends of the dowel to form a hanging loop.

Flowery watering can

Redolent of summer meadows, this folk art design transforms a plain watering can into an attractive ornament. To complete the gift, slip a glass jar inside to take water for cut flowers.

WHAT YOU NEED

Master pattern **F43(a)** • small galvanised metal watering can about 22 cm high • Matisse Folk Art background colour: lichen grey • Jo Sonja's artist's colours: rich gold, yellow oxide, warm white, naphthol red light, Turner's yellow, red earth, Norwegian orange, pine green, raw sienna, brown earth, raw umber • metal primer • water-based matt or satin varnish • paintbrushes: 25 mm decorating, no. 2 round, nos 12 and 8 flat, no. 00 liner • tracing paper • fine-tipped marker pen • masking tape • transfer paper • paint palette • old toothbrush • hard pencil (or empty ballpoint pen)

● *Technique pages 334–5, 343–4*

❶ PREPARING THE SURFACE

1 Follow the methods described in the folk art techniques section to prepare the metal surface for painting.
2 Using the decorating brush, apply three smooth coats of lichen grey, allowing each coat to dry thoroughly before applying the next.

❷ SPATTERING

1 Mix rich gold paint with a little water to a smooth, light consistency.
2 Dip the ends of the toothbrush bristles in the paint. Spatter gold lightly and evenly over the entire exposed surface of the watering can by holding the brush in one hand and drawing the thumb of your other hand towards you, across the bristles.
3 Allow the paint to dry thoroughly.

HINT

Practise spattering paint on to a sheet of scrap paper until you are confident of your technique.

❸ TRANSFERRING THE DESIGN

1 Trace the design from the master pattern using the tracing paper and the fine-tipped marker pen.
2 Place the traced design on the surface of the watering can so that it is centred between the handle and the spout, and secure it in position with masking tape.
3 Slip a sheet of transfer paper under the tracing paper and transfer the design to the can using the hard pencil or the empty ballpoint pen.
4 Repeat steps 2 and 3 to transfer the design to the other side.
5 Trace or photocopy the verse of Shakespeare from the master pattern on to a strip of tracing paper. Secure the tracing paper in position around the base of the watering can with small pieces of masking tape.

6 Slip a strip of transfer paper under the tracing paper and transfer the lettering to the watering can. Repeat or shorten the verse, as space permits.

❹ PAINTING THE DESIGN

Background wash

1 Using the no. 8 flat brush, paint a soft wash of Turner's yellow around the bases of the plants, in some places allowing it to reach about a third of the way up the can. The wash should be very transparent.
2 Allow the paint wash to dry.

Red anemones

1 Mix red earth, naphthol red light, Norwegian orange and Turner's

RED ANEMONES

Paint the petals first, then the centres. Float a shadow around the petal bases and detail the centres. Lastly, paint the buds and leaves.

PRIMROSES

Use two strokes for each petal and lightly shade the bases. Fill and detail the centres and then paint and highlight the leaves.

Make each petal with two strokes and allow them to dry.

2 Using a side-loaded no. 8 flat brush, float brown earth around the bases of the petals, butting up against the centres of the primroses.

3 Paint the centres in pine green. When they are dry, outline them with yellow oxide and paint a warm white dot in the middle of each one.

4 Paint the leaves with a round brush triple-loaded with pine green, yellow oxide and brown earth. When they are dry, side-load the flat brush with Turner's yellow and float highlights on the edges.

Floated shading

1 When all the flowers are dry, float a shadow around the base of the design using the no. 12 flat brush side-loaded with raw umber. Keep the loaded side of the brush on the outer edge of the design.

2 Using raw umber and the no. 12 flat brush, float another shadow at the top of the design, keeping the loaded side on the top outer edge.

3 Repeat steps 1 and 2 on the lower rim of the watering can, above and below where you plan to paint the Shakespearean verse.

Lettering

1 Mix some brown earth to an inky consistency with water and, using the liner brush, paint the words of the Shakespearean verse around the base of the watering can:

When daisies pied and violets blue
And lily-smocks all silver-white,
And cuckoo-buds of yellow hue
Do paint the meadows with delight…

2 When the lettering is dry, use rich gold to paint a shadow line under each letter.

⑤ FINISHING

1 Paint bands of rich gold around the top and bottom of the can, along the edges of the handles and around the spout. Apply at least two coats.

2 Using the decorating brush, cover all exposed surfaces with four to six coats of water-based varnish.

---

yellow on the round brush and paint the petals. Allow them to dry, then paint them again for greater depth and coverage.

2 When the petals are dry, paint the centres of the anemones with Turner's yellow.

3 Allow the centres to dry, and then add circles of pine green.

4 Side-load the no. 8 flat brush with brown earth and float a shadow around the bases of the petals, butting up against the centres.

5 Paint tiny dots of double-loaded warm white and Turner's yellow on and near the centres.

6 Paint the leaves and buds with a double-loaded round brush, using pine green and yellow oxide. When they are dry, repeat.

7 Apply the same colour to the stems, using the liner brush.

Daisies

1 Mix warm white and yellow oxide to make cream and, using the round brush, paint the petals.

2 Base-coat the centres in Turner's yellow. When they are dry, add Norwegian orange detailing.

3 Side-load the no. 8 flat brush with raw sienna and float a shadow around the bases of the petals.

4 Outline the lower edge of the centre of each daisy with brown earth.

5 Brush-mix pine green, warm white and yellow oxide and use this mixture to paint the leaves and stems. Use the round brush for the leaves and the liner brush for the stems.

Primroses

1 Using the round brush, paint the primrose petals with double-loaded yellow oxide and Norwegian orange.

Beaded butterfly evening bag

The fine beadwork on this evening bag is complemented by the cross-stitch butterfly design, which is sewn in metallic thread. This gift is the perfect accessory for any formal occasion, and it will draw admiring glances whenever it is used.

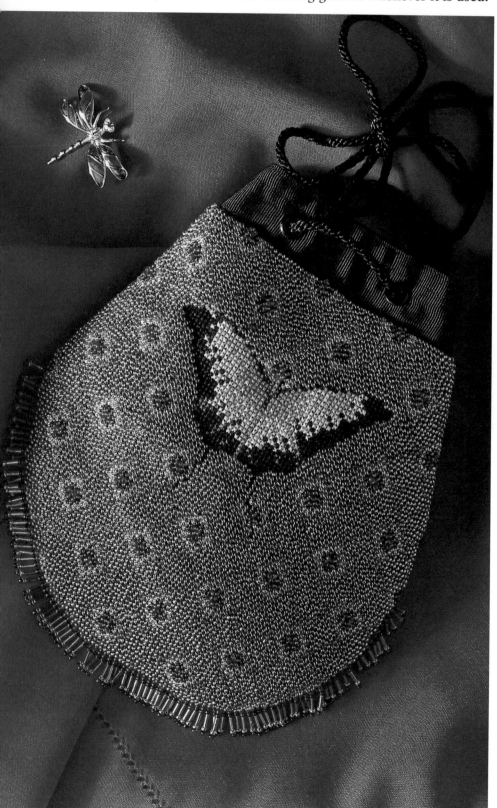

WHAT YOU NEED

Master pattern **J72(a)** • 30 cm x 30 cm black aida cloth (14 gauge) • 30 cm x 30 cm backing fabric (silk dupion or similar) • 60 cm x 30 cm medium-weight iron-on interfacing • 60 cm x 30 cm lining fabric • 40 cm black petersham ribbon, 40 mm wide • 2 m black silk cord • sewing threads (black and to match lining) • needles: size 24 crewel, size 10 beading • 8 medium black eyelets • eyelet punch • scissors • sewing machine • dressmaking pins

Stranded cotton: DMC colours 310 (black), 333 (purple), 959 (pale aqua), 995 (dark turquoise), 996 (turquoise), 3021 (brown)
Metallic thread: DMC Fils métallisés Art 271 black; Art 278 purple 4012, pale aqua 4052, dark turquoise 4065, turquoise 4033, brown 4251
Glass seed beads: Mill Hill colours 020 (bright blue) – 1 packet, 024 (antique rose) – 9 packets, 217 (ice blue) – 3 packets, 252 (purple) – 3 packets, 332 (green) – 1 packet.
Frosted glass beads: Mill Hill colour 60020 (bright blue) – 1 packet
Small bugle beads: Mill Hill colour 70020 (bright blue) – 1 packet
● *Technique pages 292–301, 309*

❶ PREPARING THE FABRIC

1 Oversew or zigzag the raw edges of the black aida cloth to prevent fraying.
2 Fold the fabric in half and in half again to locate the centre vertical and horizontal lines, and mark them with coloured tacking. The intersection of these lines is the centre of the fabric.

❷ EMBROIDERING THE BUTTERFLY DESIGN

1 Locate the centre of the master pattern by joining the opposite arrows

at the mid-point of each side of the pattern. Count from this centre line to locate the base line of the butterfly.
2 Using two strands of DMC stranded cotton with one strand of the Fils métallisés metallic thread, embroider the butterfly in cross-stitch, following the master pattern and the associated colour key.

❸ ATTACHING THE BEADS

1 Following the master pattern and colour guide, work one small section of beading at a time. Begin with the sections around the butterfly to give you a reference point.

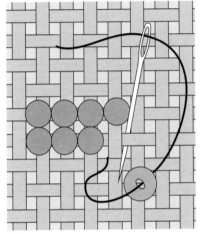

2 Using the beading needle, secure one strand of black thread at the back of the work. Bring the needle up in the bottom left-hand corner of the first square, thread on a bead and finish the stitch in the upper right-hand corner of the square.
3 Selecting beads according to the colour guide, continue to stitch from left to right, keeping a regular tension on the thread. The beads will lie correctly when stitched in this way.
4 Stitch the beaded design with single beads, except where the symbol ▮▮ is marked on the master pattern. In this case, pick up two beads on the needle but stitch the thread over only one square, as elsewhere. This will create a raised effect.

❹ CONSTRUCTING THE BAG

1 Cut around the work, leaving seam allowances of 1.5 cm around the curved part and 3 cm along the straight edge at the top.

2 Using the trimmed beaded piece as a pattern, cut out an identical shape from the backing fabric, two identical shapes from the interfacing and two from the lining fabric.

3 Cut the petersham ribbon in half. Place one piece along the top edge of the beaded section and stitch it in place as close to the beads as possible.
4 Iron one piece of interfacing on to the wrong side of the backing fabric, and then iron the second piece over the first piece.
5 Lay the other piece of petersham ribbon on the right side of this stiffened backing piece, 3 cm down from the straight edge, and stitch it in place.
6 Placing right sides together, sew the beaded section and the prepared backing fabric around the curved edge, leaving the top open. Stitch as close to the beaded area as possible. Turn to the right side.
7 With right sides facing, sew the two lining pieces together around the curved edge.
8 Place the lining bag inside the beaded bag, matching the side seams.

Trim the raw edges at the top of the bag so that the grosgrain ribbon stands above the other fabrics.
9 Fold the ribbon over the raw edges, pin, and stitch as close to the edge of the ribbon as possible. Then topstitch the ribbon close to the folded edge.

❺ FINISHING THE BAG

1 Position the eyelets 6.5 cm apart, starting 1 cm in from the seams. If you do not have an eyelet punch, your local shoe repairer may be able to do this for you.
2 Thread the black silk cord through the eyelet holes, starting and finishing at the back of the bag. Close the bag by pulling up the cord.

❻ MAKING THE FRINGE

1 At the point where the lighter backing fabric begins to fold in on itself (about 9 cm from the top of the beading), start to make the beaded fringe that goes around the bottom.
2 Work the fringe around the lower curve of the bag following the instructions in 'Making the bead fringe'.

MAKING THE BEAD FRINGE

Secure a double strand of black thread at the point where the fringe is to begin. Thread six beads on to the needle, following the colour guide (right). Take the thread round the last bead and back up through the other five beads to the starting point. Continue around the bag to the other side, butting each stitch up to the preceding stitch.

Painted apple plate

Make this beautiful and extremely decorative plate for your parents to display with pride. It can be hung on the wall or used as a practical platter for serving fruit, nuts or chocolates.

WHAT YOU NEED

Master pattern G46(a–b) • raw-wood plate, diameter 30 cm, rim about 5 cm wide • artist's acrylic paint: green, olive green, forest green, avocado, jade green, medium green, cream, moon yellow, titanium white, cadmium yellow, naphthol red, oxblood, black, burgundy wine, deep burgundy, country red, cadmium red, russet, orange, red • water-based satin varnish • palette • paintbrushes: no. 5 round, no. 8 flat, no. 00 liner • fine sandpaper • tracing paper • transfer paper • pencil • hard pencil • plate hanger (optional)
● *Technique pages 334–5, 343–4*

① PREPARING THE PLATE

1 Prepare the raw wooden surface of the plate for painting, following the methods described in the folk art techniques section.
2 Using the flat brush, apply two coats of green to the plate, sanding lightly between coats.
3 Make a tracing of master pattern G46(a). Centre the design carefully and transfer it on to the rim and inner circle of the plate.
4 Using the round brush loaded with black paint, outline the design and fill in the leaves. Use the flat brush to fill in the rest of the area. Allow to dry thoroughly.
5 Trace and transfer master pattern G46(b) on to the plate, centring the apples on the rim. Note that pattern b covers almost all of pattern a.

② PAINTING THE DESIGN
The leaves

1 Load the round brush with avocado and stroke in the leaves that lie under the apples and over the previously painted black leaves. To create a more realistic effect, paint complete leaves, allowing the paint to extend over the apple designs rather than trying to paint around them. Allow to dry.
2 With the liner brush loaded with jade green paint, roughly outline each leaf, using a loose and curvy line to put some movement into the design.

Preparing the apples

1 Unless otherwise stated, use the round brush to paint the apples.
2 Apply enough coats of white to all the apples to make them completely opaque. Allow to dry.

Green apples

1 Paint a base coat of olive green over the titanium white.
2 *First shade:* Create a medium green shade by mixing equal amounts of olive green and medium green. Use this mixture to shade the lower two-thirds of each apple, and then dry-brush the edge of the colour out into the base coat.
3 *Second shade:* Using medium green, dry-brush the lower third of each apple.
4 To create the stalk depression, place an open comma stroke of the medium green (first shade) at the top of each apple, blending the outer edge of the stroke into the base coat. Then apply a smaller stroke of medium green (second shade) and blend the outer edge.
5 *First highlight:* Using cadmium yellow, dry-brush several shape-following strokes on to the shoulder of the apple.
6 *Second highlight:* Dry-brush a small white highlight in the centre of the yellow area.
7 *Floated shade:* Using a flat brush, float forest green on the shaded outer edge and the inside of the stalk depression of each apple.

Red apples

1 For the dark red apples, follow steps 1 to 7 for 'Green apples', substituting the following colours:
base coat – naphthol red;
first shade – burgundy wine (transparent);
second shade – deep burgundy;
first highlight – cadmium red;
second highlight – white;
floated shade – russet.
2 For the light red apples, follow steps 1 to 7 for 'Green apples', substituting the following colours:
base coat – cadmium red;
first shade – country red;
second shade – burgundy wine (transparent);
first highlight – orange;
second highlight – olive green;
floated shade – red.

Cut apples

1 Paint all the cut apples with a base coat of cream. If necessary, re-trace the core pattern.
2 With the liner brush, paint a thin cadmium red line around the outside edge to represent the skin. It is more realistic if this line is a little uneven.

3 Using olive green thinned with water, paint the outer core lines and the seed pods. Allow to dry.

4 Mix together a small amount of burgundy wine and olive green and stroke in the seed cases. Mix in more burgundy wine to produce a dark brown shade and paint the apple seeds, leaving a tiny highlight on each middle seed.

5 Paint the stalks the same dark brown, then add a highlight to each stalk with the original mixture of burgundy wine and olive green.

6 Dry-brush some moon yellow shadows on to the cut surfaces.

Flowers

1 Using the round brush, paint the petals in titanium white.

2 Paint the centres with a double load of cadmium yellow and oxblood mixed with a touch of white.

❸ FINISHING

1 Allow all the paint to become completely dry.

2 Apply several coats of varnish.

3 If the plate is for display, attach a commercial hanger to the back.

Painting guide

Apples are the focal points of this design: green, dark red and light red apples, together with cut apples, cluster around the rim of the plate on a bed of rich, dark foliage, with contrasting sprays of pale apple blossom.

NOTE

The light source for this design is deliberately inconsistent in order to make the light appear to move around the plate.

Log cabin quilt

Show your parents how much you care by making them this country-style quilt, based on a traditional design. They'll be proud to display your handiwork in a guest bedroom, as a wall hanging, or thrown over a favourite sofa.

70 cm x 110 cm fabric (for the centre squares and binding) • 6 light-coloured fabrics, each 60 cm x 75 cm • 6 dark-coloured fabrics, each 90 cm x 90 cm • 5.2 m backing fabric, 90 cm or 110 cm wide • 180 cm x 260 cm wadding • sewing threads to match or tone with the fabrics • dressmaking pins • about 30 large safety pins • sewing needles • tape measure • ruler • rotary cutter and cutting surface (or sharp scissors) • sewing machine • masking tape
● *Technique pages 292–301, 305–6*

SIZE
Finished measurement (after binding): about 170 cm x 250 cm
Number of pattern blocks: 96
Pattern block measurement (after joining): 20.5 cm x 20.5 cm

❶ PREPARING THE FABRIC
1 Prewash all fabrics to check for shrinkage and colourfastness.
2 From each of the six light-coloured fabrics, cut 16 strips, 3.5 cm x 75 cm.
3 From each of the dark-coloured fabrics, cut 16 strips, 5 cm x 90 cm.
4 From the fabric for the centre squares, cut a strip 45 cm x 110 cm and set it aside for the binding. From the remaining piece of fabric, cut 96 squares, 5.5 cm x 5.5 cm. These will form the centres of the 96 blocks.

❷ CUTTING THE STRIPS
1 Take one strip of each of the six light fabrics and place them one on top of the other. Do the same with each of the six dark fabrics, keeping the two stacks separate.

| | 72 | | | | |
| 5.5 | 7.5 | 11 | 13 | 16.5 | 18.5 |

2 Using the rotary cutter, carefully cut through all six layers of light fabric to make strips measuring 5.5 cm, 7.5 cm, 11 cm, 13 cm, 16.5 cm and 18.5 cm. Keep the strips in six same-size stacks.

| 7.5 | 11 | 13 | 16.5 | 18.5 | 22 |
| | | | 88.5 | | |

3 Carefully cut through all six dark fabrics to make strips measuring 7.5 cm, 11 cm, 13 cm, 16.5 cm, 18.5 cm and 22 cm, keeping these in same-size stacks also.
4 Repeat steps 1 to 3 for the remaining 15 light and 15 dark strips.

❸ SORTING THE STRIPS
A block is made from 12 strips of fabric, each a different colour and size, together with one centre square. The quilt is formed by joining 96 blocks together, eight blocks wide and 12 blocks long. The blocks are worked in groups of six so that even amounts of each fabric are used. To make sure that each block is formed in a different order, sort your piles as follows.
1 Arrange the six stacks of light-coloured fabric in a row from largest

HINT
Accumulate the fabrics and cut the strips over a period of time. Store strips of the same colour in separate plastic bags until you are ready to use them.

COMBINING THE STRIPS
Altogether, there are 96 blocks in the quilt, and 13 different fabrics in each block. The strips are sewn to the central square in the order shown by the numbers in the diagram below. The fabrics are carefully cut and sorted so that no two blocks are pieced together in the same way.

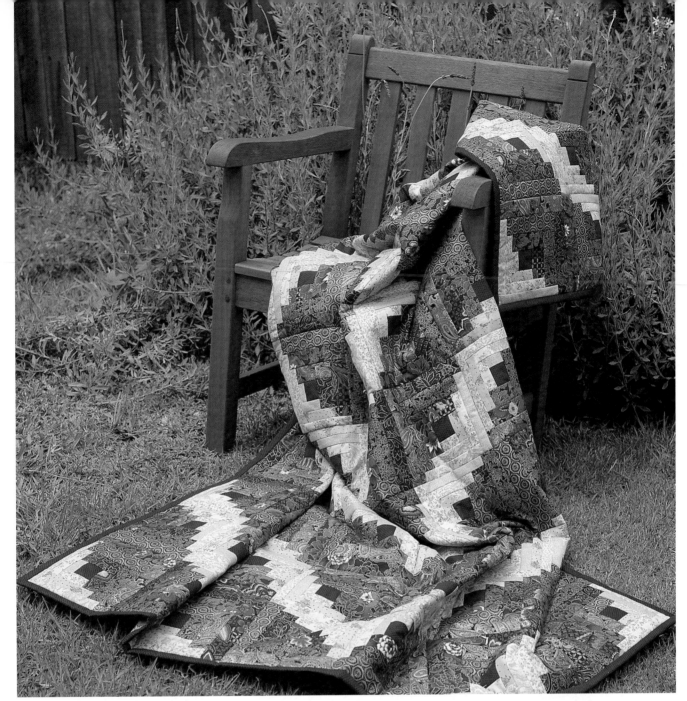

to smallest. Arrange the six stacks of dark fabric in the same way.

2 Leave the first stack of light strips and the first stack of dark strips as they are. Move one strip from the top of the second light stack to the bottom of that stack. Do the same thing with the second dark stack.

3 Move two strips from the top of the third light stack to the bottom of the stack. Do the same thing with the third dark stack.

4 Continue in this way along the rows of stacks, each time increasing by one the number of strips you move to the bottom of the piles. When you have finished, you will have 12 stacks

of fabric, each with a different colour on top of each stack.

5 Take one strip from the top of each stack, plus one square centre piece. These 13 pieces form one block. Continue to take one strip from each stack plus a square piece until you have six groups of 13 pieces.

❹ MAKING THE BLOCKS

1 Working with one group of 13 pieces at a time, sew the smallest light-coloured strip to one edge of the centre square, right sides facing. Finger press the seam away from the square.

2 Rotate the centre square 90° in an anti-clockwise direction. Sew the second smallest light strip to the edge formed by the second side of the square and the end of the first strip.

3 Rotate the centre square twice more, sewing the first and second smallest dark strips to the remaining sides of the square in the same manner as the light strips on the other sides of the square. You should now have a square enclosed by two light-coloured and two dark-coloured strips.

4 Continue in this way until you have sewn 12 strips (six light and six dark) around the centre square. The completed block should make a square measuring 22 cm x 22 cm.

5 Repeat steps 1 to 4 to make five more blocks.

6 Complete all 96 blocks, cutting out fabric strips and assembling six blocks at a time. Make sure you vary the order of the strips in the stacks so that each block is different.

5 LAYING OUT THE DESIGN

1 Arrange the blocks in a rectangle, eight blocks wide and 12 blocks long. The quilt illustrated has been worked

---

HINT

If you lose track of which strip you sewed last and don't know where to sew the next one, look for the edge with two seams. This is the edge to which to sew your next strip.

in a 'barn raising' pattern, but if you prefer, you can create your own design by laying out the blocks in a different pattern. Pin and then sew the blocks together in rows, right sides facing. Press the seams flat.

2 With right sides facing, pin and sew the rows together. Press all the seams flat.

6 ASSEMBLING THE QUILT

1 Cut the backing fabric into two equal lengths of 2.6 m. With right sides facing, sew the lengths together along the selvages with a flat seam.

2 Place the quilt front on the backing fabric and, keeping the seam in the centre, trim the backing fabric so it is 5 cm larger all around than the front.

3 Trim the wadding to the same size as the front fabric.

4 On a hard surface, lay out the backing, with the wrong side facing up, smoothing out any wrinkles. Pull the fabric taut and fix it to the surface with masking tape. Place the wadding on top and then the quilted front, right side up, smoothing out any wrinkles as you work.

5 Using large safety pins, pin through the three thicknesses of fabric, right around the fabric, leaving about 15 cm between safety pins.

6 Starting from the centre of the quilt, tack the three layers together in a sun-ray pattern to prevent the layers moving as you work. Remove tape.

7 Set a long machine stitch and sew along the seam lines between the blocks, feeding the quilt under the foot with the printed fabric uppermost. Manoeuvre the quilt as you go so that you can stitch right along a seam line to the other side without a break in the stitching.

---

8 Remove the tacking and trim the edges, leaving about 1.5 cm of wadding showing. This excess wadding will be covered by the binding.

7 BINDING THE QUILT

1 From the reserved piece of centre square fabric, cut eight strips 5.5 cm wide, across the width of the fabric. With right sides facing, stitch the short ends of the strips together to make two strips 8 cm longer than the long sides of the quilt, and two strips 8 cm longer than the short sides of the quilt.

2 Turn both edges of the bindings 7.5 mm to the wrong side and press.

3 Unfold one of the pressed hems. With right sides facing and raw edges together, sew one edge of each side binding to the front of the quilt, through all thicknesses, 7.5 mm from the edge. Use the crease in the binding as a guide.

4 Turn the side bindings to the back of the quilt. Turn under along the crease and slipstitch the binding along the line of machine stitching.

5 Sew the remaining strips of binding to the top and bottom of the quilt, following step 3 above. At each end, extend the binding about 1 cm.

6 Turn the raw edges under at the ends of the bindings and slipstitch the binding to the back of the quilt.

HOMEMAKERS, HOSTS & HOSTESSES

Every home needs
a multiplicity of things,
both useful and decorative.
A hand-made gift for
a new home or to show
your appreciation to
your host or hostess will
be especially treasured.

Tulip cushion

Any homemaker will appreciate the elegance of this Art-Deco-inspired cushion cover. The tulip design is worked in cutwork embroidery.

Master pattern H54(a) • 50 cm white linen, 115 cm wide • cushion pad, 45 cm x 45 cm • 3 skeins white stranded enbroidery cotton • needle: size 7 crewel • coloured sewing thread • tracing paper • pencil • dressmaker's carbon paper • sharp scissors • sewing machine
● *Technique pages 292–301, 313, 343–4*

① PREPARATION

1 Cut two pieces of white linen 45 cm x 45 cm, and machine stitch the edges carefully with zigzag stitch to prevent them from fraying.
2 Fold one square in half and then in quarters to find the vertical and horizontal centre lines. Tack along the lines with coloured thread.
3 Trace the design from the master pattern on to tracing paper.
4 Pin the traced design to the fabric square with the tacked centre lines, matching the centre lines of the fabric and the design. Place the fabric on a firm working surface.
5 Slip the dressmaker's carbon paper between the fabric and the design and transfer the design on to the fabric with a stylus or the pointed end of a knitting needle.

HINTS

● *To make the cushion larger or smaller, enlarge or reduce the design with a photocopier.*
● *Cover the cushion pad with a coloured fabric to suit the home-maker's decor.*

❷ EMBROIDERING THE DESIGN

1 Use three strands of cotton throughout. Establish the design with stranded cotton and running stitch, working the buttonhole stitch bars as you go.

2 Following the stitch guide, work buttonhole stitch, making sure that the ridge of the stitches lies against the area to be cut away.

3 Carefully cut away the fabric where indicated, making sure that you cut under the linking bars and as close as possible to the buttonhole stitches without actually nicking them.

❸ MAKING THE CUSHION

1 Place the two squares together, with right sides facing and all edges even. Pin, tack and stitch the front of the cushion to the back, leaving a 1.5 cm seam allowance and an opening at one side. Trim the corners and the seam. If the fabric has become soiled with handling, hand wash it in warm water using a good detergent, and dry flat.

2 Press the seams flat through a damp cloth. Turn the cushion through to the right side and press it carefully through a damp cloth.

3 Insert the cushion pad and close the opening with slipstitch.

Stitch and cutting guide
Establish the design with running stitch, working the button-hole stitch bars as you go. Complete the embroidery following the stitch guide at the right, then carefully cut away the fabric where indicated. Remember that the ridge of the buttonhole stitches must lie against any area that is to be cut away.

- - - Stem stitch
⊥⊥⊥⊥ Buttonhole stitch
▦▦▦ Bars
▱ Cut-away fabric

Sweet home sampler

This sampler is a delightful way to mark the acquisition or completion of a new home. It will remind the homemaker in future years of a very special and happy occasion.

WHAT YOU NEED

Master patterns J70(a–b) • 45 cm **x** 50 cm aida cloth (14 gauge) • stranded cotton: Anchor colour nos 1 (white), 10 (pink), 95 (lilac), 262 (dark green), 264 (light green), 301 (yellow), 371 (brown), 382 (dark brown), 890 (gold) • coloured tacking thread and needle • needle: size 24 tapestry • embroidery hoop • picture frame, 40 cm **x** 45 cm • A2 white backing board • A2 mounting board • linen carpet thread or fine, strong string (for mounting) • craft knife • steel rule or straight edge • tracing paper • scissors • pencil • tape measure • spray glue

● *Technique pages 309, 343–4*

❶ MAKING THE SAMPLER

1 Iron the aida cloth and hand over-sew, or machine zigzag, the raw edges.
2 Mark the vertical and horizontal centre lines with tacking stitches.
　　3 Following the stitch and colour guide on the master pattern, first embroider the border design. This then becomes a point of reference for the remainder of the design.

Choose one or two complementary colours for the names and dates – more colours will make the lettering hard to read.

4 Complete the design, working a small area at a time and following the stitch and colour guide carefully.

❷ PERSONALISING THE SAMPLER

1 On tracing paper, rule a straight line as a guide. From the master pattern for cross-stitch letters, trace the letters of the homemaker's name or names, and the date of moving in or completing work on the house. Leave spaces the width of two cross-stitches between letters and four cross-stitches between words. You will be able to fit only about 10 characters across the sampler, so abbreviate the names and use an ampersand (&) if necessary. Mark the mid-point of your tracings.

2 Match the mid-point of the names to the centre point of the sampler in the space provided at the top of the sampler. Embroider the letters using colours of your choice, starting from the middle and working outwards to the sides.
3 Repeat step 2 for the date, working in the space provided at the bottom of the sampler.

❸ FRAMING THE SAMPLER

1 Press the sampler on the wrong side through a damp cloth, making sure that you do not stretch the fabric or the stitching.
2 To frame the sampler, follow the steps described in 'Wedding day sampler' (pages 194–5).

NOTE
On the sampler illustrated, the spaces for names and dates are filled in with extra embroidery to balance the design. Omit as much of the pattern as is necessary to fit in the information.

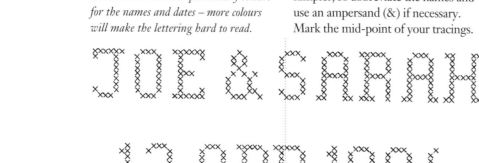

Country lace curtain

Long-wearing and easy to launder, this white cotton curtain will make a kitchen, bathroom or laundry window into a pretty feature. You can make the curtain to any width you like by repeating the pattern.

Left: One pattern section, as the curtain will hang.
Top: Border pattern, as the curtain is worked.
Top right: Detail of stitches that make up pattern.

For a curtain 55 cm wide and 47 cm long
Coats Mercer crochet cotton no. 10, 5 balls (20 g) • **1.50 mm steel crochet hook**
● *Technique pages 320–2*

CHECKING THE TENSION

Before you begin crocheting the curtain, check your tension so that the measurements of the finished curtain will be as close as possible to the specified size. You should have 44 stitches and 16 rows to 10 cm over 1 tr, 2 ch mesh. Check carefully. If you have fewer stitches, use a smaller hook; if more, use a bigger hook.

❶ CROCHETING THE CURTAIN

(worked sideways)
Using crochet hook and cotton, make 171 ch loosely.
1st row: (wrong side) miss 5 ch, 1 tr in next ch, 2 ch, miss 2 ch, 1 tr in each of next 4 ch, (5 ch, miss 5 ch, 1 tr in each of next 4 ch) twice, (2 ch, miss 2 ch, 1 tr in next ch) 10 times, 1 tr in each of next 12 ch, 2 ch, miss 2 ch, 1 tr in each of next 13 ch, (2 ch, miss 2 ch, 1 tr in next ch) 20 times, 1 tr in each of next 6 ch, (2 ch, miss 2 ch, 1 tr in next ch) 3 times, 1 tr in each of last 9 ch.
2nd row: 9 ch, miss 4 of these ch, 1 tr in each of next 5 ch, 1 tr in each of next 10 tr, 2 tr in next sp, 1 tr in next tr, 2 ch, 1 tr in next tr, 2 tr in next sp, 1 tr in each of next 4 tr, 2 ch, miss 2 tr, 1 tr in next tr, 2 ch, 1 tr in next tr, 2 tr in next sp, 1 tr in next tr, (2 ch, 1 tr in next tr) 18 times, 2 ch, miss 2 tr, 1 tr in each of next 7 tr, 2 ch, miss 2 tr, 1 tr in next tr, 2 tr in next sp, 1 tr in next tr, 2 ch, miss 2 tr, 1 tr in each of next 7 tr, 2 ch, miss 2 tr, 1 tr in next tr, (2 ch, 1 tr in next tr) 10 times, 1 tr in each of next 3 tr, 2 ch, 3 tr in next

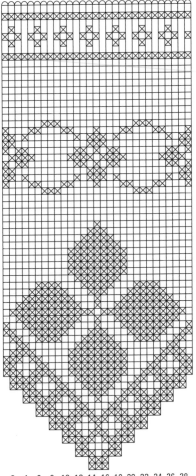

2 4 6 8 10 12 14 16 18 20 22 24 26 28

sp, 1 tr in next tr, 2 ch, miss 2 tr, 1 tr in next tr, 3 tr in next sp, 2 ch, 1 tr in each of next 4 tr, 2 ch, 1 tr in next tr, turn.
3rd row: 5 ch, 1 tr in first tr, 2 ch, 1 tr in each of next 4 tr, 5 ch, miss 3 tr, 1 tr in next tr, 2 tr in next sp, 1 tr in next tr, 5 ch, miss 3 tr, 1 tr in each of next 4 tr, (2 ch, 1 tr in next tr) 11 times, (2 ch, miss 2 tr, 1 tr in next tr) twice, 2 tr in next sp, 1 tr in each of next 4 tr, 2 tr in next sp, 1 tr in next tr, (2 ch, miss 2 tr, 1 tr in next tr) twice, (2 ch, 1 tr in next tr) 18 times, 2 tr in next sp, 1 tr in each of next 4 tr, 2 tr in next sp, (1 tr in next tr, 2 ch) twice, miss 2 tr, 1 tr in each of next 4 tr, 2 tr in next sp, 1 tr in each of next 7 tr,

2 ch, miss 2 tr, 1 tr in each of next 9 tr, 1 tr in top of turning ch.
Working in patt from graph,
4th row: patt to last 24 sts and 5 ch, 1 tr in each of next 3 tr, 14 ch, miss 4 tr, 1 tr in each of next 4 tr, 2 ch, 1 tr in next tr, turn.
5th row: 5 ch, 1 tr in first tr, 2 ch, 1 tr in each of next 4 tr, 5 ch, 4 tr in 14 ch sp, 5 ch, 1 tr in each of next 4 tr, patt to end.
Cont in patt from graph until row 29 is complete, noting that rows 2 to 5 incl form patt for border on straight edge.
Rep rows 2 to 29 incl twice, or, for a wider curtain, rep these rows until you reach the desired measurement, ending with a 29th row.
Fasten off.

❷ MAKING UP

Press very lightly with a warm iron through a slightly damp cloth.

Painted pot plant holder

Reminiscent of a romantic bygone era, this painted aluminium plant holder features a design of violets in a traditional folk art style. Filled with an appropriate flowering plant, it makes an attractive gift to delight any homemaker.

WHAT YOU NEED

Master pattern **H55(a)** • aluminium container, about 18 cm high • Folk Art acrylic colours: taffy base coat, raspberry wine, thicket, wicker white • Folk Art metallic paints: pure gold, silver sterling, blue sapphire, regal red • Folk Art pure pigment: dioxazine purple • water-based clear matt varnish spray • paint palette • paintbrushes: no. 8 flat, no. 8 round, no. 00 liner, 40 mm decorating • medium abrasive paper • lint-free cloth • tracing paper • transfer paper • masking tape • hard pencil (or empty ballpoint pen) • fine-tipped marker pen • soft artist's eraser
● *Technique pages 334–5, 343–4*

❶ PREPARING THE CONTAINER

1 Prepare the surface of the pot plant holder for painting, following the methods described in the folk art techniques section.

2 Using the decorating brush, apply two or three even coats of taffy base coat, allowing the paint to dry well between coats.

3 With tracing paper and a fine marker pen, trace the design from the master pattern.

4 Centre the working pattern on the side of the container and secure it with masking tape. Using transfer paper and the hard pencil, transfer the design to the container.

VARIATION

This charming old-fashioned flower design could easily be adapted for painting on to any object – a jewellery box or a silk scarf, for example. Simply enlarge or reduce the design as required and use suitable paints.

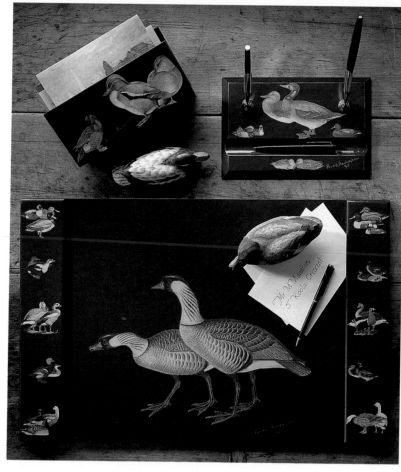

wallpaper paste and one part PVA glue to the surface where the image is to go, and a small amount of the mixture to the right side of the image.

3 Massage and mould the image on to the surface, adding more glue if necessary. With gentle pressure, use the roller over the image to distribute the glue evenly.

4 Remove all the excess glue with a wet sponge and allow to dry.

5 Apply two coats of artist's acrylic medium to the surface, allowing each coat to dry thoroughly before applying the next.

6 Follow steps 2 to 5 until all the images are in place.

❸ VARNISHING AND SANDING

1 Varnish the entire surface of each object, allowing at least 24 hours between coats and sanding each layer after the tenth coat, as described in the découpage techniques section.

2 When the surfaces are completely smooth and you cannot feel the edges of the images (about 20 coats), apply three more coats of varnish, sandpapering between coats with fine abrasive paper.

❹ FINISHING

1 Taking one object at a time, mix equal parts of beeswax and cabinetmaker's polish and warm the mixture. Using a lint-free cloth, apply the wax to the surface a little at a time.

2 Wipe vigorously with a damp cloth. Polish with a soft, dry cloth.

Découpage desk set

Découpage techniques can transform inexpensive office items such as a letter rack, an in-tray, a pen holder and a blotter pad into an elegant desk set to dress up a home study.

WHAT YOU NEED

Desk items suitable for painting • selection of suitable images • artist's acrylic paint, in a colour to suit the images • artist's acrylic gloss medium (sealer) • polyurethane gloss varnish • 3 small paintbrushes (for sealing, gluing and painting) • 20 mm imitation sable brush (for varnishing) • wet-and-dry abrasive paper in various grades • sanding block • wallpaper paste • PVA glue • roller • clear beeswax • cabinetmaker's polish • lint-free cloth • Blu-Tack • small sponge • fine, curved scissors • scalpel
● *Technique pages 329–31*

❶ PREPARATION

1 Seal the images with artist's acrylic medium and allow them to dry.

2 Prepare the surfaces of all objects following the methods described in the découpage techniques section.

3 Paint all objects with artist's acrylic paint. Allow them to dry, then sand lightly with medium abrasive paper.

4 Wipe the surfaces with a lint-free cloth and apply a further coat of paint, brushing in the opposite direction to get a good coverage. Allow all the objects to dry thoroughly.

❷ FIXING THE IMAGES

1 Lay out all the objects and arrange your images on them until you are satisfied. Try to see each item as part of a total design and arrange your images accordingly. Keep the images in place with Blu-Tack until you are ready to glue them down.

2 Working on only one object at a time, apply a mixture of three parts

Fuchsia cushion

The delicate tonality of the shadow appliqué design makes this pretty cushion the perfect finishing touch for a newly decorated bedroom. The fuchsia design is overlaid with sheer fabric and the detail is picked out with fine embroidery.

WHAT YOU NEED

Master pattern H56(a) • 75 cm white cotton voile or similar sheer fabric, 115 cm wide • 40 cm white flannelette, 90 cm wide • 20 cm x 20 cm bright pink homespun cotton • 20 cm x 20 cm green homespun cotton • 10 cm x 10 cm purple homespun cotton • 10 cm lightweight iron-on interfacing • 4 m pink organza ribbon, 20 mm wide • 2 m purple organza ribbon, 15 mm wide • round cushion insert, 30 cm diameter • 2 buttons, 12 cm diameter • sewing threads: purple, pink, green, white • stranded embroidery cotton: green • needle: crewel no. 8 • dressmaking pins • compass • 25 cm embroidery hoop • scissors • fabric glue • tracing paper • dressmaker's transfer pencil • pencil • sewing machine
● *Technique pages 292–301, 302, 307–12, 343–4*

❶ CUTTING OUT

1 Using a pencil and tracing paper, trace all the pattern pieces for the fuchsia appliqué design from the master pattern.
2 With the transfer pencil, transfer the traced pattern shapes on to the wrong side of the iron-on interfacing. Roughly cut around the shapes, leaving about 2 mm of interfacing outside the cutting lines.
3 Place the interfacing shapes for the bud and outer petals of the flowers on the wrong side of the pink fabric and press with a hot iron to fuse the interfacing to the fabric. Similarly, iron the interfacing shapes for the inner petals on to the wrong side of the purple fabric and those for the leaves on to the wrong side of the green fabric.
4 Cut out the interfaced shapes along the cutting lines, taking care with the

parts of the design that butt against each other.
5 With a compass, mark out a circle with a radius of 17 cm on the tracing paper and cut it out. Use this circle as a pattern to cut out a circle of flannelette and a circle of voile.

6 Fold the paper circle in half and trace the semicircle on to another piece of tracing paper. Elongate each end of the semicircle by 4.5 cm to make a squat arch shape. Cut out this shape and use it as a pattern to cut two pieces of flannelette and two pieces of voile. These pieces will become the back of the cushion, overlapping in the centre to form a flap though which to slip the cushion insert.

❷ ASSEMBLING THE DESIGN

1 Referring to the photograph for colour and position, arrange the various flower parts on the right side of the flannelette circle.
2 When you are happy with the arrangement, place a small amount of fabric glue on the wrong side of each of the appliqué pieces and fix them to the flannelette circle.
3 Place the voile circle on top of the flannelette so that the appliqué pieces are sandwiched between the voile and the flannelette. Tack lightly around the edge of the circle to hold the two pieces in position.
4 Place both layers of fabric in an embroidery hoop and tighten the hoop so that both fabrics are taut.

Before being glued on to the flannelette, the fabric flower and leaf parts are ironed on to interfacing to give them body.

5 Stitch around each piece of appliqué in a small, even running stitch, using single sewing threads in colours that match the different parts of the appliqué design. (The stitches should not pierce the coloured fabric; rather, they should sit right on the edges of the various pieces.) Also use running stitch to define the details shown as dotted lines on the pattern.
6 With purple sewing thread, work the stamens in backstitch and the ends of the stamens in either French knots or satin stitch.
7 Use two strands of green embroidery cotton to work along the stems in backstitch.

❸ MAKING UP THE CUSHION COVER

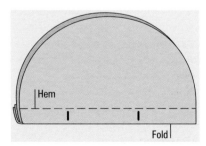

1 Assemble the pieces for the back, placing the voile over the flannelette. Neaten the straight edges with zigzag stitch and then fold them over to the bottom edges of the jug, overlapping the pieces at random and being especially careful around the lemon motifs.

6 Let all the work dry completely and then paint dark green swirls all over the blue tissue paper.

7 Add texture by scrunching up small pieces of lemon yellow and orange tissue paper and sticking them randomly over the outer surface.

❹ FINISHING

1 Paint the inside of the jug dark yellow. Cover the handle with a layer of lemon yellow tissue paper and the base with a layer of blue tissue paper.

2 Outline the edges of the handle with stripes of dark green paint.

3 Cut a number of small rectangles (about 3 cm x 1.5 cm) from the white paper. Paste these over the rim at intervals to make a chequered pattern, and allow them to dry thoroughly.

4 Apply two coats of clear acrylic varnish, allowing the first coat to dry thoroughly before applying the second. If the jug is to be used for fresh flowers, fit a glass jar inside.

NOTE

It is impossible to make the jug symmetrical, so do not try to do so – a rustic, handmade look is much more interesting and effective. However, as the final step in moulding the wire, take care to make the circular base as even as you can around the rim and slightly concave, so that the finished jug will sit firmly.

Home noticeboard

An appropriate gift for the home lover – a smart noticeboard on which to keep messages, postcards, photographs, appointment cards and all the other pieces of household paperwork. It would look equally good in the kitchen or in the home office.

WHAT YOU NEED

Master pattern H57(a) • 5 mm thick polyboard, 594 x 447 mm • red felt, 674 x 527 mm • 6 m black ribbon, 10 mm wide • 17 black drawing pins • cushion frame moulding, 20 mm x 12.5 mm x 2445 mm • stapler with 5 mm max. staples • PVA wood glue • 2 mirror clips • clear gloss varnish • varnish brush • tracing paper, about 620 mm x 470 mm • pencil • cross-cut saw • mitre box • corner clamps (if available) • panel pins • ruler • 2 mirror clips and screws
● *Technique pages 338–342*

❶ PREPARING THE BOARD

1 Lay the felt on a firm surface. Place the polyboard on top so that there is an equal amount of felt showing on each side.

2 Fold the excess to the back of the board, then attach the felt to the back of the board by first stapling it at the approximate centre of each side as shown. Gently stretching the felt as you go, gradually work towards the corners, finishing with a neat fold. Keep the staples about 25 mm apart and approximately 5 mm from the edge of the board. Trim the surplus

felt with the craft knife and ruler taking care not to cut into the board.
3 With tracing paper and a pencil, trace off a template for the complete board using the quarter template supplied (turning the tracing paper over for two of the quarters).

4 Turn the board over so that the felt side is uppermost, and use the template as a guide to fix the ribbons in position ensuring that all the staples are within the rebate area marked on the template, and that the ribbons are fairly taut. Trim the ends of the ribbons after fixing.
5 Fix the drawing pins to the crossed ribbons but not to those around the edges of the board.

❷ MAKING THE FRAME

1 Using the saw and mitre box, cut the frame sides and ends from the cushion moulding to the following dimensions, but before cutting, check the board's dimensions in case the felt has made the board slightly thicker: two pieces 620 mm long and two pieces 475 mm long.
2 Make sure both pairs are the same length. Glue and, if possible, clamp the frame together making sure that the corners are square before the glue sets. Leave to dry.
3 Paint the frame with two coats of clear gloss varnish, leaving it to dry between coats.

❸ FINISHING

1 Fit the board inside the frame and hold at the back with three or four

panel pins along each side.
2 Finally attach mirror clips to the top of the board.

a

Felt covered
board

b

45°   Rebate   c

NOTE
To check on the exact cutting size for the moulding to frame the board, add together measurement 'a' and twice 'c' plus 2 mm, for one side and 'b', twice 'c' plus 2 mm for the other. Cut two of each.

Parchment window tracery

The art of paper cutting, which originated in China, is not difficult; with a little practice, anyone can make interesting items like this window decoration. The tracery is designed to hang in a window so that it will cast intricate shadows as the light shines through it.

WHAT YOU NEED

Parchment (or calligraphy paper), A4 size • **pencil** • **fine black marker pen** • **tracing paper** • **masking tape** • **small sharp-pointed scissors** • **scalpel or craft knife** • **cutting board** • **stapler** • **white eraser** • **ruler** • **pin** • **corrugated cardboard** • **sewing thread or nylon fishing line** • **needle**

● *Technique pages 343–4*

❶ TRANSFERRING THE PATTERN

1 Using the marker pen, carefully trace the master pattern (below) on to the tracing paper.

2 Fold the sheet of parchment in half widthwise and use a ruler to

HINT
Entertain children by helping them to make a simple paper-cut gift for a teacher. Trace the three flowers from the middle of the design and enlarge and simplify them so that they can be cut out with safety scissors.

make a sharp crease along the fold. Open the paper out.

3 Place the tracing paper under one side of the creased parchment, matching the fold in the parchment with the fold line on the master pattern, and lightly trace the design on to the parchment with a pencil.

4 Referring to the photograph, lightly shade the areas to be cut out. Refold the parchment along the crease line and staple it around the outer

edge to hold the two halves firmly together. Trim excess parchment to about 2 cm from the staples.

❷ CUTTING OUT THE DESIGN

1 With the points of the scissors, puncture a shaded area of the paper near the centre, away from the cutting line. This is your starting point for cutting. Cut the pattern out, removing the smaller areas in the centre first and the outer edge of the pattern last.

MASTER PATTERN

If it is difficult to see the design lines when transferring the master pattern on to the parchment paper, improvise a light box by taping the pattern to the window and then taping the parchment in place on top.

To make sure both sides of the decoration are identical, transfer the design on to one side of the parchment paper and then fold the parchment in half along the fold line. Use a pencil to shade in the parts of the design to be cut out.

Do not cut out the unshaded diamond shape at the top of the design, as this is the point from which the decoration is hung.

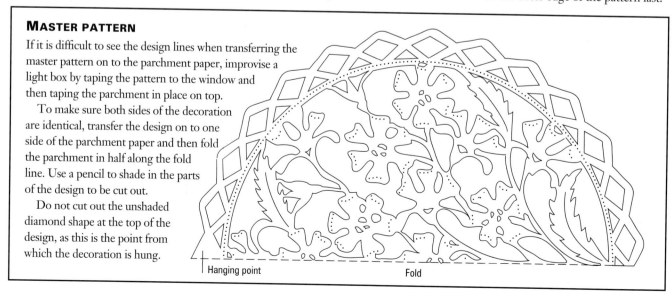

Hanging point   Fold

WHAT YOU NEED

Master pattern **H75(a–d)** • pair
of sheets and pillowcases in pure
cotton • fabric paints: dusty green,
olive green, pastel pink, deep pink •
stencilling paintbrushes: 2 large,
2 medium • stencil film or treated
manila cardboard: 1 piece about 45
cm x 20 cm, 1 piece about
30 cm x 15 cm • spray adhesive •
tracing paper • dressmaker's carbon
paper • craft knife • ballpoint pen •
cutting mat or board • rag
● *Technique pages 337, 343–4*

❶ PREPARING THE LINEN

1 Wash and iron the bed linen.
Put the bottom sheet aside.
2 Fold the top sheet in half lengthwise and mark the centre of the top
edge, where the stencilling is to go.
(The design goes on the part of the
sheet that is turned back on the bed.)
Fold the pillowcases widthwise and
mark the centres of the long sides.

❷ MAKING THE STENCILS

1 Trace the master patterns on to
tracing paper and, using dressmaker's
carbon paper and ballpoint pen, transfer the rose designs on to the stencil
film or treated manila cardboard.
2 Using the craft knife and the cutting board, cut out the designs.

❸ STENCILLING

1 Open the top sheet out and place
the part to be stencilled on a hard
surface, smoothing out any wrinkles.
2 Spray the back of the stencil with
adhesive and centre the design on the
sheet, about 10 cm from the top edge.
Position it so that the rose design is
nearest the edge of the sheet and the
scroll faces into the sheet.
3 Using pastel pink fabric paint and a
large stencil brush, stencil in the roses,

NOTE
*When stencilling the pillowcases,
slip a sheet of light card inside
each one to ensure that no paint
seeps through to the back.*

the scrolls and the circles. Using a
medium stencil brush and deep pink
fabric paint, add shading to the roses.
4 Wipe the stencil with a clean rag
and spray it again with adhesive.
Apply the stencil to the next part of
the sheet, making sure that the second
design is level and aligned with the
first design. Repeat step 3.
5 Continue applying the stencil and
stencilling the pink parts until you are
near the side of the sheet. When you
can no longer fit a complete motif
on to the sheet, turn your sheet and
arrange the stencil down the side.
Continue stencilling down the sides
as far as you think is appropriate for
a turnback (about two stencil lengths).

6 Position the large corner stencil to
stencil a rose in each corner. When

you have stencilled all the pink parts
of the design, allow the paint to
become completely dry.
7 Make sure the stencil is quite clean,
then spray it with adhesive again.
Reapply it to your design, aligning
the parts already painted under the
corresponding parts of the stencil.
With a large stencil brush and olive
green fabric paint, stencil the leaves.
8 When you have stencilled all the
leaves, use a medium stencil brush to
apply dusty green shading randomly
to some of the leaves, and then use
the deep pink fabric paint to 'bronze'
some of the leaf tips.
9 Repeat the stencilling procedure
with the pillowcases, using the smaller
stencil designs.

❹ FINISHING
When the paint has completely dried,
seal it following the instructions given
by the manufacturer.

HINT
*To make this gift for a really
special person, look for linen that
has lace inserts, like that used in
the set illustrated. This type of
linen is expensive, but it is a
beautiful way to show a homemaker how much you care.*

STENCILLING THE DESIGNS
The same stencilling method is used for both the top
sheet and the pillowcases, but the layouts differ.
In the linen illustrated here, the design
is repeated three times across the top
of the pillow and twice down the
sides; on the sheet, the stencil is
repeated six times across the top
and twice down the sides. The rose stencil
is used in the corners.

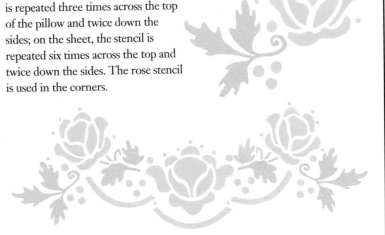

Découpage memorabilia box

Most of us hoard small mementoes, and they often become lost among our everyday objects. This colourful memorabilia box is a great place to store those precious bits and pieces, and it makes an attractive display item as well.

WHAT YOU NEED

Old wooden or craft wood box • suitable images • beeswax stick • artist's gesso • artist's acrylic paint in a colour to tone with images • artist's acrylic gloss medium (sealer) • polyurethane gloss varnish • 3 small paintbrushes (for sealing, gluing and painting) • 25 mm imitation sable brush (for varnishing) • wet-and-dry abrasive paper: fine and coarse • rubber sanding block • wallpaper paste • PVA glue • Blu-Tack • rubber roller • clear beeswax • cabinetmaker's polish • pieces of thick kitchen sponge • lint-free cloth • fine curved scissors • scalpel • screwdriver
● *Technique pages 329–31*

❶ PREPARATION

1 Before you begin, mark the top, bottom and front of the box on the inside so that you can reassemble the box accurately. Then remove any hinges and brass corners.
2 Check all surfaces and fill in any crevices with the beeswax stick.
3 If you are using a craft wood box, seal all the surfaces with artist's acrylic medium before sanding to prevent the release of formaldehyde.
4 Sand all surfaces lightly with wet-and-dry abrasive paper. Apply a coat of artist's gesso and allow to dry.
5 Seal the surfaces of the box and the images with artist's acrylic medium. Allow them to dry thoroughly.

❷ FIXING THE IMAGES

1 Make paper templates of all surfaces and arrange the images on them. Attach the images with Blu-Tack and rearrange them until you are happy with the design. The focus of the design should appear on the top and front of the box. With the curved scissors,

carefully cut the images to the required size and shape.
2 Mix three parts wallpaper paste and one part PVA glue. Working on one side at a time, apply plenty of the mixture to the surface of the box and a small amount to the right side of the images.
3 Massage and mould the images into the surface, adding more glue if necessary. Where images are placed on the corners of the box, mitre the corners and trim away any excess paper so that the edges fit together flush with no overlap. (You need not be so careful if metal corners are to be replaced on top.) Use the rubber roller to spread the glue evenly. Remove excess glue from the surface of the images with a wet sponge.
4 Repeat this procedure until images have been applied to all surfaces.
5 Before the glue has dried, gently run your fingernail along all the edges of the box to lightly score the paper. Using extreme care, peel back the top layer of paper and run a sharp scalpel blade down the score line to remove the excess paper, at the same time ensuring that the paper abuts neatly and that there are no gaps.
6 When the glue is dry, apply two coats of artist's acrylic medium to the surface, allowing each coat to dry thoroughly before applying the next.

❸ VARNISHING AND SANDING

Varnish the entire surface of the box, following the instructions in the découpage techniques section.

❹ FINISHING

1 Paint the inside of the box with artist's acrylic paint. Allow the paint to dry, then seal it with two coats of artist's acrylic medium.
2 Screw the hinges and brass corners (if any) back into place.
3 Mix equal parts of beeswax and cabinetmaker's polish and warm the mixture. Apply the mixture to the surface of the box, a little at a time.
4 Wipe over vigorously with a damp cloth and polish with a soft, dry cloth.

Placemats for a country kitchen

Mix and match odd fabric remnants to make these unusual padded and quilted patchwork table mats. Perfect for breakfast or an informal lunch, they are very easy to sew. The amounts of fabric specified will make one mat.

● Technique pages 292–301, 305–6

WHAT YOU NEED

20 squares assorted cotton fabric prints, 8 cm x 8 cm (for the patchwork) • 38 cm x 44 cm plain cotton fabric (for the backing) • 30 cm x 36 cm craft wadding • sewing thread • dressmaking pins • tape measure • pencil • scissors • sewing machine

❶ SEWING THE PATCHWORK

1 Check that all the patterned pieces are cut squarely along the straight grain of the fabric, and that they are all the same size (8 cm x 8 cm).

2 Lay out the fabric squares in four rows of five to decide how you want the patchwork to look. Number the squares lightly with a pencil on the wrong side of the fabric to guide you when you are sewing them together.

3 With right sides facing, and following your numbered sequence, stitch together the five squares that make up each row, using a 1 cm seam allowance. Press the seams open.

4 Again following the numbers, and with right sides facing, stitch the four rows together using a 1 cm seam allowance. Press the seams open.

❷ QUILTING THE PATCHWORK

1 Centre the patchwork right side up on the wadding and pin it in place. There should be a 2 cm margin of wadding all around the patchwork. If necessary, trim the wadding to this measurement.

2 Quilt the patchwork fabric to the wadding by machine stitching along the patchwork joins.

❸ ATTACHING THE BACKING

The corners of the backing are mitred over to the front of the place mat to form a border around the patchwork.

1 Trim the backing fabric to make a rectangle 38 cm x 44 cm. Press the edges under 1 cm all round to the wrong side. Turn over another 3 cm all round and press.

2 Unfold the fabric. Using the press lines as guides, mitre each corner neatly to form a border 3 cm wide. Stitch the diagonal mitring seams from the corners to the 1 cm press lines, leaving 1 cm to be folded under to make the inner edge of the border.

3 Turn the backing right side out, push the corners out, and press flat. Press down the 1 cm seam allowance around the inner edge of the border.

4 Insert the quilted patchwork, right side up, into the backing piece and tuck the edges under the border.

5 Pin and topstitch around the inner edge of the border, sewing through all layers of fabric.

HINT
Be adventurous when you are choosing fabrics for making the patchwork. In the placemats illustrated, bold stripes and checks are combined with small floral prints to produce a very unorthodox but colourful effect.

European Easter eggs

There are many ways to paint and decorate eggs, so you can please everybody with these seasonal gifts. Children will be able to make some of the eggs for a host or hostess.

WHAT YOU NEED

Eggs (hen, duck or goose) • egg cup or egg carton • dye or artist's acrylic paints and gesso • PVA glue • clear polyurethane gloss varnish • small paintbrushes (for painting, gluing and varnishing) • tweezers
Blown eggs: needles: medium and large straw • small bowl • white vinegar • warm water
Red glitter egg: red paint • red glitter • 20 cm gold braid or ribbon, about 12 mm wide
Dried flower egg: small dried pressed flowers • pale green paint • 20 cm ribbon, 12 mm wide
Découpage-style egg: pale pink paint • small pictures from wrapping paper • fine, curved nail scissors
Beaded egg: small coloured beads and sequins • paint in a colour to suit the decorations
Icing flower egg: pink paint • small icing flowers and leaves (from a cake-decorating supplier)
Stencilled egg: small flowers, leaves or grasses, or fabric cut-outs • dye • bowl for dye solution • egg white • linseed oil or varnish • stocking • strong thread • rubber gloves
● *Technique pages 329–31, 334–5*

❶ PREPARING THE EGGS

If you intend to spend a great deal of time creating a design and you want it to last, it is best to use blown eggs (eggs from which the yolks and whites have been removed). Blown eggs will keep indefinitely, if they are completely clean and dry on the inside.
1 Use an egg at room temperature and shake it vigorously so the yolk becomes detached.

2 With a darning needle, make a hole at each end of the egg. Carefully enlarge the hole at the blunt end by breaking off tiny pieces of shell with the point of the needle until the hole is big enough to insert the blunt end of a wooden skewer.
3 Insert the needle through the larger hole and move it about to break up the yolk further. Lean over a bowl and place your lips firmly over the smaller hole. Blow the contents of the egg through the larger hole—once they start to move, they will flow easily.
4 Mix a solution of one cup of warm water and one teaspoon of vinegar in a bowl, and immerse the egg until the shell contains one or two tablespoons of the liquid. Hold your finger and thumb over the holes and shake the

egg to wash the inside thoroughly. Then gently blow the solution out of the large hole.
5 With the blunt end facing down, place the egg shell in an egg cup or carton to drain. Do not start decorating the egg shell until the inside of the egg is completely dry.

❷ COLOURING THE EGGS

Most of the eggs in this project have been given a base coat of colour before the design is added. Eggs can be coloured with various mediums.
1 Dyeing with commercial dyes is one of the easiest ways. Dyes requiring boiling should not be used on blown eggs. Cold water dyes are suitable for dyeing both blown and hard-boiled eggs. To dye your eggs, follow

mixture to the boil and simmer for about 15 minutes. Strain the mixture and allow to cool thoroughly before adding blown or hard-boiled eggs.

❸ DECORATING THE EGGS

The methods of producing the designs in the photograph are described below. These are only some of the possible ways to decorate eggs. With a little imagination, you can easily create your own designs.

Red glitter egg

1 Apply two coats of red paint to the egg and allow the paint to dry.
2 Coat the blunt half of the egg with glue and sprinkle it with red glitter. Carefully balance the egg in the dimple of an egg carton or in an egg cup and allow it to dry.
3 Repeat step 2 with the other half of the egg, making sure you leave a 5 mm band around the middle of the egg free from glue.
4 Brush the centre strip with glue. Place the ribbon or braid around the egg and press it gently but firmly into position. Allow it to dry.

Dried flower egg

1 Apply two coats of pale green paint to the egg and allow it to dry.
2 Using a fine brush, carefully dab a little glue on to the backs of the dried flowers.
3 Using tweezers to pick up the flowers, arrange them on the egg and gently press them into place.
4 Tie the ribbon in a bow and glue it in position. Coat the entire surface with the clear varnish.

Découpage-style egg

1 Apply two coats of pink paint to the egg and allow it to dry.
2 Cut out a selection of small pictures from wrapping paper or books. Choose images printed on thin paper – they are easier to mould around the egg, and will give a smoother surface.
3 Apply glue liberally to the wrong sides of the shapes and press them on to the egg, smoothing out any air bubbles or lumps of glue. Wipe away any excess glue. Allow the glue to dry.

VARIATION

You can decorate eggs very simply using a batik technique. Draw a design in crayon or candle wax on the egg before immersing it in the dye. The area covered with crayon or wax will resist the dye.

4 Seal the egg by applying two or three coats of clear varnish.

Beaded egg

1 Apply two coats of paint to the egg and allow it to dry thoroughly.
2 With a very fine paintbrush, dab glue on to beads and sequins. Arrange the beads and sequins on the egg with tweezers. Allow the glue to dry.
3 Seal the the egg with two or three coats of clear varnish.

Icing flower egg

Follow the steps for decorating the beaded egg, but use cake decorations instead of beads.

Stencilled egg

1 Brush the undersides of small flowers, leaves, grasses or fabric cut-outs with egg white and arrange them on the egg, pressing the coated sides on to the surface of the egg.
2 Carefully slip the egg into a stocking and tie up the stocking tightly enough to hold the decorations in place.
3 Immerse the egg in a dye bath for the time stated in the manufacturer's instructions.
4 Leave the egg in the stocking and hang it up to dry. Remove the egg just before the stocking is quite dry, and carefully peel off the decorations.
5 When the egg is completely dry, rub it with linseed oil or coat it with varnish to give a shiny effect.

the manufacturer's instructions. Allow the eggs to dry completely before you begin decorating them.
2 Eggs can also be painted with artist's acrylic paints. Before you start, it is best to paint your egg with artist's gesso to give a smooth, clean surface on which to paint. Apply two coats of paint, allowing the paint to dry thoroughly between coats.
3 You can also experiment with dyes made from vegetable matter, such as onion skins (which produce a yellow dye), beetroot or spinach. Different teas also produce interesting hues. The amount of organic matter used determines the intensity of the colour. Cover the organic material with water and add a small amount of brown vinegar to 'set' the colour. Bring the

Wreath of nuts & leaves

This softly coloured wreath is studded with cones, seedpods and nuts to evoke the autumn.

Vine wreath base (from florist's suppliers) • dried oak leaves on small branches • dried salal leaves (from florist's suppliers) or bay leaves • poppy seedheads, cedar roses or small cones • hazelnuts on wires • hot glue gun and glue sticks • 20 cm thin pliable wire
● *Technique pages 332–3*

❶ DRYING THE FOLIAGE
Air dry the oak and bay leaves following the methods described in 'Flower and foliage drying'.

❷ MAKING THE WREATH
1 Make a hanger across the back of the wreath with wire.
2 Build up the background by pushing small branches of salal leaves into the base. Intersperse with oak or bay leaves. Make sure that the top and sides are covered and that the base is

> **HINT**
>
> *To wire nuts: stand the nuts in Plasticine and drill a small hole using a fine drill. Push a short length of florist's wire into the hole and glue in place using a hot glue gun.*

concealed. Allow some branches to hang into the centre of the circle and some to overhang the outside edge. Once you are happy with the arrangement, glue the leaves into place using the hot glue gun.
3 Glue small groups of cedar roses or cones randomly around the wreath ensuring that some of the groups are towards the inner side, some on top and some towards the outer edge. Be sure to glue the cedar roses or cones

to the base, not to the leaves, or they will not be secure. Turn the wreath as you work to ensure a balanced result.
4 Place groups of wired hazelnuts close to the cedar roses or cones and fix in place by pushing the wires through the vine base and twisting the wire round the vine at the back. Arrange the poppy seedheads fanning them out around the cedar roses or cones and when you are pleased with the result glue them in place.

EDIBLE GIFTS

Whether it be a spicy chutney or a traditional cake, a homemade delicacy is a gift for any occasion. There's a tasty treat here to suit every palate, from the conservative to the adventurous.

Nibbles & appetisers

Everybody likes to nibble on something before dinner. Here is a selection of recipes you can prepare at home for gifts. Most are perishable and should be stored in the refrigerator.

Marinated olives (left) look very attractive when the layers are built up carefully inside ornamental glass jars. Glazed chilli nuts (right) are the perfect accompaniment for tall, cool drinks – present them to a host instead of wine or after-dinner mints.

Glazed chilli nuts

Make sure you have the trays and the ingredients ready before you start, as you will have to work quickly once the caramel is cooked.

WHAT YOU NEED

200 g toasted almonds
250 g granulated sugar
½ teaspoon chilli powder
60 ml water

1 Preheat the oven to 180°C and toast the almonds for approximately 8–10 minutes, or until golden.
2 Lightly oil two baking trays.
3 In a heavy-based saucepan or frying pan, dissolve sugar and chilli powder in the water over low heat, stirring constantly. Bring to the boil and simmer until the mixture is golden.
4 Stir in the toasted almonds and continue stirring for 2–3 minutes until they are well coated in the caramel.
5 Pour immediately on to one of the trays and quickly separate the nuts with oiled tongs. Using an oiled knife, push the nuts off the tray on to another lightly oiled tray, keeping the nuts well separated.
6 Allow the caramel to set before storing the nuts in screwtop jars.
● Makes 200 g.

Marinated olives

The following recipe is only a guide. The quantities will vary depending on the size and number of your jars.

WHAT YOU NEED

Oranges
Assorted medium-sized olives
(Kalamata, green, stuffed)
Fresh bay leaves
Fresh sprigs of thyme
or rosemary
Peeled cloves of garlic
Medium-sized green chillies
Virgin olive oil

Chocolate, date & almond torte

This scrumptious mixture will fill three 12.5 x 6.5 cm cake tins – give two away and keep one for yourself.

For the cake
200 g toasted almonds
200 g dark cooking chocolate
250 g seedless dates
6 egg whites,
at room temperature
150 g caster sugar
For the chocolate coating
500 ml double cream
500 g dark chocolate,
chopped roughly

1 Preheat the oven to 180°C. Lightly grease and line the three cake tins with three layers of non-stick baking paper, bringing the paper up above the sides of the tins.
2 Chop the almonds, chocolate and dates, using a large, sharp knife.
3 In a large mixing bowl, whisk the egg whites with a pinch of salt until stiff. Fold in the sugar gradually.
4 Fold in the chopped almonds, chocolate and dates and spoon the mixture evenly into the prepared tins.
5 Bake in the oven for 45 minutes. Leave to cool in the oven, with the door open. Don't worry if the cake looks cracked when you turn it out – the chocolate coating will cover these imperfections.
6 *To make the coating:* Bring the cream to the boil and pour over the chopped chocolate in a large saucepan or bowl, stirring until the chocolate has melted and the mixture is smooth and glossy.
7 Coat the tops and sides of the cakes with the chocolate mixture. Place on a rack over a plate in the refrigerator until the chocolate has set.
8 Recoat each cake with the coating mixture – which may need to be reheated over a pan of hot water – and smooth the sides for a glossy effect.
● You can make variations of the torte by substituting walnuts for almonds and dried figs for dates.

Place the torte on a broad satin ribbon. Bring the ribbon up to the top, loop it around itself and secure underneath with sticky tape. Nest the torte in foil, tissue or rice paper.

Many Indian sweets are linked to religious festivals and other special days.

Barfi

Barfi are Indian sweets that are traditionally decorated with edible silver paper and given to friends and relatives during Divali, one of India's most colourful festivals.

600 g demerara sugar
250 ml water
375 g full cream powdered milk
1 teaspoon cardamom
seeds, lightly pounded
½ teaspoon ground nutmeg
550 ml double cream
50 g pistachio nuts, chopped

1 Make a sugar syrup by putting the sugar and water into a heavy-based saucepan and bringing it to the boil, stirring to dissolve the sugar.
2 Simmer the mixture over medium heat, stirring constantly, for 25–30 minutes until the syrup is sticky and forms a thick thread.
3 Meanwhile, put the powdered milk, cardamom seeds and nutmeg into a bowl. Add the cream and combine the ingredients with your hands until the mixture resembles breadcrumbs.
4 When the syrup is ready, pour it into the milk mixture, mixing it in quickly with a wooden spoon.
5 Pour into a biscuit tray lined with non-stick baking paper. Allow to cool. Scatter with chopped pistachios and then refrigerate until set.
6 Cut the barfi into squares or diamond shapes and decorate.
● Makes about 30 pieces.

Remove the fruit cakes from the tins when they are almost cool and decorate them with glazed fruits and nuts.

Festive fruit cake

Bake this cake as a gift to celebrate any festive occasion.

WHAT YOU NEED

250 g dried figs or stoned dates
250 g glacé pineapple
125 g dried apricots
125 g whole green glacé cherries
125 g whole red glacé cherries
2 teaspoons grated orange zest
200 ml ginger ale
250 g macadamia nuts
2 eggs
100 g brown sugar
90 g melted butter
1 teaspoon vanilla essence
75 g plain flour
1 teaspoon cardamom powder
½ teaspoon baking powder
Pinch salt
2–3 tablespoons dark rum

1 Preheat the oven to 150°C. If using figs, chop them roughly, but leave dates whole. Chop the pineapple and apricots roughly. Put these fruits into a bowl with the cherries and orange zest. Soak overnight in the ginger ale.
2 The following day, drain the ale from the fruit and mix in the nuts.
3 Lightly grease three 12.5 cm cake tins and line the sides and bottoms with three layers of baking paper.
4 Beat the eggs in a bowl until they are light and foamy.

5 Add the sugar, butter and vanilla. Continue beating until the ingredients are well combined.
6 Sift the dry ingredients and fold them into the creamed mixture, then fold in the fruit and nuts. Spoon the mixture into the prepared tins.
7 Bake for 1¼ hours, or until a skewer inserted into the centre of the cake comes out clean.
8 Remove the cakes from the oven and spoon the rum over the tops.

Boiled pineapple fruit cake

Crushed pineapple and spices liven up a favourite old recipe.

WHAT YOU NEED

450 g crushed pineapple
375 g mixed dried fruit
100 g demerara sugar
125 g butter
1 teaspoon cinnamon
½ teaspoon allspice
1 teaspoon bicarbonate of soda
150 g self-raising flour
175 g plain wholemeal flour
Pinch salt
75 g sunflower kernels
3 eggs, beaten

1 Preheat the oven to 150°C. Put the pineapple, dried fruit, sugar, butter, cinnamon, allspice and bicarbonate of soda into a saucepan and stir over a medium heat until the sugar has dissolved and the butter melted. Bring to the boil, then simmer gently for 10 minutes. Remove the mixture from the heat and allow to cool.
2 Grease two 15 cm cake tins and line them with three layers of non-stick baking paper.
3 Sift together the flours and salt. Stir into the fruit mixture with a wooden spoon, along with the sunflower kernels and beaten eggs.
4 Spoon into the prepared tins and bake for 1½ hours or until a skewer inserted in to the centre comes out clean. Allow to cool in the tin, then turn out and decorate with glazed fruits and nuts.

Panforte

This nougat-like cake, originally a Christmas treat, has been a Sienese speciality since medieval times. It is now exported all over the world.

WHAT YOU NEED

50 g walnuts
50 g hazelnuts
200 g blanched almonds
200 g mixed glacé fruit
25 g mixed candied peel
15 g glacé ginger
200 g plain white flour
1 tablespoon cocoa
½ teaspoon ground coriander
½ teaspoon ground cinnamon
¼ teaspoon mixed spice
4 tablespoons honey
150 g icing sugar
1 tablespoon water
Rice paper

1 Preheat the oven to 150°C and line two 20 cm shallow cake tins with rice paper. If you cannot find rice paper, line the tins with aluminium foil lightly brushed with oil.

Arrange wedges of panforte neatly in a flat basket lined with a paper doily, wrap in cellophane and tie with a bow.

2 Roast the nuts on a baking tray in the oven until they are golden brown. Remove from the oven, allow to cool and then chop roughly.

3 Cut up the fruit and mix together in a bowl with the nuts, peel, ginger, flour, cocoa and spices.

4 In a small saucepan, combine the honey, icing sugar and water. Bring to the boil and cook until the syrup reaches 112–116°C measured with a sugar thermometer, or until a small drop of syrup hardens when dropped into a cup of cold water.

5 Add the syrup to the fruit and nut mixture and combine well – the mixture should be stiff and sticky.

6 Spoon the mixture evenly into the lined tins and top with more rice paper, pressing down with your hands to even out the mixture. Place the tins in the oven and bake for 30 minutes.

7 Remove the panforte from the tins and allow to cool.

8 When cool, cut into thin wedges and dust thickly with icing sugar.

Tsoureki

Delight your host and hostess at Easter with this spectacular traditional Greek Easter bread.

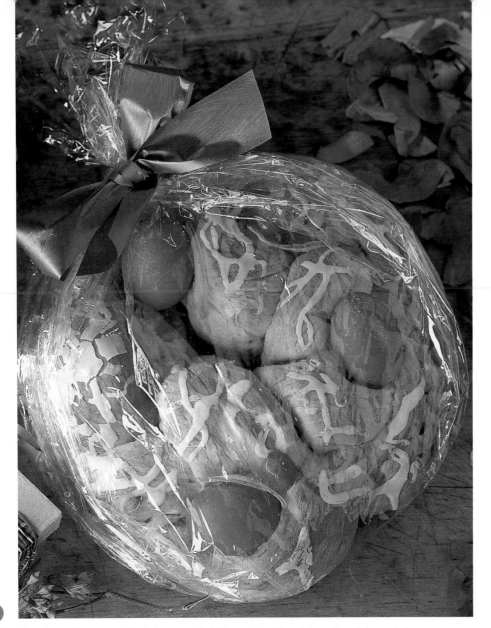

Eggs have always symbolised the renewel of life, and the Church has adopted the symbol to represent the Resurrection. Red eggs feature importantly in Greek Easter celebrations.

WHAT YOU NEED

3 eggs
1 tablespoon vinegar
Red egg colouring
700 g plain flour
2 sachets (14 g) dry yeast
½ teaspoon salt
75 g caster sugar
1 teaspoon cinnamon
200-250 ml warm milk
125 g melted butter
2 eggs, beaten
50 g almonds, chopped
50 g sultanas
50 g chopped mixed peel
Icing sugar

1 *To colour the eggs:* Put the raw eggs into a saucepan and cover with cold water. Add the vinegar and the red egg colouring. Bring gently to the boil, simmer for 10 minutes, then remove pan from heat. Leave the eggs in the steeping mixture for about 2 hours, and then drain.

2 To make the dough, put all the dry ingredients into a large mixing bowl. Make a hole in the centre and pour in the warm milk, the melted butter and the eggs. Mix well, adding more milk if necessary.

3 Turn the dough out on to a floured board and knead it until it is quite smooth and shiny.

4 Put the dough in a lightly greased bowl and let it rise in a warm place for about an hour, or until it has doubled in bulk. Press two fingers into the dough. If the depression made by your fingers remains, the dough is ready.

5 Knead the dough again and turn out on to a floured surface. Gently knead the almonds, sultanas and mixed peel into the dough, then divide it into three pieces and roll each piece into a long rope.

6 Plait the three ropes together and shape them into a circle on a greased baking tray. Place the prepared coloured eggs, unpeeled, at evenly spaced intervals in the hollows of the plait.

7 Cover the dough and leave it to rise again for about an hour.

8 Preheat the oven to 190°C. Bake the plait for 30–35 minutes. Remove the tsoureki from the oven and leave it to cool on a wire rack.

9 When cool, drizzle the bread with glacé icing, made from sifted icing sugar and a little water.

Biscotti

Italian biscotti are a delicious accompaniment for morning coffee.

WHAT YOU NEED

50 g pine nuts
275 g plain flour
100 g caster sugar
½ teaspoon bicarbonate of soda
Pinch of salt
2 sprigs rosemary
Zest of 1 orange, finely grated
80 g unskinned almonds
2 eggs, beaten
1 egg, beaten with
a little water

1 Preheat the oven to 180°C. Spread the pine nuts on an oven tray and toast them for 8–10 minutes.
2 Put the flour, sugar, bicarbonate of soda and salt into a bowl. Finely chop the rosemary leaves and add to the dry ingredients along with the grated orange zest, almonds and toasted pine nuts. Combine the ingredients well.
3 Add the eggs and mix to a dough.
4 Divide the dough into four and roll into thickish 'sausages' on a lightly floured surface.
5 Place on a greased baking tray, brush with egg wash and bake for 20 minutes. Leave on tray to cool. Cut at an angle into slices about 1 cm wide.
6 Brush the slices with the egg wash once again and bake at 150°C for a further 10 minutes.
● Makes about 48 biscotti.

Brownies

This famous American chocolate-and-nut slice is always a hit.

WHAT YOU NEED

125 g butter
125 g dark chocolate
4 eggs
350 g sugar
1 teaspoon vanilla essence
150 g plain flour
75 g walnuts
Icing
150 g dark chocolate, chopped
45 g butter

Italian biscotti (top left) and almond bread (bottom centre) are classic twice-cooked biscuits. Brownies (bottom left) and gingerbread men (top right) aren't really biscuits – but they're just as tempting, and so are stuffed dates (top centre) and jaffa fudge (centre).

1 Preheat the oven to 180°C. Line a 27 x 17 cm biscuit tin with non-stick baking paper.
2 Melt the butter and chocolate in a bowl over steaming water. Remove from the heat and allow to cool.
3 Beat the eggs with a pinch of salt until light and foamy. Gradually beat in the sugar and vanilla essence.
4 Quickly combine the cooled chocolate mixture and the eggs, using a wooden spoon. Fold in the flour, then the nuts.
5 Spoon this mixture into the prepared tin and bake in the oven for 35–40 minutes. Remove the brownies from the oven and allow them to cool in the tin.
6 *To make the icing:* Melt the chocolate and butter in a small bowl over boiling water. Mix well, and then leave to cool a little. Spread icing over the top of the brownies with a spatula and allow to set.
7 Cut into squares and place the brownies in a box between layers of greaseproof paper.
● Makes about 24 brownies.

Stuffed dates

Tasty and unusual titbits to accompany after-dinner coffee.

WHAT YOU NEED

20 fresh dates
Glacé pineapple or dried apricots
Toasted slivered almonds
Grated zest of 2 oranges
100 g granulated sugar

2 Lightly bruise the herbs with a pestle and mortar and add to the oil. Seal and leave to steep for two weeks.
3 Strain the oil through muslin or cheesecloth into sterile bottles.
4 Add a sprig of fresh herb to each bottle, then seal and label the bottles. Keep in a cool, dark place.
● Makes 750 ml.

Herb vinegar

Use the finest vinegar to enhance the delicate flavour of the herbs.

WHAT YOU NEED

25 g fresh herbs
750 ml white wine or champagne vinegar
1–2 sprigs fresh herbs

1 Lightly bruise the herbs with a pestle and mortar, or with the back of a spoon on a wooden board.
2 Combine the herbs with the vinegar in a non-metallic container. Cover the mixture and leave it to infuse for a couple of weeks.
3 Strain through double cheesecloth into clean sterile bottles.
4 Add a fresh sprig or two of the herb you have used for the infusion to each bottle. Cork and label the bottles.
● Makes 750 ml.

Vinaigrette

A classic vinaigrette to accompany avocados, artichokes or asparagus.

WHAT YOU NEED

500 ml virgin olive oil
or light olive oil
100 ml red or white
wine vinegar
2 teaspoons Dijon mustard
Coarse sea salt to taste
6 whole peppercorns
1 bay leaf
Fresh thyme
1 whole head of garlic

1 Put the oil, vinegar, mustard and salt into a sterile screwtop or cliptop jar. Shake well. Add peppercorns, bay leaf and thyme.

2 Slice the head of garlic lengthwise in half, removing any excess papery coating. Float one half in the jar. Use the other for another vinaigrette.
● Makes 600 ml.

Fruit vinegars

Rasberry vinegar can be diluted with iced water to make a cool and refreshing drink.

WHAT YOU NEED

500 g soft fresh fruits
(raspberries, strawberries,
blueberries)
750 ml white vinegar

1 Combine the fruit and vinegar in a bowl and stir well to lightly bruise the fruit. Cover the mixture and leave it to infuse for a few days.
2 Put the mixture into a saucepan. Bring it to boiling point, and then remove immediately from the heat and allow to cool.
3 Strain the mixture through double muslin or cheesecloth into sterile jars. Seal the jars and label them.
● Makes 750 ml.

Variation

Peaches, plums and pears can also be used to make fruit vinegars. Slice the fruit in half, leaving a few of the stones attached. After a few months, filter off the vinegar. The fruit may be eaten as a pickle with cold meats and the vinegar used traditionally.

Red chilli vinegar

Flavoured vinegars add piquancy to vinaigrettes and sauces.

WHAT YOU NEED

2–3 long red chillies,
washed and dried
750 ml white wine vinegar

1 Cut one of the chillies in half lengthwise and place in a 750 ml bottle with the other two chillies.
2 Pour in the vinegar and then cork the bottles firmly and label them.
● Makes 750 ml.

Garam masala

Grind spices in a coffee grinder. Clean out before and after using.

WHAT YOU NEED

3 tablespoons coriander seeds
3 tablespoons cumin seeds
3 teaspoons cardamom seeds
1 tablespoon black peppercorns
3 cinnamon sticks
10 cloves
½ teaspoon grated
nutmeg (optional)

1 Dry roast the seeds separately in a hot frying pan, shaking constantly. Remove from the heat just as they begin to smoke. Place in a bowl and leave to cool.
2 Blend the seeds and the remaining ingredients (other than the nutmeg) to a fine powder in a coffee grinder, adding the nutmeg if desired.
3 Store the garam masala in sterile screwtop jars.
● Makes about 50 g.

Garam masala (front) will be a welcome addition to your hostess's kitchen.

Pickles

A gift of homemade pickles is a nostalgic reminder of the days when every housewife pickled and preserved garden produce.

Preserved peppers in oil

Preserved peppers with a hint of garlic make a colourful addition to any meat dish.

WHAT YOU NEED

3 large green peppers
3 large red peppers
Salt
1¾ litres white vinegar
1 or 2 cloves garlic,
cut in slivers
30 g fresh parsley
250 ml olive oil

1 Cut the peppers into five or six segments, removing the membrane and seeds. Wash and dry well. Place the segments in a bowl and sprinkle liberally with salt. Put a plate on the top and weigh down with a heavy weight. Allow to stand overnight.
2 The following day, drain the peppers well and return them to the bowl. Cover them with the vinegar and put a plate on top to ensure that the pepper segments are submerged in the vinegar. Allow to stand for about 8 hours or overnight.
3 Drain the peppers and pack them into sterile jars, distributing the garlic slivers and parsley evenly throughout. Cover with oil and seal.
4 The following day, check the oil level and top up if necessary. Cover tightly and store in the refrigerator for a month before giving as a gift.
● Makes about 1.5 litres.

HINT
Pickles need to mature for at least four weeks to allow their full flavour to develop before you present them as gifts.

Preserved lemons

In the Middle East, this is a common way of preserving lemons. Both the skins and the juice add a unique flavour to salads and fish.

WHAT YOU NEED

Fresh lemons
Coarse sea salt

1 Wash and scrub the lemons to remove any wax.
2 Put them in a bowl of salted water and allow to stand for 24 hours. Drain well and dry.
3 Make two cuts, at right angles to each other, through each lemon from

Left to right: Pickled oranges with a hint of honey, preserved lemons from the Middle East, giardiniera from Italy, garlic-flavoured preserved capsicums and piquant pickled eggplant – marvellous presents to give your weekend host.

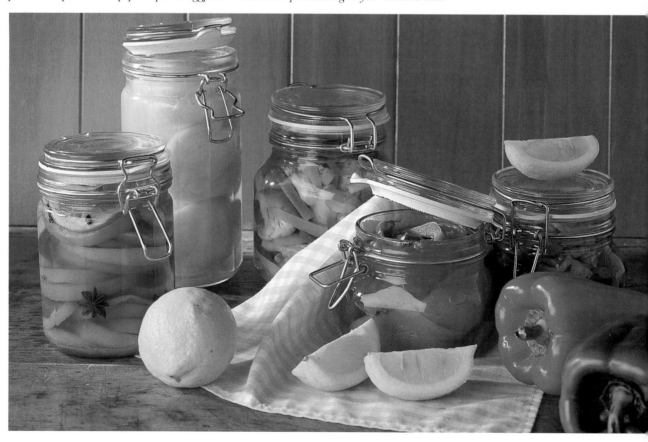

the stem end – do not cut them all the way through.

4 Put a teaspoon of salt into the centre of each lemon.

5 Push three or four lemons into a sterile ½-litre jar with a wooden spoon. Cover with water and seal.

6 After a couple of days, the lemons will have softened slightly; at this stage you can pack in another lemon or two.

7 When the jar is well packed, set it aside for a month. Don't worry if a film forms over the lemons; it can easily be washed off.

● You can also use this method to preserve very ripe limes.

Giardiniera

Fresh vegetables are pickled to make this colourful, delicately flavoured antipasto from Italy.

WHAT YOU NEED

350 g cauliflower florets
200 g green beans
200 g Lebanese cucumbers
3 large carrots, peeled
3 peppers (1 green, 1 yellow, 1 red)
150 g small onions
125 ml olive oil
125 ml water
250 ml white wine
1¼ litres white vinegar
3 tablespoons sugar
3 tablespoons salt
4–5 bay leaves
½ tablespoon peppercorns

1 Wash and dry the cauliflower florets. Top and tail the beans and cut into halves. Halve the cucumbers lengthwise and then slice each half into thirds. Cut the carrots into thin strips. Remove the membrane and seeds from the capsicums and cut into strips about 5 mm wide. Cut the onions into quarters.

2 Put the oil, water, wine, vinegar, sugar, salt, bay leaves and peppercorns into a large pot and bring to the boil. Simmer until the sugar and salt have dissolved. Remove from the heat and leave to cool for 5 minutes.

3 Drop the prepared cauliflower,

carrots, beans and onions into the pickling solution and place a plate on top to ensure that the vegetables are fully submerged.

4 When completely cool, add the cucumbers and capsicums. Leave for 3–4 hours with the plate on top.

5 Pack into sterile jars and cover completely with the pickling solution.

● Makes about 2.25 litres.

Pickled oranges

These oranges are delicious with ham, roast duck or pork.

WHAT YOU NEED

8 oranges, unpeeled
1 teaspoon salt
250 ml water
450 g sugar
250 ml malt vinegar
90 g honey
1 small knob ginger, peeled and chopped
1 teaspoon ground cinnamon
½ teaspoon five-spice powder
8 whole black peppercorns
8 cardamom pods
2 star anise
12 cloves

1 Wash the oranges thoroughly and put them into a large pot or saucepan together with the salt. Cover with water and bring to the boil. Reduce the heat and leave the fruit to simmer for about 40 minutes.

2 Drain the oranges, allow them to cool, and then cut them into slices about 5 mm thick.

3 Put the remaining ingredients into a saucepan and bring to the boil. Reduce the heat and simmer gently for 10 minutes.

4 Add the orange slices and bring the mixture back to the boil, stirring occasionally. Reduce the heat and simmer gently for another 15 minutes.

5 Remove the saucepan from the heat and allow the mixture to stand for approximately 10 minutes.

6 Ladle the oranges into warmed sterile jars. Seal and label the jars. Keep refrigerated once seal is broken.

● Makes about 1.5 litres.

Piquant pickled aubergine in oil

A scrumptious taste with sun-dried tomatoes on Italian bread.

WHAT YOU NEED

2 kg aubergines, peeled
200 g cooking salt
750 ml white vinegar
1 tablespoon sugar
1 tablespoon salt
15 whole black peppercorns
Olive oil
4 small red chillies
4–6 cloves garlic, peeled
6 sprigs fresh oregano

1 Cut the aubergines into lengthwise slices about 5 mm thick. Place them in layers in a large earthenware dish, sprinkling salt on every slice. Finish off with a layer of salt. Place a flat plate on top of the aubergines, weigh it down with a heavy weight, such as a bag of potatoes, and leave for several hours. Take out the slices and squeeze them to remove excess liquid.

2 Mix the vinegar, sugar, salt and peppercorns in a saucepan and bring the mixture to the boil.

3 Drop a quarter of the aubergine slices into the boiling vinegar and simmer for 30 seconds. Remove and place on paper towels. Repeat until all the slices have been blanched. Make sure that they are well dried. Put them in a bowl and dress with olive oil.

4 Place the aubergine slices in layers in sterile jars, distributing the chillies, garlic cloves and oregano as you go.

5 Fill the jars with olive oil, pressing down to remove any air bubbles. Use a skewer to release any remaining trapped air.

6 Check the oil level the following day and top with more oil if necessary. Seal and store in a cool dark place.

● Makes about 1.2 litres.

HINT
When you are making pickles, remember to use only stainless steel equipment.

Preserves & chutneys

What nicer contribution to a picnic or special dinner than a spicy chutney, an unusual mixture of dried fruits preserved in mustard, a continental treat like olive paste or tapenade of figs, or a jar of tomatoes that you have dried and bottled yourself?

Red pepper marmalade

Red pepper marmalade is a tasty addition to pork, ham or chicken.

WHAT YOU NEED

12 large red peppers
2 tablespoons salt
675 g sugar
375 ml white vinegar

1 Wash the capsicums, remove the seeds and the membrane and chop finely. Sprinkle with the salt and allow to stand for 2–3 hours in a colander.
2 Put the drained capsicum in a heavy-based saucepan with the sugar and vinegar. Cook for about an hour, stirring occasionally, until thick.
3 Spoon into warm sterile jars and seal. Refrigerate once seal is broken.
● Makes about 1 litre.

Apricot chutney

Apricots, garlic, chillies and ginger mingle to stimulate the taste buds.

WHAT YOU NEED

500 g dried apricots
8 large cloves garlic, peeled
4 medium chillies, chopped
1 medium-sized knob
fresh ginger, peeled
and chopped
400 g brown sugar
500 ml red or white
wine vinegar
½ teaspoon salt
150 g sultanas

1 Cover the apricots with water and soak the fruit overnight.
2 The following day, put the garlic, chillies and ginger in the blender together with some of the soaking water and blend until smooth.
3 Put this mixture in a preserving pan or large saucepan, together with the apricots and their soaking liquid.
4 Add the sugar, vinegar and salt. Bring to the boil and simmer over the lowest heat for about ½ hour.
5 Add the sultanas and cook for a further ½ hour or until the chutney is thick and glossy. Allow to cool.
6 Place in sterile jars and store in the refrigerator.
● Makes about 850 ml.

Tomato chutney

Try this fiery South-East Asian variation of a familiar condiment.

WHAT YOU NEED

2 tablespoons black
mustard seeds
625 ml malt vinegar
4–6 kg ripe tomatoes, peeled
300 ml olive oil
4 tablespoons cumin seeds
200 g fresh ginger, peeled
and chopped
20 cloves garlic, peeled
10 fresh red chillies, chopped
2 tablespoons
turmeric powder
2 tablespoons sambal oelek
250 g palm sugar
100 ml fish sauce

1 Soak the black mustard seeds overnight in the malt vinegar. Drain the seeds and discard the vinegar.
2 Preheat the oven to 180°C, and roast the tomatoes in some of the oil for about 1½ hours.
3 Toast the cumin seeds in a hot frying pan for a few minutes. Shake the pan occasionally and watch that the seeds do not burn.
4 Put the cumin and mustard seeds and all the other ingredients except the oil into a blender and purée.
5 Simmer in a saucepan for about 45 minutes, stirring frequently.
6 Add the roasted tomatoes with their juices and the remaining oil.
7 Cook the chutney for a further hour, stirring frequently and adding more oil if necessary.
8 Spoon into sterile, screwtop jars.
● Makes about 3 litres.

Olive paste

Anchovy-flavoured olive paste can be spread on bread or tossed through a salad or hot pasta.

WHAT YOU NEED

300 g pitted black olives
18 anchovy fillets
130 g capers
4 cloves garlic, roughly chopped
1 teaspoon freshly
ground black pepper
½ teaspoon salt
125 ml olive oil

1 Put the black olives, anchovy fillets, capers, chopped garlic, pepper and salt into a food processor.
2 Process until smooth, dribbling in the olive oil gradually as you go.
3 Spoon into sterile, screwtop jars.
● Makes about 500 ml.

Fig tapenade

This Provençale condiment goes well with barbecued lamb chops.

WHAT YOU NEED

125 g dried figs
175 g pitted Kalamata olives
Juice of 1 lemon
2 tablespoons olive oil
45 g anchovies
50 g capers

1 Put the figs into a bowl, cover with boiling water and leave to soak until soft. Remove the figs and chop them into small pieces with a sharp knife.
2 Put the figs in a food processor with the remaining ingredients and process to a fine pulp. Spoon the fig tapenade into a sterilised jar.
● Makes about 220 ml.

Left to right: Apricot chutney, tomato chutney, tomatoes in olive oil, olive paste, red pepper marmalade (top), mustard fruits (bottom), and fig tapenade – there's something here to suit every friend's palate and taste buds.

Mustard fruits

Mustard fruits are delicious with game, ham or roast pork.

500 g sugar
375 ml water
250 g dried apricots
250 g dried peaches
250 g dried figs
250 g dried mango
1 cinnamon stick
4 cloves
6 black peppercorns
6 coriander seeds
125 ml white wine vinegar
50 g hot mustard powder

1 Put 400 g of the sugar with the water into a saucepan and gently heat until the sugar has dissolved. Add the fruit and spices, and cook over a low heat for 15–20 minutes.

2 In another saucepan, dissolve the remaining sugar with the vinegar and cook for about 10 minutes, until it forms a thick syrup. Allow to cool.

3 Mix the mustard powder with enough of the syrup to form a paste. Stir in the remaining syrup and then combine it with the cooked fruit compote. Mix well.

4 Return to the boil, allow to cool, and then pour into warm, sterile jars.

● Makes about 1.5 litres.

Dried tomatoes in olive oil

Use either plum or cherry tomatoes – the cherry tomatoes don't take as long to dry. Red and yellow cherry tomatoes look very attractive mixed together.

2 kg vine-ripened tomatoes
10 g fresh thyme or oregano
10 g coarse sea salt
1 tablespoon sugar
8 cloves garlic, peeled
1–2 bay leaves
Capers (optional)
Olive oil

1 Preheat the oven to 50°C. (For preference use a convection or fan-assisted oven.)

2 Wash and dry the tomatoes, halve them lengthwise and arrange them cut-side-up on cake racks.

3 Finely chop the fresh herbs and sprinkle them over the tomatoes, together with sparing quantities of salt and sugar.

4 Put the racks into the oven. Remember to put a tray underneath to catch any liquid.

5 Leave to dry for 24–36 hours. The time will vary depending on your oven and the moisture content of the tomatoes. The tomatoes should be dry but still fleshy. Do not let them become too withered.

6 Remove and allow to cool, then place in sterile glass jars with the garlic and a bay leaf or two. Add the capers if desired.

7 Cover the tomatoes with oil, tapping the jar on a bench top to remove any air bubbles. Seal the jars tightly and store in the refrigerator.

● Makes about 750 ml.

Drinks

A bottle of homemade cordial is a refreshing gift, especially at the height of summer. A tablespoon or two of cordial added to iced water makes a delicious cool drink.

Blackcurrant liqueur (second from left) makes a luxurious gift. Ginger syrup (left), Earl Grey tea & lemon syrup (centre) and Fifty-fifty cordial are great for family parties.

Earl Grey tea & lemon syrup

Dilute with water and lots of ice for an instant iced tea drink.

WHAT YOU NEED

2 Earl Grey tea bags
600 ml boiling water
700 g sugar
25 g citric acid
4 large unwaxed lemons

1 Put the tea bags and water into a saucepan. Allow to stand for 10 minutes, then remove and discard the tea bags.
2 Add the sugar to the pan, heat gently until the sugar has disolved.
3 Transfer to a sterile bowl and stir in the citric acid.
4 Pare the rind from the lemons, squeeze juice and add both to bowl.

5 Cover the bowl with a clean cloth to prevent evaporation and leave for 8 hours or overnight.
6 Strain into sterile bottles and seal.
● Makes about 1 litre.

Blackcurrant liqueur

Blackcurrant liqueur is the basis of the aperitif known as Kir. To make Kir, pour a teaspoonful of the liqueur into a wine glass and top with white wine or champagne.

WHAT YOU NEED

2 cups blackcurrants
Small cinnamon stick
2 cups brandy
½ cup sugar

1 Put all the ingredients into a sterile jar and mix well. Seal and shake well. Store in a dark, cool place for a month

or two, shaking the jar well every other day.
2 Strain the mixture through a muslin cloth into sterile bottles and seal.
● Makes about 1 litre.

Ginger syrup

Here is a soft drink that will please the most discriminating taste.

WHAT YOU NEED

900 g sugar
Juice of 3 lemons
1 dessertspoon ground ginger
1 teaspoon tartaric acid
4.5 litres water

1 Mix together all the ingredients in a very large bowl, stirring until all the sugar has dissolved.
2 Strain and pour into sterile bottles. The syrup will be ready in 2–3 days.
● Makes six 750 ml bottles.

Fifty-fifty cordial

Mix with fizzy mineral water and ice for a refreshing summer drink.

WHAT YOU NEED

4 oranges
4 lemons
2 kg sugar
30 g Epsom salts
75 g tartaric or citric acid
2 litres boiling water

1 Grate the citrus zest and squeeze the juice into a large bowl. Add sugar, salts, acid and zest. Add the boiling water and allow to stand overnight.
2 The following day, pour into sterile bottles and seal.
● Makes five 750 ml bottles.

size. It is especially useful for cutting fabric for patchwork, appliqué and quilting. However, remember that rotary cutters are very sharp and can cause deep cuts in hands or furniture.
• Always use a cutting mat under the fabric. A self-healing mat with a rough surface that prevents the fabric from slipping is best.
• Always use a ruler (plastic or steel) to guide the cutting wheel.
• Iron the fabric before cutting and smooth it out over the cutting mat so that there are no wrinkles to cause uneven cutting lines.
• Holding the ruler down firmly with one hand, push the cutter blade away from you in one movement, pressing into the cutting mat and keeping the blade tight against the ruler.
• Retract the blade after each cut.

Scalloped edges

1 To calculate scallop size, measure the edge to be scalloped, excluding seam allowances. Keeping the size proportionate, work out how many scallops will fit along the edge. Scallops should be about a third as high as they are wide. Make a cardboard template of the scallop shape.
2 Tack tissue paper or tear-away fabric stabiliser to the wrong side of the fabric edge.

3 Centre the template on the fabric edge and mark around it on the right side of the fabric. Then mark scallops right along the edge on either side of the centre scallop.
4 Machine finishing: Zigzag along the scalloped edge with a small open zigzag stitch. Trim away excess fabric, and then machine a second row of zigzag stitches over the first to give a close satin stitch finish.
5 Hand finishing: Staystitch by hand or machine about 3 mm inside the

marked scallops. Cut around the scalloped edge and finish the raw edges with closely worked buttonhole stitch.

Machine sewing

STAYSTITCHING

Staystitching is a reinforcing stitch, usually made through a single layer of fabric, to prevent stretching during assembly of a garment. It is generally placed just inside the seamline on curved or angled seams, and is done as soon as the pattern has been removed and before any further handling.

SEAMS

Seams are the basic structural elements of a garment, and must be formed with care. For most seams the right sides of the fabric are placed together, but occasionally the wrong sides are facing. The standard seam width is 1.5 cm (15 mm), but always check the pattern in case a seam requires a special width. Seams should be backtacked at the beginning and end for reinforcement.

Seam assembly

1 Pin the seam, matching notches and other markings along the seamline. Place pins perpendicular to seamline, with tips just beyond the seamline and heads toward seam edge.
2 If necessary, sew a row of tacking stitches close to the seamline, removing the pins as you tack. (Note that with most seams, only pinning and machining are necessary.)
3 Backtack (make a few reverse stitches) to secure the thread, then

stitch forward along the seamline. Backtack at the end of the seam for a few stitches. Clip off the threads close to the stitching.
4 If you used tacking stitches, remove them. Either press the seam open or press it closed in one direction.

Corner seams

To reinforce a corner seam, reduce the stitch length for about 2 cm on each side of the corner.

Trimming a seam

To trim a seam, cut away some of the seam allowance. Trim a seam in this way when the full seam allowance would interfere with the fit of the garment or with further assembly.

Grading a seam

When a seam forms a garment edge or is to be enclosed, grade it so that the seam lies flat and does not make a bulky ridge. Trim the seam allowance (see above), and then cut a little more from the seam allowance that will fall farthest from the garment side.

Trimming a corner

1 When you reach the point, pivot the machine needle and take one stitch across to the next edge. Pivot the needle again and continue the seam along the other edge.

Stitch across at point

2 Trim the seam allowance across the point, close to the stitching, then taper it on each side. The more elongated the point, the further back the seam allowance should be trimmed, so that when the point is turned right side out the allowance will not overlap and create bulk.

Clipping and nicking

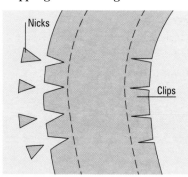

Nicks

Clips

Clip and nick curved seams before pressing so that they lie flat. Clips are slits cut into the seam allowances of convex curves so that the edges can spread. Nicks are wedges cut from the seam allowances of concave curves to allow the edges to draw in.

Understitching

Understitching keeps a facing and its seamline from rolling to the garment's right side. It is done after the seam allowances have been trimmed and

graded, and clipped or nicked. Working close to the seamline on the right side, straight stitch through the facing and the seam allowances.

Finishing seams

Seam finishes are techniques used to neaten the raw edges of seams and prevent fraying. Depending on the assembly procedures used, seams may be pressed before or after neatening.

The most commonly used seam finishes are overlocking and zigzagging, both of which may be used on either open or closed seams.

Seam finishing techniques not as widely used are turned and stitched, hand overcasting, machine overedging, bias binding and pinking; these are special decorative finishes.

French seams

French seams are self-enclosed seams that do not need a separate seam finish. They are especially appropriate for sheer fabrics, in which the seams are visible from the right side of the finished garment. They look best if the finished width is 5 mm or less.

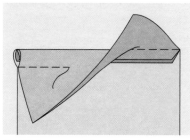

1 With wrong sides of fabric together and a 1.5 cm seam allowance, stitch 1 cm from edge. Trim seam allowance to 3 mm.
2 Press the seam open. Fold right sides together, with the stitched line exactly on the edge of the fold, then press again.
3 Stitch on the seamline, which is now 5 mm from the fold.
4 Press the seam to one side.

Bias bound seams

Binding produces a neat, well finished seam. It is sometimes used to finish seams in unlined jackets or coats.
1 Trim any notches from seam edge and wrap binding around it. Press.

SEAM FINISHES

Closed overlocked seam

Closed zigzagged seam

Open overlocked seam

Open zigzagged seam

Turned and stitched seam

Hand overcast seam

Pinked seam

2 Stitch close to the edge of the top fold, catching the underneath fold in the stitching.

BIAS STRIPS

Bias strips are strips of fabric cut on the true bias (i.e. at a 45° angle to the crosswise and lengthwise grains). Bias strips are used for such things as hem facings, piping, corded piping and binding raw edges. Commercial bias binding is available in a variety of colours and widths.

Cutting bias strips

1 Find the true bias by folding the fabric diagonally so that an edge on the crosswise grain aligns with the selvage (lengthwise grain).
2 Press the fold and then open it out. With a ruler and fabric marker, mark lines on the fabric parallel to the crease for the required width of the bias strips. Cut along the lines.

Joining bias strips

1 Right sides together, pin two strips at right angles with a 6 mm seam

allowance. Stitch the seam, starting and finishing at junctions of seamline.

2 Press seam open. Trim away the protruding corners of seam allowances to align with edge of strip.
3 Repeat steps 1 and 2 to join as many strips as you need.

Binding a raw edge

1 Cut a bias strip four times finished width of required bind and about 8 cm longer than the edge to be bound (join strips if necessary). Press strip lengthwise in half, wrong sides together. Open out, then fold edges in to meet centre line and press.

2 Unfold one edge of bias strip. With right sides together, pin bias strip to fabric, aligning raw edges. Turn back starting end 1 cm. Stitch binding to fabric along fold closest to edge until you are within 8 cm of starting point.

3 Trim away excess binding at this end, leaving a 1 cm overlap at starting point. With bind ends overlapped, continue stitching through all layers to complete.
4 Press seam allowances into binding. Bring remaining folded edge of bind-

ing to wrong side of garment, enclosing raw edges. Place fold on stitching line. Pin in place, taking care not to stretch bias binding.

5 Slipstitch folded edge of binding into stitching. Slipstitch binding ends together where they overlap.

MITRING

The key to successful mitring is accurate pressing of the folds at the corner.

1 Press fabric to wrong side on seamlines of crosswise and lengthwise edges, forming corner. With a fabric marker, mark both raw edges at the point where they cross.

2 Unfold fabric and lightly mark or crease a diagonal line from junction points through corner of pressed seamline to form mitre stitching line.

3 Fold fabric diagonally (on bias), right sides together, aligning edges. Stitch mitre along diagonal line, backtacking at beginning and end.

4 Trim mitre, leaving a 6 mm seam allowance. Press seam open, then turn to right side and press.

Mitring a bias facing

A bias facing may be formed either by cutting bias strips of fabric or by using commercial hem facing (bias). Cut fabric bias strip 60 mm wide, joining strips if necessary. Press both cut edges to wrong side for 6 mm.

1 Trim fabric seam allowance to 6 mm along edges to be faced. Unfold one edge of bias facing. With right sides together, pin facing to edge of fabric, marking a pivot point on facing seamline at corner.

2 Remove facing and staystitch for a short distance along foldline at marked point to reinforce. Clip seam allowance to point, being careful not to cut stitching.

3 With right sides of fabric and facing together, pin and stitch along foldline of facing, pivoting around corner at clipped point.

4 Trim seam allowances at corner. Carefully fold facing so it is at right angles to itself. Press lightly.

5 Fold garment, with right sides together, so facing edges are even. Stitch along the diagonal press line. Trim off the point leaving a 6 mm seam allowance.

6 Press open the the seam allowances at the edges. Turn the facing to the wrong side and press.

PIPING AND CORDED PIPING

Piping and corded piping are often used as decorative inserts or trims – for example, around hemlines. Both can be purchased, but the range of colours and fabrics is limited, so it is often preferable to make your own.

Piping

Desired exposed width

1.5 cm seam allowance

1 Cut a bias strip twice the desired exposed width, plus twice the seam allowance (i.e. 3 cm).

2 Fold strip in half lengthwise, with wrong sides together. Stitch in 1 cm from raw edges to hold.

Corded piping

1.5 cm

1 Fold a corner of fabric or paper over cord and pin, encasing the cord snugly. Measure 1.5 cm out from pin and cut.

2 Use the cut piece as a gauge for measuring width of bias strips.

3 Wrap the cut bias strip around the cord, with right side of fabric out and edges together. Using a zip foot, stitch close to the cord.

Attaching piping and corded piping

1 Mark hemline and trim hem allowance to 1.5 cm. Attach piping to right side of hem, aligning raw edges. Stitch in place. (For attaching corded piping, use zip foot.)

2 Cut facing (fabric) for required width and shape of hemline. Sandwich piping between hem and facing, aligning cut edges. Stitch a seam 1.5 cm from edges. (For corded piping, stitch as close as possible to cording.)
3 Trim, grade and clip turnings where required. Understitch facing if necessary.

4 Press facing to inside of garment so that piping forms trim at hem. Hem facing in place along neatened edge.

TUCKS

A tuck is a stitched fold of fabric. Tucks are usually decorative, but they can also be used as shaping devices.

Marking tucks

Mark either the stitching lines or the foldline of each tuck with thread (tailor's tacks or threadline), or use a suitable marking tool. Ensure that markings are indicated on the side of fabric where tucks are to be formed.

Stitching tucks

When you have marked the tucks appropriately, press them to the inside or the outside of the garment, as required by the design. Matching the stitching lines, pin the tucks in place and then stitch.

Marking tucks by pulling threads

Tucks can also be marked by pulling a thread of the fabric to mark tuck foldline. This is an accurate method when tucks are on straight grain of fabric. Use this method when tucks are to be formed across the width or length of fabric or tucked insert.
1 Pull a single thread from edge to edge of fabric and press along each pulled threadline.
2 Stitch desired finished width of tuck from foldline, and press tucks according to the design effect that is required.

Marking tucks with a cardboard gauge

A cardboard marking gauge can eliminate the need for marking the stitching lines of tucks.
1 Cut a cardboard strip the desired width of tuck plus space between stitching lines. From one end of gauge, mark down finished width of tuck and cut a notch.

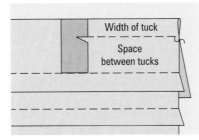

2 Place the unnotched end of the gauge on the stitching line of the previous tuck. The upper edge will then lie along the next tuck foldline and the notch will indicate the stitching line.

Making pin-tucks with a sewing machine

You can make very fine pin-tucks with a sewing machine. They are formed by using a twin needle (needles vary in size) with two top threads and a pin-tucking foot (these come with varying numbers of grooves). Consult your sewing machine manual for the correct settings.

BUTTONHOLES

Buttonholes can be either machine stitched or sewn by hand.

Machine buttonholes

Mark buttonhole. Consult your sewing machine manual for the correct settings. Machine using buttonhole foot and cut buttonhole opening with sharp, pointed scissors or seam unpicker.

Handworked buttonhole

1 Mark buttonhole. Use sharp scissors or a seam unpicker to cut along buttonhole through all fabric layers.
2 Tack around outline of buttonhole with a small running stitch to reinforce. Hand overcast raw edges through all layers to prevent fraying.

3 Work buttonhole using buttonhole stitch along straight edge, turning work and fanning stitches around end of buttonhole facing opening (i.e. where button pulls).

4 To form bar tack, make several straight stitches across remaining end of buttonhole. Work small horizontal buttonhole stitches over these stitches.

Appliqué

Appliqué is a great way of using up scraps of fabric left over from other sewing projects. You can produce beautiful appliqué work either by hand or with a sewing machine.

FABRICS

Smooth-surfaced fabrics of light or medium weight are best for appliqué work. Do not use loosely woven or extremely bulky fabrics. Press out all wrinkles and creases before using, and make sure that the appliqué fabric has the same washing requirements as the background fabric.

SCISSORS

You need two pairs of sharp scissors: a pair of medium-sized dressmaker's scissors for general cutting, and a pair of small, pointed embroidery scissors for close trimming.

CUTTING

Before cutting, assemble the fabric pieces and decide which piece will be used for each appliqué.

1 Pin the cutting template to the right side of the fabric and trace a dotted line around it. Remove the template and mark a 5 mm seam allowance outside the dotted line.
2 Cut out the appliqué piece outside this outer seam allowance line, leaving a generous margin all round.

3 Staystitch just outside the inner seamline (the dotted line), using 2 mm

stitches. Trim the appliqué by cutting out along the outer marked lines. Clip and nick the seam allowances around the curves and corners.

SEWING BY HAND

1 Finger press the seam allowance to the wrong side along the marked seamline of the appliqué and tack the folded edge as you go, keeping the stitching within the seam allowance.
2 Pin the appliqué to the background fabric and hold it in place with vertical tacking. Secure the appliqué with a fine slipstitch along the folded edges. Alternatively, use a decorative embroidery stitch, such as running stitch or cross-stitch, to secure the appliqué. Remove the tacking.

SEWING WITH A MACHINE

Appliqués may be sewn down with straight or zigzag stitch. First adjust the stitch tension and foot pressure to suit the fabric you are using.

Straight stitch method

1 Fold the seam allowance to the wrong side and tack in place.
2 Position and pin the appliqué on to the right side of the background fabric. Hold the appliqué in place with vertical tacking to prevent it from shifting while you stitch.

3 Using a stitch length of 2–2.5 mm, straight stitch along the folded edges of the appliqué. Use a handsewing needle to take the top thread ends through to the wrong side, and fasten them off together with the bottom threads. Remove the tacking.

Zigzag method

1 With the seam allowance exposed, position, pin and tack the appliqué in place on the right side of the background fabric. Straight stitch directly over the marked seamline.

2 Using embroidery scissors, trim away the seam allowance, cutting as close to the stitching line as possible.

3 Sew short, narrow zigzag stitches over the raw edges and the straight stitching. Take the top threads to the wrong side and fasten off with the bottom threads. Remove tacking.

Heirloom sewing

Around the turn of the century the techniques we now call heirloom sewing were practised widely, even on everyday garments and household linen.

PREPARING THE FABRICS

As the items you make will have to be laundered and ironed, it is advisable to pre-shrink the fabric and lace before starting work.

Most fabrics used in the projects in this book can be gently handwashed in warm water using quality soap flakes. Rinse the fabric well and hang it out to dry, without distorting the fabric.

Iron the fabric while it is still damp, so that it is easier to press out any creases. Lightly spray fine fabrics with starch before final pressing.

ROLL AND WHIP

This technique is used to neaten the raw edges of fabric laces and to provide a firmer edge for joining two lace edges together. This ensures that the joined laces do not pull apart.

1 Using the zigzag setting on your sewing machine (stitch width at 3) and with the wrong side of the fabric facing up, stitch along the raw edge of the fabric, stitching no more than 3 mm on to the fabric and completely off the fabric on the right-hand side.
2 As you begin to work, the edge of the fabric will roll over to form a firm edge. You may not be able to control the way the fabric rolls, but do not worry, as this edge will be covered by additional trims.

ROLL, WHIP AND GATHER

This technique is the same as rolling and whipping, except that a quilting thread is enclosed in the rolled edge of the fabric.
1 Lay the fabric with the wrong side facing up.
2 Place a quilting thread along the edge of the fabric and under the presser foot of your machine.
3 Zigzag carefully over, but not through, the quilting thread and over the raw edge of the fabric, as for roll and whip. The thread will be encased by the rolled fabric edge.

4 Gather the fabric by gently moving it along the quilting thread, spreading the gathers evenly.

ATTACHING FABRIC TO FABRIC

1 Take two pieces of fabric, both with edges rolled and whipped.
2 Place the two rolled and whipped edges together with right sides facing, so that the upper edge is just to the left of the lower one. (The pieces are

sewn in this way so that the rolled edges are not sitting right on top of each other, thus creating bulk.)
3 Zigzag over the two edges, making sure the stitching goes off the edge of the fabric to the right.

ATTACHING ENTREDEUX TO FABRIC
Stitching in the holes

1 Before you begin, check the length of the zigzag stitch by placing the entredeux under the presser foot of the machine and moving the needle by hand. Adjust the stitch length so that the needle points accurately into each successive entredeux hole.
2 Cut away the batiste (fabric edging) along one side of the entredeux. Roll and whip the edges of the fabric piece.
3 With right sides together, place the trimmed edge of the entredeux on the fabric, with the entredeux just to the left of the fabric edge. Start sewing by positioning the needle in one of the entredeux holes, then zigzag along the edge, always sewing off the right-hand edge of the fabric.

Stitching in the ditch

1 Without trimming the batiste edge, lay the entredeux on the fabric, right sides together.
2 Stitch right beside the entredeux holes, using a straight stitch.
3 To finish the raw edge, trim the batiste and fabric to 3 mm and zigzag along the edge.

ATTACHING LACE TO FABRIC

Widen your zigzag stitch to cover the entire lace heading. If it is not covered, the lace can change shape.

1 With right sides together, place the lace just inside the rolled and whipped edge of the fabric.
2 Zigzag along the edge, making sure that the stitch covers the whole width of the lace heading and goes off the edge of the fabric on the right-hand side.

ATTACHING LACE TO ENTREDEUX

1 Trim away one of the batiste edges from the entredeux.
2 Butt the trimmed side of the entredeux to the edge of the lace and zigzag along, sewing into the holes of the entredeux and making sure that the stitch covers the lace heading.

GATHERING LACE

Laces with a straight woven edge have a strong, straight thread along the edge (the heading). Pick this thread out of the lace near one end with a pin and pull it up, spreading the gathers evenly as you go. To keep the heading as flat as possible, take a thread from the top and the bottom.

JOINING TWO STRAIGHT LACE EDGES TOGETHER

1 Butt the two lace edges together, but do not overlap. Place the laces under the machine presser foot so that the join is right in the middle.
2 Begin zigzagging, adjusting the stitch width and length to suit the laces you are sewing. Aim for a stitch that is not too noticeable, but that still secures the laces together firmly. Do not make the stitches too close together or the seam will be bulky.

HEIRLOOM LACES

As the name heirloom sewing suggests, an article produced by these methods is intended to last through generations and represents a big investment of love, care and patience. To achieve the best result, we recommend that you use laces made from natural fibres.

Two types of insertion and edging laces have been used to make the heirloom sewing projects in this book – woven lace and fabric lace (also called Swiss embroidery), which has a recognisable fabric background. Broderie anglaise lace is a type of fabric lace.

Entredeux

Faggoting

Beading

Fabric lace

Edging lace

Edging lace

Insertion lace

Quilting

Quilting is an enduringly popular craft that can be as simple or as elaborate as your level of skill permits. Start with small, easily manageable projects and work up to larger ones.

A quilted effect is obtained by hand or machine stitching two layers of fabric together with a soft filling between them, which makes the finished article warm. The anchor stitching is usually worked in a regular pattern to create a subtly textured surface.

Although quilting is usually associated with making bed quilts, it can also be used to make garments, such as dressing gowns and vests, and home accessories, such as oven cloths, cushions and wall hangings.

FABRICS
Fabrics used for the top layer of a quilt should be smooth, light-weight to medium-weight, and opaque (not see-through). Heavy or stiff fabrics will not take up the contours of the quilting. The backing fabric can be decorative like the top layer, or it can be a solid colour. For a bed quilt it should not be too smooth or the quilt will slip off. Fabrics should be pre-shrunk and checked for colour-fastness.

FILLING
The most common quilt filling is cotton or polyester fibre wadding, both of which are light-weight, warm and easy to quilt. Polyester wadding is more stable than cotton wadding, requiring less quilting to hold it in place, and gives a more puffy quilted surface. Thicker wadding requires less stitching, but it is much more difficult to hand quilt. If you are not sure, seek the advice of your supplier.

Loose filling is also available, both in cotton and polyester, or you can use kapok or shredded foam.

NEEDLES
For hand quilting, use quilting needles or betweens. Use as small a needle as you can work with on your fabric; the smaller the needle, the smaller your stitching will be. For machine quilt-

ing, use a fine, sharp needle (a 60 or 70 jeans needle is ideal) and a walking foot so the layers feed evenly through the machine without puckering.

THREADS
Use a strong thread. Quilting thread is cotton thread coated with a glaze, but you can use an all-purpose cotton or polyester thread instead. For a richer look, use a lustrous silk twist.

CUTTING THE FABRIC
Make the quilt top at least 10 cm longer and wider than the finished quilt to allow for 'shrinkage' caused by the quilting. The more quilting you do, the more the quilt will 'shrink'.

The backing fabric should be 5 cm larger all round than the front. With thicker wadding and more extensive quilting, cut the fabric with a larger allowance than specified above, since the take-up will be greater.

PREPARING THE WADDING
1 Cut the wadding to the same size as the quilt top.

2 To join sections of wadding, split one edge of one of the wadding pieces to be joined and cut back a 2 cm strip from the upper side.
3 Repeat step 2 on one edge of the second piece, but this time remove the strip from the lower side. Overlap the edges and join the sections together

by machining through both thicknesses with a long, lightly tensioned straight stitch.

ASSEMBLING THE QUILT
The success of a quilting project depends on the accuracy and care with which you work these early construction stages.
1 Lay the backing material, wrong side up, on a hard, flat surface. Pull it taut and fix the corners of the backing to the working surface with masking tape. Spread the wadding on top, stroking it with the edge of a ruler to get rid of wrinkles. Lay the top layer, right side up, over the wadding.
2 Pin through all three layers, starting at the centre and moving out towards the edges.

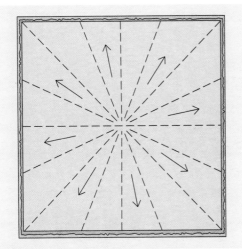

3 Using large tacking stitches, tack the three layers together in a sunburst pattern or a rectangular grid. Start in the centre and work towards the edges. Make sure that you use enough tacking stitches so that the layers remain smooth and do not shift. Remove the masking tape and pins.

4 Fold the excess backing up and over so that the raw edge of the backing butts against the raw edge of the top layer. Fold it again about 10 mm over the edge of the top layer. Pin the folded material in place.

5 Tack the folded edge through all three layers. This very important step helps to prevent the edge of the quilt from stretching out of shape.

HAND QUILTING

Always place the layered fabric in a quilting hoop before stitching. Wear a thimble on your middle finger and use a fine, even running stitch.

1 To secure the thread at the start, knot the end of the thread and insert the needle from the top through all three layers. Pull the thread from underneath so that the knot slips through the top layer and lodges in the wadding. Trim any thread that is visible at the surface.

2 Start at the centre of the quilt and work outwards, adjusting the layers to remove puckers as you go. Take a few stitches at a time, pushing the needle through with your middle finger. To be sure the needle penetrates all layers, hold your other hand under the layers so that you can feel the tip of the needle each time a stitch is taken. Remove the tacking as you go.

3 To end a line of quilting, make a knot on top of the quilting surface. Insert the needle one stitch length away and run the needle through the batting for a short distance. Bring the needle up and gently pull the thread so that the knot slips through the top layer. Trim the thread as close to the surface of the fabric as possible.

MACHINE QUILTING

Quilting by machine gives a durable and evenly worked result. It also takes only a fraction of the time that hand quilting does. Machine quilting is especially suitable for small projects because they are easy to manoeuvre.

For a large piece of quilting, you will need to modify your sewing area and plan the sequence and direction of your quilting carefully.

To modify the sewing area

Move your sewing machine to an open area. Raise a large piece of board or wood on two sawhorses or chairs to the same level as the sewing machine.

Place this surface flush with and to the left of the machine and use it to support large, heavy quilted pieces.

Quilting direction

Plan machine quilting so that the bulk of the piece always lies to the left of the needle. Roll up the bulk to the right of the needle tightly enough to fit under the sewing machine arm as it becomes necessary.

General instructions

1 When you are constructing the quilt, make sure you have tacked the layers generously so that they do not shift as they are being fed through the machine. Around the area where you are quilting, use safety pins to secure the layers even more firmly. To avoid unsightly puckers, keep the stitch tension and the foot pressure low. Set the stitch length to about 2 mm.

2 Feed the quilt through the machine as evenly as possible. Smooth the quilt in front of the needle as you sew. When you need to stop stitching to rearrange the quilt, stop the machine with the needle in the down position to avoid jumps in the line of stitching.

Securing thread ends

1 Try to avoid starting a new thread in the middle of a line, starting always from an outside edge if possible. However, if you do need to secure thread ends in the middle of the work, leave long thread ends on both top and bottom of the quilted surface. Thread one end through a needle and run the needle through the wadding for a short distance. Bring the needle out and cut off the thread end close to the quilted surface.

2 Run the other thread end through the wadding in the same way. Thread ends that finish on the edges of the quilt do not need to be secured, as the edge finish will keep them in place.

FINISHING

Quilted pieces are usually finished and the loose threads around the edges secured with a fabric binding, which may be cut on the straight or the bias.

Embroidery

Embroidery is a craft you can do almost anywhere – in an armchair, on the bus, or during work breaks. Most stitches are easy, and you will rapidly be able to develop your own designs.

PREPARING THREADS

Use threads no longer than about 50 cm, because long threads can be damaged by stretching and knotting as you pull them through the fabric.

Stranded cotton

Stranded cotton comes with several strands (usually six) loosely twisted together. Many projects specify how many strands are to be used for the stitches, and you need to separate this number from the rest.

To detach the number of strands you need, cut a length of stranded yarn and at one end separate out the required number of strands. Hold the separated strands in your mouth and the rest of the strands in one hand. Hold the rest of the cotton length in your free hand and gently pull the divided strands apart, moving your free hand slowly down the thread length to control the twisting action.

Doubling single-strand cotton

If you need to double strands of perle cotton, do not fold the length in half. Instead, cut two separate lengths and insert them side by side into the eye of the needle.

SECURING THE THREAD

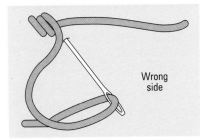

1 To start working with a new embroidery thread, hold the end of the thread against the wrong side of the fabric and work embroidery stitches over about 4 cm of this end.
2 To secure the embroidery when you come to the end of a thread, take

the thread to the wrong side and work it back under about 4 cm of worked stitches. Trim with sharp scissors.

USING AN EMBROIDERY HOOP

An embroidery hoop holds the fabric taut, reducing distortion and helping you to keep your stitch tension even. Hoops are made of wood, plastic or metal in a range of diameters.
1 To put the fabric in the hoop, place it over the inner ring of the hoop. Adjust the screw on the outer ring so that it fits snugly over the inner ring and the fabric. Place the fabric in the hoop so that the fabric threads run straight in both directions. To protect delicate fabrics, place tissue paper on either side of the fabric before securing the frame, then tear the paper away from the working area.
2 To avoid marking the fabric, take it out of the hoop when finishing work for the day. Release the screw and press down the fabric at the edges of the hoop, at the same time easing up the outer ring.

HOLDING THE NEEDLE

1 Insert the needle using a stabbing motion when possible – this will help you to keep an even stitch tension.

Push the needle straight down and pull the thread through, then bring the needle straight up again.

2 To work looped stitches, such as chain stitch or fly stitch, bring the needle up, and, before you pull the thread through, use your free hand to guide it around the needle.

EMBROIDERY STITCHES

This section contains instructions for working the stitches you will need to make the projects in this book.

Backstitch

This stitch can be used as a straight outline stitch or as the baseline for other decorative stitches.

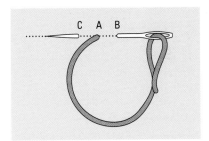

1 Working from the right to the left, bring the needle out at A, insert it at B, and exit at C. The distance between points C and A and points A and B should be equal.

2 Repeat this sequence to form next stitch, entering at A of previous stitch. Keep all stitches the same length.

Bullion knot

This stitch can be used as a filling stitch or for outlining. It is also used to form grub roses.

1 Bring the needle up at A. Insert it at B and exit again at A, but do not pull the thread through. Twist the thread around the point of the needle the number of times specified in the instructions for the project.

2 Carefully pull the needle through both the fabric and the twists.
3 Without distorting the twists, pull the thread towards point B so the coil lies flat. Pull the working thread tight and use the point of the needle to pack the threads in the coil together evenly. Reinsert the needle at B.

Buttonhole stitch wheel

This stitch is often used for embroidering flower motifs.

Work basic buttonhole stitch in a circle, inserting the needle into the same hole at the centre for each stitch.

Chain stitch

This stitch is used for outlining. It is also occasionally used for filling areas.

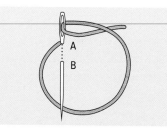

1 Bring the needle out at A, insert it back into the same hole at A and bring it out at B, carrying the thread under the needle point, before pulling it through. To work the next stitch, insert the needle at B.

2 Continue stitching in this manner, always inserting the needle into the hole made by the emerging thread.

3 To end the row, take a small stitch through the last loop.

Colonial knot

A colonial knot is similar to a French knot. Colonial knots can be worked closely together to fill an area, or can be scattered more freely.

1 Bring the needle up at A. Holding the needle in one hand, take the thread in the other and wind it around the needle in a figure of eight.

2 Pull on the thread to tighten the loops and take the thread down to the back of the fabric by inserting the needle into the fabric close to point A. Pull the thread through.

3 Scatter the knots as desired within the design area. The knots can be made larger by increasing the number of figures of eight that are wound around the needle.

Coral stitch

This is a simple outline stitch punctuated with small knots along the row.

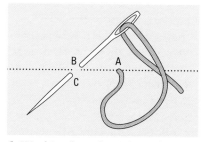

1 Working from the right to the left, bring the needle up at A. Insert the needle at B and then, taking up a few threads of the fabric, slant the needle out at C.

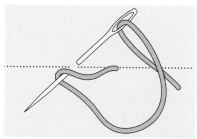

2 Loop the thread over and around the point of the needle, and then pull the needle through to secure the stitch and form the knot.

3 Continue in this way until the end of the row, spacing the knots evenly or in a more random fashion, as the design dictates.

Couching

This stitch is used to outline a design or to give more weight to a single line. It is worked with two threads: the laid thread and the couching thread. The couching thread is stitched over the laid thread to attach it to the fabric.

1 Securing them on the wrong side, bring up the desired number of laid threads at the right end of the design. Use your left thumb to hold and guide these threads as you couch over them.
2 Bring the couching thread up at A, just below the laid threads. Insert it at B, directly above the laid threads, and bring it up at C, further along the line. Point C now becomes point A of the next stitch.
3 Repeat steps 1 and 2 until the laid threads are completely anchored. Ensure that the distance between each stitch is equal.
4 To finish, bring the ends of the laid threads to the back of the work and secure by taking them back under the last few couching stitches.

Cross-stitch

Cross-stitch is usually worked in rows of even, slanted stitches, moving first from right to left to work part of each

stitch, and then from left to right to complete the stitches.

Cross-stitch can also be worked as a single stitch by working right to left and left to right stitches alternately. Take care that the top stitches all slant the same way.

Feather stitch

This is a looped stitch that is worked alternately to the left and then to the right of a centre line.

1 Working from top to bottom, bring the needle up in the centre at A. Insert the needle at B, slightly lower and to the right. Angle the needle out at C on the centre line, carrying the working thread under the needle point, and pull through.

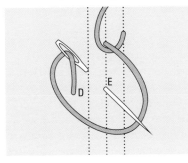

2 Insert the needle at D, slightly below and to the left of point C. Angle it out at E along the centre line. Carry the thread under the needle point and pull it through.

3 Continue in this way, alternating the looped stitches to the left and the right of the centre line.
4 To end the row, take a small stitch over the last loop.

Long-armed feather stitch

This stitch is worked in a similar way to basic feather stitch.

1 Bring the needle up in the centre, at A. Insert it at B, slightly higher and to the right, then angle the needle out at C along the centre line. Carry the thread under the needle point and pull through. The distance between all points should be the same.

2 Insert the needle at D, slightly higher and to the left of point C, and then angle it out at E on the centre line below point C.

3 Carry the thread under the needle and pull it through. Continue in this way to the end of the row.
4 To finish off the row, take a small stitch over the last loop.

Fly stitch

Fly stitch is a single looped stitch, similar to feather stitch. It can be scattered about or used as a border.

1 Bring the needle up at A, then insert it directly across at B and angle it out again at C. The distance between the points should be equal. Carry the thread under the needle point and pull through.
2 Complete the stitch by inserting the needle at D, over the loop.
3 Continue forming the stitches in this way, placing the stitches in a random manner or in a row, depending on your design.

French knot

This stitch is used like seeding stitch, but it is more raised and textured.

1 Bring the needle up at A. Holding the thread taut with one hand, wrap the thread around the needle twice. Gently pull the thread so the twists are tightened against the needle.
2 Insert the needle near point A and pull it through, making sure that the thread end is still held taut.
3 Scatter the knots as you wish within the design area. You can make French knots larger by increasing the number of twists around the needle.

Herringbone stitch

This stitch, which is a form of cross-stitch, is often used as a border. You can work a second row of herringbone stitch in another colour over the first, in the spaces between the stitches.

1 Working from left to right, bring the needle up at A. Make a slanting stitch towards the top right, inserting the needle at B. Bring the needle out a short distance back, at C.

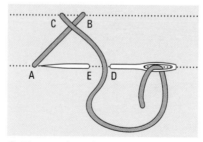

2 To complete the stitch, insert the needle at D, below and to the right of B, then bring the needle up at E to start a new stitch.
3 Repeat steps 1 and 2, keeping the the length of the stitches, and the spacing between them, even.

Lazy daisy stitch

Lazy daisy stitch is a single looped stitch, normally worked in a circle to give the appearance of petals.
1 Bring the needle out at A, insert it back into the same point, and bring it out at B. Carry the thread under the needle point, then pull it through.

2 Insert the needle at C over the chain loop, then bring the needle out at D to begin the next stitch.
3 Repeat steps 1 and 2 until you have completed all of the 'petals'.

Pistil stitch

A variation of the French knot, this stitch looks like the pistil of a flower.

1 Bring the needle out at A. Then pick up the thread and wind it twice around the needle.
2 Return the needle to the back of the work at B, the required distance from point A, pulling the thread taut around the needle as you pass it through the fabric.

Running stitch

This is an easy-to-work outline stitch. It can be the same length on both sides or longer on the right side.

Satin stitch

This is a solid filling stitch.

1 Working from left to right, bring the needle up at A and insert it directly above at B. Bring the needle out again at C, close to point A.
2 Continue in this way until the whole area is filled. Keep the stitches smooth and even.

Slanted satin stitch

This stitch is worked in a similar way to basic satin stitch.

1 Start in the centre of the shape to establish the angle of the slant. Work across to fill one side of the shape, taking shorter stitches to fill in any corners. Then start again at the centre and work the other way to fill the other side.
2 When the shape you are filling is a large one, slanting satin stitches may straighten out as you work. To prevent this, take great care to insert and bring out the needle at precisely the same distance, both top and bottom, from the previous stitch.

Padded satin stitch

This stitch gives the same effect as basic satin stitch, except that the stitched area is slightly raised. The padded area is made up of an outline of split stitches and then of two layers of satin stitches, the second worked diagonally over the first.
1 Work a row of split stitches right around the area to be filled.

2 Work horizontal satin stitch to fill the outlined area, making sure that you cover the split stitches.

3 Work a second satin stitch layer at an angle to the first. Take special care to keep the outline edges even.

Seeding stitch

This is one of the simplest filling stitches. It can be scattered around the design area or worked in clusters.

1 Bring the needle up at A, make a tiny stitch down at B and bring the needle up at C.
2 Make another small stitch, the same size and parallel to the first. Scatter seeding stitches as desired, changing the direction of the stitches.

Shadow stitch

This is one of the few embroidery stitches that are worked from the wrong side. Fine, sheer fabric is used so that the work will show through to the right side. Because only one strand of thread is used, stitches must be small to create the shadow effect.

1 Using only one strand of thread, secure the thread by working a few running stitches on the wrong side along one of the design lines.

2 Continuing to work on the wrong side of the fabric, make a small backstitch on one line. Keeping the thread lying down the centre of the design, carry it over to the opposite line and make another small backstitch.

3 Continue working the design in this manner, checking the right side of the work as you stitch to make sure there are no gaps between stitches. Adjust the length of stitches where necessary to accommodate varying shapes of the design, but always keep them as small as possible. A herringbone stitch will be formed on the wrong side of the work and a backstitch outline on the front.
4 To finish off, weave the thread back along a side edge of a few completed shadow stitches.

Spider's web stitch

This circular motif can be used to represent flowers. Before you start, divide the circle into nine equal parts.

1 Bring the needle out at A and insert it at D. Then bring it out at the centre over the working thread and pull it through.
2 Insert the needle at G and bring it out at I.

3 Insert the needle at C. Bring it out at the centre, over the working thread, and pull it through.
4 Insert the needle at F and bring it out at H.
5 Insert the needle at B. Bring it out at the centre over the working thread and pull it through.
6 To make the last spoke, insert the needle at E and exit at the centre.
7 Weave or whip to finish.
• *Weaving:* Start from the centre and pass the needle over and under the spokes in an anti-clockwise direction until all the spokes are covered.
• *Whipping:* Carry the needle under and back over a spoke, then under that

spoke and the next one ahead. Work around the web, always moving the needle back over one spoke and forward under two until all of the spokes are covered.

Split stitch

This stitch is worked in the same way as stem stitch, except that when the needle emerges it splits the working thread. The final effect resembles a thin chain stitch. Although outlining is its most common use, split stitch can also be used in solid runs.

1 Working from left to right, bring the needle up at A and then take it down at B.
2 Bring the needle back up at C, through the laid thread, so that it splits the centre of the laid thread.
3 Continue, keeping the stitch length even except around curves, where it should be shortened slightly.

Stem stitch

Primarily an outlining stitch, this stitch is often used to work plant stems in floral designs as well.

1 Working from left to right, bring the needle out at A. Insert it at B and bring it out at C, half a stitch length back.

2 Repeat this sequence, keeping the thread below the needle and to the left. Keep stitches even in length.

Straight stitch

This is a single satin stitch that can be of any length and worked in any direction. It can be used to cover straight design lines, or scattered to make an open filling. Be sure that the thread is not carried too far on the wrong side between the stitches.

Worked in a circle, a cluster of straight stitches resembles a stylised flower, the centre of which can be filled in with French knots.

1 Bring the needle up at A and take it to the back at B.
2 Work as many straight stitches as needed for the desired design.

Whipped stitch

Whipped stitch is a simple, decorative variation of running stitch. A second thread (often in a contrasting colour) is woven under the running stitch without picking up any of the fabric. It is very effective when several rows are worked under each other.

CUTWORK EMBROIDERY

In cutwork embroidery, the design is outlined with buttonhole stitch and then portions of fabric are cut away from the inside of the design.

Cutwork embroidery uses two main stitches – running stitch and buttonhole stitch – both of which are easy. However, great care and precision are needed, particularly when working bars and cutting the fabric. Fine, sharp needlework scissors are essential.

1 Using either embroidery floss or perle cotton, establish the design with running stitches.

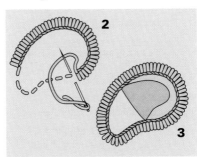

2 Work over the running stitch with a fine, close buttonhole stitch. Make sure that the ridge of the stitching lies against the line that is to be cut away.
3 Working from the wrong side, use fine needlework scissors to cut away the enclosed area close to the base of

the stitches. Be very careful not to cut into any of the stitching.

Working a bar

1 Mark the design with running stitches until you come to a bar position. Carry thread across design area and take a small stitch. Bring thread back and take another stitch. Take thread across design area again.

2 Work buttonhole stitch over these three laid threads, without catching the fabric underneath, then continue working running stitch around the rest of the motif.
3 Outline the whole design with fine buttonhole stitch, as for basic cutwork. Cut away the enclosed area close to the ridge of the stitches, being careful not to cut the worked bar.

SILK RIBBON EMBROIDERY

Silk ribbon embroidery is worked like thread embroidery, but because the ribbon is flat and wide, some special techniques are needed.

Work the stitches with about 30 cm of ribbon at a time. You can increase this length slightly as you become more experienced, but remember that overworked and worn ribbon is much harder to manipulate.

Two basic types of needles are used in silk ribbon embroidery: chenilles and tapestry needles. Both types have large eyes to accommodate the rib-

bon. For the most successful results with ribbon embroidery, use good-quality silk ribbon. Synthetic ribbons tend to twist and do not lie smoothly.

Threading the needle

1 Pass the end of the ribbon through the eye of the needle.
2 Thread this end on to the point of the needle, piercing the ribbon about 1 cm from the end.
3 Pull back on the long end of the ribbon until the ribbon locks firmly on to the head of the needle.

Securing the ribbon

1 At the start of the embroidery, bring the ribbon through to the front of the work, leaving a small tail on the wrong side. To secure the ribbon, pierce this tail with the needle as you work the first stitch or two.
2 At the end of the work, weave the ribbon in behind the stitching if possible. If not, cut it off, leaving a tail that can be caught up when you begin the next part of the embroidery.

Flat straight stitch

The following technique ensures that the silk ribbon stitches will lie flat and untwisted against the fabric.
1 Bring the needle up at A. Hold the ribbon flat against the fabric, under your thumb, directly opposite the required position of the stitch.

2 Spread the ribbon by placing the needle under the ribbon and then sliding it back along the ribbon with an upward pressure to the point where the ribbon emerges from the fabric.

3 Make the stitch the required length, and then pass the needle back down through the fabric at B.

4 Keeping your left thumb in position as long as possible, form the ribbon loop over it. Pulling the ribbon firmly at this point should remove any twists in it. Slide your thumb from the loop and gently tighten the stitch.

Making a silk rose

1 Take about 50 cm of 25 mm wide silk ribbon and fold over the corner. Roll the end of the ribbon several times to cover the folded edge.

2 Stitch the side of the roll firmly to the inside of the ribbon, about one-third of the way up the roll, and then stitch right through the bottom of the roll several times to hold it firm.

3 Turn the free end of the ribbon away from the roll, then roll the rolled up ribbon to the left, towards the turned away ribbon. Stitch through the side and the base several times.

4 Continue in this way, rolling and stitching the ribbon, until the rose is the desired size.

5 To finish, cut the end of the ribbon at an angle, tuck in the corner and raw edges, and stitch it in at the base.

BLOCKING

When you have finished your embroidery, check whether the fabric has stretched out of shape. This is likely to happen on loose-weave fabrics and on canvas, or where your stitching tension is tight. If there is little or no distortion of the fabric, you need only give your work a light steam-press from the back, using a damp cloth to stabilise the shape and even out the stitching surface.

Canvas and other fabrics that have become badly distorted should be blocked to restore the original shape. Cover a board larger than the embroidery with polythene. If your work has a selvage, cut nicks along it to ensure that it stretches evenly. Dampen the fabric and place it face down on the board. Lightly hammer a tack into the unworked area at the

top of the fabric, near the centre. Stretch the fabric gently down, keeping the threads vertically aligned, and hammer in a second tack at the centre of the bottom edge. Do the same in the centre of the two sides. Then, working outwards from the centre, hammer in tacks along all four edges, gently stretching the fabric as you go. Check the straightness of the threads and adjust if necessary. Let the fabric dry before removing.

Needlepoint

Needlepoint is rather like painting – once you have learned to make the stitches, you can create pictures in any style, from traditional to contemporary, from delicate to bold.

Needlepoint is the name usually given to embroidery worked on canvas. As the stitches must be worked into the holes between the woven threads, they can be worked only diagonally or parallel to the horizontal and vertical woven threads of the canvas. Despite this restriction, many different stitches can be formed. The stitches used to make the projects in this book are described in the following pages.

CANVAS

Canvas is made up of lengthwise and crosswise threads woven to produce precisely spaced holes between threads. The intersections of these threads are known as meshes. The thickness of the woven threads and the size of the holes vary with different sorts of canvases. This difference is called the gauge; a fine-gauge canvas has more threads to the centimetre than a large-gauge canvas.

Canvas is usually made from cotton, but can also be made in various synthetic materials. There are very fine-gauge canvases made from silk. Some canvases are woven from single threads, and some from double threads. Double-thread canvas is stronger than single-thread canvas, and stitches of different sizes can be worked on the same piece.

HINT

If you are unfamiliar with any of the stitches described here, it is a good idea to practise them on scrap canvas until you have learned the 'rhythm' of the stitches. This is especially important for the more complicated stitches where you have to insert the needle into the back of the canvas and out at the front following a sequence of numbers.

Binding the edges

As canvas has a tendency to unravel, selvages should be trimmed off and edges bound with masking tape or bias binding. Attach bias binding with a medium zigzag machine stitch.

YARN

Needlepoint can be worked with various yarns. The most commonly used are tapestry wool, viscose and cotton. Use thick yarns for large-gauge canvas and finer yarns for fine-gauge canvas. The yarn should slide through the canvas without distorting the fabric or damaging the yarn, but should be thick enough to cover the canvas when the stitches are formed.

Securing the yarn

To secure the yarn at the start of your work, allow 5–6 cm of yarn to remain at the back of the canvas. Hold this yarn end against the canvas and catch it in with the first few stitches. When the end is secured, clip off the excess and continue to work the rest of the stitches.

To secure the yarn at the end of the work, bring the needle and yarn to the back of the canvas. Weave the yarn through the underside of the last few stitches, and then trim off the excess.

STITCHES

Binding stitch

Binding stitch is used for finishing edges and for sewing seams together. It must be worked neatly and evenly.

To form binding stitch, follow the sequence of numbers in the diagram, taking your needle to the back of the work at the odd numbers and through to the front at the even numbers. After you have made the starting stitches (nos 1–8), a 'rhythm' will be established of crossing three threads diagonally forward and two threads diagonally back.

Byzantine stitch

Byzantine stitch is worked in steps moving across the work area. The steps are usually made up of rows of four, five or six long, slanted stitches.

1 Starting at the upper left corner of the area to be covered, work a row of four to six long, slanting stitches horizontally across the canvas.

2 Under the last stitch, work the same number of stitches vertically.

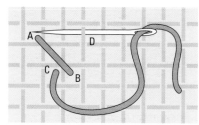

3 Continue to work in this manner, creating 'steps', until you reach the bottom of the area to be worked. Begin a new row by fitting the steps of the new row into the steps of the preceding row.

Herringbone stitch

Herringbone stitch forms a tightly woven texture. It is like cross-stitch, except that the stitches cross off-centre. All rows are worked left to right.

1 Starting at the upper left of the area to be worked, bring the needle out at A, down over two canvas meshes, and in at B. Take the needle under one lengthwise thread, out at C, up over two meshes, and in at D.

2 Pass the needle back under one lengthwise thread and start working the next stitch.

3 Begin each new row of stitches in the canvas hole directly below the start of the stitches in the row above.

Leaf or fir stitch

Leaf or fir stitch can be worked singly, or in groups or rows. Turned sideways or upside down, it makes a feather.

1 Work the side stitches first, as in the example illustrated, starting at A and working through to G.

2 Work five top stitches, fanning them out to form the top of the leaf. Then complete the leaf by working the side stitches on the opposite side.

3 Start a new leaf six holes away from the start of the previous leaf, and repeat steps 1 and 2 above.

4 With each new row, reverse the working direction, positioning the new row so that the tops of the leaves fit into the base leaves of the row above. When working from left to right, form the leaves in a clockwise direction, as described in steps 1 and 2 above. When working from right to left, reverse the working order and form the leaf anti-clockwise.

JACQUARD STITCH

This stitch is worked diagonally from the top left to the bottom right. It is made up of rows of spaced Byzantine stitch with rows of continental stitch filling the spaces between.

1 Starting at the top left, work steps of Byzantine stitches across the work (normally four to six stitches per step).

2 Work more steps of Byzantine stitch, leaving a stepped row of blank canvas between each row.

3 On each row of exposed mesh, work continental stitch (see instructions under 'Tent stitch' later in this section). Work the rows from the bottom up, turning the canvas around the other way for each row so you are always working in the same direction.

4 On horizontal steps, form the stitches in the usual way, bringing yarn out at the base (point A) and in at the top (point B). On the vertical rows, reverse the direction, bringing the yarn out at the top (point C) and in at the base (point D).

Long-armed cross-stitch

Long-armed cross-stitch (sometimes called Greek stitch) is made up of short and long stitches. The long stitches are usually worked over twice the number of canvas meshes as the short stitches.

1 Bring the needle out at A and up over two meshes, and insert it at B. Bring the needle out again, two meshes to the left, at C.

2 Insert the needle at D, which is four canvas holes away from point A. Pass the needle back under two canvas threads and out at E to start the next stitch. Always end a row with a short stitch (as stitch A–B).

3 To begin a new row, turn the work upside down. Working from left to right, begin with a short (A–B) stitch.

Mosaic stitch

Mosaic stitch produces a block-like pattern through repetition of the same three stitches. Rows of these stitches can be worked either horizontally or diagonally across the canvas.

Worked horizontally

1 Working from right to left and starting at the upper right of the area to be covered, work one tent stitch

(points A to B), then a longer stitch across two canvas meshes (points C to D), and then another tent stitch (points E to F). This forms one block.

2 Begin the next block one canvas hole to the left. Continue to end of row, leaving needle at back of canvas at the end of each row.

3 Turn the canvas upside down. Align the blocks of the new row with the blocks of the previous row, as shown in the diagram.

Worked diagonally

1 Starting at the upper left of the area to be worked, work the first row of blocks diagonally across the canvas, skipping one canvas hole between each block.
2 At the end of the row, leave the needle at the right side of the canvas and work the second row in the reverse direction. Work successive rows up and down the canvas, fitting

the new mosaic blocks into the spaces left between the blocks of the preceding row.

Reverse mosaic stitch

This stitch can be worked in one colour or two.

1 Work rows of mosaic stitch diagonally, missing every second row.

2 Turn the work 90° so that the upper right is now the upper left. Repeat step 1 to fill in the spaces.

Norwich stitch

This stitch can be worked in various sized squares, as long as the square always has an uneven number of threads. The diagram shows how to work Norwich stitch over a nine-thread square. If you intend working the stitch over a different number of threads, plan it on graph paper first.
1 Bring the needle up at 1 and down at 2. Continue in this way, following

NINE PATCH

Nine patch is a square design consisting of five triple cross-stitches worked in one colour and four clusters of diagonal stitch worked in another colour (making nine components all together). The design is worked over a nine-thread square.

1 Working over a three-thread square, stitch a triple cross-stitch following the sequence of numbers in the diagram above. Bring the needle to the front of the work at the odd numbers and to the back at the even numbers.

2 Work the other four triple cross-stitches in the same manner, being careful to position them in the right holes so that the diagonal stitches will fit exactly between them.
3 Using a different coloured yarn, work the diagonal stitches between the triple cross-stitches, as shown in the diagram. Take care to cross over the correct number of canvas threads, and make sure all stitches are slanted in the same direction.

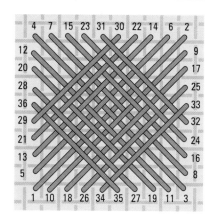

the sequence of numbers exactly until point 34. Ensure that you bring the needle to the front of the canvas at the odd numbers and down to the back at the even numbers.
2 Bring the needle up at point 35, weave the needle under stitch 29–30, and insert the needle at point 36. Secure the yarn.

Ray stitch

Ray stitch consists of seven stitches radiating from a common canvas hole and forming a square. Expanded ray stitch is made up of thirteen stitches, forming a rectangle. The colour of the yarn can be alternated with each square or row of squares.

1 Begin at the upper left-hand corner of the area to be covered and work rows from left to right and from right to left alternately. Work each ray stitch in a counter-clockwise direction, following the numbers from 1 to 7; each stitch begins at a number and ends in the canvas hole, A, that is common to all stitches. Fan each ray stitch as shown in the diagram.

2 Point 7 of the first ray stitch now becomes the common hole, A, of the new stitch. At the end of each row, reverse the working direction and place the new stitch units below those just completed.

Diamond ray stitch

This is a variation on ray stitch. The outer stitches can be worked in a dif-

ferent colour to achieve the distinctive diamond pattern when several rows are worked in a block.

Rhodes stitch

Rhodes stitch is used for large areas and to fill in backgrounds. Diagonal stitches are superimposed to make a pattern of raised square blocks. Each block consists of straight stitches across the square, following each other anti-clockwise so that they all cross the same central point.

1 Begin each square (a nine-thread square in this example) at the bottom left-hand corner (point 1). Insert the needle at 2, carrying the needle under the square and out at 3.
2 Fill every hole around the square in this way, following the sequence indicated by the numbers 1 to 36.

Tent stitch

A tent stitch is a diagonal stitch formed over one canvas mesh. There are three kinds of tent stitches, each with its own stitch name – the half cross-stitch, the continental stitch, and the basketweave stitch. The basketweave and continental stitches are more durable than the half cross-stitch and give more coverage on the back of the canvas. The half cross-stitch is more economical of yarn and distorts the canvas less.

Half cross-stitch

Half cross-stitch is worked from left to right. The needle is carried horizontally across the back of the work, forming horizontal stitches on the back of the canvas.

1 Starting at the upper left, bring the needle out at point A and in at point B. Continue to work the stitches in this way to the end of the row.
2 Work the last stitch and leave the needle at the back of the canvas.

3 Turn the canvas upside down and form the new row in line with the stitches of the row just completed.

Continental stitch

Continental stitch is a form of tent stitch that can be worked horizontally from right to left or vertically from top to bottom. In both methods of working, a diagonal stitch is formed on the back of the canvas.

1 To work continental stitch horizontally, start at the upper right-hand corner of the area to be worked. Form each stitch by bringing the needle out at A and inserting it at B. When you come to the end of each row, finish the last stitch and leave the needle at the back of the canvas.
2 Turn the canvas upside down and

work the stitches of the new row directly in line with those in the row you have just completed.

1 To work continental stitch vertically, start at the top corner of the area to be covered and work a row of stitches down the canvas. When you come to the end of the row, leave the needle at the back of the work.

2 Turn the canvas upside down to reverse the working direction, and form the new row of stitches beside the first. Repeat until the area is filled.

Basketweave stitch

Basketweave stitch is worked in rows alternately down and up the canvas.

1 Starting from the top left-hand corner of the area to be worked, bring the needle out at A and insert it again at B. Work stitches in a diagonal row, skipping one canvas hole between stitches. To work down, hold the needle vertically, as shown.

2 Form the first stitch of an up row by bringing the needle out through the hole directly below the beginning of the previous stitch.

3 To work an up row, hold the needle horizontally between stitches. Form the first stitch of the next down row beside the last stitch of the previous down row.

Window eyelet stitch

A window eyelet is made up of four ray stitches radiating from a central cross-stitch (worked last). The stitches are worked in the numerical sequence shown, so that each ray finishes with a corner stitch on top. The window eyelet illustrated here has been worked over a nine-thread square.

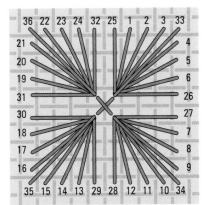

1 Over a nine-thread square, work the stitches in the sequence shown, coming up to the front of the work at the numbered points and taking the needle back down at the common hole of the individual ray stitches.
2 Finish the pattern by working a cross-stitch in the centre.

Crochet

Crochet uses a small number of simple stitches to create a variety of patterns and textures. It can be worked with threads and yarns ranging from very fine to quite coarse.

These instructions are for right-handers; if you are left-handed, substitute right hand for left and vice versa. As a left-hander, you will find the diagrams easier to follow if you look at them through a mirror, which will give you the correct position for the left hand.

BEGINNING THE WORK
Holding the hook
There are many different ways of holding a crochet hook, and most people develop a style of their own as they become more experienced. The following is a common method.

Hold the hook like a pencil, with the thumb and index finger on either side of the flat portion of the hook and the middle finger resting against the thumb.

Holding the yarn

Wrap the ball end of the yarn around the little finger of your left hand. Take it under the fourth and third fingers, then over the top of the index finger, leaving about 5 cm of yarn between finger and hook. Use your index finger to keep the yarn taut so that you can manipulate the yarn easily and with an even tension around the hook.

Slip knot
Most crochet begins with a slip knot, which secures the yarn to the hook. Make the knot about 15 cm from the yarn end.

1 Wind the yarn once around two fingers and over the fingers again to the left of the first thread. Using the hook, pick up the second thread through the first one.

2 Pull the second thread through the first one to form a loop.
3 Keeping the hook inside the loop, pull both yarn ends and draw in the loop until it is close to the hook, but not too tight.

WORKING A CHAIN
Chain stitch is used to form the foundation row in crochet work, and is also an integral part of many crochet pattern stitches.

1 Hold the slip knot between the thumb and middle finger of the left hand. Keeping the yarn taut over the index finger, pass the hook under the yarn. Draw the yarn through the loop on the hook to form a new loop. The new loop should be loose enough for you to draw the next chain through.

2 Repeat step 1 until the required number of chains are completed. When counting chains, remember that the loop still on the hook is not counted as a chain.

Turning chains
At the beginning of each row, a certain number of chains must be added to bring the work level with the first stitch of the new row. The exact number of chains to be added depends on the height of the stitch you are using. (See the instructions that follow for working basic stitches.)

BASIC STITCHES
Slipstitch (slst)
Slipstitch is a short stitch, used for joining and shaping. It is sometimes worked along an edge to strengthen it and minimise stretching.

Insert hook in chain or stitch. Wrap yarn over hook and draw a loop through both chain and yarn loop on hook.

Double crochet (dc)

Double crochet is often used to finish edges, and sometimes to join crochet pieces together. When turning double crochet use one chain.

Insert hook into stitch or chain, yarn over hook, and draw yarn through stitch or chain. Draw yarn through both stitches on hook. Double crochet complete.

Half treble (htr)

Half treble is not often used. It makes a firm, attractive fabric with a pronounced ridge. When turning half treble, use two chains.

1 Wrap yarn over hook, and then insert hook into stitch or chain.

2 Draw loop through stitch or chain. You should now have three loops on the hook.

3 Wrap yarn over hook and draw through all three loops on hook. Half treble complete.

Treble (tr)

Treble is a compact stitch and is the most commonly used. When turning treble, three chains are used.

1 Wrap yarn over hook and then insert hook into stitch or chain from front to back.

2 Draw loop through. You should have three loops on the hook.

HINTS

- *To keep edges straight, never work into last stitch of previous row, as the turning chain counts as the first stitch of each row.*
- *Count the stitches after each row to make sure you have worked the correct number.*

CHECKING THE TENSION

Before starting to make a crochet project, it is important to check the tension. Make a test swatch, as instructed in the pattern. Place the swatch on a flat surface, insert two pins, 10 cm apart, into the swatch, and count the stitches between. Place the pins vertically to count rows and horizontally to count stitches.

After checking your tension, if you find your work is too loose, change to a smaller hook. If it is too tight, change to a larger hook. With practice, you will be able to achieve the correct tension.

3 Wrap yarn over hook. Draw loop through first two loops only, leaving two loops on hook.

4 Wrap yarn over hook and draw it through last two loops on hook. Treble complete.

WORKING A ROUND

1 Chain required number of stitches and join them into a ring by slipstitching into the first chain.

2 If working first round in double crochet, begin round with one chain. If working first round in treble, begin round with three chains. Work number of stitches required into ring.

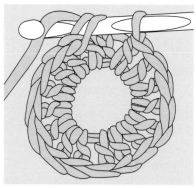

3 When round is complete, close with a slipstitch in top of beginning chain, unless otherwise directed.

INCREASING

For all stitches, make a single increase by working two stitches into one. The illustration shows double crochet.

For all stitches, double increase by working three stitches into one. The illustration shows double crochet.

DECREASING

1 To decrease one stitch in double or half treble, insert hook into next stitch. Wrap yarn over hook and draw yarn through.
2 Insert hook into next stitch. Wrap yarn over hook and draw yarn through three loops on hook.

To decrease several stitches at the beginning of a row, omit turning chain and work slipstitches for required number of decreases. Work one double crochet into next stitch and continue in pattern. Do not work the slipstitches on the return row.

JOINING YARN

Yarns should never be joined by knotting them together. Instead, use the following method.

1 Work to final two loops of last stitch at the end of a row with first yarn, and then draw new yarn through these two loops to complete stitch.

CROCHET ABBREVIATIONS

alt	alternate
beg	begin, beginning
ch	chain
cont	continue
dc	double crochet
dec	decrease, decreasing
dtr	double treble
htr	half treble
inc	increase, increasing
patt	pattern
rem	remain/ing
rep	repeat
rnd	round
sk	skip
sp	space
slst	slipstitch
tog	together
tr	treble
ttr	triple treble
yoh	yarn over hook
★	Repeat the stitch instructions between the asterisks as many times as there are stitches to accommodate them.
( )	Work the series of steps within parentheses according to the instructions that follow the parentheses.

2 Trim first yarn to 5 cm. Make a chain and turn. Lay the ends of the new and old yarn together over the work and crochet over the top of them for four or five stitches.

FINISHING

1 Trim off the yarn to 10 cm. Pull this end through the last loop and tighten the loop.

2 Using a tapestry needle, weave the yarn into the back of the work below the top row of stitches for 3–5 cm. Trim off the remaining yarn.

Knitting

Knitting is a relaxing pastime, and a wonderful way of creating handmade garments with a touch of individuality. It is also a good first craft for children, as it is safe and simple.

NEEDLES

Whether you use plastic, metal or wooden needles depends on personal preference and availability. Stitches slide well along metal needles, but they tend to be noisy and their rigidity may cause problems for arthritic knitters. Plastic needles are quieter than metal ones and easier to handle. Bamboo and wooden needles are more expensive, but their ease of handling and superior performance make the extra cost worthwhile if you intend doing a lot of knitting.

Needle thickness is expressed in millimetres (mm). The size of the stitch increases with the thickness of the needle. In general, work thicker yarns with large needles and thinner yarns with smaller ones. If the needles are too large for the yarn, the knitted fabric will be loosely structured; if the needles are too small, the stitches will be too compact and rigid.

Needle length depends on the size of the project. Needles should be long enough to hold all stitches comfortably. Very large projects may be easier to work on circular needles.

CASTING ON

Casting on forms the first row of stitches and one selvage of the finished article. Three common methods of casting on are described here.

For all methods, form the first stitch by making a slip knot. To form a slip knot, make a loop 15 cm from the end of the yarn. Insert the needle into the loop, draw the yarn from the ball end of the wool through the loop and tighten the knot.

Knitting on

This method forms a versatile selvage that is soft when worked through the front of the loops and firm when worked through the back.
1 Hold the needle with the slip

knot in the left hand. Insert the right needle through the front of the loop and take the yarn around the needle.

2 Draw the yarn through to form a second loop. Transfer the new loop to the left needle and knit into it to form the next new stitch. Continue forming new stitches in this way until you have made the required number.

Cable cast-on

This is worked in the same way as knitting on, but each new loop is made by inserting the needle between the two previous stitches instead of into the last loop. This gives an edge that is both elastic and decorative.
1 Make the first two stitches as for knitting on. For each new stitch after that, insert the right needle between the two previous stitches.

> ### HINT
> *With practice you will develop your own way of holding the needles and handling the yarn. The methods described here can be adapted to suit what feels most comfortable for you.*

2 Take the yarn around the needle as for knitting on, draw through a new loop and transfer it to the left needle.

3 Continue forming new stitches between loops until you have made the required number.

Single cast-on

This method uses only one needle. It forms a loose selvage that is particularly good for hem edges, for buttonholes or for lacy knitting patterns.

1 Hold the needle with the slip knot on it in your right hand. Wrap the yarn from the ball end around your left thumb, then grasp the yarn firmly between the palm of your hand and the tips of your fingers.

2 Turn your hand so that the back of your thumb is facing you. Insert the needle from front to back through the loose loop that is formed.

3 Slip your thumb out of the loop and at the same time pull the yarn downward to close the loop around the needle. Continue making stitches in this way until you have made the required number.

BASIC STITCHES
There are only two basic stitches in knitting – the knit stitch and the purl stitch. All other stitch patterns are made by combining and varying these two stitches. For some examples, see 'Basic stitch patterns' on page 326. Knitting methods vary from place to place, and people generally develop a style of their own. One of the more common methods follows.

Knit stitch

1 Grasp the needle with the stitches in your left hand. The first stitch should be about 2 cm from the tip. Take the yarn around the little finger of your right hand, under the next two fingers and over the top of the index finger, extending it about 5 cm from the first stitch on the needle.
2 Holding the yarn behind the work, insert the right needle into the front of the first stitch from left to right (the needle tip pointing towards the back).

With your right index finger, loop the yarn around the right needle and over the top in an anti-clockwise direction.

3 Draw the loop on the right needle forwards through the stitch, at the same time pushing the stitch on the left needle towards the tip. With practice you will be able to coordinate these two movements smoothly and increase your speed.

4 Allow the stitch on the left needle to slip off, while the new stitch (the loop you have just made) remains on the right needle.
5 Repeat steps 1 to 4, pushing the stitches forward on the left needle with your thumb, index and middle fingers, and moving the stitches back on the right needle with your thumb.

Purl stitch
1 Grasp the needle holding the stitches in the left hand, as described in step 1 for knit stitch.
2 Holding the yarn in front of the work, insert the right needle into the

front of the first stitch, from right to left (the needle tip pointing slightly upward). With your right index finger take the yarn backwards over the right needle, then forward and under it.

3 Draw the loop on the right needle backwards through the stitch and at the same time push the stitch on the left needle towards the tip. With practice you will be able to coordinate these two movements smoothly and increase your speed.

4 Allow the stitch on the left needle to slide off the needle. The new stitch (the loop you just made) remains on the right needle.
5 Repeat steps 1 to 4, pushing the stitches forward on the left needle with your thumb, index and middle fingers, and moving the stitches back on the right needle with your thumb.

CASTING OFF
Plain cast-off is the easiest and most versatile method of casting off.
1 Knit the first two stitches at the

beginning of the row in the stitch pattern you have been working.

2 With yarn behind the work, insert the left needle into the first stitch.

3 Pull the first stitch over the second stitch with the left needle and then let it slip from the needle. Knit the next stitch on the left needle in pattern.

4 Repeat steps 2 and 3 until you have cast off the desired number of stitches.

INCREASING, OR ADDING STITCHES
Knit increase

Bring the yarn forward, in front of the right needle. Insert the needle knitwise in the first stitch and knit a new stitch through the first stitch. Put the new stitch back on to the left needle and knit it in the normal way, placing it, at this stage, on the right needle as usual.

Purl increase

Holding the yarn behind the right needle, insert the needle purlwise

in the first stitch and purl a new stitch through it. Place the new stitch back on to the left needle and purl it, placing it on the right needle as usual.

DECREASING, OR REDUCING STITCHES
Knit decrease

Knit two stitches together (K2 tog) through the front of both loops.

Purl decrease

Purl two stitches together (P2 tog) through the front of both loops.

JOINING WITH A SEAM ALLOWANCE

Joining pieces with a seam allowance is ideal where the edges of the knitted piece are uneven, such as shoulder seams that have been cast off in steps. It is also suitable for taking in a garment or for shaping curved seams because the stitches can be formed at any distance from the edge.

CHECKING THE TENSION

Knitting instructions always specify a tension; that is, the exact number of stitches (and sometimes rows) per 10 cm using the specified needles, yarn and stitch pattern. The size of the finished article is based on the specified tension, so it is important to make sure you knit at the tension specified.

1 Before beginning any new project, make a test swatch at least 15 cm square, using the recommended yarn and needles and working in the specified stitch.

2 Place the completed swatch right side up on a flat surface (the ironing board is a good place to work) and pin the edges, taking care not to stretch the sample.

3 To check the horizontal tension, insert two pins 10 cm apart on a row and count the stitches between them. It is easier to count stitches on the knit side of stocking stitch, where each loop represents one stitch. When counting stitches for garter stitch, count the loops in one row only.

4 To check the vertical tension, insert two pins 10 cm apart vertically and count the rows between them. It is easier to count rows on the purl side of stocking stitch, where each two ridges equals one row. In counting rows for garter stitch, every ridge equals one row and every furrow equals another.

5 If there are too many stitches or rows in your tension square, knit another sample using needles one size larger; if there are too few stitches, try using needles one size smaller. The time taken to get the tension right will be well spent, because an error of even one stitch per 10 cm multiplies to a substantial size difference over a wide area. However, do not use needles more than one size away from that specified. If you cannot match the stated tension, choose another pattern.

Backstitched seam

Hold the two pieces together with right sides facing. Using a knitter's needle and a length of the yarn used in the knitting, backstitch the seam, taking in two knitting stitches at a time.

Slipstitched seam

1 Using a crochet hook of appropriate size and a length of the yarn used in the knitting, draw a loop through a corresponding stitch on each section.
2 Insert the hook through the next two stitches and draw a loop through both stitches and the loop on the hook. Repeat steps 1 and 2 along the length of the seam.

JOINING EDGE TO EDGE

Joining knitted sections edge to edge makes a smooth, bulkless seam that is almost invisible.

Flat seam on garter stitch

1 With right sides facing up, lay the two knitted pieces side by side with corresponding stitches aligned.
2 Sew stitch by stitch, placing the needle under the horizontal loop next to the edge stitch on one section, then under the corresponding loop on the other.

Flat seam on rib

1 Place the knitted pieces together with right sides facing and corresponding stitches aligned.
2 Attach the yarn at the right-hand end. Bring the needle up through the centre of the next two corresponding edge stitches and down through the next two. Continue stitching in this way to the end of the seam.

EMBROIDERY ON KNITTING
Knitting stitch
Knitting stitch is best worked with yarn of the same thickness as the knitted garment. Take care not to pull the embroidery yarn too tightly.

1 Bring the needle from the back through the centre of the stitch below the one to be covered. Then take the needle from right to left under both strands of the stitch above the one to be covered. Bring the needle back to the start of the stitch and take the needle behind the two strands in the

---

BASIC STITCH PATTERNS

The following knitting stitch patterns are the easiest to create and are ideal for beginners.
Garter stitch is the simplest stitch pattern, and is normally produced by knitting every stitch of every row. It has a pebbly surface, identical on both sides, and a loose structure that stretches equally in both directions.
Stocking stitch is the most versatile stitch pattern, and is produced by knitting one row and purling the next. It is smooth on the knitted side (which

is usually considered to be the right side) and pebbly on the purled side. The fabric stretches more crosswise than lengthwise. Stocking stitch is used for jumpers and dresses, and for knitted accessories such as hats, gloves and socks.

Stocking stitch – knitted side

Stocking stitch – purled side

Rib stitch is produced by alternating one or more knit stitches with one or more purl stitches in one row, then purling the knit stitches and knitting the purl stitches on the return row. This produces a pattern of vertical ridges that is identical on both sides when knit and purl stitches are knitted in equal numbers. Rib stitch has considerable crosswise elasticity and is especially suitable for welts (cuffs and waists) of garments, where the ribbing ensures a snug fit.

Rib stitch

Garter stitch

row below. Take the needle across into the centre of the next stitch.

2 Repeat step 1 until you have made the required number of stitches.
3 To finish, bring the needle back to the start of the stitch and through to the back of the work.

Cross-stitch embroidery

Cross-stitch embroidery on knitting should be worked with a finer yarn than that with which the garment is knitted. Be careful not to pull the embroidery yarn too tightly.

1 Bring the needle up under a purl strand connecting two knit stitches. Cross diagonally into the stitch one above and one to the right. Take the needle down behind the purl strand into the stitch below.

2 Cross to the left diagonally to complete the cross, and then take the needle through to the back. Pass the needle diagonally behind the next knit stitch on the left and bring it out again under the next purl stitch.

POMPOMS

1 To make a pompom, you need two identical circles of cardboard with holes cut out of the middle. To determine the size of the cardboard circles, estimate the desired diameter of the finished pompom; add 1.5 cm to this measurement to allow for trimming, and add the diameter of the centre hole. (The diameter of the centre hole is a quarter of the finished diameter of the pompom.) For example, to make a pompom with a finished diameter of 8 cm, you will need two cardboard circles with diameters of 8 cm + 1.25 cm + 2 cm (11.25 cm), with centre holes of 2 cm diameter.

2 With the two circles flat together, wind the yarn round and round the cardboard until the centre hole is filled up and you can no longer push the yarn through.

3 Place the point of a pair of scissors between the two circles of cardboard and cut around, keeping the scissors between the cardboard circles.

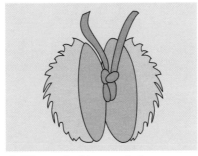

4 Wrap a double strand of yarn round between the two circles of cardboard, knot it firmly and cut away the cardboard. Trim the pompom.

KNITTING ABBREVIATIONS

alt	alternate
beg	beginning
cc	contrasting colour
cont	continue
dec	decrease
foll	following
gst	garter stitch
inc	increase
incl	including, inclusive
K	knit
K-wise	knitwise (insert needle as though to knit)
K2 (3) tog	knit two (or three) stitches together
l	left
mc	main colour
P	purl
P-wise	purlwise (insert needle as though to purl)
P2(3) tog	purl two (or three) stitches together
patt	pattern
psso	pass the slipped stitch over
r	right
rem	remain/remaining/remainder
rep	repeat
rsf	right side facing
sl	slip a stitch, without working it, from left needle to right needle
st	stitch
stst	stocking stitch
tbl	through back of loop (enter stitch from the back instead of the front)
wsf	wrong side facing
ybk	yarn back (take yarn to back of work)
yfwd	yarn forward (take yarn to front of work)
work even	continue work without increasing or decreasing
★ ★	Repeat the instructions between the asterisks as many times as there are stitches to accommodate them.
( )	Repeat instructions enclosed in parentheses the number of times indicated after the parentheses.
[ ]	Instructions within square brackets explain the method of working a particular stitch or technique.

Knotted lace

Knotted lace looks complex, but it is based on a very few simple stitches. It is important that loops be of an even size, so practise the stitches before attempting a project.

BASIC LOOP

You must form a row of basic loops along the edge of the fabric before beginning to make the pattern (rather like casting on in knitting). Always work from left to right when working on a straight edge. Basic loops should be uniformly small and evenly spaced.

1 Thread the needle with a thread about 60 cm long. Holding the end of the thread between the thumb and forefinger of your left hand (right hand if left-handed), place the thread behind the fabric. Insert the needle into the fabric from the front, 2 mm from the edge and under the thread. Do not pull the needle through.

2 Hold the doubled-over thread near the eye of the needle. Loop the threads under the point of the needle from right to left, and down towards the eye of the needle.

3 Pull the needle through in an upward direction. Pull the knot tight. You have now made a basic knot.

4 To make the first basic loop, insert the needle from the front of the work, 2 mm along from the first knot, and repeat the basic knot, this time leaving a loop about 2 mm high. Continue in this way until you have completed a row. Do not cut the thread.

5 Turn the work over and work a turning loop into the first loop. Then work the second and subsequent rows by inserting the needle through the loops of the previous row.

CLOSED LOOP AND BOW

1 Work a foundation row in an even number of basic loops and turn the work over.

2 Work a small turning loop into first loop. Into the same loop work a long loop, one and a half times higher than the basic loop. Place the needle through the front of the loop. Do not pull it through.

3 Taking the thread from the knot end, pass it over the point of the needle from left to right. Pull the thread through and pull it tight. You have now made a closed loop.

4 Make another loop of the same height into the next basic loop.

5 Place the needle behind all the long loops and pass the thread over the needle from front to back. Pull all the threads tight together in the middle.

6 Put the needle through the top of the last long loop and work another closed loop.

7 Work another loop of the same height into the next loop and close it with a closed loop knot.

8 Repeat steps 4 to 7 until the end.

SMALL TURNING LOOP

This is a small loop made like a basic loop and worked into the first loop when turning. It is not part of a row.

BRIDGING LOOP

This is a small loop made like a basic loop and worked into a large loop. It is not worked on the next round.

PICOT

A picot is made by working a number of loops into the same large loop. Small picots produce a scalloped effect and large picots make a fan shape.

INCREASING AND DECREASING

If the foundation rows are correct, you should not need to increase or decrease. If you do need more loops, increase by working two knots into one loop. To decrease, miss a loop or make one knot through two loops.

JOINING THREADS

1 Cut the thread about 5 cm from the last knot worked. Over this knot make another with a new thread.

2 Work into next loop, catching the cut end of previous thread with the knot. This will make a double loop.

3 Keep the thread ends at the back of the work. On the next round, work into the double loop before trimming the thread.

Découpage

Découpage is a time-consuming but satisfying craft. Take great care at every stage of the work, and the result will look as though the images are floating in translucent porcelain.

Découpage is the art of decorating hard surfaces with cut-out paper images. It originated in eighteenth century Venice, and enjoyed a popular revival a hundred years later in the England of Queen Victoria.

The printed images are glued on to the surface of the object, and then many coats of varnish (often 30 or more) are applied until the images are completely submerged and their edges cannot be felt.

Anything with a hard, smooth surface can be ornamented with découpage. Boxes, old suitcases, violin cases, wooden screens, trays, wooden bowls, chairs and tables are all suitable. Small objects like blown eggs can also be découpaged.

EQUIPMENT AND SUPPLIES
Preparing the surface
You will need sandpaper, wood putty (filler) or beeswax, gesso, rust guard for protecting metal surfaces, sealer, and inexpensive paintbrushes.

Preparing the images
You will need fine, sharp scissors (long-bladed and curved cuticle), a scalpel, a cutting board or mat, artist's acrylic gloss medium (for sealing), and Blu-Tack.

Fixing the images
You will need wallpaper paste, PVA glue, a brush, sponges, and a small rubber roller with rounded edges.

Varnishing
You will need a chiselled imitation sable paintbrush (or any other good-quality brush that does not shed its bristles), about 25 mm wide, good-quality polyurethane gloss varnish, wet-and-dry abrasive paper of several grades of fineness, a sanding block (rubber or cork), lint-free cloths, and mineral turpentine.

Waxing
You will need cabinetmaker's polish, clear beeswax or liquid car wax, and soft cloths. Alternatively, finish découpage projects with a micromesh kit, available from craft suppliers.

CHOOSING IMAGES
The images are a major part of découpage, so choose carefully. Make sure the images are clear and consistently coloured. Ideally, images should be on thin, non-porous paper because thicker surfaces will need many more coats of varnish to submerge them and therefore will make a raised, uneven surface, which will spoil the overall effect.

Books are an excellent source of images. You can also use magazine pictures, as long as they are well sealed so that the printing on the other side will not show through. If you use wrapping paper, avoid the folded kind, as the creases will show, and seal the paper well before applying.

PREPARING THE SURFACE
Before applying découpage, ensure that surfaces are non-porous and extremely smooth. If you do not take the time to prepare surfaces well, the result is likely to be less than perfect.

Wood

1 Remove old paint or varnish with paint stripper. Wash with mild deter-

gent to remove all dirt, grease and wax. Fill cracks or indentations with wood filler or a beeswax stick.

2 Sand all surfaces thoroughly to ensure a smooth working surface. If the surface is not smooth enough, apply several coats of artist's gesso, allowing coats to dry thoroughly between applications. Sand until the surface feels like smooth ivory.
3 Apply wood sealer to all surfaces.

Metal
1 Remove any rust with a wire brush or sandpaper. Clean the surface with methylated spirits. For larger objects, you can save hours of preparation and achieve a better finish by taking the object to a professional sandblaster to have it sandblasted and sealed.
2 Apply a coat of rust-inhibiting metal primer. Lightly sand the surface and apply a coat of sealer or rust-resistant paint.

Porous surfaces
Apply several coats of gesso to any surface that will soak up varnish. Polystyrene foam is eroded by varnish, so ensure that the surface is well finished with gesso and sealer.

SEALING THE IMAGES
Before they are fixed in place, images must be sealed to prevent varnish from seeping under the paper. Sealing also preserves the colour and prevents the image from stretching and wrinkling when it is glued down. Always seal images before cutting them to exact size. Photographs with non-porous backs do not require sealing.

1 Apply artist's acrylic gloss medium sparingly to the back of the image and allow to dry.

2 Apply a similar coat to the front and allow it to dry thoroughly.

LAYING OUT THE DESIGN

Do not cut away the background from the images until you are completely happy with the design, as you may want to use some of the background images elsewhere in your design.

1 Before you fix the images to the prepared surface, take time to arrange the pictures on paper templates or on the object itself. Fix the images with Blu-Tack and rearrange them until you are satisfied with the design.

2 So that you have enough paper to grasp without damaging the image, before trimming the outside edge of an image, remove any enclosed background areas by cutting a hole through the top surface and bringing the scissors up from under the paper.

3 Cut away the excess background, feeding the paper smoothly through the scissors to produce a crisp edge. If the image does not have too many curves, you can use a scalpel instead.

CAUTION

To achieve good results, the printed images must be neatly and accurately cut out, so use sharp, good-quality instruments. However, be careful – especially with scalpels, which are very sharp. To prevent the scalpel from slipping when cutting straight edges, hold it firm against the edge of a steel ruler.

RULES FOR VARNISHING

- Always wear a mask or respirator to avoid breathing in fumes.
- Use goggles to protect your eyes.
- Work in a well-ventilated, dust-free area where you can leave your découpage to dry, and work in good light to ensure even coverage.
- Varnish away from direct sunlight.
- Varnish in dry weather, as dampness and humidity can cause a misty effect in the varnish.
- Keep the brush clean and free of excess varnish as you work by washing it in turpentine. Clean the brush thoroughly after each application.

GLUING

It is essential that the pictures be glued securely to prevent varnish from seeping under the image and lifting it. It is also essential to remove every trace of glue from the surface before you begin varnishing.

1 Mix three parts wallpaper paste and one part PVA glue. Unless the images are very small, apply the glue to the hard surface rather than the image, as the glue can make the paper stretch and tear. Be generous with the glue

and work with only one image at a time. On curved surfaces use wallpaper glue only, mixed to a thick, jelly-like consistency. This mixture will give you more time to work on the image and mould it on to the shape.

2 Place the picture on the surface and add a small amount of glue to the upper side of the image. Massage the picture carefully to smooth out any lumps of glue and air bubbles from under the paper.

3 With gentle pressure, run the roller over the picture to distribute the glue evenly. Always roll from the centre of the image out towards the edges, and roll in one direction only, not backwards and forwards.

4 Wipe excess glue from the top of the image with a well-wrung-out sponge. Difficult glue smears can be removed with a solution of water and a little vinegar or lemon juice.

5 When all the images are in place and the glue is thoroughly dry, use

coloured pencils to conceal any white edges that appear around the images. This ensures that the images will blend together in the finished piece.
6 Apply a coat of sealer over the images and the surface of the object.

VARNISHING

The aim of varnishing is to build up the background to the level of the images, so that the images appear to be inlaid in the surface.

Initial coats

1 With a lint-free cloth, remove surface dust before varnishing. Using an imitation sable brush, apply a generous coat of varnish to the surface, brushing out from the centre in one direction only.
2 Remove any excess varnish from the brush and then lightly apply the tip of the brush to the work in order to remove air bubbles and excess varnish. Allow the varnish to dry for at least 24 hours.
3 When dry, rub lightly with a lint-free cloth to remove surface dust particles. Apply another coat of varnish, brushing at right angles to the first coat to ensure good coverage.
4 Repeat steps 1 to 3 until a good depth of varnish has built up and you are sure that a light sanding will not damage the paper images. This will take at least 10 coats. Leave to dry for 24–48 hours.

Upper coats

Sanding between coats will remedy the lumps and bumps that start to appear after varnishing.
1 Using no. 600 wet-and-dry abrasive paper wrapped around a rubber block,

and a little water, sand the varnished surfaces lightly in one direction. Do not use a circular motion, as this will scratch the surface. Concentrate on the images, sanding back the varnish on top of the image at each sanding and allowing the background varnish to continue building up.
2 Remove all residue with a sponge and a lint-free cloth and then varnish again, allowing each coat to dry thoroughly. Change the direction of sanding between coats and keep the abrasive paper moist.

3 Repeat steps 1 and 2 as often as necessary to achieve a uniform thickness of varnish. The varnish must be built up until you can no longer feel the edges of the images. The number of coats needed will vary, depending on how thickly the varnish is applied and how thick the image is. All crevices must be filled with varnish; this can take anywhere between 10 and 30 coats of varnish. Pay particular attention to any areas of the design where many images are superimposed. Perseverance and patience are required at this stage.
4 When you are satisfied that the surface is absolutely flat, apply three further coats of varnish, polishing the surface with no. 1200 wet-and-dry abrasive paper between applications to produce a very smooth, dull finish.

WAXING

1 Mix together equal amounts of beeswax and cabinetmaker's polish and warm the mixture (microwaving on high for 20 seconds is an ideal method). Spread the wax evenly over the surface with a soft, lint-free cloth, working on a small area at a time.

2 Before the wax dries too hard, wipe the surface with a damp cloth, using a brisk, circular motion. Polish with a soft, dry cloth.
3 If necessary, apply a second coat of wax to achieve a hard, glossy appearance. Wax the object again from time to time to maintain the smooth, silky finish.

MICROMESHING

If you intend your project to last a long time – and perhaps be handed down through generations – you may wish to finish the project using micromesh techniques, rather than waxing. Micromesh kits contain products to cut and polish the varnish, creating the effect of fine porcelain. This glow will last indefinitely, whereas ordinary polishes need to be reapplied every six months or so. Micromesh kits are available from craft shops.

PROBLEMS AND SOLUTIONS
Air bubbles

Using a scalpel, carefully make a small slit, preferably on a design line or any other unobtrusive place. Lift each edge of the cut and insert a little glue beneath the image. Press the glue further under the image and then press it towards the slit to expel air and excess glue. Allow the glue to dry, and camouflage the area if necessary with an oil-based pencil.

Build-ups and drips

Do not sand these off, as sanding will leave dark marks. Slice off the excess varnish with a scalpel and allow the underneath varnish to dry thoroughly. Then carry on varnishing.

Sanding through varnish

Stop sanding immediately. Colour with an appropriate oil-based pencil, smudge, seal, and continue varnishing.

Flower & foliage drying

Dried flowers make a charming way of preserving nature's beauty. Handle plant material gently, and let your imagination run riot when you are arranging flowers in a posy or picture.

Foliage and flowers suitable for dried floral arrangements can be prepared in a number of ways. Most of the floral art projects in this book use flowers and leaves that have been pressed, air dried or silica gel dried.

PICKING THE FLOWERS

The early morning of a dry day is the best time to pick flowers for drying. Pick only blooms in perfect, blemish-free condition, and make sure that they are free of moisture.

PRESSING

This method is used to preserve foliage and flowers that are fairly flat when in their natural state – such as maidenhair fern, pansies, freesias, anemones and simple daisies – and that are to be used in flat arrangements, such as pictures, and on objects like candles and book covers. Most leaves retain their colour while they are being pressed, but the chlorophyll that gives leaves their green colour disintegrates when exposed to light. You can preserve the colour of leaves by spraying them with light-fast natural dyes, which are available from most florists and florists' suppliers.

1 Spread out the plant material evenly on several sheets of absorbent paper (newspaper will do). Make sure the sprays do not overlap, otherwise they will stick together.

2 Place several layers of absorbent paper over the flowers and foliage. Cover the entire surface with something fairly heavy, such as a sheet of thick glass or large books.

3 Leave in a well-ventilated place, checking occasionally to make sure

the leaves and flowers are not sticking to the surface of the paper. The length of time plant material takes to dry depends on humidity and the thickness of the material, but check after about 10 days, and then every few days after that. Two to three weeks is a normal drying time in summer, but it may take up to six weeks in winter.

AIR DRYING

This is the simplest and most common method of preserving plant material, but it should be used only for foliage and flowers that do not wilt easily, such as straw flowers, paper daisies, baby's breath, globe amaranth, statice, delphinium, lavender and hydrangeas.
Do not use this method for flowers that are very fleshy or have long stems or large heads, because shrinkage will alter their shape.

1 Sort the leaves and flowers into small bunches and remove any excess foliage from the lower stems.

2 In a dry, warm, dark and airy place, either stand the bunches upright in an empty container or secure the ends of the stems with string and suspend them upside down. The plant material will take a week or so to dry, depending on the size of the individual pieces and their moisture content.

SILICA GEL DRYING

Silica gel is a chemical compound that absorbs moisture. When dry, it takes the form of fine blue crystals, which gradually turn pink as they absorb moisture. The crystals can be used over and over again if you dry them in a warm oven after each use and store them in an airtight container.

Plant material dried with silica gel retains its form and colour very well. Suitable flowers for silica gel drying include roses, zinnias, anemones, poppies, shasta daisies, gerberas and Canterbury bells. Only flowers of the same or similar varieties, which will dry in the same time, should be placed in the same container of gel.

1 Cover the bottom of a plastic airtight container with a layer of silica gel 2 cm deep.

2 Study the shape and bulk of the flowers and decide which way they should lie. Some will dry best when laid upright, some face down, and others when laid sideways. If you want to preserve long flower heads (such as delphiniums) that are likely to be squashed by the weight of the gel, support them from below with notched pieces of cardboard.

Stencilling

Stencilled motifs can add an individual touch to any number of simple household items.

MAKING STENCILS

Cut stencils from sheets of semi-transparent acetate film or treated manila cardboard. Transparent film is easier to use, because you can trace the design straight on to it and can see what is happening through the film. If you use cardboard, you will need to waterproof it first by saturating it in a mixture of equal parts of linseed oil and turpentine. Leave it to dry for about 30 minutes, then remove excess linseed oil with a paper towel.

1 If you are using clear film, trace the design directly on to the material, using a fine-tipped permanent marker pen. If you are using cardboard, trace the design on to tracing paper and then, using transfer (graphite) paper and a stylus or empty ballpoint pen, transfer the design on to the cardboard. (See page 343 of 'Tracing, transferring & scaling'.)

2 Place the stencil material with the traced design on a cutting mat or any other suitable surface. Using a craft knife, cut along the lines of the traced design. Work from the centre of the design outwards. Always cut towards your body and away from the hand you are using to steady the stencil.

3 When cutting around curved edges, swivel the plastic or cardboard around the knife to create flowing edges, rather than trying to manoeuvre the knife around the curve.

4 If you accidentally cut beyond the guideline, repair both sides of the stencil with strips of masking tape.

POSITIONING THE STENCIL

Apply a light mist of spray adhesive to the back of the stencil and attach it to the surface to be decorated. The adhesive will hold the stencil in place and help to prevent paint from bleeding under the edges of the stencil and ruining the crisp outline. When the stencil starts to unstick, apply another light coat of adhesive. Alternatively, secure the edges of the stencil with masking tape.

APPLYING THE PAINT

The paint is applied to the surface of the object through the holes in the stencil material. The idea is to build up the colour on the object gradually. Colours can be blended and textures controlled by a range of methods.

Pouncing

This is the traditional method of stencilling. A stiff stencilling brush is used to stipple paint on to the surface. If you do not have a stencilling brush, trim the bristles of an ordinary, wide, round paintbrush.

1 Dip the brush into the paint, and remove the excess paint by tapping the brush on to scrap paper.

2 Holding the brush vertically, apply the paint to the stencil cut-out with a light, up-and-down pouncing movement. Begin lightly and do not overload the brush with paint. If you apply too much paint it may bleed under the outline of the stencil.

Rolling

This is an alternative method of applying paint that produces a smooth, flat finish. Dip a small foam roller into the paint and roll it backwards and forwards on some scrap paper until it is nearly dry. Apply the roller to the stencil cut-out.

Sponging

This method allows you to control the texture of the paint. Use a fine, uniformly textured, synthetic sponge for a smooth finish, and a natural sponge for a more textured finish.

1 Fold the sponge to make a small pad. Dip it lightly into the paint and then force out any excess paint by dabbing the sponge on a paper towel.

2 Using either an up-and-down pouncing motion or a light swirling motion, fill in the stencil cut-out.

Soft brushing

Using a softer stencil brush allows you to blend several colours in a gentle, controlled way.

1 Dip the brush into the paint and remove any excess by moving the brush backwards, forwards and in a circular motion on a paper towel. Make sure that the paint is evenly distributed on the bristles to a depth of a few millimetres.

2 Holding the brush upright, apply the colour using a soft circular motion, as if you were dusting the surface of a table.

3 Repeat steps 1 and 2 with other colours, allowing the colours to blend into each other in some places.

AEROSOL SPRAY PAINTS

These paints can be applied in thin, even coats, giving a smooth, regular finish. Always use aerosol sprays in a well ventilated area.

1 Attach newspaper or lightweight card to the outside edges of the stencil with masking tape to protect the area immediately surrounding the stencil from paint drift.

2 For the best results, release the paint in short, sharp bursts using a pumping action, while holding the can directly in front of the stencil and about 15 cm away from it.

CARING FOR STENCILS

• Wipe off any excess paint as soon as you remove the stencil from the work. Make sure any remaining paint is dry before you apply the stencil again.

• Store stencils in plastic envelopes for using again.

Woodworking

Learn basic woodworking skills, and you will be able to make toys and household articles. Make sure your working area is large enough to work comfortably and store tools neatly.

TIMBER

Timber is generally either softwood or hardwood. There are also a number of sheet materials made from wood or wood pulp. These include plywood, particle board or chipboard, medium density fibreboard (MDF) and hardboard. All these materials have their own special characteristics and limitations, so the type of timber to be used has been specified in each project. If you wish to substitute one wood for another, make sure that it is suitable for the job.

WORKBENCH

Any firm working surface, such as a bench in the garage or an old, sturdy table, can be used as a workbench.

MEASURING TOOLS

To ensure your work is accurate, you will need the following tools.
- A steel tape for measuring
- A steel rule for measuring, for using as a straight edge when cutting with a knife, and for determining whether a surface is even
- A try-square for marking and testing right angles

CAUTION

Working with wood can be dangerous, as tools are sharp and wood can splinter and chip. It is important to wear suitable clothes and use the appropriate safety equipment.
- *Wear sturdy shoes that cover your feet completely.*
- *Wear safety goggles whenever flying debris or dust might be hazardous to your eyes.*
- *Always clamp wood firmly so that you are confident that it cannot shift while you are working on it.*

- A spirit level for testing whether surfaces are level or 'plumb'. If the air bubble in the glass indicator on the spirit level is dead centre, the surface you are testing is level.

VICES AND CLAMPS

Portable vices, which are attached to the bench with thumb screws, and G-clamps (also known as C-clamps), are very useful for holding wood steady and for clamping glued sections together until they are dry.

HANDSAWS

There are various types of handsaws. Each type is suitable for performing specific tasks.

Coping saw

Designed for cutting curves and holes close to the edge of a piece of wood, a coping saw has a fine, removable blade that is held taut in a U-shaped frame. (A hacksaw is similar in design, but is used for cutting metal.)

1 With the wood clamped firmly in a vice, grip the handle of the saw with both hands. Following the marked guide line carefully, aim to make one continuous cut if possible.
2 The blade of a coping saw can be rotated around its axis. As you progress around the curve, periodically rotate the blade to follow the direction of the cut.

3 To cut out a circular section, drill a hole inside the circle large enough to accommodate the width of the blade. Unclamp the blade from one end of the frame, thread the blade through the hole and reclamp the blade. Proceed as outlined in steps 1 and 2.

Crosscut panel saw

This saw is used to cut large blocks of timber, as well as sheet materials such as plywood, chipboard and fibreboard. It has a long, flexible blade designed to cut across the grain of the timber. The flexible blade allows you to adjust the cutting line if it begins to wander. The saw leaves a rough cutting edge, which must be sanded smooth.

1 Grip the handle with your index finger pointing down along the handle to stabilise and guide while you cut. Place the saw at the beginning of the cutting line.
2 Cut a starting groove by making a few short cuts back towards your body. Use the thumb of your free hand to guide and steady the blade.
3 Hold the saw in the starting groove at an angle of 45° to the cutting surface (this is the angle at which the

POWER SAW SAFETY

- Keep the electric cable well away from the blade. Plug the cable into a circuit breaker so that the current will be cut off if the saw cuts into the cable.
- Check that the blade is the right way round when fitting it.
- Do not remove the saw from the wood until it has stopped.
- Switch off the power and pull the plug from the socket whenever the saw is not in use, even for short spells.
- Keep children out of the room while you are using the saw.
- Wear safety goggles or spectacles when cutting, as flying dust can damage your eyes.
- Make sure the blade will not cut anything underneath the piece you are working on.
- Never use blades that are damaged, blunt or bent.
- Replace the cable if the sheathing is damaged. Check that the outer sheathing runs right into the saw housing and the plug.

teeth of the saw are designed to cut) and saw backwards and forwards in

long, easy strokes, allowing the weight of the saw to do the work.

Fretsaw

This saw is used for detailed work. It is similar to the coping saw, except that it has a finer, more flexible blade.

1 Sit in front of the work and hold the saw upright in one hand.
2 Use your free hand to hold the timber steady, and cut on the downstroke.

Keyhole or pad saw

A keyhole saw is used to cut out shapes that are too far from the edges of the timber to be cut with a coping saw. A keyhole saw has a narrow replaceable blade that is clamped into a wooden or metal handle. It is gripped like a screwdriver.

1 Within the shape to be removed, drill a hole large enough to accommodate the saw blade.
2 Insert the blade into the hole and cut with a back and forth motion.

Rip saw

A rip saw is designed to cut along the timber grain. It is similar to the crosscut panel saw, but has coarser teeth. It

is unsuitable for cutting across the grain, as the teeth leave a jagged edge. Grip the rip saw in the same way as the panel saw, but hold it at an angle of 60° to the cutting surface.

Tenon saw

This is an excellent, general-purpose saw. It is a short, fine-toothed crosscut saw with a reinforced metal spine to hold the blade rigid. It cuts accurately and smoothly, and is especially good for cutting joints.

1 Grip the handle with your index finger lying alongside the handle.
2 Saw using a back and forth motion, applying light pressure on the forward stroke. To keep the tenon saw level so that you cut square to the timber, make sure that your forearm is in line with the spine of the saw.

POWER SAWS

Power saws take the physical effort out of sawing and get the job done in a fraction of the time that it would take using a handsaw.

Hole saw

These are sold as attachments for power drills. They come in a range of diameters and will cut perfect holes up to 6 cm in diameter. Holes can be cut to greater depth if you stop from time to time and clear out waste wood before proceeding.

Jigsaw

Jigsaws are speedy, powerful and highly manoeuvrable. A jigsaw fitted with the right blade can cut straight lines and intricate curves in wood, laminate or metal.

MITRE BOX

A mitre box is a saw guide used for cutting the precise 45° angles required for making mitred right-angled joints. It consists of a simple wooden frame with two raised sides, in which there are pre-cut slots to guide the blade of the saw.

1 Clamp the wood firmly against the far side of the mitre box and use a tenon saw to cut it. If you are mitre-cutting moulding, ensure that it is clamped the right way around.
2 Make sure that you hold the saw horizontally to avoid cutting into the sides of the guide slots.

DRILLS

Wheelbrace drill

This type of drill is used to make holes up to 6 mm in diameter. Grip the straight handle with one hand and use the other hand to turn the drive wheel.

Brace

A brace is used to drill holes with a diameter greater than 6 mm and a depth of more than 38 mm. Grip the rounded handle with one hand to hold the brace steady and turn the offset handle with your other hand.

Power drill

With a power drill you can drill holes in almost any surface in a fraction of the time taken by a hand drill.

Drill bit

A bit is the detachable drilling tool that fits into the end of the drill. Drill bits come in various thicknesses, depending on the size of the hole you want to make. The bit is inserted into the jagged jaws of the drill (called the chuck). The jaws are then tightened by means of a chuck key inserted in the barrel of the drill.

Drilling holes for screws

When drilling holes for screws, always use a drill bit smaller than the diameter of the solid core of the screw. For softwoods use a smaller bit than for hardwoods, so that the screw has to bite deeper into the wood and thus will hold the work securely.

Countersinking screws

Drill a hole in the usual way. Change to a drill bit 1 mm larger in diameter than the screw head, and drill a shallow depression at the top of the screw hole. The head of the screw will now lie flush with the surface. Alternatively, use a countersink bit.

SCREWDRIVERS

Screwdrivers have either flat blades for screwing conventional, single-slot screws, or special heads for cross-slotted screws (Phillips screwdrivers).

1 Choose a screwdriver that is the right size for the screw. If the blade is too narrow, it will distort the screw head; if it is too wide, the blade will tend to slip, damaging the wood.
2 When using a screwdriver, always hold it so that the blade is squarely in the slot of the screw.

PLANES

A plane is used to finish wood to an exact size. Planing is always done in a forward direction away from the body and following the grain of the wood.

Make sure that the wood is clamped firmly and that the plane blade is not set too deep, otherwise it will dig into the surface.

1 Hold the plane by the handle and the small knob at the front.
2 As you make each stroke, smoothly transfer downward pressure from the front to the back of the plane.

Planing the end grain

1 Clamp the end firmly in the vice to avoid vibration.
2 Plane from each end, towards the centre of the timber to prevent the wood from splitting.
3 Check frequently that the planed end is square and level, using a try-square and a straight edge.

CHISELS

A chisel is used for cutting joints, rebates and shallow recesses, or for shaping work. If your chisel is kept sharp, hand pressure should be sufficient for most jobs. If a great deal of wood is to be removed and more pressure is required, use a wooden mallet to tap the end of the chisel.

CAUTION

The sharpness of a chisel and the force applied to it make it one of the most dangerous tools to use.
- *Take considerable care to clamp the timber firmly so that it will not slip as you work and so that you have both hands free.*
- *Always work away from your hands and your body.*
- *Never place a chisel where it might be knocked to the floor, as the sharp blade could cause serious injury to feet.*

NAILS AND SCREWS

Nails

Nail length depends on the type of wood you are using. For hardwoods, use a nail length that is twice the thickness of the timber; for softwoods, select a nail length three times the thickness of the wood.

Lost head wire nails are round nails with heads shaped like a bullet. These heads can be punched below the surface of the wood.

Oval wire nails have heads that are hammered flush with the surface of the wood. They should be inserted so that the longer axis of the head aligns with the grain of the timber.

Panel pins are very fine nails that are used for most of the light projects in this book.

Screws

Countersunk screws are used most often in woodwork because they can be tightened to 'set' flush with the surface of the wood.

Raised-head screws are usually made from shiny plated metals, and are used when appearance is important. They are screwed only down to the countersunk rim, leaving the rounded head exposed and raised.

Round-headed screws are most often used with hardware fittings that are not countersunk. If a washer is placed under the head, these screws can also be used for toy wheels or other moving parts.

Self-tapping screws are used for fixing thin metal whenever it is not practicable to use a nut-and-bolt. First drill a hole in the metal slightly smaller than the thread of the screw so that the screw will fit in firmly.

When using a chisel to pare or trim wood to shape, work at a slight angle to the vertical, using both hands in the same way as for cutting across the grain. Shave away a thin slice of wood with each stroke.

1 Clamp the wood firmly, so that you have both hands free.

2 To cut with the grain, keep the bevelled side of the chisel facing up. Use one hand to guide the blade and the other to apply pressure. Work away from your body and your hands.
3 When cutting across the grain, work from directly above the timber surface. Hold the chisel with your thumb on top of the handle to provide

the pressure, and carefully guide the blade with the index finger of your other hand.

HAMMERS

A cross-pein hammer has a flat, tapered end (the pein) opposite the striking head, and is used for light work. A claw hammer has a heavier head and a 'claw' for pulling out old or crooked nails.

When you use a hammer, grip it so that the end of the handle extends about 4 cm behind your hand. First tap the nail gently to embed it in the timber, and then swing from the elbow, keeping your wrist straight and allowing the weight of the hammer to do the work. If the nail is hit at any appreciable angle, it will bend.

To avoid bruising the wood with the hammer when you are driving home a nail, lay a small piece of waste wood over the head of the nail and hammer it flat against the working timber. Alternatively, use a nail punch. Choose a punch with a point slightly smaller than the head of the nail. Centre the point of the punch on the nail and tap the punch with the hammer until the nail head is flush with the surface of the wood.

Removing nails

Place a small block of scrap timber under the hammer head to avoid bruising the timber. Slide the claw of the hammer under the head of the nail until the nail is held tight, then pull the handle back.

Hammering a small nail or tack

1 Hold the nail, pin or tack steady between your thumb and index finger, and tap it gently with a cross-pein hammer until the nail stands upright by itself. Hammer the nail home.
2 If the nail is too short to hold, push it through a piece of stiff paper or the teeth of a fine comb. When the nail is nearly home, tear away the paper or slide away the comb.

PUNCHES

Punches are used for driving panel pins or wire nails below the surface of the timber, or to finish driving in nails where you do not want to mark the surface with a hammer head.

RASPS

Rasps are steel rods covered with raised abrasive metal teeth. They are useful for shaping wood, but are not suitable for finishing, as the metal teeth do not produce a smooth surface. A good general-purpose rasp for woodworking is one about 25 cm long with one flat and one convex side.

FILES

Files are like rasps, except that they have much finer teeth. They produce a smooth finish but will not remove large quantities of wood.

SANDPAPER

A more accurate name for sandpaper is glasspaper. It is heavy-duty paper covered with granules of glass or other hard, abrasive material. It is generally sold in sheets, which can easily be torn into more manageable pieces. Used for smoothing wood, sandpaper is available in various grades, from coarse to very fine.

When sanding wood, first use a coarse paper, and then progressively finer papers, until the timber surface is smooth to the touch. Always work along the grain. To sand flat surfaces, wrap the glasspaper around a sanding block of cork or light timber.

COMPLEX CUTTING WITH BASIC TOOLS

For some projects in this book, you can cut curved edges or holes using only a panel or tenon saw, a drill, a chisel, a rasp and a file.

Convex curves

1 Cut the curves roughly to shape, cutting across the corners of the wood and close to the drawn curve.

2 Go on cutting off corners until you are as close to the curve line as you can get without cutting into it. Finish the curve with a rasp and a file.

Concave curves

1 Make a series of cuts perpendicular to the edge of the wood, passing through the waste area as far as the marked curve.
2 Cut away the waste between the saw cuts with a chisel.

3 Use a chisel to pare the curve close to the marked line. Finish off with a curved rasp and a file.

Small circular holes

1 Drill a series of adjacent holes just inside the marked circumference.
2 Cut the wood between the holes with a chisel and remove the centre.
3 Using the chisel, pare the wood back to the circumference and finish off with a curved rasp and a file.

Large circular holes

1 Drill a series of adjacent holes within the waste area, in a triangular pattern large enough to take the blade of a panel or tenon saw. Remove the resultant rough triangular shape.
2 Saw radial cuts to the marked circumference. Cut away the waste between the saw cuts with a chisel.
3 Use a chisel to pare the curve close to the marked line. Finish off with a curved rasp and a file.

Tracing, transferring & scaling

If you take the time and trouble to transfer patterns accurately and neatly, it will be much easier to assemble and finish your project to a professional standard.

There are several ways of transferring an outline or a design from a master pattern to the material you are going to work with. The method you use depends on what material you are transferring the pattern to. If the material is transparent or semi-transparent, the best method is to trace the design directly on to the material using an appropriate marker.

If you cannot see through the material, first trace the pattern on to tracing paper and then transfer this working pattern to the material using one of the methods described below.

DIRECT TRACING

To trace a pattern directly on to transparent plastic (as when making stencils), use marker pens especially designed for the purpose, such as the pens used on whiteboards or overhead transparencies.

To trace on to transparent or semi-transparent fabric, place the design under the fabric and trace the lines with a marker. You may find it easier to see the design lines if you use a light box or tape the fabric and working pattern to a window. To trace on to fabric, choose the most suitable marker from the following.

• A water-soluble marker pen washes out in cold water after use.
• A fade-out pen can be used when you cannot wash out the fabric. Marks last up to 48 hours. You should, however, check by marking a piece of scrap fabric and leaving it for two days. Examine the fabric in different lights, including fluorescent, to make sure the marks have disappeared.
• A silver or white marker pencil (or quilter's pencil) can be sharpened to a fine point. Marks can be removed with a fabric eraser.
• A hard lead pencil gives a fine line, but the marks may prove difficult to remove completely.

• A chalk-based dressmaker's pencil has the disadvantage that the marks can brush out, sometimes while you are still working.

TRANSFERRING FROM TRACING

First trace a working pattern from the master pattern on to tracing paper.

Wood, metal, paper and cardboard

Use transfer (or graphite) paper, available from artists' suppliers.
1 Using small pieces of masking tape at each corner, attach the tracing paper to the surface to be decorated.
2 Slip the transfer paper underneath the tracing paper and, using light pressure, trace over the design lines with the tip of a hard pencil or an empty ballpoint pen. You can remove transferred lines with a pencil eraser.

Fabric
Dressmaker's carbon paper
If you need to transfer detailed design lines, one of the easiest methods is to use dressmaker's carbon. Carbon paper comes in several colours, so choose a colour that will show on the fabric. The marks made by dressmaker's carbon paper can sometimes

---

CAUTION
Before you mark your work, always test a fabric marker on a scrap of the fabric you are using to make sure the marks can be removed when you have finished the work. When using water-soluble markers, rinse the fabric under cold water until the marks have completely disappeared. Using hot water or an iron is likely to set the chemicals in the marker, making it impossible to remove the marks.

POSITIONING DESIGNS ON FABRIC

1 Fold and quarter the fabric and crease along the lines. If the crease line will not hold, tack along the fold lines. Pin or tape the fabric to a flat surface.

2 Find the centre of the design and fold and quarter the traced pattern so that the folded midpoint corresponds with the midpoint of the design. Place the pattern on one quarter of the fabric, aligning centre points.

3 Open the pattern out so that the pattern fold lines correspond with the fabric fold lines. Fix the pattern down with masking tape, and then transfer the design to the fabric using the appropriate method.

be difficult to remove, so it is best used when the design lines are to be covered with stitching.

1 Place the pattern in position on the right side of the fabric and pin at the corners. Carefully slip the carbon paper, carbon side down, between the fabric and the pattern.

2 Draw over the design lines using a tracing wheel or a stylus.

Transfer pencil

Some transfer pencils are marketed as water-erasable, but test them on your fabric before you use them.

1 Trace the design on to tracing paper and then turn the paper over and trace over the design lines with the transfer pencil.

2 Place the tracing paper in position on the fabric with the transfer pencil lines against the fabric. Press down on the paper for a few minutes with a warm iron (not hot).

3 Lift the iron to the next area of the paper (do not slide). Without moving the tracing paper, lift a corner to make sure the transfer has taken.

Pricking out

An alternative method of marking simple design outlines is to prick out the design by hand or machine.

To prick out by hand, trace the design on to tracing paper using an ordinary pencil. Pin the tracing in position on the right side of the fabric. Lay the

pattern and the fabric over a thick wad of fabric, such as a blanket. Prick holes with a needle through the tracing paper, along the lines of the design. Use a fabric marker to mark dots on the fabric through these holes. Remove the tracing paper and join up the dots on the fabric.

To prick out a simple design very quickly with a sewing machine, remove both the top thread and the bobbin thread from the machine, set the stitch length to about 3 mm and 'stitch' along the design lines. Then trace over the outline of holes left by the needle with a suitable washable fabric marker.

SCALING

Sometimes you will want to enlarge or reduce a design – for example, to repeat a stencil design on various articles. The simplest way to do this is to use a photocopier with an enlarging function to to copy a pattern or design to the size you want. However, if you do not have access to a photocopier, use the following method to make your design larger.

1 Decide how much bigger you want the design to be and make a note of the desired width. Draw a small grid over

the design and then rule a rectangle around the design.

2 Tape the design to the lower left-hand corner of a sheet of paper. Rule a diagonal line from the bottom left corner of the rectangle to the top right corner, extending the line past the top corner on to the sheet of paper. Extend the base of the rectangle to the desired width of your enlargement. Rule a line from this point at right angles to the base of the rectangle, extending it until it crosses the diagonal. Rule the remaining sides of the enlarged rectangle and remove the original design.

3 On to the enlarged rectangle, measure and rule the same number of rows and columns as you ruled over the original design, so that you have an identical grid, but with larger squares than the original.

4 Working square by square, copy the design lines from the original grid on to the corresponding squares on the larger grid. You may find that it is easier to transfer the lines if you first mark dots where the design lines intersect the squares and then connect the dots.

5 To make a design smaller, draws a grid smaller than the design and follow step 4.

1

2

3

4

Gifts & crafts index

Gifts are listed alphabetically, with the principal crafts shown in italics and additional crafts shown in italics and parentheses. The symbol • denotes a gift that is 'quick and easy' to make.

Techniques index

This index covers the techniques section (pages 292–344), which describes the principal crafts required to make the projects. Use it to quickly find the instructions for individual techniques.

General index

Go to 'Garden gifts' to find something for a keen gardener, or look under 'Clothing' if you want to make a gift for the fashion-conscious.

Key to master pattern pieces

A1 Daisy & bee baby's outfit: *a* Skirt back & front, *b* Front yoke, *c* Back yoke, *d* Sleeve, *e* Sleeve binding, *f* Collar front, *g* Collar back, *h* Bonnet crown, *i* Bonnet brim

A2 'B is for Baby' quilt: *a* Butterfly, *b* Bird, *c* Bear, *d* Bunny, *e* Heart, *f* Bow, *g* Top border, *h* Side & bottom border

A3 Classic christening gown: *a* Front panel, *b* Skirt, *c* Back yoke, *d* Side yoke, *e* Sleeve

A4 Rocking horse overalls: *a* Pants front, *b* Pants back, *c* Front yoke, *d* Back yoke, *e* Leg band

A6 Baby's bootees in soft leather: *a* Front, *b* Side/back, *c* Sole

A7 Jingle bears: *a* Bear shape

B8 Raggedy Anne doll: *a* Head, *b* Front body, *c* Back body, *d* Arm, *e* Leg

B9 Doll's dress: *a* Front, *b* Back

B10 Push-along duck: *a* Body, *b* Wing, *c* Foot, *d* Wheel

B12 Edward Bear suit: *a* Front, *b* Back, *c* Sleeve, *d* Hood front, *e* Hood back, *f* Ear, *g* Paw pad, *h* Mitten

B13 Soft animal toys: *a* Octopus, *b* Koala, *c* Pig, *d* Whale, *e* Frog

B14 Soft rattles for a baby: *a* Handle, *b* Sphere segment

C15 Toddler's table & chairs: *a* Table top, *b* Table leg, *c* Table leg support, *d* Chair back, *e* Chair seat, *f* Chair side/legs, *g* Chair cross bar supports

C16 A very special Christmas stocking: *a* Stocking, *b* Collar, *c* Appliqué design

C17 Mouse bookends: *a* Body, *b* Head, *c* Arm, *d* Foot, *e* Tail

C18 Cuddly cow sweatshirt: *a* Cow design

C19 Personalised bedroom name plates: *a* Painting design

C20 Mummy's little helper's apron: *a* Front & back, *b* Shoulder frills

C21 Rock-a-bye doll's cradle: *a* Head, *b* Foot, *c* Side

C22 Balloon shorts: *a* Front/back

C23 Benjamin Bear: *a* Side head, *b* Back head, *c* Front head, *d* Ear, *e* Front body, *f* Back body, *g* Legs, *h* Foot pad, *i* Arm, *j* Paws

D26 Crazy patchwork evening bag: *a* Patchwork design

D27 Stylish soft rucksack: *a* Base, *b* Bag flap, *c* Pocket flap

D28 Sea-side towel & tote bag: *a* Large seaweed, *b* Small seaweed, *c* Shells, *d* Clam

D29 Pastoral poppy tray: *a* Poppy design

E32 Cream-on-cream cushion: *a* Embroidery design

E35 Monogrammed linen handkerchief *and* Monogrammed towels: *a* Alphabet

E37 Space-saving kitchen tea-towel airer: *a* End piece

E74 Crinolined lady lampshade: *a* Crinolined lady, *b* Daisies, *c* Forget-me-not, *d* Hyacinth

F38 Man's summer nightshirt: *a* Front, *b* Back, *c* Sleeve, *d* Facing, *e* Collar

F39 Rose bouquet blanket box: *a* Large rose design, *b* Small rose design

F40 Connoisseur's wine rack: *a* Scallop pattern, *b* Heart shape

F41 Director's chair: *a* Large strawberry design, *b* Small strawberry design

F42 Rosebud nightgown: *a* Front skirt, *b* Back skirt, *c* Yoke, *d* Sleeve, *e* Yoke facing

F43 Flowery watering can: *a* Flower design & verse

G45 Sewing box: *a* Base, *b* Back panel, *c* Lid front, *d* Lid top, *e* Rear top, *f* Side, *g* Divider, *h* Shelf, *i* Shelf front, *j* Cotton reel holder

G46 Painted apple plate: *a* Background design, *b* Rim design

G47 Iris garden apron: *a* Iris design

G48 Quilted oven cloth & mitt: *a* Mitt pattern

G49 Oak & acorn drawer liners: *a* Oak & acorn design, *b* Bow design

G50 Wooden towel rail: *a* Side piece

G76 Marquetry bookmark: *a* Cat design

G77 Sunflower wall hanging: Circles – *a* 4.5 cm diameter, *b* 3.75 cm diameter, *c* 3.25 cm diameter

H51 Director's chair cover: *a* Main piece, *b* Side piece

H52 Decorative hat & coat rack: *a* Plaque shape with cut-out for mirror

H54 Tulip cushion: *a* Tulip design

H55 Painted pot plant holder: *a* Violet design

H56 Fuchsia cushion: *a* Fuchsia design

H58 Simple wooden tray: *a* End piece

H75 Rose-trimmed bed linen: *a* Rose design (sheet), *b* Corner design (sheet), *c* Rose design (pillowcase), *d* Corner design (pillowcase)

I60 Broderie anglaise nightshirt: *a* Front yoke, *b* Front skirt, *c* Back yoke, *d* Back skirt, *e* Sleeve, *f* Front band

I61 Folk art kitchen canisters: *a* Large canister design, *b* Medium canister design, *c* Small canister design, *d* Grapevine design

I62 Chrysanthemum tablecloth: *a* Chrysanthemum design, *b* Scallop pattern

I63 Fast food station for birds: *a* Side panel

I65 Garden carry box: *a* Large strawberry design, *b* Small strawberry design

I66 Coat-hanger for a wedding dress: *a* Coat-hanger cover with embroidery pattern

I67 Satin bridal horseshoe: *a* Horseshoe shape

J68 New baby sampler: *a* Cross-stitch design, *b* Alphabet

J69 Embroidered table linen: *a* Cross-stitch design

J70 Sweet home sampler: *a* Cross-stitch design, *b* Alphabet

J71 Wedding day sampler: *a* Cross-stitch design, *b* Alphabet

J72 Beaded butterfly evening bag: *a* Butterfly design

J78 Ribbon & needlepoint pincushion: *a* Stitch guide

J79 Needlepoint cushion: *a* Stitch guide

Acknowledgments

Jean Alderton:
A calendar for all seasons

Penny Anderssen:
Découpage desk set

Diana Brandt:
Pastoral poppy tray

April Briscoe:
Folk art frames for baby photos

Ruby Brown:
European Easter eggs

Margaret Burch:
Dried flower wreath

Vicki Carr:
Log cabin quilt

Marilyn Carter:
Doll's dress

Margo Cavill:
Découpage memorabilia box

Coats Patons Crafts
(Coordinator Barbara Lennon):
*Balloon cardigan & striped jumper,
Cot blanket, Breakfast tea cosy,
Child's hat & scarf, Embroidered
table linen, Man's luxury jumper,
Man's scarf & hat, New baby
sampler, Rainbow jumper, Sweet
home sampler, Wedding day sampler*

Kate Coombe:
*Iris garden apron, Painted apple
plate, Personalised bedroom name-
plates, Strawberry garden chair*

Chris Dawson:
*Beginner's flower press, Country-style
dish rack, Decorative hat & coat rack,
Elegant indoor planter box, Fast food
station for birds, Marble kitchen
board, Mouse bookends, Push-along
duck, Rock-a-bye doll's cradle, Sewing
box, Space-saving kitchen tea-towel
airer, Toddler's table & chairs,
Wooden towel rail*

Edward Dew:
Home noticeboard

Elena Dickson:
*Coat-hanger for a wedding dress,
Delectable lace collar*

DMC (Coordinator
Effie Mitrofanis):
*Country lace curtain, Lacework
jug cover*

Stephanie Donaldson:
*Table centrepiece of dried flowers,
Wreath of nuts & leaves*

Rachel Dulsom:
Beaded butterfly evening bag

Jan Eaton:
*Chrysanthemum tablecloth, Daisy &
bee baby's outfit, Tulip cushion*

Brigitte Eckardt:
*Candles with pressed flowers,
Framed wedding bouquet,
Old-fashioned botanical picture*

Rosemary Evans:
Marquetry bookmark

Kate Finnie:
Printed T-shirts

Kate Finnie & Paula McPhail:
Fairy wings & wand

Janet Grice:
'B is for Baby' quilt

Christine Harris:
*Cuddly cow sweatshirt, Fuchsia
cushion, Monogrammed towels,
Sunflower wallhanging*

Alan Hayes:
Sweet-scented solutions

Amanda Ho:
Raffia bag, Raffia sunhat

Colleen Hughes:
*Quilted oven cloth & mitt,
Traditional rag rug*

Mark Hunter:
Plaited leather belt

Aristea Kaydos:
Raggedy Anne doll

Elizabeth Kaydos:
*Découpage pencil box, Faux finish
bedside table*

Deborah Kneen:
*Flowery watering can,
Luxury handkerchief bag,
Rose bouquet blanket box*

Denise Lawson:
Stylish soft rucksack

Dianne Leeson:
*Balloon shorts, Edward Bear suit,
Fine woollen summer shawl,
Jingle bears*

Sandra Levy:
Parchment window tracery

Marion Loveridge:
Garden carry box

Jessica Maude:
Brilliant bead jewellery

Lyn McBride:
Découpage picture frame

Lorell McIntyre:
Painted pot plant holder

Paula McPhail:
*A very special Christmas stocking,
Director's chair cover, Easy mothball
bags, Hand-covered photograph
album, Herb-filled sleep pillow,
Man's summer nightshirt, Mummy's
little helper's apron, Old-time lavender bags, Placemats for a country
kitchen, Rocking horse overalls, Satin
bridal horseshoe*

Beryl Miller:
Soft animal toys

Jennifer Newman:
*Monogrammed linen handkerchief,
Ribbon & lace bridal garter*

Judy Newman:
Handmade hatboxes

Diana Oakley:
*Broderie anglaise nightshirt,
Classic christening gown, Rosebud
nightgown*

Alison Park:
Needlepoint cushion

Marie Platt:
Cream-on-cream cushion

Judy Pullen:
Seagrass basket, Seagrass mat

Albert Richardson:
Basic window box

Susan Roach:
Sculpted floral hair slide

Frances Robinson:
*Connoisseur's wine rack, Dolls' house,
Miniature furniture, Simple wooden
tray, Treasure chest*

Sheridan Rogers &
Katharine Blakemore:
Edible gifts

Skye Rogers:
*Leafy lemon jug, Painted mat,
Snappy sneakers*

Lyn Silver:
*Aromatic beeswax candles,
Birdseed rings, cakes & bells,
Fragrant pot pourri*

Nerida Singleton:
*Chic fabric necklace, Découpage key
chain, Liberty-print hair accessories*

Di Skarratt:
*Elegant Victorian bows, Flower seeds
in homemade packets, Fragrant herbs
in a terracotta pot, Kindergarten
carry bags, Plastic bag dispenser,
Pot plant with bow, Romantic flowers
in a pot, Soft rattles for a baby,
Trimmed hand towels, Wind chimes*

Mike Spiller:
Sporty peg players

Ruth Stoneley:
Crazy patchwork evening bag

Madeleine Strongman:
*Crinolined lady lampshade, Garden
sculpture, Rose-trimmed bed linen,
Sea-side towel & tote bag, Stencilled
writing paper & envelopes*

Yvonne Theriault:
Folk art kitchen canisters

Tonia Todman:
*Baby's bootees in soft leather,
Handmade writing paper,
Hanging flower basket, Sea-shell
picture frame, Trinket box*

Gerry Warlow:
Benjamin Bear

Jenny Wilkinson:
*Embroidered baby's vests, Party
pinafore dress*

40-700-2